The Gender Conversation

Evangelical Perspectives on Gender,
Scripture, and the Christian Life

National Library of Australia Cataloguing-in-Publication entry:

Title: The Gender Conversation: evangelical perspectives on gender, scripture, and the Christian life / editors: Edwina Murphy, David Starling; contributor: Timothy George.

ISBN: 9780992275594 (paperback)

Notes: Includes bibliographical references.

Subjects: Gender identity--Religious aspects--Christianity. Religion and civil society. Christian life.

Other Creators/Contributors: Murphy, Edwina, editor. Starling, David, editor. George, Timothy, 1950-

Dewey Number: 261.83576

The Gender Conversation

Evangelical Perspectives on Gender, Scripture, and the Christian Life

EDITED BY EDWINA MURPHY AND DAVID STARLING

FOREWORD BY TIMOTHY GEORGE

MORLING **PRESS**

WIPF & STOCK
An Imprint of WIPF and STOCK Publishers

THE GENDER CONVERSATION
Evangelical Perspectives on Gender, Scripture, and the Christian Life

© **Morling Press and Wipf and Stock Publishers 2016**

First Published in Australia in 2016

Morling Press
122 Herring Rd Macquarie Park NSW 2113 Australia
Phone: +61 2 9878 0201
Email: enquiries@morling.edu.au

www.morlingcollege.com/morlingpress

Wipf and Stock Publishers
199 W. 8th Ave., Suite 3
Eugene, OR 97401 United States of America

www.wipfandstock.com

ISBN: 978-1-4982-9895-7

Designed by Brugel Images & Design **www.brugel.com.au**

Cover image source: Freepik.com

Contents

Part Seven

Gender, Biology, and Identity

Part Eight

Gender, Mission, and the Reign of God

Epilogue

Reference List

Additional Resources

Videos from the Symposium are available online

www.vimeo.com/ondemand/genderconversation

Available to download from 1 December 2015

Single video:

Buy or Rent (available for 48 hours)

Entire series of videos:

Buy or Rent (available for 1 week)

Contributors

Matthew Andrew is a PhD student and research fellow at Morling College, where he is engaged in research on divine impassibility and violence. Before commencing his research he was in pastoral ministry for seven years, both in Sydney and on the Central Coast of NSW, where he currently resides with his wife and children.

Caroline Batchelder is a member of the theology faculty at Alphacrucis College. Her doctoral dissertation (completed through Morling College) was a literary-theological study of the figure of the Servant in the "Servant Songs" of Isaiah, with interests in the topics "image of God" and "justice," and in inner-biblical allusion.

Michael Bird is a graduate of Malyon College and the University of Queensland. He has previously taught at Highland Theological College and the Brisbane School of Theology, and is currently a Lecturer in Theology at Ridley College in Melbourne. He is the author and editor of over twenty books.

Miyon Chung is a Korean-American Lecturer in Theology at Morling College. Before coming to Morling in 2014, she taught at Torch Trinity Graduate University (2002–2013). Her global commitments include working with Asia Pacific Baptist Federation, Baptist World Alliance, and Lausanne.

John Dickson is the minister of St Andrew's Anglican Church in Roseville and an honorary fellow of the Macquarie University Ancient History Department. He has written more than a dozen books, including a recent book on the question of women preaching, entitled *Hearing Her Voice: A Biblical Invitation for Women to Preach.*

Megan du Toit has been interested in gender since she was born with a twin brother. Both her honours theses (English and Theology) arose from her experience of gender. As an ordained Baptist pastor, PhD candidate in theology, and mother of two sons, questions of gender occupy her mind constantly.

Timothy George is the founding dean of Beeson Divinity School of Samford University. He has served until recently as the chair of the Doctrine and Christian Unity Commission of the Baptist World Alliance, and is active in Evangelical–Roman Catholic Church dialogue. He is the author of more than twenty books, as well as numerous articles and book sections, and is the general editor of the Reformation Commentary on Scripture.

Geoffrey Harper, originally from Dublin, is a lecturer in Old Testament at Sydney Missionary and Bible College. His doctoral dissertation (completed through Morling College) was on intertextual allusion in the book of Leviticus. He and his family live in Croydon and attend Petersham Baptist Church. In his spare time, Geoff enjoys fishing, reading, good coffee and playing Lego with his kids.

Beth Jackson is currently the Associate Pastor, Children and Families at Epping Baptist Church. Beth's current research interests revolve around child theology and contextual missiology and she is pursuing a PhD with Oxford Centre for Mission Studies in these areas.

Michael Jensen is the rector of St Mark's Anglican Church, Darling Point. He is a graduate of Sydney's Moore College and Oxford University. His doctorate was published as *Martyrdom and Identity: The Self on Trial* in 2010. He has published a number of other books and writes monthly for *Eternity* magazine.

Hefin Jones served as Associate Pastor of Chatswood Baptist Church from 2007–2015 and has recently accepted an appointment to the faculty of a seminary in South East Asia. He previously served as a pastor in both South Africa and Australia. His dissertation was on the place of faith and justification in apocalyptic readings of Galatians.

Gayle Kent is a Lecturer in Pastoral and Practical Studies and the Dean of Students at Morling College. She has a Master of International Education (School Leadership) and a Master of Arts (Christian Studies). She also serves on the pastoral team at Macquarie Chapel Presbyterian Church.

Lyn Kidson has had many years of ministry experience. She has completed both a Masters of Divinity (SMBC) and an MA in Early Christian and Jewish studies at Macquarie University. At present Lyn is a PhD candidate at Macquarie University and her research focus is on 1 Timothy in its literary, social, and historical contexts.

Karina Kreminski is Lecturer in Missional Studies at Morling College. Before that she was leading a church in Sydney for thirteen years. She was ordained in 2002 and recently attained her doctorate in the formation of a missional church. She teaches and preaches at church events and also loves to mentor emerging leaders.

John McClean teaches Systematic Theology and Ethics at Christ College, Sydney. He has written a book on the theology of Pannenberg and an introduction to doctrine, and is working on one about the doctrine of revelation. He is the convenor of the Gospel, Society and Culture Committee of the Presbyterian Church in NSW.

Margaret Mowczko is vice president of the Sydney chapter of Christians for Biblical Equality. She received the Paul Dovico Prize from Macquarie University for her MA thesis on Phoebe and the role of deacons in the early church. Marg is an award-winning writer and blogs at newlife.id.au.

Edwina Murphy is Lecturer in Church History at Morling College, having previously served as an evangelistic intern and associate pastor. She has published a devotional, *Ancient Wisdom Living Hope,* and a number of scholarly articles on Cyprian. She is married to Peter and they have two children.

Anthony Petterson has been a full-time lecturer at Morling College since 2006, teaching Old Testament and Hebrew. He is married to Megan and has two teenage and two young-adult children. He has published *Behold Your King: The Hope for the House of David in the Book of Zechariah,* and *Haggai, Zechariah & Malachi,* an Apollos commentary.

Andrew Sloane is Director of Postgraduate Studies at Morling College. He began at Morling as Lecturer in Old Testament and Christian Thought. He studied medicine and practised briefly as a medical doctor before studying theology. Andrew has previously ministered in Baptist churches and has been on faculty at Ridley College in Melbourne.

David Starling lectures in New Testament and Theology at Morling College. He has written several books, including *UnCorinthian Leadership* and *Hermeneutics as Apprenticeship* (forthcoming). David and his wife Nicole are involved together in serving God at Macquarie Baptist Church, together with their four children.

Nicole Starling is a postgraduate student and adjunct lecturer in Church History at Morling College. She has previous degrees in law and social sciences, and has published articles on gender, history, and apologetics in *CASE* journal and the *Journal of Religious History.* She is currently working on a chapter for a forthcoming multi-author volume on the history of Australian preaching.

Justine Toh is Senior Research Fellow at the Centre for Public Christianity. She worked at Reuters and Fairfax Digital before completing her doctorate in cultural studies at Sydney's Macquarie University in 2009. She speaks and writes about Christianity and everyday life and can be contacted at jtoh@ publicchristianity.org.

Kamal Weerakoon is a Presbyterian Church minister, a member of that church's Gospel, Society and Culture Committee, and a research fellow at Morling College, working toward an interdisciplinary PhD in missiology and intercultural studies.

Patricia Weerakoon is a medical doctor, academic, sexologist, and writer. Previously she was director of an internationally renowned graduate sexual health program at the University of Sydney. She has translated her passion to bring good holistic sexual health to all people into practical sex education, sex research, and sex therapy.

Foreword

Timothy George

In 2005, I published an essay in *Christianity Today* titled "A Peace Plan for the Gender War: How to Love Your Egalitarian or Complementarian Neighbor as Yourself." This article received a lot of attention, not because I had made an original contribution to this hotly contested debate within the evangelical church, but rather because I called for a reframing of the discussion. What we needed was a kind of engagement that would allow for genuine dialogue and mutual learning to take place.

My comments were directed not to the church at large or to society in general, but to evangelical believers committed to a high view of the authority of Scripture. For example, I assumed that evangelical Christians, along with Catholic and Orthodox believers, would (or should) affirm marriage as a lifelong covenantal union between one man and one woman—as Genesis teaches, Jesus believed, and Paul affirmed. I also assumed that evangelical believers would (or should) uphold the sacredness of every human life, including children still waiting to be born. Such matters, of course, cannot be taken for granted. A fuller discussion of "gender" would need to include these and many other matters not covered in my article and barely touched on in this volume.

In this wider context, the egalitarian/complementarian question might seem to some too parochial, a bit of "inside baseball" as we say in North America. The fact remains, though, that this continues to generate controversy, often with more heat than light, and still constitutes a church-dividing issue within many ecclesial communities and denominational families. There is no shortage of passionate arguments and book-length advocacy statements on both sides of this polemical divide. But what we have in this volume is quite rare: a symposium of earnest Christians, colleagues and friends, who both speak and listen carefully to one another in a spirit of conviction and humility.

In this volume, the discussion often returns to this question: What does the Bible mean by what it says? The technical term for such a quest is *hermeneutics,* and the contributors to this volume are skilled interpreters, adept at "correctly handling the word of truth" (2 Tim 2:15). The arguments put forth here do not resolve the difficult exegetical questions that have surfaced in the vast literature on this debate, but they do show how such a discussion can be conducted in a charitable manner, with respect and goodwill on all sides. In a too-wordy age of raucous rhetoric and self-referential theology, such an engagement is a worthy achievement indeed.

Speaking at Regent College some years ago, Mary Stewart Van Leeuwen challenged her audience to remember that issues raised in gender discussions could not be resolved by arguments, organization, and church political strategies alone. Such matters, she said, require serious, prayerful engagement. The essays in this volume have been undertaken in such a spirit. By doing so, they make a signal contribution to the spirituality of dialogue. Dialogue does not require compromise or the abandonment of convictions. But it is a call to speak the truth in love, to express our disagreements in the context of community. In this way, we forge friendships and walk humbly with our God. In this way, we magnify Jesus Christ—crucified, risen, and reigning—the Lord of all our disputes.

Introduction

David Starling and Edwina Murphy

Among the many books on gender that have been published within evangelical circles in recent years, the vast majority presuppose and perpetuate a state of affairs in which the complementarian/egalitarian schema functions not only as a distinction but also as a divide: the published books, in almost all cases, either advocate for one view against the other, or bring together proponents of the two main alternative views to debate the issue, trading arguments back and forth. Occasionally we hear calls for a better conversation between evangelical egalitarians and complementarians, but the increasingly tribal nature of contemporary evangelicalism's institutions means that conferences and publications reflecting this sort of conversation are still few and far between. Nevertheless, the discussions and debates continue with some vigour, online and in the flesh, and books on the subject continue to engage the interest of readers.

The Gender Conversation aims to offer something that is (sadly!) rare in all this flurry of publishing, debate, and discussion: a book that arises out of a genuine, affectionate, and mutually respectful face-to-face conversation between contributors who know one another and work together in the service of the gospel. The book had its genesis in conversations among the faculty of Morling College and reflects the ethos of an institution whose faculty and student body are composed of men and women who share an evangelical understanding of the gospel but differ on its implications for how we view issues of gender. Its chapters began as papers delivered at a day conference held at Morling in September 2015, which brought together Morling faculty members and other fellow-evangelicals within our circles of contact, to discuss issues of gender, theology, and Christian living. We encouraged the contributors to engage critically with each other's ideas, but to interact with each other in a genuine conversation—aimed at deepening mutual understanding and respect, highlighting common ground, clarifying points of difference, and learning from one another—not merely a debate in which each party aims to score points at the expense of the other.

The day conference began with a short, historically themed paper by Edwina Murphy entitled "How To Have a Conversation," which serves as an overture to this volume. It is followed by the eight parts which make up the main content of this book. Each part brings together a collection of short pieces on its theme by three different contributors, followed (in the case of Parts One to Seven) by brief responses that each contributor offers to the other two.

The papers in Part One focus on what is said and implied about gender within the Genesis 1–3 narratives of creation and fall, and the issues that arise in interpreting and applying them today. Two papers offer contrasting answers to the question of whether the Genesis narratives imply an ordered relationship between the first man and the first woman that precedes the fall and the judgements pronounced in Genesis 3; the third explores the intertextual relationship between the creation and fall narratives of Genesis 1–3 and the cultic and legal texts of Leviticus (which would have constituted a key component of the matrix within which ancient Israelite readers encountered the Genesis text).

Part Two, entitled, "Gender, Scripture, and Family," discusses the ways in which our created maleness and femaleness ought to be expressed in the gendered roles of husbands and wives, mothers and fathers, sons and daughters, and brothers and sisters within the family. The biblical texts under discussion in these chapters include the household codes of the New Testament epistles and the gospel texts that record the teachings of Jesus about marriage and singleness.

In Part Three, on "Gender, Scripture, and Church," the focus shifts to the church, and the significance of gender difference for functions which men and women perform and the offices in which they serve. A key focus within all three chapters is the interpretive questions raised by the much-debated instructions of Paul in 1 Timothy 2.

The unifying theme of Part Four, on "Gender, History, and Hermeneutics," is the way in which historical tradition and situation affect our reading and application of Scripture in matters relating to gender, both in defining women's roles and in appropriating biblical imagery. It brings together papers on female martyrs and confessors in the early church, female preaching in early colonial Australia, and the relationship between (female) Zion and the (male) Servant within the interpretation history of Isaiah.

Part Five deals with the implications of cultural context for how we read and apply Scripture in matters relating to gender. The conversation within these chapters touches on both the general, theoretical issues raised in the "Christ and culture" discussion and the particular, practical issues that arise out of reading Scripture within, for example, a nineteenth-century Korean context or a post-Christendom Australian context.

Part Six, on "Gender, Power, and Politics," takes as its theme the implications of the gospel for our contributions to the wider, public debates about the ethics and politics of gender that take place within our culture. The chapters include an exploration of the difference that "a child in the midst" makes to discussions of gender and power, a searching reflection on how the gospel of Jesus Christ brings good news to the victims of abuse and violence within the household, and a brief foray into the aesthetic and ontological presuppositions of an authentically Christian contribution to gender-political discourse.

In Part Seven, the contributors explore the complexities of the relationship between our created maleness and femaleness, the cultural practices and understandings of gender within which we are socialised, and the sense of gender identity that individual men and women experience. The contributors bring to the discussion a rich, inter-disciplinary combination of theological, medical, and cultural-studies perspectives; the result is a searching and nuanced discussion in quest of an adequate Christian understanding of issues including intersex experience, gender dysphoria, and contemporary genderqueer and transgender ideologies.

Finally, in Part Eight, the volume concludes with two papers from the evening plenary session of the conference, relating the discussion of gender to the wider question of the redemptive purposes of God for his creation and the way in which they have been fulfilled in Jesus, followed by a brief epilogue from the editors reflecting on the outcomes of the conversation and offering suggestions for how it might fruitfully be continued.

The conference was a rich and stimulating day for all who were able to be part of it. We are deeply grateful to all those (especially Sheree Brugel, Merry Ann Shabalala, and the whole cast of contributors) whose efforts made the day such a success, to the team at Morling Press (particularly Sheree, as commissioning editor, and Margaret Wilkins, as copy editor) who gave such expert assistance in converting the conference presentations into a book, and to James Stock and his colleagues at Wipf & Stock, who embraced the opportunity to come alongside us in extending the reach of the book's distribution. Our hope in publishing the book is that the blessings and benefits of the conference will be extended to many more, for the good of God's people and the furtherance of his mission in the world.

Overture: How To Have a Conversation

Edwina Murphy

One of my husband's favourite books when he was growing up was *The Bike Lesson*. Small Bear receives a new bike, but he's not allowed to ride it until his father teaches him how. Unfortunately, Papa Bear is incapable of riding a bike and each disastrous attempt—riding into a tree, down a ravine— is followed by a variation on the refrain: "That is what you should not do. So let that be a lesson to you." When the son is finally allowed on the bike, he starts riding with ease and doubles the somewhat sheepish father home. There is apparently a behavioural principle that says you shouldn't teach a skill by showing someone how *not* to do it. But it worked for the Berenstain Bears, and so I thought it might work for us today.

In that vein, I am going to highlight a few famous conversations, or colloquies, from the history of the church—and who doesn't love church history?—in the hope that we can avoid the mistakes of the past and have a fruitful conversation today.

Now I would like you to think back to the dawn of the Reformation. In 1517, Martin Luther famously nailed his Ninety-Five Theses to the door in Wittenberg. Four years later, he was on trial at the Diet of Worms, taking his stand on the authority of Scripture:

> Unless I am convinced by the testimony of the Scriptures, or by evident reason, (for I put my faith neither in Pope nor Councils alone, since it is established that they have erred again and again and contradicted one other), I am bound by the scriptural evidence adduced by me, and my conscience is captive to the Word of God. I cannot, I will not recant anything, for it is neither safe nor right to act against one's conscience. Here I stand! I can no other. God help me. Amen.[1]

Scripture, not the church, was to be the basis of authority. In the meantime, Zwingli had started his own program of reform in Zurich. His first sermon was on 1 January, 1519. He began with Matthew 1:1, preaching directly from the Greek text, and subsequently worked his way right through the book. The Bible was the foundation. All one needed to do was clear away the accretions of church teaching and tradition and the truth would be clear. Sola Scriptura! What could possibly go wrong?

Well, it wasn't too long before Luther and Zwingli were disagreeing over one of the central practices in the church—the Lord's Supper. They probably could have continued quite happily writing abusive treatises and slandering each other in public, but there was a serious problem. The decision of the Second Diet of Speyer, held in 1529, meant that the spread of Lutheranism was banned. The Lutheran princes protested, hence the term "Protestant." One of them, Philip of Hesse, was keen to gain doctrinal agreement with the Reformed churches, thus enabling the Lutherans and the Swiss Reformed to unite against the military threat of the Catholics. So

---

1   Atkinson, *The Trial of Luther*, 161–62. The words "Here I stand! I can no other" are not in the earliest manuscripts, but they do make for a dramatic ending.

he arranged the Marburg Colloquy. Here's how Philip of Hesse's chancellor opened the proceedings:

> My gracious prince and lord has summoned you for the express and urgent purpose of settling the dispute over the sacrament of the Lord's Supper. Although much has been written about the matter, it is the desire of my gracious prince and lord that no one display his own particular feelings, rather that everyone seek the glory of God, the common Christian welfare, and brotherly concord. And let everyone on both sides present his arguments in a spirit of moderation, as becomes such matters.[2]

These are words that we might well adopt for our conversation today—that we don't just trumpet our own opinions, but seek God's glory, the common good of Christians, and brotherly and sisterly unity in a spirit of moderation. High aspirations indeed! And yet, I promised an example of what not to do. Don't worry—Luther hasn't spoken yet.

Luther replied that it certainly was a good idea, although he had rejected it two years earlier because he felt that everything had been said on both sides. Now, however, he wished to obey the wishes of the most pious prince, adding: "Although I have no intention of changing my mind, which is firmly made up, I will nevertheless present the grounds of my belief and show where the others are in error."[3] Not a positive start. Luther's conviction and determination, so crucial in the face of the opposition at Worms, were to prove less helpful in conversation with would-be allies at Marburg. Luther then proceeded to throw in a few unfounded accusations linking the teaching in Strasbourg to the Arian heresy. Zwingli refuted those, saying he had made his opinion on justification quite clear in his work "On the Clarity and Certainty of the Word of God." The title reflects the optimism of the

---

2   "Marburg Colloquy, 1529," in Ziegler (ed.), *Great Debates of the Reformation*, 73.
3   Ibid.

early reformers. As it turned out, Scripture was not quite as clear as first thought . . .

The debate hinged on Jesus's words: *Hoc est corpus meum.* "This is my body." Luther wrote the phrase on the table in chalk, then covered it with a velvet cloth to be removed at an appropriately dramatic moment. How much clearer could Scripture be? "This is my body!" Luther denied that the words could be taken in any other way than their literal meaning, rejecting Zwingli's metaphorical approach.

I don't think that anyone could rightly accuse either Luther or Zwingli of not holding to the authority of Scripture, and yet they disagreed over its interpretation. It seems today that some evangelicals avoid listening to the opinions of others who disagree with them, dismissing them out of hand as not submitting to the Bible. I think this has to stop. Name-calling may have a distinguished pedigree in the history of the church, but it is one tradition we can do without. Reasoned exegesis of Scripture can lead to different positions, although that's not to say that any interpretation whatsoever is acceptable. We might want to remember Augustine's caution, that since love is the fulfilment of the law, "Anyone who thinks that he has understood the divine scriptures or any part of them, but cannot by his understanding build up this double love of God and neighbour, has not yet succeeded in understanding them."[4]

Ironically, the hope still harboured by Melanchthon, Luther's associate, of reuniting with the Catholics may have led to his unwillingness to accommodate the Reformed here. So, with no agreement reached on the issue of the Lord's Supper, both sides were persuaded to come back the next day, state what they could affirm together, and promise to seek the truth in brotherly love. But it was more a desperate attempt to salvage something, and soon the old animosity returned.

---

4   Augustine, *De Doctrina Christiana* (*On Christian Doctrine*), 1.36.40.

That sticking point, which Lutherans later abandoned anyway, prevented the two groups of reformers from uniting, with the result that they continued squabbling amongst themselves and fighting against the Catholics—Zwingli himself was killed in battle. Having rejected the authority of the Roman Catholic Church, they also developed their own rigid theological systems—only Luther, it seems, was permitted to follow his conscience; others had to toe the line. While Catholic missionaries went to Japan and China, Protestants gave little thought to the rest of the world. It's my hope that instead of being caught up in scoring points against one another, we keep in mind the bigger picture. My focus should not be on convincing a fellow Christian to adopt the Edwina Jane Murphy perspective on life, the universe, and everything. Instead, I should be working together with other Christians, even those who fall slightly short of my comprehensive theological understanding, to take the hope of Jesus to a broken world.

The 1054 Schism is another great example of how not to have a conversation, although no-one really noticed there was a schism until one hundred and fifty years later. Over the centuries, the Eastern and Western sides of the church had been drifting apart. They spoke different languages—Greek and Latin. They had different practices. For example, the East had married clergy; the West thought that was licentious. The West used unleavened bread; in the East, the yeast represented the humanity of Christ and so they thought the West was denying this aspect of Christ's nature. And, of course, they were both unhappy about the filioque clause in the Nicene Creed. The original version said that the Holy Spirit proceeds "from the Father." The Western version was modified to read "from the Father and the Son." The East were outraged that the West would change a creed agreed upon at an ecumenical council without consultation; the West were incensed that the East had removed a clause from the creed—it had been there for so long they had forgotten it wasn't original. So the situation was rather sensitive.

The Normans had conquered southern Italy, and enforced Latin rites in all the churches. In retaliation, the Patriarch of Constantinople, Michael

Cerularius, closed down the Latin-rite churches in his territory. The pope, Leo IX, wasn't too happy about this, so he sent someone to negotiate. Given the delicate situation, you can imagine that he might have chosen someone fluent in Greek with excellent diplomatic skills. But, of course, he sent a head-kicker who spoke only Latin and was committed to the supremacy of the pope (another thing the Eastern churches weren't too keen about). Cardinal Humbert marched into Hagia Sophia, laid down a bull of excommunication on the altar, and stormed back out. Unsurprisingly, Cerularius returned the favour.

After 1204, when Crusaders sponsored by Venetian merchants didn't quite make it to the Holy Land and spent three days looting, raping, and killing their Eastern brethren in Constantinople, the relationship really was in tatters. Later attempts to restore it failed because even when the negotiators managed to come to an agreement, the people in the Eastern churches wouldn't accept it. The wounds were too deep. And they were not going to give up their identity. Of course, whatever other concessions might be made, the Roman Catholic Church was not going to budge on the primacy of the pope. In the wake of Vatican II, the anathemas have been removed, faults acknowledged on both sides, and the relationship is on the mend. It has, however, taken almost a millennium. I hope we'll make progress a little faster than that!

To have a conversation you need to learn other people's language, and listen, not just speak. You need to be sensitive to their traditions and way of looking at the world. (Of course, other people have traditions; we only have biblical practices!) Also, if you want to be friends with someone, it helps if you don't beat them up.

If we go even further back, into Old Testament times, we see that sometimes just the way we use our words can identify what side we're on. In Judges 12, the Gileadites have just fought the Ammonites, Israel's enemies, and won. (I pass over the unfortunate episode of Jephthah's daughter.) Then the Ephraimites, who refused to help in the first place, complained about not being part of the victory. So they went into battle against their brothers, saying, "You Gileadites are renegades from Ephraim and Manasseh" (Judg 12:4). And so, we have God's people fighting among themselves.

Now, the Gileadites are winning the day and they capture the fords of the Jordan. Some survivors want to get back home to Ephraim but, of course, they say they're not Ephraimites. Who knows if they're telling the truth? They are, after all, fellow Israelites. So the Gileadites come up with a great idea—they get them to say the word "Shibboleth." Its literal meaning is the part of a plant containing grain, like an ear of corn. It can also mean, in other contexts, a stream. But they're not talking about farming or water supply. You see, the Ephraimites can't pronounce the "Sh" sound, and so they say "Sibboleth." That gives them away, and the Gileadites were able to slaughter over 40,000 of them in the end. We're not aiming for that kind of outcome today.

We shouldn't be envious when other Christians are successful. We shouldn't rejoice in the defeat of our brothers and sisters in Christ—they're not the enemy! Let's not divide ourselves into tribes, using coded language to identify who's in and who's out, who we'll accept and who we'll reject, but rather think of ourselves, together, as the people of God. If our battle is against principalities and powers, then in addition to putting on the full armour of God, we are also called to "keep on praying for all the Lord's people" (Eph 6:10–18). If we are faithful in praying for one another, we'll find it easier to keep our swords pointed in the right direction.

If Luther could be wrong, and Zwingli could be wrong, and even Calvin could be wrong, if those giants of the faith were sometimes in error, then perhaps there is the slightest chance that not everything I think is correct. The possibility remains that I can learn by listening to others as we study God's word together. As Cyprian, third-century bishop of Carthage, says:

> No-one ought stubbornly to do battle in defence of
> an opinion once acquired and long held; but should
> rather eagerly embrace another viewpoint if it is an

improvement and of greater benefit. For when we are being offered improved counsel, we are not being defeated, we are being instructed. This is especially true when it is a question of those matters that concern the unity of the church and the truth of our faith and hope.[5]

> WE WORRY TOO MUCH ABT FIGHTING OUR OWN BROTHER IN CHRIST INSTEAD OF COMING TOGETHER TO FIND THE TRUE SOURCE OF KNOWLEDGE. WE WOULD RATHER PROVE OUR POINT TO BE JUSTIFIED INSTEAD OF FIGHTING FOR THE TRUTH TO BE SPOKEN FROM GOD'S WORD.

---

5   Cyprian, *Epistle* 71.3.2.

Part One

Gender, Scripture, and Creation

Genesis 3—The Creation of Order, or Frustration of the Creation Order?

Anthony Petterson

In 1 Corinthians and 1 Timothy the teaching about relationships between men and women in church is grounded in God's work in creation. A crucial point in the contemporary debate is whether responsibility and authority are given to Adam in Genesis 1 and 2 before the fall (the complementarian position), or Adam's "rule" is only a consequence of the fall and imposed on marriage as a source of oppression from which Christ liberates his followers (the feminist/egalitarian position). In this paper I argue that there are at least ten aspects of the account in Genesis 1–3 that support the conclusion that the man (Adam) was given responsibility to lead his wife (Eve) before the fall and that God's punishment in Genesis 3 does not establish order, but frustrates the created order. I grant that some points will be more convincing than others but, taken together, I think they present a strong case. Indeed, many feminist scholars agree with this reading, but because they do not share evangelical convictions about the authority of this part of God's word, they dismiss or question its relevance for today.[1] While this part of the Bible is dissonant with our culture, my experience is that it is also often caricatured and misinterpreted, or made to say more than it does. Furthermore, the terminology that interpreters use in their exegesis and discussion of gender relationships often inflames and provokes tension, rather tha[...] [...] the paper.

[handwritten annotation: GOD'S DIVINE PURPOSE IS EQUAL W/ MAN & WOMAN. NOT ONE OR THE OTHER.]

Before looking at the evidence for order in the man and the woman's relationship before the fall, it is crucial to observe their equal status and importance. First, male and female are both created in the image of God (Gen 1:27), and represent his rule together. As a couple they are commissioned to "be fruitful and increase in number; fill the earth and subdue it." Indeed, both male and female are indispensable to the fulfilment of this divine purpose. In Genesis 2, the oneness or unity between the man and woman is underlined in a couple of ways. Crafted from the man's rib, the woman is "bone of his bones and flesh of his flesh" (vv. 22–23). She is made of the same substance as man.[2] In addition, in marriage the man and the woman become "one flesh" (v. 24). While this certainly entails sexual union, it is more a statement of the new kinship relationship between husband and wife—the man and the woman effectively become blood relations.[3] To be united (or to "cleave") speaks of the permanency of the relationship.

Within this relationship of husband and wife there is also evidence of an order. The following points indicate the man is given responsibility to lead his wife before the fall and that she was to offer him willing assistance to fulfil God's commission together.

First, the sequence of creation in Genesis 2 with the man created first indicates the husband leads in the relationship from the beginning (the

---

1   For instance, Clines, *Eve*, 37, says: "if that is what the text says we cannot accept the text" (cf. 46–47). Or Gellman, "Gender," (335), "feminist theology . . . can proceed only by boldly declaring independence from its being able to read the biblical text in a favourable light."

2   Kraus, *Gender Issues*, 25, notes the word translated "bone" can also be translated "self" or "selfsame."

3   Wenham, *Genesis*, 1.71.

man is created from the dust of the ground in v. 7, and the woman is later created from the rib of the man in v. 21). Paul refers to this aspect of the Genesis narrative in both 1 Cor 11:8 and 1 Tim 2:13. Some object to this point contesting that if the sequence in which God creates is significant, then this would give animals authority over humans. However, Paul's claim seems to be about the narrative sequence in Genesis 2–3, where events in the story are carefully arranged in order to convey meaning. The panorama of Genesis 1 is crafted so that the creation of humanity on the sixth day crowns God's work and the Sabbath forms its supreme goal, hence the sequence is animals then humans.[4] In Genesis 2, where the narrative zooms in on the creation of humanity, the sequence in which the man and the woman are created is designed to convey an understanding of their relationship to each other— that the man is the leader. This leadership is seen later when he is the one to initiate a new family (v. 24). Elsewhere in Genesis 2–3, sequence is highly significant and reflects an order in creation (see points five and six).

Second, the prohibition against eating from the tree of the knowledge of good and evil is spoken to the man alone (in 2:17). He has the responsibility to mediate this command to his wife after her creation and protect her from disobeying it. Presumably this command could have been given to both of them after the creation of the woman, or given again to the woman by God after her creation, but the account as it stands implicitly gives the man this responsibility to which he is later held to account (see points five and six).

Third, the woman is created for the man to resolve a deficiency in his experience, namely that he was alone and needed "a helper suitable for him" (2:18). On its own, the word "helper" might not entail order if it means helping alongside.[5] However, the immediate context indicates that the man is helpless without her to fulfil God's command to fill the earth. She does much more than come alongside; the purpose of her creation is to meet and remedy the man's deficiency (cf. 1 Cor 11:9). The man is not said to be

---

4   Blocher, *In the Beginning*, 57.
5   Meyers, *Rediscovering Eve*, 73. Meyers argues that *kĕnegdô* ("suitable" NIV) means "on a par with," yet ultimately meaning must be determined from context.

a helper of the woman, which would make it clearly mutual. Instead, she is created as "a helper suitable for him." Some argue that because God is said to be helper (e.g., Exod 18:4; Ps 46:1; cf. Isa 30:5), it cannot be understood in terms of order. However, this objection holds only if "helper" is understood in terms of value and status, rather than in terms of function. Instances of God helping humanity demonstrate that at times, God may respond to a person's cry for help and place himself under them for their benefit. This does not affect his divinity (status or ontology), just as the incarnation did not diminish the Son's divinity. Nor does being a "helper" diminish the woman's humanity as one who is to bring glory to God—being a "helper" is a role with special dignity.

MAN SHOULD BE THE AUTHORITATOR.

Fourth, when the woman is brought to the man after her creation, he is the one who takes the active role in speaking. Furthermore, he is the one who twice names his wife, once before the fall and the other afterwards. First in 2:23 he calls her "woman," and in 3:20 she is named "Eve." This may not seem significant until it is recognised that in the ancient Near East, giving a name is often an authoritative act.[6] In Genesis 1-2, it connects to the task given to humanity to rule over the animals (in 1:26 and repeated in 1:28), which Adam demonstrates in 2:19-20 by naming them. It is a task which reflects the image of God, since on three days God names parts of creation (Gen 1:5, 8, 10). In this context, naming is undoubtedly an authoritative act. Two objections are often made to this—first, would not this make the woman the same as the animals? Clearly not, in the light of Genesis 1 where the woman also is given authority over the animals, and in the light of Genesis 2 where she alone matches the man. Second, some point out that, since Hagar names the LORD in Gen 16:13, name giving is simply discernment rather than an authoritative act. This observation seems to be true for Hagar, since the name she "discerns" is consonant with her recent experience of the Lord as the God who sees ("El Roi"). However, naming is much more than discernment for the man in Genesis 2–3. When the man names the living creatures here, the text is explicit that "whatever the man called each living creature, that was its

---

6   See for instance, von Rad, *Genesis*, 83: "Name-giving in the ancient Orient was primarily an exercise of sovereignty of command." Also Wenham, *Genesis*, 1.68.

name" (v. 19). Because the man's naming carried authority, the name stuck, so to speak.[7] Indeed, throughout the rest of the Bible, the women continue to be "woman" and the first woman continues to be called "Eve." However, the name that Hagar gives the Lord is never again used in Scripture—it did not stick. This is precisely because she does not have authority to name the Lord. God is not named by human beings, whether male or female, but he reveals his own name when he sees fit (e.g., Exod 3:14–15). While Adam's naming of his wife and Hagar's naming of God use similar Hebrew expressions, each context indicates a very different type of naming.

Fifth, when the man and the woman hide from the Lord after eating from the tree, the Lord calls for the man first (3:9–12), then the woman (3:13). This implies the man had responsibility for his wife, even before the punishment is placed on them. God does not confront the couple together, which would be expected if responsibility were evenly distributed. This is all the more notable since earlier they were made "one flesh" (2:24). Related to this, and sixth, the pattern of evasion and punishment in Genesis 3 supports seeing an earlier order having been established in Genesis 1–2. In terms of evasion, the man blames the woman (3:12), and the woman then blames the serpent (3:13), each seeking to evade their God-given responsibility. When God announces punishment, he speaks first to the serpent (3:14–15), then the woman (3:16), then the man (3:17–19). This ordering in the narrative suggests seeing a man/woman/animal order having been established in creation.[8]

Seventh, while Eve is clearly portrayed as the first human to sin by eating first from the tree (3:6), when God confronts each of them, only the serpent and the man are accused of doing wrong (3:14, 17). Obviously the woman is understood to have been involved in the wrongdoing (3:13) and bears her own punishment (3:16), but the man and the woman are viewed as a unity for whose joint actions the man is ultimately responsible. Again, this implies the man had responsibility for his wife prior to the fall.

---

7   Gellman, "Gender," 331–34.
8   See further, Wenham, *Genesis*, 1.50–51.

Eighth, the man's sin is not only that he ate from the tree about which God commanded him not to eat, but also that he "listened to" his wife (3:17).[9] Of course he does not stand condemned for doing what all good husbands should! God's condemnation indicates the man failed to exercise his God-given responsibility to lead his wife in the ways of the Lord. He passively followed his wife when she was deceived by the serpent and then openly disobeyed God's word. The comment that he "was with her" when she ate (3:6) underlines his negligent failure.

Ninth, the punishment of death that was first spoken to the man as a warning in 2:17, is finally spoken to him as part of his punishment in 3:19. Clearly death will engulf both the man and the woman (and animal life), but the climactic judgement is spoken to the man as part of his punishment because he is the one who ultimately bore responsibility for their act of rebellion. Similarly, in 3:24 only the man is said to be driven out of the garden, but clearly the woman is to be understood as driven out as well, otherwise the events of 4:1 would have been impossible. The narrative again points to the leadership of the man in the relationship. Indeed, in readings of Genesis 1–3 elsewhere in Scripture, responsibility is consistently placed at the feet of Adam (e.g., Rom 5:12–21; 1 Cor 15:22, 45–49; 1 Tim 2:14). This only makes sense if Adam is understood to have responsibility for Eve before the fall (i.e., in Genesis 1–2).

Tenth, other punishments reinforce the design God had already established in the pre-fall creation, but now life continues with pain and toil. It seems likely this is the case for the marriage relationship as well. So, childbirth is implicit in 1:28, but now it will be with great pain (3:16). Work is part of God's good purpose in creation (2:15), but now it is experienced as painful toil (3:17–19). Similarly, order is not introduced into the marriage relationship in 3:16, but now as a consequence of sin, the God-intended relationship of the husband's responsibility to lead and the wife's willing assistance to fulfil God's commission has been disrupted.

---

9   The verb (*šāmaʿ*) translated as "listened to" (NIV) can also be translated "obeyed."

As a consequence of sin, the woman will now desire to rule over her husband and he will assert his rule.[10]

In these ten ways, a close analysis of the text of Genesis 1–3 supports seeing that before the fall the man was given responsibility for his wife Eve and authority to be used to lead her in the ways of the Lord, and that God's punishment in Genesis 3 does not establish order, but frustrates the created order. Unfortunately in the discussion of the implications of this, it is often taken to mean that Genesis 1–3 is demeaning to women who are portrayed as inferior to men and open to male abuse. In our contemporary culture, words like "subordinate," "hierarchy," and "patriarchal" are value laden, and in my view prove unhelpful in furthering discussion, since they are mostly used with a pejorative sense.[11] Even the word "submission" now has connotations of sexual slavery, which subverts its usefulness in explaining the Bible's picture of male and female relationships in marriage. Language that clarifies is to be preferred to that which seeks to win points, and it is paramount that evangelical Christians communicate clearly here. At a time when there is massive confusion on gender in our society, when reports of domestic violence are on the increase, and women are increasingly only valued in terms of their ability to contribute to the economy, in my view it is more important than ever that evangelicals come to one mind on what the Bible is teaching on gender and speak with one voice.

In terms of the character of male leadership or what the NT calls "headship" in marriage, it is crucial to recognise that in Genesis it is patterned on God himself. Not only the male, but male and female are to exercise dominion over the earth as agents of God and reflect his compassion and loving care. In Genesis 1, God's rule is benevolent, demonstrated in his concern for blessing both humanity and the wider world (1:28; 2:3). This means the husband's "leadership" (entailing authority) is exercised in love

---

10   See Mathews, *Genesis*, 248–51.
11   See also Block, "Marriage and Family," 41.

(cf. Eph 5:25), with "willing assistance" on behalf of the wife.[12] There may be better ways of describing this, but it seems to me that these terms avoid reading a value of each partner in the relationship.[13] The text of Genesis nowhere says or implies that the woman is inferior, or of less worth in the relationship, even if she fulfils a different role. The assertion, often taken to be self-evident, that order in a relationship is demeaning to the party who is under the authority of another again fails to see that the type of leadership envisaged in Genesis is not one that limits human freedom, but promotes it. Many human relationships require order to flourish, like an employee and their boss, or a coach and their football team, or an orchestra and their conductor, or a parent and their child—these authority structures do not entail that the boss, the coach, the conductor, or the parent are of greater human value or superior, nor that those under their leadership are inferior, subservient, abused, or oppressed. Why is any order in the marriage relationship so often assumed to be detrimental?

Similarly, it is sometimes asserted that order in the marriage relationship is abusive or will foster abuse. Yet a generation of social change in which the traditional "patriarchal" ordering of marriage has been largely dismantled in the modern West can hardly be said to have swept away the problems of intimate partner violence and abuse; in fact, recent media in Australia report the incidence of abuse has increased, not declined—how is this to be explained? It is likely that abuse was under-reported in earlier generations when women were generally much more financially dependent on their husbands. At the same time, another key factor must surely be that the kind of protective male leadership set forth in the Bible has generally been despised and ridiculed in the broader culture. Interestingly, social science research shows that there is an inverse relationship between church

---

12   Block, "Marriage and Family," 43–44: "we do a disservice to the biblical record if we are preoccupied with the power the *'āb* [father/husband] wielded. In healthy and functional households the male head was neither despot nor dictator. . . [instead, the OT] views leadership in general to be a privilege granted to an individual in order to serve the interests of those who are led."

13   Block, "Marriage and Family," 43–44, notes: "This emphasis on the responsibilities associated with headship over the household (as opposed to its privileges and power) is consistent with the overall tenor of the Old Testament, which views leadership in general to be a privilege granted to an individual in order to serve the interests of those who are led."

attendance and domestic violence among Protestant men.[14] It would be fascinating to explore whether feminism as an ideology is failing to prevent the abuse of women because in rejecting male leadership what is also rejected is an expectation of active care, protection, provision, and love that male leadership should entail. While it is sadly true that "patriarchy" often tips over into the control and abuse of women (as Gen 3:16 foreshadows), feminism in itself does not seem to provide the solution to this abuse. Ultimately the real solution to this serious problem is found in Christ who, forgoing selfish use of power and egoistic pursuit of status, shows how authority can be exercised in love and in service that expressly seek the good of the other (cf. Eph 5:25–33; 1 Pet 3:7).

The pattern for marriage relationships in Genesis 1–3 is sometimes made to say more than it does. In his commentary on Genesis, Mathews rightly states that "Genesis cannot be viewed as a paradigm for all man-woman relationships in society. To apply it universally to other social contexts such as government, education, or commerce, would be unwarranted, for chaps. 2–3 do not address such institutions."[15] These chapters primarily concern marriage. In addition, within the marriage relationship, gender roles are not spelled out in detail; rather, they are only broadly defined. In the punishments on the woman and the man (Gen 3:16–19) there is focus for the man on the responsibility that he bears in their marriage to lead her in the ways of the Lord and protect her from evil, along with his agricultural pursuits (which in the curse suggests crops, but the wider context of Gen 1 also indicates livestock—e.g., 1:24–25). The focus of the woman's role is on children (cf. 1:28), and the companionship she provides her husband to fulfil God's commission together (cf. 2:18). That the man bears responsibility to lead the marriage does not mean that he cannot delegate aspects of it to her, nor that the woman does not have any power in the relationship.

---

14   Tracy, "Domestic Violence," 573–94.
15   Mathews, *Genesis*, 220.

Other places in the OT, such as Proverbs 31, show the wife of noble character engaged in commercial activities in the wider society in addition to the affairs of her household.[16]

Robert Morgan rightly observes that "some disagreements about what the Bible means stem not from obscurities in the texts, but from the conflicting aims of the interpreters."[17] A close analysis of Genesis 1–3 shows at least ten points that together indicate the man is given the responsibility to lead his wife before the fall, to which she was to offer willing assistance to fulfil the Lord's commission together. While this has sometimes been seriously misconstrued to bolster male status and justify abuse, no serious reading of Genesis can justify this. On the contrary, the presentation in Genesis of a husband's loving leadership should be seen in care, protection, and provision for his wife. Genesis's presentation of different gender roles may jar for many in our contemporary culture, but here is another point at which followers of Jesus are called to be counter-cultural.

---

16   Meyers, *Rediscovering Eve*, 185, notes that women's control of and expertise in household technologies would have given them personal and social power, and considerable influence.

17   Quoted in Thiselton, *New Horizons*, 49.

Response: Margaret Mowczko

Anthony and I are in agreement on his points concerning the essential equality of men and women. However, there are several others in his paper that I disagree with, points that appear to be inferences without a basis in the biblical text.

For example, Anthony makes the statement:

> . . . the prohibition against eating from the tree of the knowledge of good and evil is spoken to the man alone (in 2:17). He has the responsibility to mediate this command to his wife after her creation and protect her from disobeying it . . . [T]he account as it stands implicitly gives the man this responsibility to which he is later held to account.[18]

The biblical text says nothing at all about the man being given a responsibility to mediate God's command; and the text says nothing at all about the man being given a responsibility to protect the woman from disobeying it. It could just as easily be inferred that God repeated his command to the woman once she was made.

---

18   See page 17, above

We know that God spoke to the woman as well as to the man. In Genesis 1:28–30 we read that God spoke to both men and women together; and in Genesis 3 we read that he spoke to the man and to the woman individually. Moreover, he held each accountable and responsible for their own actions (Gen 3:9–12, 13, 16, 17–19). None of God's statements in Genesis 3 suggests that he held the man accountable for supposedly failing to protect the woman.

Throughout Scripture we see that God continues to speak in various ways to men and to women, sometimes even repeating his instructions. For example, God gave Samson's mother certain instructions, and then repeated them to Samson's father. Did God repeat his command to Eve? We simply do not know how she learned of it.

Hagar is a woman mentioned in both Anthony's paper and mine. In Genesis chapters 16 and 21, on two separate occasions, and in two different ways, God spoke to Hagar. Hagar named God "El Roi" based on her first astonishing encounter with him. The fact that the name is recorded in Scripture indicates God's approval of the name. It also allows the significance of the name to continue, even if no-one actually calls God by that name. In fact, very few people actually call God by his name (cf. Exod 3:13–15). Interestingly, God gave Solomon a name that no-one seems to have used, "Jedidiah" (2 Sam 12:25). Yet this name is not dismissed, or considered as lacking credence, just because no-one uses it.

My biggest concern with Anthony's paper was the emphasis he placed on the man being created first and the woman second, and the supposed relevance of this order today. The idea that a "first" person has more authority than a "second" person challenges what Jesus taught about his kingdom. In Jesus's kingdom the humble are exalted, the lowly are the greatest, the last are first, and the first are last. We corrupt these basic kingdom principles when we place hierarchies in marriage and ministry.

Response: Geoffrey Harper

Much gender-debate literature that I read misses the nub of the issue for, apart from extremists, no-one is arguing that women are ungifted, or that they ought not to be involved in ministry, or that they are ontologically inferior to men. Thus I appreciate that Anthony focuses on what I think is at the centre of current debate—that is, whether asymmetric authority is intrinsic to creation order or whether it is a violation of that order. That seems to be, to my mind at least, the dividing point between complementarians and egalitarians.

The core of Anthony's paper adduces ten points from Gen 1–3 to support the (complementarian) view that Adam, before the fall, was given "responsibility for his wife Eve and authority to be used to lead her in the ways of the Lord." Although Gen 1–3 is subtle, Anthony makes a good case for this reading. However, as these arguments are both frequently made and rebutted in the literature, I want to focus my comments instead on some ancillary points he makes.

First, Anthony notes that Gen 1–3 is "often caricatured and misrepresented, or made to say more than it does." I wholeheartedly agree, although I would like to add that both sides are guilty here. Egalitarians and complementarians alike frequently (mis)use Gen 1–3 simply to proof text prior convictions. Genesis must be allowed to speak on its own terms.

Second, and towards that end, Anthony helpfully situates the specific issue of authority *difference* within Genesis's broader aim to highlight *sameness*. As he rightly notes, both men and women are created in the image of God, together they are to rule and to be fruitful, each is essential to the other. This, like many aspects of Gen 1–3, functions to create significant dissonance with broader ANE views. In other creation texts that come to us from the deserts of the Levant none focuses on the creation of women. Only the origin of men or of generic humanity is explicitly discussed. Genesis seems written to counter such neglect and is thereby highly subversive in its original context. The text's affirming stance towards women is often lost in the heat of battle, which is unfortunate, because it is a point both sides can agree on.

But third, Anthony also distinguishes function from ontology; difference and sameness are not mutually exclusive. Thus he critiques the notion that "order or hierarchy in a relationship is demeaning to the party who is under the authority of the other." It is a pity Anthony could not flesh this out more within the scope of his paper because such non-intuitive thinking really is at the heart of the gospel. It's little wonder that Jesus had to correct the faulty thinking of his disciples time and again regarding their equation of leadership authority with lording it over others.

Lastly, Anthony draws attention to another pertinent point for current discussion—that is, the use of terminology with pejorative associations. While one could argue that words are being misunderstood, I think the horse has already bolted. Much better, then, is Anthony's call for "language that clarifies" in order to allow evangelicals to properly communicate rather than aggravate.

Is a Gender Hierarchy Implicit in the Creation Narrative of Genesis 2:4–25?

Margaret Mowczko

Introduction

For much of its history, the church has used the second half of Genesis 3:16 as a definitive statement on the status of women. In this verse God tells the first woman that even though she will have a desire for her husband, he will rule over her. In recent decades, however, many Christians have looked again at this verse, and have interpreted Genesis 3:16 as God's prediction or description of what will happen in relationships between men and women, now that sin has entered the world. This verse is not God's mandate or endorsement of patriarchy.

Despite this revision of Genesis 3:16, some Christians maintain that a gender hierarchy, with men being in charge, is God's will and design for society and marriage. They appeal to a reading of Genesis chapter two to support their view, and believe a gender hierarchy is implicit in the created

WOMAN ARE A REPRESENTATIVE OR REFLECTION OF THE REDEEMED CHURCH.

order of the man being formed first, and the woman second.[19] I will argue, however, that the narrative in Genesis 2 does not imply a gender hierarchy, but instead contains profound statements concerning the equality of the first man and woman.

While this paper mostly focuses on Genesis 2, I will begin with a brief look at what Genesis 1 says about men and women. I will also briefly discuss whether Paul believed that a gender hierarchy is implicit in the created order, or if he taught that the created order is somehow significant in human relationships. But I'd like to begin with a caution.

The first few chapters of Genesis contain important foundational truths about God and his world, and our place in it. Genesis 1 and 2 tell us, in only a few words, the nature of humankind, including the purpose and function of men and women. As well as being sparing in detail, these two chapters are somewhat enigmatic. They raise more questions than they answer, and so we all have our own ideas and pet theories about how certain things may have played out. We must stay with the text, however, and see what is actually being stated. We must allow the text to communicate what the original authors intended to convey.

Genesis Chapter One

The author of Genesis 1 tells us about God's creation of the world, including his creation and commissioning of men and women. Here we read that God took the earth and that he made it into something beautiful and functional.[20] Verses 26–28 tell us the purpose and function of humanity:

---

19   *Recovering Biblical Manhood and Womanhood* (*RBMW*), edited by John Piper and Wayne Grudem, is a volume containing twenty-six chapters written by twenty-three authors who believe in a gender hierarchy in marriage and in the church. Nineteen of the essays include the argument that the permanent subordination of women is based on the created order given in Genesis 2. Affirmation 3 of "The Danvers Statement," included in RBMW, states "Adam's headship [i.e., authority] in marriage was established by God before the Fall, and was not a result of sin." The authors of "The Danvers Statement" provide Genesis 2:16–18, 2:21–25, 3:1–13, and 1 Corinthians 11:7–9 as the Bible verses which they believe support their view of male authority. While some of the narrative in Genesis 2 and 3 is told with a spotlight on the first man, I will contend that the text nowhere indicates that the first woman is in anyway less than him in status, function, or authority before the fall.

20   Walton, *Genesis*, 84.

TRINITY

Then God said, "Let [us] make humankind (Hebrew: *'ādām*) in our image, according to our likeness; and let them have dominion over the fish of the sea, and over the birds of the air, and over the cattle, and over all the wild animals of the earth, and over every creeping thing that creeps upon the earth."

> "So God created humankind (*'ādām*) in his image,
> in the image of God he created them;
> male and female he created them."

God blessed them, and God said to them, "Be fruitful and multiply, and fill the earth and subdue it; and have dominion over the fish of the sea and over the birds of the air and over every living thing that moves upon the earth." (Gen 1:26–28 NRSV)

There are several points that I want to highlight from this passage. In these verses we read:

- both men and women were created by God in his image and likeness;

- both men and women were blessed by God;

- both men and women were spoken to by God and given certain commands:

  - to procreate;

  - to have dominion over the earth;

  - to rule the animals.

These verses tell us that there was a differentiation between male and female humans at creation.[21] There is no differentiation, however, in the

---

21   See N. T. Wright's *Women's Service in the Church: The Biblical Basis* for his comment that animals and aspects of plant life, as well as humans, were created as male and female.

status and purpose of men and women. According to Genesis 1, men and women are equal in being and equal in function. Both are commanded to procreate, and to rule over God's created earth and the animals, as his image bearers and regents.[22] Note that, there is no indication that either men or women have a greater or lesser responsibility in obeying these commands. Note also that, while men and women are commanded to rule animals, nowhere in this chapter, or the next, does it say that some humans were to rule other humans. Thus, according to Genesis 1, men and women are also equal in authority. I won't elaborate further on the statements in Genesis 1, but we need to keep them in mind as we look at Genesis 2.

IN LIFE OR IN MARRIAGE

It is unwise to conflate the different creation accounts in Genesis 1 and Genesis 2. Yet, since we have these two accounts in the canon of Scripture, as well as a third, much abbreviated, version in Genesis 5:1–2, we should not read any of these passages in isolation. We should read these accounts with the understanding that the others bring. Furthermore, Genesis 1:26–28 is relatively straightforward in its message regarding men and women; Genesis 2 is less straightforward. One principle of interpreting Scripture is to use the clearer, easier-to-understand passages to help us understand the less clear passages. So, keeping Genesis 1 in mind, we turn to Genesis 2.

The Human in Genesis Chapter Two

In Genesis 2 we are told that the creation of the first human occurred before the first woman was made. Throughout most of this chapter, this human is called in Hebrew *hā'ādām*. The English translation of *hā'ādām* as "the man" in many Bible versions gives the impression that this person was male, but *hā'ādām* more specifically means "the human." The text does not elaborate on the sex of the first human before the operation mentioned in Genesis 2:21. His sex only becomes apparent afterwards when he is referred to as *'îš* for the first time. (*'îš* is the Hebrew word often used for an adult male

---

22   In the culture of the OT, rulers of vast empires erected images of themselves in areas where they were not physically present. These images represented "their power and rulership over far reaching areas of their empires." Hess, "Equality With and Without Innocence," 81. As God's image bearers we are representatives of God and his dominion, even though he is not "physically" present.

person.) Some suggest that we are meant to understand that this first human was an androgyne before the operation, having a male and a female side. Whatever the case, this person was alone, and this was a problem. So God declares that he will make "a helper as his partner" (Gen 2:18 NRSV).

DO NOT AGREE.

Naming the Animals

Immediately after declaring that he will make a helper, God does something that at first glance seems strange. According to Genesis 2:19, God makes the animals and brings them to the human so he can give them names. Some have stated that the act of naming the animals shows that the first human was granted with a special kind of authority, which extended to having authority over the woman, despite the fact that God had not yet made her. Naming the animals cannot have been an example of a male exercising an exclusively masculine authority, however, because as we saw in Genesis 1 women were also given authority to rule the animals (Gen 1:26–28). Also, the act of naming in the Bible does not necessarily imply authority. For instance, Hagar (the Egyptian slave of Sarah) gave God a name: a significant name that has been recorded in Scripture (Gen 16:13–14). Yet it cannot be supposed that Hagar had authority over God just because she gave him a name.

The task of naming the animals may have been designed to highlight the fact that, as yet, there was no other creature which was like the human. Consequently, at the conclusion of the naming exercise, the text states that the human had "not found a helper as his partner" (Gen 2:20 NRSV). Genesis 2 makes it clear that the woman is distinct from the animals. So the presumption of some—that the human's task of naming the animals also meant he was authorised by God to name the woman and thus have authority over her—is contrived and baseless.[23] Nevertheless, Adam did give the woman the name "Eve" after the fall (Gen 3:20). Calling her *ʾiššâ* ("woman") to compare her to *ʾîš* ("man") before the fall (Gen 2:23) was not an act of naming.

---

23   For example, Raymond Ortlund writes, "God charged the man with naming the creatures and gave him the freedom to exercise his own judgment in each case. In doing so, Adam brought the earthly creation under his dominion. This royal prerogative extended to Adam's naming of his helper." "Male-Female Equality and Male Headship, Genesis 1–3," 92.

The Surgical Removal of the Human's "Side"

God solves the problem of the human's solitude and need of help by making another human being. In Genesis 2:21, we read that God performed surgery on the first human and that he took something *out* of him. Traditionally this something has been referred to as a rib; however, the Hebrew word used here typically refers to a "part."[24] The corresponding Greek word in the Septuagint is *pleura* meaning "side," a word mostly used in the context of the human body.[25] A literal translation of Genesis 2:21–22 in the Septuagint reads: "[God] took one of his sides . . . And the Lord God built the side (*pleura*) which he had taken from Adam into a woman." Again, this may suggest we are meant to understand that the first human had a male and female side. HUN...

When the first human woke, something of his was missing. Something had been taken out and had become an integral part in the making of the first woman. When he sees the woman for the first time, the man makes several statements, one of which is: "she was taken out of man!" (Gen 2:23d ESV). This losing of a significant body part to the woman makes the concept of the created order of man first, woman second, less clear cut and decisive.

A Helper for Him

This first woman was made to help the man. In English, the words "help" and "helper" can have a broad range of connotations. "Help" can refer to a simple, modest act, or it can refer to something much more significant and vital. The Hebrew word for "helper" used in Genesis 2:18 and 20 is *ʿēzer,* and it is always and only used in the Old Testament in the context of a necessary, and powerful assistance.

---

24   The Hebrew word *ṣēlāʿ* is used forty-one times in the Old Testament, but it is only translated as "rib" and "ribs" in Genesis 2. See George Wigram, "צלע [*ṣlʿ*]."

25   Bauer/Danker, "πλευρά [*pleura*]," 824.

'ēzer is used twenty-one times in the Old Testament.[26] Apart from the two occurrences in Genesis 2, *'ēzer* is used three times in the context of people helping (or failing to help) in life-threatening situations; sixteen times it is used in reference to God as a helper. All of these texts are talking about a rescuing, powerful kind of help. In Exodus 18:4 we read that Moses named one of his sons Eliezer, which in Hebrew means "My God is my helper" (*'elî* = "my God"; *'ēzer* = "helper"). This verse explains that Moses gave his son that name because God had powerfully delivered Moses from Pharaoh's sword. Despite the consistent use of *'ēzer* as having a vital and strong sense in the Bible, when used about the first woman, its interpretation has been unfairly diminished to fit with typically lowly cultural views of women.[27]

When I first received my copy of the Septuagint, I was curious to see what Greek word the translators had used to translate *'ēzer*. Would it have the same vital and strong sense? I was delighted to discover that *'ēzer* had been translated as *boēthos* in Greek. *Boēthos* is a noun made up of two words which mean "cry out" and "run." The cognate verb *boētheō* means "to run to the aid of those who cry out for help . . ."[28] *Boēthos* and its cognates are used ten times in the Greek New Testament.[29] There is nothing in these New Testament verses that imply servitude or domesticity. Rather, they all refer to a strong, rescuing, even a divine, help. Furthermore, *boēthos* and its cognates are used over one hundred times in the Septuagint where they also always have a strong sense.[30] Considering the consistent use of *boēthos*, it is utterly unjustified to diminish the meaning when used to describe the first woman. She was made to be a vital and strong help for the man. Genesis 2 does not explain how she was to help the man, but presumably it was to alleviate the problem of the human's aloneness and to partner with him in the joint commission given in Genesis 1: to procreate, to subdue the earth, and rule the animals together. GOD WANTS US TO SERVE & HELP OUR HUSBAND IN A WAY THAT IS BIBLICAL.

---

26   Genesis 2:18–20 (twice); Exodus 18:4b; Deuteronomy 33:7; 33:26; 33:29a; Psalms 20:2; 33:20; 70:5; 89:17; 115:9–11 (three times); 121:1–2 (twice); 124:8; 146:5; Isaiah 30:5; Ezekiel 12:14; Daniel 11:34; Hosea 13:9.

27   This section adapted from Mowczko, "A Suitable Helper."

28   Perschbacher, "*Boētheō*," 72.

29   Matt 15:25; Mark 9:22–24; Acts 16:9; 21:28; 27:17; 2 Cor 6:2; Heb 2:18; 4:16; 13:6; Rev 12:16.

30   Cf. Mowczko, "Every verse in the Septuagint that contains 'boēthos.'"

Subordinate, Suitable, or Similar?

Despite the strong sense of the Hebrew and Greek words behind the English word "helper," some maintain that the first woman was not the equal of the first man.[31] The Hebrew and Greek words which qualify the word "helper"—words often translated into English as "suitable" in Genesis 2:18 and 20—indicate, however, that she was his equal. ~~AGREED.~~

The Hebrew word (technically, a prepositional phrase) used here is *kĕnegdô*. The Hebrew lexicon *Brown, Driver, and Briggs* translates Genesis 2:18 as "I will make him a help corresponding to him i.e. *equal* and adequate to himself" (emphasis added).[32] The *Gesenius Hebrew-Chaldee Lexicon* notes that *kĕnegdô* "is often used of things which are like one another." Thus the word means "similar." The first woman was a helper or strength, equal and similar to the first man.

The prefix of *kĕnegdô* (the inseparable preposition *kĕ-*) has a somewhat similar range of meanings to the Greek preposition *kata* and, in Genesis 2:18 of the Septuagint, *kĕnegdô* is translated into Greek simply as *kata*. *Kata* often has the meanings of "according to" and "corresponding with."[33] In verse 20, however, the translators chose to use a different Greek word, *homoios*, to translate *kĕnegdô*. *Homoios* means "similar" or "having the same nature."[34] It seems that the translators chose to use two different words, *kata* and *homoios*, to express the breadth of meaning of *kĕnegdô*. This is a helpful translation choice.[35]

---

31   For example, Raymond Ortlund writes "So, was Eve Adam's equal? Yes and no. She was his spiritual equal and, unlike the animals, 'suitable for him.' But she was not his equal in that she was his 'helper.'" "Male-Female Equality and Male Headship, Genesis 1–3," 91. With Ortlund's statement in mind, John Walton comments on the Hebrew word for "helper": "Nothing suggests a subservient status of the one helping; in fact, the opposite is more likely. Certainly 'helper' cannot be understood as the opposite/ complement of 'leader.'" *Genesis*, 176.

32   Brown, "נֶגֶד [*neged*; corresponding to]," 617.

33   *Kata* often has the meaning of "according to," etc., when it occurs with an accusative noun or substantive, as it does in Genesis 2:18.

34   Bauer/Danker, "ὅμοιος, [*homoios*]" 706. LSJ has several definitions for *homoios* including "resembling," "the same"; "of the same rank or station," etc., and notes that the word is used in geometry of equal angles. Liddell/Scott/Jones, "ὅμοιος, [*homoios*]" 1124–1125.

35   Gesenius comments that the translation of *kĕnegdô* in Genesis 2:18 and 20 of the Septuagint is "well rendered". Gesenius, "נֶגֶד [*neged*]."

The ideas expressed in *kĕnegdô* are of similarity, correspondence, mutuality, equality. There is not the slightest sense of subordination here. The idea of similarity continues with the man's description of the first woman. When he sees her for the first time he doesn't remark on their differences, he comments on their profound similarities and kinship: "This at last is bone of my bones and flesh of my flesh . . ." (Gen 2:23a).[36]

There is nothing whatsoever in the expression *'ēzer kĕnegdô* that implies a subordination of the first woman, or an authority of the man over the woman. Instead, *'ēzer kĕnegdô* has the meanings of strength and similarity. [37] Each of the creation accounts in Genesis chapters one, two, and five, highlights the similarity and equality of men and women.

Paul and the Created Order

The first woman was made to be a helper for the first man, but does this mean that God's will is that she, and all women, are to serve and provide unreciprocated assistance to men? There are Christians who claim just that, and they usually cite 1 Corinthians 11:8–9 to support this notion: "Indeed, man was not made from woman, but woman from man. Neither was man created for the sake of woman, but woman for the sake of man" (NRSV). These are true statements; however, this is not Paul's last word on the subject.

✢ 1 Corinthians 11:2–16 is written as a chiasm and should be read as such.[38] The statements in the first part of the chiasm must be read with the corresponding statements in the second part. The corresponding verses of 8–9 are verses 11–12 which state, "Nevertheless [or, except that], in the Lord, woman is not independent of man nor man independent of woman. For just as woman came from man, so man comes through woman; but all things come from God" (NRSV). ✢

---

36   Walton writes, "Given all the lexical data and the fact that Adam refers to woman as taken from his "bone" and "flesh," it is more likely that the text portrays God as taking a handful of bone and flesh out of Adam's side to use in the construction of Eve. Another suggestion goes so far as to suggest that Yahweh divides Adam in half, making one half (side) the woman." Genesis, 177.

37   "What God had intended then was to make a 'power' or 'strength' for the man who would in every way 'correspond to him' or even 'be his equal'." Kaiser, "Genesis," 94.

38   See Mowczko, "The Chiasm in 1 Corinthians 11:2–16."

Rather than insisting that women were created to unilaterally serve or assist men, Paul writes that men and women are mutually dependent on each other (1 Cor 11:11). And rather than placing an importance on the created order, Paul nullifies its significance by pointing out that even though the first woman's source was the first man, every other man since has been born from a woman (1 Cor 11:12). Paul did not advocate for a gender hierarchy or gender "roles" based on the created order; he advocated for mutuality and equality between the sexes.

In 1 Timothy 2:13–14, the created order is mentioned once more in the Bible. These verses tell us what we already know from Genesis 2 and 3, that "Adam was formed first, then Eve; and Adam was not deceived, but the woman was deceived and became a transgressor (1 Tim 2:13–14 NRSV). I suggest that these verses contain a correction to a twisted version of the creation of Adam and Eve that was being taught in the Ephesian church. There are several indications in 1 Timothy that the heresy in Ephesus had some similarities with some forms of proto-Gnostic heresies (e.g., 1 Tim 6:20; cf. 1 Tim 1:3–4;4:7).[39] The Gnostics were fascinated with the creation accounts and their myth-like elements; and their own elaborations on creation were a far cry from the biblical accounts (cf. 1 Tim 1:6–7).[40] The correct information given in 1 Timothy 2:13–14 is not a reason for disallowing a woman to do something that neither a man nor a woman should do: namely, to teach in an unacceptable manner (as indicated by the Greek word *authentein* in 1 Timothy 2:12.)[41]

---

39   Albert Wolters (a complementarian) has studied the nouns related to the infinitive *authentein* (a key word in 1 Timothy 2:12) and has noted, ". . . the word *authentēs* played a prominent role in Gnosticism; for example it was the name of the supreme deity in the systems of early Gnostics Cerinthus and Saturninus (first and second centuries AD)." In endnote 88 of his paper Wolters comments that it is striking that eight of the twenty-nine occurrences of *authentia* (another cognate noun of *authetein*) refer to Gnostic sources. Wolters has demonstrated a clear link between the nouns *authentēs* and *authentia* with first and second century Gnosticism. "A Semantic Study of *authentēs* and its Derivatives," 50, 64.

40   Cf. Wieland, *The Significance of Salvation: A Study of Salvation in the Pastoral Epistles*, 74–78.

41   See Mowczko, "The Consensus and Context of 1 Timothy 2:12" for more on 1 Timothy 2:12ff.

No Shame

Finally, I want to look at the last statement in Genesis chapter two. The statement that the first couple were naked and unashamed has baffled me. Why did the author choose to make this particular point? *Perhaps* this point is connected with the social construct called honour-shame which was, and is, pervasive in patriarchal cultures. The honour-shame dynamic typically allows only men to gain honour for their family, usually through public acts of bravery or benefaction. Women, on the other hand, must stringently maintain the supposed virtue of "shame" by being sexually chaste, so as not to bring dishonour to their family. (This "shame" is not like embarrassment, but is supposedly part of a virtuous woman's demeanour in honour-shame cultures.) In such cultures, honour is more valuable than life, and nothing is more ruinous than a "shame-less" woman. The more patriarchal the culture, the more women are covered up in shapeless clothing, silenced, and hidden at home guarding their chastity and preserving their shame. Elsewhere in the biblical texts there is evidence that honour-shame was part of society,[42] but in Genesis 2:25, despite the man and the woman being completely uncovered, there was no shame. Perhaps there was no shame because there was no patriarchy. Sin had not yet entered the world, and the man was not yet ruling, or exercising authority, over the woman.

[handwritten: WRONG]

[handwritten: THERE WAS NO CULTURE @ THIS POINT... THEY WERE THE 1ST. THAT'S WHY GOD CLOTHED THEM.]

Conclusion

Genesis chapter two says nothing whatsoever about the first man having more authority than the first woman, let alone having authority *over* the woman. Rather, the remarkable language in Genesis 2 is of similarity, affinity, and correspondence between the couple. There is sexual differentiation, but there is no mention of a differentiation in roles in either chapter one or two of Genesis, and there is no hint that the woman was subordinate to the man.

---

42 For example, many Bible women, even if they feature in a narrative, are not named but identified by their relationship to a man.

In 1 Corinthians 11, Paul played down any significance of the created order and pointed out that, while the first woman came from man, every other man has come from a woman, and all have God as their source. Paul also taught that, for those who are "in the Lord", man is not independent of woman, nor woman of man. Just as the first man needed someone to help him to fulfil God's commission, we continue to need each other. Men need the help of women, and women need the help of men. This mutual, reciprocal service and assistance, as well as our shared origin, makes for true complementarity.

Response: Anthony Petterson

I am in wholehearted agreement with Margaret when she argues that Genesis 1 and 2 demonstrate the equality of men and women. Indeed, this is the view of complementarians and egalitarians. There are, however, two significant points of disagreement between us. First, I think that there is order in the relationship between the man and the woman before the judgement pronounced in Gen 3:16. However, I think it is our second point of disagreement that impacts the first and that is the character of this ordering. Margaret describes the ordering that I have argued for in Genesis 1–3 as "gender hierarchy" and "subordination of women," with women to "serve and provide unreciprocated help to men." These terms and descriptions are loaded and to many people they have connotations of oppression and/or abuse. I do not understand the ordering between the man and the woman in Genesis 1–2 to be framed in these terms; rather the man is given a responsibility to lead his wife for her good and in her interests.

In terms of exegesis, Margaret raises doubts about our English translations. She argues that they unequivocally give the impression that the first created person was male. She would prefer to translate *hā'ādām* as "the human." However, the Hebrew means "the man" and this is how it would have been understood by ancient readers. It is certainly not true that the man's sex only becomes apparent in Gen 2:21. While Margaret does not go as far as Trible and Bal to argue the first human is undifferentiated sexually (an "earthling"), she does float the possibility that "the first human had a male and female side."[43] Gellman shows how the argument of Trible and Bal fails exegetically.[44] The woman is not separated out from an intermixed body. Genesis 2:22 states the woman is "made" or "fashioned" or "built" (*bānâ*) from a piece of "the man." God is not said to refashion the man in any way, just to close up the place with flesh (v. 21). Indeed, straight after the operation, he is still called "the man" (2:23; 3:9, 12, 20). Furthermore, the man is conscious of having the same identity before and after the operation since when he is introduced to the woman he exults and exclaims that he has found what he was looking for (2:23). There is no sense in which he has lost something or that his identity has changed in any way.

Our disagreement over the woman as "helper" is more in how this is conceived. I agree that she is created "to procreate, to subdue the earth, and rule the animals together." Where we disagree is that because she was created as a helper, that this does not imply order. Margaret says that helping does not imply "servitude" and "domesticity." Again, these seem like loaded words. If "servitude" is slavery, I agree; there is no sense in which the woman is created as the slave of the man. No complementarian I know argues that. But if "servitude" simply means service—how can helping not involve service of the other?

Finally, that "Adam and his wife were both naked, and they felt no shame" in Gen 2:25 simply anticipates the account of the fall in Genesis 3 where, upon eating, they realise their nakedness and try to cover themselves (3:7) and hide from the Lord in shame (3:10). To argue "there was no shame because there was no patriarchy" does not pay enough attention to the flow of the narrative and injects an extraneous idea.

---

43   Bal, *Lethal Love: Feminist Readings of Biblical Love Stories*, 112–13; Trible, *God and the Rhetoric of Sexuality*, 80.

44   Gellman, "Gender," 323–24.

Response: Geoffrey Harper

Margaret touches on several crucial matters for understanding Gen 1–3 that I am in substantial agreement with. She rightly argues that we must endeavour to stay with the text in order to hear what the original author(s) wanted to convey. She ably demonstrates one aspect of that intent by highlighting Gen 2's "profound statements concerning the equality of the first man and woman." This is certainly a key note in Gen 1–2 and, as mentioned in response to Anthony's paper, it is unfortunate that this substantial point of agreement is often lost in the heat of debate. In conversations such as this it is vital to recognise points of similarity even while continuing to discuss differences.

At the same time there are aspects of Margaret's argument that I think require clarification. First, her contention that *'ēzer* ("helper") has a "vital and strong sense" in the Old Testament needs to be qualified. David Clines demonstrates in his detailed study of the term that, even while those described as *'ēzer* may at times have a superior status, they nevertheless become secondary to the project of the one being helped.[45] It would be useful to hear how Margaret would integrate Clines's study (and conclusions) into her broader thesis.

---

45   Clines, *What Does Eve Do*, 27–37.

Secondly, Margaret's argument regarding 1 Tim 2 remains somewhat unclear to me—although I appreciate the impossibility of doing justice to such a hotly contested text within the confines of a short paper. Margaret contends that the problem Paul corrected in Ephesus was a twisted form of the creation account. His ban was therefore a move to counter false teaching. However, if that was the case then why did Paul command women alone to be silent (2:12), especially when the only false teachers explicitly mentioned in 1 Timothy are male (1:3, 20, etc.)? Either Paul is being unbelievably sexist, or there is a better way to understand his appeal to creation order.

Third, I find Margaret's suggestion that the first human was an undifferentiated "androgyne" unpersuasive. On this she seems to follow Phyllis Trible's exegesis (or perhaps, more tangentially, that of Rashi).[46] This line of reasoning seems to me to be a case of special pleading. While *'ādām* can mean "human" or "humanity" it also simply means "man." Contextually, "man" works better in Gen 2 as signifying the one for whom woman is made as a counterpart. If the ancient author had really wanted to convey the idea of an androgynous being then the more ambiguous term "living being" (cf. 2:7) would have made the point more clearly.

Lastly, Margaret perhaps claims more than is strictly warranted at times. For example, she asserts that "[a]ccording to Genesis 1, men and women are equal in being and equal in function." While that holds true at one level it breaks down at another. Men and women together receive the command to be fruitful, yet they perform profoundly different, non-transferable, functions within the overall achieving of that end. Genesis 1 seems to sit comfortably with equal beings fulfilling complementary roles within God's design. Could the same dynamic hold true vis-à-vis authority? Texts like Deut 17 suggest so, for the king was to exercise authority over men and women while at the same time being regarded as an equal among brothers (Deut 17:15, 20). Asymmetric authority *and* equality of being—seemingly not a contradiction but rather part of the God-ordained fabric of Israelite life.

---

46   Cf. Trible, *Rhetoric of Sexuality*, 98.

First Things First: Reading Genesis 1–3 in Its Pentateuchal Context

G. Geoffrey Harper

Genesis 1–3 is foundational for Christian theology and practice. Accordingly, these chapters are called upon to defend, and to undermine, a diverse range of positions on matters extending from the age of the earth through to sexuality and gender. Yet, unless adequate care is taken, interpretation of Gen 1–3 can end up shaped more by contemporary questions and assumptions than original purpose. As C. S. Lewis memorably quipped, "What we think we see when we are looking into the depths of Scripture may sometimes be only the reflection of our own silly faces."[47]

Now, I take it as granted that as responsible exegetes we want to see more than our own reflections as we approach Gen 1–3, especially considering the importance of clear biblical thinking when it comes to matters related to gender. So how can we approach this pivotal text so as to clearly hear what it has to say while at the same time minimising the distorting effects

---

47   Lewis, *Reflections*, 121.

of contemporary assumptions? Teasing out one answer to that question is the focus of this essay. What I want to propose is that other parts of the Pentateuch can provide a window into the meaning and purpose of Gen 1–3 that at the same time evades current preoccupations. The particular avenue I want to explore is the one offered by the Pentateuch's cultic and legal texts. This approach may be surprising to some because the Western church has generally excelled in marginalising this part of Scripture.[48] Yet that may well prove to be to our loss for, as I hope to demonstrate, careful consideration of the connections between creation and cult can provide important new data for theological discussion—including the topic of gender that is the concern of this current volume.

Parallels between Creation and Cult

In recent Pentateuch scholarship there has been a growing appreciation of the intertextual connections which link creation and Israel's tabernacle cult. The literature devoted to the topic is becoming increasingly vast.[49] For my purposes, however, it will be sufficient to draw out a few examples to demonstrate the link. Having done so, I will then be able to discuss the implications of these parallels for reading the Pentateuch in general and for approaching Gen 1–3 in particular.

The first text I want to consider is Exod 25–31, 35–40. These two blocks of material which frame the account of the golden calf incident in Exod 32–34 detail instructions for the tabernacle and record its subsequent construction. Although often skimmed, or even skipped entirely, by readers bored with the seemingly endless detail, these chapters are crucially important for the theology of the Pentateuch. A large measure of that significance is conveyed through the use of language and concepts which parallel Gen 1–3.

---

48   Not many of us will have had our first exposure to the Bible come though detailed study of the Book of Leviticus—as is the case for Jewish children (cf. Wenham, *Leviticus*, vii). For exploration of the reasons behind Western neglect of cultic texts, consult Brueggemann and Hankins, "Wellhausen's World," 15–31.

49   For a very useful introduction to the discussion, see the collection of seminal essays in Morales, *Cult and Cosmos*.

The following points serve to illustrate the case:[50]

1. Instructions for the tabernacle (Exod 25–31) are given in seven blocks of divine speech, each unit beginning with the words, "And Yahweh said."[51] The language is evocative of the repeated phrase in Gen 1, "And God said." Further indicating a connection is that the seventh unit in Exod 25–31 is a command to observe the Sabbath (31:12–17; cf. Gen 2:1–3).

2. In Gen 1:2 the hovering "Spirit of God" anticipates the coming creation. The next unambiguous reference to the "Spirit of God" is found in Exod 31:2–5 which indicates that the Spirit was a primary agent in the construction of the tabernacle and its furnishings.

3. The tabernacle's entrance faced east (Exod 27:13–15). Thus as people approached the presence of Yahweh therein they had to come from the east, ritually reversing the direction of sinful humanity's eastward banishment (Gen 3:24; 4:16; cf. 11:2).

4. The tent itself was bedecked with images of trees, flowers, and fruit (Exod 25:31–36; 28:33), all suggestive of a verdant garden.[52]

5. The lampstand which stood in the holy place had six branches and was covered with buds, blossoms, and flowers (Exod 25:31–40). Not surprisingly, many have seen here a stylised tree of life.[53]

6. The curtain which barred access to the holy of holies was embroidered with images of cherubim (Exod 26:31–33), perhaps recalling the cherubim that had been stationed to bar access to the garden in Gen 3:24.

---

50   While each parallel on its own may not persuade, the cumulative weight of connections is compelling.

51   Translations throughout are my own unless otherwise stated.

52   The association of gardens with temples was commonplace in the ancient world. A lush garden in close proximity to a temple was a picture of the fruitfulness and prosperity made possible by the indwelling deity.

53   E.g., Stuart, *Exodus*, 577. Stuart suggests that the lampstand's incorporation of features from different species was a way of representing the primordial tree (577, fn. 352).

7. The description of the tabernacle's completion in Exod 39–40 echoes words and phrases from the creation account.[54]

Gen 1:1–2:3	Exod 39–40
God saw all that he had made, and it was very good (Gen 1:31a)	Moses saw all the work, and behold, they had done it; as Yahweh had commanded, so had they done it (Exod 39:43a)
Thus the heavens and the earth were completed in all their vast array (Gen 2:1)	So all the work on the tabernacle, the Tent of Meeting, was completed (Exod 39:32)
God had finished the work he had been doing (Gen 2:2a)	So Moses finished the work (Exod 40:33b)
God blessed the seventh day (Gen 2:3a)	Moses blessed them (Exod 39:43b)

In these ways, the building of the tabernacle at the end of Exodus forms an inclusio with the building of the world in Gen 1.[55] Yet the climactic filling of the tabernacle with Yahweh's glory (Exod 40:34–35) creates a new narrative tension within the storyline of the Pentateuch, for all, including Moses (v. 35), are excluded. How, then, can sinful humanity re-enter the now immanent divine presence from which it had been barred since Gen 3? The book of Leviticus in its canonical setting addresses the dilemma. Perhaps not surprisingly, therefore, allusion to Gen 1–3 continues to be important throughout Leviticus.

In Lev 16, for example, a passage that sits at the structural and theological heart of the book (and indeed of the Pentateuch), several important allusions to Gen 1–3 become evident. The specific wording used

---

54   Adapted from Nihan, *Priestly Torah to Pentateuch*, 54.

55   Thus for Weinfeld, Gen 1:1–2:3 and Exod 39:1–40:33 are "typologically identical" ("Sabbath," 503).

to prescribe Sabbath rest (v. 31) and total cessation from work (v. 29)[56] links Lev 16 to Gen 2:1–3.[57] This connection serves to recall the original creation in its "very good" state (Gen 1:31).[58] On the Day of Atonement, therefore, Israel corporately experienced "seventh-day" time. But this occasion also uniquely required the high priest to enter into the very presence of Yahweh (Lev 16:12–14). As Aaron did so he ritually reversed the trajectory of humanity's banishment; his approach towards the divine presence was *from* the east[59] and necessitated going past the cherubim embroidered upon the curtain (cf. Exod 26:31–33). Moreover, on this day only, Aaron was to dress in a linen tunic (*lbš* + *kuttōnet*, 16:4), meaning that as he approached Yahweh he was clothed as Adam and Eve had been in the post-fall garden (*lbš* + *kuttōnet*, Gen 3:21).[60] Thus Aaron's entry into the most holy place functioned as a representative return of an excluded humanity. With this confluence of sacred time and sacred space Lev 16 portrays the restoration of a lost world on a microcosmic scale and hence becomes the (partial and temporary) resolution to the narrative tension raised by Gen 3.[61]

The restoration hinted at in Lev 16 takes on a spatial dimension in Lev 26. Here, allusion to Gen 1–3 in vv. 3–12 is used to convey the potential blessing that life in the land holds for Israel. That blessing is painted in specifically edenic terms. In Canaan the people will enjoy abundant fruit from trees (v. 4; cf. Gen 1:29; 2:16), they will be fruitful and will multiply (v. 9; cf. Gen 1:28). Moreover, wild beasts will be banished (v. 6; cf. Gen 3:13, 15), restoring the

---

56   Balentine (*Leviticus*, 134) notes that only the Sabbath and the Day of Atonement require *absolute* cessation of work.

57   The shared syntactical combination of '*śh* ("to do"), *mělā'kâ* ("work"), and *šěbî'î* ("seventh") used in conjunction with the *šbt* root occurs in the Pentateuch only nine times.

58   A connection to the seventh day of creation is supported by the use of sevenfold patterning throughout Lev 16 at structural and lexical levels.

59   The entrances to tabernacle and courtyard were situated on the east side (Exod 36:31–38; 38:13–14; cf. m. *Yoma* 1:3).

60   The combination of *lbš* + *kuttōnet* occurs only seven times in the Pentateuch (Gen 3:21; Exod 29:5, 8; 40:14; Lev 8:7, 13; 16:4). All bar Gen 3:21 are explicit references to priestly vestments.

61   Cf. Mann, *Book of the Torah*, 19: "With the expulsion of the man and woman from the garden . . . [h]uman beings are permanent exiles from the pristine space and time of Eden. There is no way back and the way ahead is uncertain. The plot of the Pentateuchal narrative, to its very end, will be concerned with the attempt to find another way human beings can live with integrity before God, at home on the earth, and within the security of divine blessing" (italics removed).

"paix originelle" between humans and animals.[62] Most significantly of all, Yahweh will "walk about" (*hlk, hithpael*) in the midst of his people as he had once "walked about" (*hlk, hithpael*) in the Garden (v. 12; cf. Gen 3:8).[63] The Promised Land is thus imagined as a new Eden; Israel is a new Adam.

Hermeneutical Implications of the Creation-Cult Nexus for Reading Genesis 1–3

While much more could be said, the above examples illustrate a wider Pentateuchal strategy to establish parallels between creation and cult. But why is this important and how ought it to shape our interpretation of Gen 1–3?

First, it is vital to acknowledge the deliberateness of the link. Multiple points of contact to the same texts signify intention on the part of an author or redactor.[64] Allusion is meant to be noticed. Therefore, for those who shaped the final form of the Pentateuch, Israel's cult and the creation of the world are conceptually connected.

Second, intertextuality works both ways. The use of words and phrases in Gen 1–3 more normally found in cultic contexts bequeath a temple-like nuance to the creation and garden narratives. Conversely, the use of creation language in descriptions of the tabernacle reveals that the founding of Israel's cult is understood to be the inauguration of a new creation. A confluence of reordered time and space, the immanent presence of Yahweh, the recreation of a new humanity who may once again enter God's presence, together signal at least a partial return to edenic conditions. Terence Fretheim captures the significance well:

> At this small, lonely place in the midst of the chaos of
> the wilderness, a new creation comes into being. In

---

62   Marx, *Lévitique 17–27*, 200.

63   The *hithpael* of *hlk* ("to walk") with God as subject appears only three times in the Pentateuch (Gen 3:8; Lev 26:12; Deut 23:15 [14]).

64   See my discussion in Harper, "Time for a New Diet," 181–184.

the midst of disorder, there is order. The tabernacle is the world order as God intended writ small in Israel . . . The people of Israel carefully encamped around the tabernacle in their midst constitutes the beginnings of God's bringing creation back to what it was originally intended to be. The tabernacle is a realisation of God's created order in history.[65]

Thus, thirdly, the textual strategy of linking cult and cosmos has significant hermeneutical implications for reading Gen 1–3. For a start, it becomes apparent that a key function of the Gen 1–3 narratives in their Pentateuchal setting is to pre-figure the tabernacle.[66] The creation of the world and its subsequent fracturing provide a conceptual backdrop that serves to emphasise the significance of the cult.[67]

More pertinent to the topic at hand, however, is that the restoration imagined by the Pentateuch's legal and cultic texts encapsulates an understanding of the original creation that is the goal of that restoration. This reality throws into even sharper relief the problem of "proof-texting." Context, as they say, is everything; responsible exegetes do well to pay it appropriate heed. Yet, from the discussion above, it becomes apparent that a contextual reading of Gen 1–3 must also include the Pentateuch's cultic texts. This is equally as true for matters pertaining to gender. Thus the creation-cult nexus brings back to the table texts that are often dismissed as being irrelevant at best, even misogynist at worst.[68] In fact, a reconsideration of the theological importance of cultic texts for gender-related issues is sorely needed. For if, as seems clear, these texts outline the microcosmic restoration and reordering of the world along creation lines then the values encoded within cannot be simply dismissed out of hand as outmoded

---

65   Fretheim, *Exodus*, 271.

66   On this see Morales, *Tabernacle Pre-Figured*, 245–277.

67   Cf. Blenkinsopp, "Structure of P," 279: "for P, what happened at Sinai is explicable only in the light of what happened in the archaic period before Israel as such came into existence."

68   See, for instance, the references to Leviticus (and to the Old Testament more generally) in Gilmore, *Misogyny*.

cultural expressions. In fact, ties to creation patterns align cultic texts with eschatological expectation. In light of this, then, the question naturally arises: what insights do the Pentateuch's legal and cultic texts afford the gender conversation? How can reading Gen 1–3 within its broader (cultic) context serve to advance or clarify the discussion?

Leviticus 18, Bestiality, and the Gender Conversation

From the foregoing discussion it is clear that reading Gen 1–3 with due sensitivity to the Pentateuch's legal and ritual texts provides a window into the creation narratives that may in turn help to mitigate the distorting effects of contemporary presuppositions. However, what parts of the Old Testament like Leviticus can contribute to the gender conversation through a clarification of Gen 1–3 is, needless to say, a topic that remains somewhat underdeveloped. Even a limited foray into such uncharted territory would require another paper. Accordingly, I must confine myself to one worked example—something akin to firstfruits offered in anticipation of a fuller harvest to come.

Leviticus 18 provides just such a test case, albeit a slightly provocative one; I offer it in a spirit of tentative suggestion as a means of stimulating further discussion. The focus in this part of Leviticus is on the renewed interpersonal relationships that ought to categorise Israel as the forerunner of a recreated humanity. The rhetoric of the legislation suggests continual relevance.[69] Towards that end chapter 18 outlines prohibited sexual unions. Understandably, the pericope has been both appealed to and denigrated for its stance on various matters, perhaps most notably its proscription of same-sex intercourse in v. 22. That said, it is the following verse outlawing bestiality that proves interesting because of its unusual phrasing.

Verse 1 of Lev 18 identifies the audience of the address: "Yahweh said to Moses, 'Speak to the sons of Israel and say to them.'" However, while the

---

69   For elaboration, see Zenger, *Einleitung*, 69.

laws that follow are addressed specifically to the Israelite menfolk,[70] v. 23 prohibits bestiality for men and for women. Yet the syntax is interesting. The command concerning men is given in the second person: "And you shall not lie with any beast" (18:23aα). But the command regarding women is given in the third person: "And a woman shall not stand before a beast in order to lie with it" (18:23b). Jan Joosten draws the following conclusion:

> The reason for this variation is that, in the concept of H, the audience of the law are the Israelite men, who are thus made responsible for their own behavior. Although women are made subject to the law, it is the men that are made responsible for their observance of the laws. The intention behind the phrase *benē yiśrā'ēl* is not, therefore, to exclude women—as if they should not hear or keep the laws—but rather to subsume them under the person of the man in whose household they live.[71]

Doubtless, for many, the immediate response to Joosten's conclusion will probably run something like this: surely Lev 18 is, at this point, simply reflecting male-oriented cultural assumptions and therefore has little or nothing to contribute to a contemporary understanding of gender roles. However, it is at least worth asking whether that is a conclusion derived from the text or from our own cultural presuppositions. This is where awareness of the wider connection between creation and cult becomes useful, because it suggests at least the possibility that Lev 18 might in some way reflect aspects of Gen 1–3.

In that regard it is interesting to note a similar dynamic at play in the garden narrative.[72] In Gen 2:17, a divine prohibition against eating is

---

70   For this understanding of the phrase *běnē yiśrā'ēl*, see Joosten, *People and Land*, 30–33. I am indebted to Joosten for my discussion of v. 23.

71   Joosten, *People and Land*, 31.

72   It is worth noting that the unsuitability of animals as (sexual) partners in Lev 18:23 is in itself an outworking of Gen 2 (esp. vv. 18–25).

issued to the man (the verbs and pronominal suffixes are masc. sg.). Yet, in dialogue with the serpent, the woman repeats the command of 2:17 verbatim but substitutes a plural form of the verb: "God said, 'You [pl.] shall not eat'" (3:3aβ). The implication is that the man communicated God's command— originally delivered to him alone—to the woman who then included herself in its proscription. Genesis 2–3 thus reflects a similar dynamic to Lev 18 with respect to men hearing divine commands and then passing them on to the women in their own "households."

If the parallel I have drawn is valid then attempts to dismiss the male-female dynamic in Lev 18 simply on the charge of cultural idiosyncrasy or even as perversion of original intent are weakened, for Lev 18, as with the rest of the Pentateuch's ritual and legal texts, is geared towards the re-establishment of creation ideals. The parallel with Genesis therefore suggests that Lev 18 reflects not a fallen and perverted way of things, but rather an order that is intrinsic to the pre-fall world of Gen 2. Such a conclusion fits with the wider tenor of Lev 18 which attempts to define appropriate sexual expression in line with the Gen 2 ideal of a husband-wife marriage (Gen 2:20–25).

Furthermore, as discussed earlier, intertextuality works both ways: Lev 18 can, in turn, open a window on Gen 1–3. For example, the question concerning whether or not Gen 1–2 supports the idea of male headship is hotly contested. Genesis is appealed to both to maintain and to deny the premise.[73] However, the parallel with Lev 18 adds new data to the discussion. As part of a wider recapitulation of primordial patterns, the dynamic in Lev 18 suggests that male headship—understood as responsibility to pass on divine commands—is intrinsic to creation order. Objections which appeal to the radical change inaugurated by the new creation are also weakened, for such claims imply that the new creation language of the New Testament takes us in a different direction from passages like Lev 18.[74] However, the direction is, in fact, exactly the same—the restoration of the world along creation lines.

---

73   See respectively Ortlund Jr., "Male-Female Equality," 95–112 and Belleville, "Women in Ministry," 25–30. See also the essays by Petterson and Mowczko in this volume.

74   So Spencer, *Beyond the Curse*, 29–42.

In this way, Leviticus adds further canonical perspective to Paul's injunction that in matters related to assessing divine revelation, "[wives] must ask their own husbands at home" (1 Cor 14:35; cf. v. 29). Read against Gen 2 and Lev 18 Paul's emphasis perhaps lies on the *responsibility* of (first-century) husbands to instruct their (generally uneducated) wives vis-à-vis divine commands.[75] Likewise, in 1 Tim 2, Paul's causal reference (*gar* ["For"]) to Adam's prior creation (v. 13) can be understood as appealing to the same dynamic—viz. the particular *responsibility* for men to pass on authoritative teaching, not women (cf. v. 12).

Conclusion

In conclusion, while the example just given may not convince everyone, it is my hope that the wider argument I am making will. The Pentateuch deliberately connects creation and cult. In this way ritual and legal texts are seen to be a reflection on, and indeed an outworking of, creation ideals. Thus, reading Gen 1–3 in its Pentateuchal context requires careful consideration of books like Leviticus. Conversely, books like Leviticus may open a window into the meaning and purpose of Gen 1–3 that has heretofore not been fully realised. More work needs to be done, but it is my hope that in utilising the perspective of these oft-ignored texts greater clarity might ensue for teasing out what it means to be male and female in God's good creation.

---

75   Cf. the views of Plutarch (*Conj. Praec.* 48; *Mor.* 145).

Response: Anthony Petterson

I find Geoff's paper compelling and an intriguing perspective on the debate. My response is not so much to critique his findings, but to offer some tentative thoughts about other implications and questions for further investigation. Many writers note the sanctuary associations of the Garden of Eden which Geoff well summarises. From this perspective, humanity is not only given dominion to rule as kings in Genesis 1, but in Genesis 2 the man is also given priestly responsibility. This is conveyed in v. 15 with the use of the verbs "work" (*'ābad*) and "care" (*šāmar*) which elsewhere only occur together to refer to the duties of the Levities in the sanctuary (cf. Numbers 3:7–8; 8:26; 18:5–6). Significantly, to "care" or "guard" is also the task transferred to the cherubim in Gen 3:24 after humanity is expelled from the garden. Alexander comments: "In all likelihood, Adam was commissioned to keep or guard the garden so that it would remain holy. This was a normal task associated with any sanctuary."[76] God's priestly purpose for the man in Gen 2:15 therefore supplements the concept of subduing and ruling that is introduced in Genesis 1.

Geoff argues that Leviticus 18 suggests male headship entails the responsibility to pass on divine commands. Interestingly, one of the key

---

76   Alexander, *Eden*, 26.

functions of Aaron and the priests in the OT is to teach the Torah (i.e., pass on divine commands). This is seen in Lev 10:11 (cf. Deut. 17:8–13; 31:9; 33:9–13; 2 Chr 35:3; Neh 8:7–9; Jer 18:18; Ezek 7:26; Hag 2:11; Mal 2:6–7). My question is whether this role of the priesthood also reflects God's concern to restore the world along creation lines. If so, is it significant that the priesthood is only ever filled by men in the OT? Does the OT priesthood also show that passing on divine commands is the role of men? Evangelical theology rejects the notion of pastors as priests because of the high-priesthood of Jesus who has offered the once-for-all sacrifice (and rightly so). However, if the other key role of the priest to pass on divine commands transfers to the pastor, it seems to me that this may also go some way to explaining the restriction of pastoral leadership in the NT to men—it reflects God's concern to restore the church along creation lines.

Response: Margaret Mowczko

I found the parallels between the tabernacle and creation in Geoff's paper fascinating. Yet, while there are echoes of the creation story in the institution of the tabernacle, we must take care how we read the tabernacle and its rituals back into the creation accounts. At best, they are a shadow of creation. Similarly, the author of Hebrews states that the regulations and sacrifices of the tabernacle were merely "a shadow of the good things to come" (Heb 10:1a). One of the main themes of the book of Hebrews is that, through Jesus, the OT priestly rituals have been superseded. As followers of Jesus, both men and women have access to the Holy Place (Heb. 10:19–22; cf. 4:16). We are not required to observe the cultic requirements of the OT law, and we do not need any other priest except our High Priest Jesus Christ. Indeed, the institution of the tabernacle has limited relevance to Christians.

The community of the ancient Israelites, like the societies of their neighbours, was predominantly patriarchal, and I agree with Geoff that this social dynamic is reflected in the OT law. The law was instituted while the effects of the fall, which included patriarchy, were in full operation (cf. Gen. 3:16b). I disagree with Geoff, however, where he claims that, as a general rule, God has given men a particular responsibility to pass on divine commands and authoritative teaching to women.

The Bible shows that several women, rather than men, were the first to receive and pass on certain divine commands and teaching. These women include Samson's mother, and then his father; Abigail, and not her husband; and Mary the mother of Jesus, and then Joseph. Other women who passed on prophetic or divine messages to men include Deborah (to the nation of Israel and to Barak the general of the army); Huldah (to men such as the High Priest Hilkiah and Josiah the king); King Lemuel's mother (to her son the king); Anna (to all in the temple who were looking for the redemption of Jerusalem); Mary Magdalene (to Jesus's other disciples); and Philip's daughters who, according to several early church writers, most notably Eusebius, were "mighty luminaries."[77] Then there is Priscilla who, with her husband Aquila, explained the "way of God" (i.e., theology), including the doctrine of Christian baptism, more accurately to Apollos. The Bible shows that God can, and does, entrust his word—with the authority it entails—directly to his daughters.

---

77   *Church History* 3.31.3.

Part Two

Gender, Scripture, and Family

What Do We Do with the Household Codes Today?

Michael F. Bird

[handwritten margin: ← COLOSSIANS 3v22; EPHESIANS 6v5]

[handwritten top right: to submit to those above us w/ love]

Introduction

Former Australian Prime Minister Kevin Rudd once appeared on the ABC talk show Q&A where he was asked by a member of the audience why he, as a Christian, doesn't believe what Jesus says in the Bible about marriage being a divinely sanctioned relationship between a man and a woman. His reply was a curt and forceful version of a *reductio ad absurdum* argument: "Well mate, if I was gonna have that view, the Bible says that slavery is a natural condition. Because St Paul said in the New Testament, 'Slaves be obedient to your masters.' Therefore, we should have all fought for the confederacy in the US civil war."[1] Rudd deployed the Pauline household codes with their recognition of the normalcy of slavery as a way of showing that biblical mandates are culturally contingent and therefore potentially replaceable

[handwritten: OT WAYS DIFFER FROM NEW]

---

[1]   JNews, "Australia Election: Rudd Defends Gay-Marriage Stance."

[handwritten: SLAVERY → OBEDIENCE (ROMANS 6v22, OR SERVANT]

with an ethical paradigm that is better informed by contemporary sciences and still upholds the basic love command of the New Testament. I have no intention here of evaluating the merits or misconceptions of Rudd's terse summary of biblical commands about sexuality and how we apply them today.[2] However, his remarks do constitute a prime example of how the New Testament household codes are frequently regarded as culturally distant, socially counterintuitive, and even morally affronting. The household codes are then fit for examination as to how one constructs biblical ethics in a post-biblical context.

The NT household codes prescribe the order of relations between masters, wives, children, and slaves (see Col 3:18—4: 1; Eph 5:22—6: 9; 1 Tim 2:9–15; Tit 2:2–10; 1 Pet 2:13—3:7).[3] It is widely acknowledged that the NT household codes were largely borrowed from Graeco-Roman cultural norms and were adopted for Christian households for the purpose of promoting familial order and social cohesion. The problem is that application of these texts to our own setting is not straightforward. Christians today do not live within a Graeco-Roman environment where the household codes were formulated and esteemed. Christians generally prefer social orders that are egalitarian rather than hierarchical. Even Christian complementarians who support male headship would not espouse the patriarchal powers normally given to a household's *paterfamilias* including the power of life and death over all members. Contemporary Christian expectations of the manner of a child's obedience to his or her parents are markedly different as to what they were in the Graeco-Roman world. Christians today overwhelmingly abhor the idea of slavery and usually have had a reformist or abolitionist stance towards its practice.

Thus it is legitimate to ask how we are to understand and appropriate the NT household codes for ourselves while recognising the normative nature of biblical commands and the complexities of applying them in

---

2   See Resource777, "Does 'Bible Say Slavery is a Natural Condition'? Response to Kevin Rudd by N.T. Wright."

3   For the post-apostolic period see *Did.* 4.9–11; *Barn.* 19.5–7; *1 Clem.* 1.3–2.1; 21.3–9.

diverse contexts. This study will briefly describe different interpretive models for understanding the NT household codes, note the primary feature of the tension that they create, and thereafter employ a redemptive-history trajectory hermeneutic to identify how we can appropriate the NT household codes for the contemporary church.

Interpretive Models for Understanding the Household Codes

The Christian household codes represent a genre of teaching addressed to the various members of a domestic dwelling. They are typified by listing members in binary pairs of husbands/wives, parents/children, and masters/slaves and then defining the mutual relations between the pairs usually in terms of obedience and submission. These codes are most likely derived from Aristotelian and Stoic ethical precepts for the governance of relationships within a household that were subsequently appropriated by Hellenistic Jewish authors and taken over by Christian authors as well.[4] A key difference is that, whereas the Stoics drew up their household management lists according to the "law of nature," Christian versions are shaped by a distinctively Christian view of identity and ethics—hence the emphasis on mutual obligations. That difference notwithstanding, what is striking is the overarching sameness between the NT and Graeco-Roman household codes. The NT household codes replicate the patriarchal and hierarchical perspectives embedded within their Graeco-Roman counterparts. John Barclay comments that "for better or worse, the code represents a christianization of traditional rulings on household relationships."[5] Not surprisingly many scholars, clergy, and lay people find this sameness disturbing or unpalatable. If the patriarchal and hierarchical nature of the household codes is a problem, then there are several strategies for dealing with it.

---

4   See Aristotle, *Politics* 1.5; Dionysius of Halicarnassus, *Ant. rom.* 2.24–27; Seneca, *Ep.* 94.1; and in Hellenistic Judaism, e.g., Philo, *Hypoth.* 7.1–9; *Decal.* 165–67; Josephus, *C. Ap.* 2.190–219; Pseudo-Phocylides 175–227.

5   John M. G. Barclay, *Colossians and Philemon*, 71.

Reject the Patriarchialising Tendencies of the Post-Apostolic Generation

Many scholars regard the household codes as deriving from a post-apostolic generation where the charismatic and egalitarian ethos of the early church was deliberately snuffed out by an emerging brand of "early catholicism." This "early catholicism" imposed patriarchal structures by forging letters in the name of the apostles in order to sanction pagan household codes as normative for Christians. The assumption is that texts like Gal 3:28 are simply irreconcilable with the NT household codes. This leads to the conclusion that the codes are later constructs of a post-apostolic church written to specifically undermine and supplant an egalitarian mode of church life. The household codes function to put women, children, and slaves in their place with apostolic and thus divine sanction.[6] On this view, the household codes are not simply awkward, they are a betrayal of a key part of the NT message about equality in Christ.

The problems with this view are twofold. First, the postulation of an "early catholicism" is a construct of late nineteenth-century German Protestantism which created the category in order to manufacture a villain for all the doctrines and ethics that were disagreeable to modern liberal theology. If there is something in the NT you didn't like, you could always dump it in the box called "early catholicism." Second, the disparity between the egalitarian texts of the undisputed Pauline letters and the household codes of the disputed letters is more imagined than real. We have to remember that the Paul who wrote Gal 3:28 also wrote 1 Cor 11:1–16 about head coverings. What is more, Colossians is a letter that contains both sorts of texts: an egalitarian text like Col 3:11 and a household code explained a few short verses later in Col 3:17—4:1. There is no evidence of an absolute disparity between equality in Christ and ordering social relationships according to cultural norms.

---

6   See, e.g., Tamez, *Struggles for Power in Early Christianity.*

Historically Contingent and Culturally Irrelevant

Another option is to regard the household codes as part of the world of the NT authors, but not necessarily prescriptive for our own time. Popular author and blogger Rachel Held Evans appears to take this approach when she writes:

> The question modern readers have to answer is whether the Greco-Roman household codes reflected in Ephesians, Colossians, and 1 Peter are in and of themselves holy, or if their appearance in Scripture represents the early church's attempt to blend Christianity and culture in a way that it would preserve the dignity of adherents while honouring prevailing social and legal norms of the day. The Christian versions of the household codes were clearly progressive for their time, but does that mean they have the last word, that Christians in changing places and times cannot progress further?[7]

The question that Evans ends with is legitimate in that the borrowing from Graeco-Roman social norms certainly implies the cultural contingency and perhaps even the ethical relativity of the NT household codes. Direct application from "then" to "now" is not straightforward. Even so, if one regards NT instruction as somehow normative for Christian ethics, it would require careful and well-reasoned judgement before setting aside such exhortations as dispensable on account of their historical situatedness. Even culturally distant texts can speak to our time whether that is through underlying principles, narrative patterns which can be emulated, or by theological configurations which remain wise and useful for our own effort to form Christ-centred communities.

---

7   Evans, *A Year of Biblical Womanhood,* 218.

Semi-Direct Transplant

A further way to understand the household codes is taken up by complementarian theologians who see them as remaining normative for Christian families. Wayne Grudem simply denies that NT authors modelled their instruction about Christian households on Graeco-Roman household codes. He claims that the similarities between the Graeco-Roman household codes and apostolic household instructions are limited to the groups named in the respective lists. What is more, he simply cannot envisage Peter or Paul giving into cultural expectations and advocating the use of sinful and sub-Christian patterns of behaviour in Christian homes just to attract unbelievers to the gospel; such would impugn the courage and integrity of the apostles.[8]

Three problems stand out: (1) The similarities between Graeco-Roman household codes and Christian household instructions are just too palpable to deny. The response that the only thing they have in common is the list of people mentioned is like saying that the only thing they have in common is their DNA. (2) Grudem's inability to imagine apostolic leaders using extant cultural norms in Christian ethics is denying what actually took place in the early churches. The fact is that some ethical teachings from the Greek and Roman world, particularly from Stoic philosophy, were regarded as wise, good, noble, and virtuous even for Christians (e.g., *enkrateia*, "self-control"). Christians have habitually robbed pagan ethics in the name of taking every thought captive to Christ. (3) Every complementarian has to admit that the application of the biblical household instructions to our own time can only be partial, indirect, or analogous. That is because the form of obedience expected of wives and children in the ancient world and the practice of slavery cannot be directly mapped onto our contemporary age with modern nuclear families, hyper-individualism, and an absence of patron-client relationships. I'm not denying that the biblical household codes can still be meaningful and relevant for us now, but their application to our present situation can only be achieved after a responsible exercise in biblical and cultural hermeneutics.

---

8   Grudem, "Wives Like Sarah, and the Husbands Who Honor Them, 1 Peter 3:1–7," 203–4.

Christian Liberalisation

Another approach, one I've argued for myself, is to regard Christian authors as appropriating and yet liberalising the Graeco-Roman household codes. This is done in the interest of preventing misconceptions of Christian groups as anti-social gatherings.[9] The household codes are not ideal, but are a necessary way of negotiating a path for Christian assemblies in a world where meetings behind closed doors were viewed with the utmost of suspicion. It is probable that Christian authors like Paul and Peter appropriated these well-known household codes for apologetic reasons because they are a means of ensuring the commendable conduct of Christian homes before outsiders (see Col 4:5; 1 Thess 4:12; 1 Pet 2:15–20). The Christian household codes concern how the lordship of Jesus Christ over a community is to be lived out before the pagan world around them. While these codes are undoubtedly patriarchal, they express that patriarchy in light of mutual obligations of honour and love and clearly censure abuses of authority. They were a necessary way of stabilising a para- or post-Jewish group that was regarded as religiously sectarian, politically subversive, and socially offensive to cultural elites and civic powers. The household codes are not intended as a mere affirmation of the status quo of pagan ethics, nor a mandate for social revolution; rather, they concern the authority of the Lord over the household of faith and the mutual obligations which follow from the subordination of all authority under the Lord. I invite you to consider how female household leaders like Chloe of Corinth (1 Cor 1:11) or Nympha of Laodicea (Col 4:15) would have regarded Paul's formulation of the household codes. Following Margaret MacDonald, I think these women leaders would have seen that the household codes afforded them a degree of protection, respectability, and stability. They would have regarded the household codes, I suspect, as an obvious and prudent instruction for the world of the emerging church.[10]

---

9   Bird, *Colossians and Philemon*, 112–17.

10   MacDonald, "Can Nympha Rule This House?" 115.

While I obviously prefer the "liberalising" view whereby Graeco-Roman household codes were adopted and amended by Christian leaders for apologetic reasons, I still believe that a tension does exist between the egalitarian texts and the household codes. This tension is not between a Pauline egalitarianism and the patriarchy of an early catholicism. Rather, the tension is that some texts enjoin Christians to be culturally radical and subversive and other texts enjoin Christians to try to be culturally normal and unobjectionable. But when are we supposed to be radical and when are we supposed to look normal? When are we supposed to subvert cultural norms and when are we called on to adopt them? When do we try to bring down the system and when do we try to be part of it? My tentative suggestion would be to prosecute a radically inclusive ethos when it comes to breaking down externally imposed cultural barriers which can attempt to impose themselves in the church, but we must be willing to ensure the survival of the church by maintaining an order and decorum that will not force state authorities to move against the church. To give but two examples, radicalness might involve deliberately cultivating multi-ethnic churches which are safe havens for asylum seekers, while the quest for survivability might entail fulfilling our obligations to register our churches as legally incorporated associations.

A Redemptive–Hermeneutic Model

The real crux of the matter is how we apply the NT household codes to our own situation today. The NT household codes need to be addressed one document at a time with a view to ascertaining their particular function and purpose within their specific literary context. Even so, there are enough similarities between their form and contents across the NT that it is possible to generalise somewhat about their appropriation for our own times. To this task I now turn.

One approach for us to consider, at least as a conversation starter, is William Webb's redemptive-movement hermeneutic.[11] Webb attempts to set up a hermeneutical method by which we can discern which biblical

---

11   Webb, *Slaves, Women and Homosexuals.*

commands remain in force and which biblical commands do not. He does that by observing how biblical texts compare with their broader culture and how they sound within the development of the canon, and then applying the developmental pattern to how Christians can now apply biblical commands in their own culture. In which case, Webb plots a way to go beyond the Bible while still following what he sees as biblically defined trajectories.[12]

In the case of the household codes, Webb argues that the theological analogies about Christ's headship over the church as a basis for male headship over women in Eph 5:22–24 and 1 Cor 11:3 are not necessarily transcultural. That is because similar theological analogies are used to justify slavery and submission to a monarchy in other biblical texts. To prove his point further he says that no man would use God's command for Hosea to expose Gomer to disgrace as a model for husbands disciplining their wives (see Hosea 2). Male headship may continue to be practised for pragmatic reasons in instances where physical protection and economic dependence are the norm, but the transcultural aspect here is that husbands and wives are to love and serve each other sacrificially.[13] On the submission of children to parents, Webb believes that some dimension of hierarchy between parents and children is normative in all cultures due to the dependency of children on their parents. Cultural factors in the ancient world meant that such submission would be lifelong, whereas such cultural factors do not exist in the present time, with the result that adult children should be expected to honour rather than obey their parents.[14] In the case of slavery, Webb maintains that Scripture does not present a finalised ethic in the area of slavery, but establishes a reformist approach to the institution even when it is treated as normal. Moreover, the NT remarks about slavery logically entail a trajectory for a better ethic that calls for the abolition of slavery. What is more, the idea that employee-employer relationships are an application of master-slave relationships is a

---

12   On the idea of having an ethic that is "better" than the Bible, Webb has courted much criticism. See Schreiner, "William J. Webb's *Slaves, Women and Homosexuals*, 46–65; Grudem, "Review Article: Should We Move Beyond the New Testament to a Better Ethic? 299–346; Reaoch, *Women, Slaves, and the Gender Debate.*

13   Webb, *Slaves, Women and Homosexuals*, 188–90, 213–16, 248–50.

14   Ibid., 212.

misnomer; there is simply no fitting analogy for the application of slavery to our modern context. The application we should make is to follow the biblical trajectory and work to abolish modern slavery and slave-like conditions throughout the world.[15]

Conclusion

The household codes represent a series of exegetical, hermeneutical, and practical challenges. I have argued in this study that the household codes were developed for apologetic and pragmatic reasons in the early church which leaves open the question of their transcultural normativity. In addition, the household codes also existed within a particular cultural tension between fostering a Christ-centred culture of equality on the one hand and attempting to ensure the survivability of Christian households by organising them according to extant norms of order and authority on the other hand. Negotiating the tension between radicalness and normalness is part of the never-ending tension by which Christians have to practise their faith amidst a surrounding and often hostile culture. Furthermore, I have followed William Webb's redemptive-movement hermeneutic to show how the household codes cannot be applied in a static fashion to our own time; rather, they must be appropriated in light of some cultural hermeneutics. Husbands and wives should love and serve each other in a context of mutual submission. Children must obey their parents in youth and honour them in adulthood. Slavery is a practice with no modern analogy and we should work for its earnest abolition.

---

15   Ibid., 247–48.

Response: David Starling

Michael's paper addresses a crucially important hermeneutical and practical question: what should we do with the NT's household codes? Important as that question is, however, we cannot address it adequately until we have first addressed the prior exegetical question: what were the *apostles* intending to do through the household codes that they embedded within their letters? If we are to read the household codes in a way that honours both the literary integrity of the letters they belong to and the authoritative nature of those letters as NT Scripture, then our first recourse in discerning the purpose of the household codes ought to be to the statements that the letters themselves make about the rationale of the instructions they contain, and the stance of the authors toward the social structures and cultural values of the world in which the NT's original readers lived.

When we read the NT household codes with those questions in mind, it soon becomes clear that there are serious questions to be asked about the assumption that Michael's paper is based on, that the household codes were simply "borrowed from Graeco-Roman cultural norms" and "adopted for Christian households for the purpose of promoting familial order and social cohesion."[16]

---

16   Cf. the critical comments on approaches such as this in Thielman, *Ephesians*, 365–69, and Arnold, *Ephesians*, 369–72.

Here and there within the surrounding context of the New Testament epistles (e.g., in the introduction to the household instructions of 1 Peter) there are certainly indications that the codes are applying the gospel to a social order that is human and contingent, not eternal or divine; there are suggestions, too, in 1 Peter and the pastoral epistles, that the public reputation of the church is a consideration that ought to add to the reasons for Christians to act with honour and integrity in their social relationships. But there is no suggestion anywhere in the surrounding contexts of the NT household codes that the authors are simply adopting the *norms* of the surrounding pagan culture as a kind of survival strategy for the church.

At some points the ethical norms that are taught within the codes clash sharply with those of the Aristotelian and Stoic traditions; at other points, they overlap somewhat, and coincide with elements of conservative popular morality, or its more enlightened and compassionate Stoic adaptations. But even where the morality of the codes overlaps with the popular morality of the time, the rationale that the New Testament authors offer as a warrant for those shared norms is a distinctively Christian rationale.[17] Paul does not say, "wives, submit to your husbands because Aristotle (or Hierocles, or Arius Didymus) thought that would be a good idea." Nor does the logic with which he supports the injunction even remotely resemble the logic of Arisotle's *Politics* or the Stoic treatises. Instead, he accompanies the instruction with an elaborate, explicit, and deeply Christian account of the way in which it is grounded in the intentions of the creator, interpreted in light of Old Testament Scripture and its fulfilment in the gospel of Christ.

There are, therefore, significant flaws in the approach that Michael proposes as the answer to his question about what we should do with the household codes today. If we are to receive the household codes as Christian Scripture, then our decision about what we should do with the codes needs to be informed by a deeper and more careful answer to the prior question of what the codes themselves are doing.

---

17   Cf. the comments on the Pauline household codes in Wright, *Paul and the Faithfulness of God*, 1108, 1375–76, and the broader discussion of the relationship between early Christian ethics and the moral norms of the surrounding culture in Starling, "Not as the Gentiles."

Response: Gayle Kent

Michael's paper highlights different interpretive models for applying the household codes of the New Testament in today's world and in the contemporary church. His paper acknowledges the difficulties in appropriating these codes and the ways that they have been regarded as "culturally distant, socially counterintuitive, and even morally affronting." Like David's paper, Michael's seeks to find a workable hermeneutic: one that will maintain a Christian view on ethics and identity as well as retain the wisdom that can come by understanding these texts' principles, narrative patterns, and theological perspectives.

A major strength of Michael's paper is the synopsis of various interpretative models and his critique of the main tensions in each. His first summary contains a definitive rejection of any model of interpretation that the household codes are post-apostolic impositions and he rightly highlights the danger of too rashly dismissing these texts. The other three summaries, while less overtly critical, outline noteworthy areas of caution in the hermeneutic challenge of applying the household codes: the difficulty posed by "cultural contingency" and "ethical relativity," the "partial, indirect, or analogous" relevance of positions, relationships, and social structures, and the complexity of the church's task to be both "culturally radical and subversive" as well as "culturally normal and unobjectionable."

Michael's preferred model for further discussion is Webb's redemptive-hermeneutic model, which encourages readers of Scripture to recognise "biblical trajectories." While not outlining these trajectories in full, Michael argues that there are common themes in Scripture which allow us to assess biblical ethics through a lens which questions both the transcultural relevance of a command and the broader trajectory of God's redemptive purposes. One of these would be the presence of headship and submission as a means for protection and dependence but not as a static acceptance of hierarchical structures. When applying this model to the household codes, marriage and parental relationships are thus repositioned with mutual submission and honour at their core. The master/slave relationship is placed within a reformist trajectory and therefore, we should avoid modern day appropriations but seek the abolition of slavery altogether.

Having the redemptive purposes of God as the fulcrum in how we relate to one another is both valid and essential. The practical outworking of this model, however, maintains the same tensions and complexities as other hermeneutic frameworks and highlights the somewhat perilous task of how and when we decide when to go "beyond" the Bible.

In some ways, Michael's preference for a redemptive hermeneutic is not that far from David's narrative-dramatic preference, for at the heart of both is the grand purposes of the gospel of Christ. There is a wise reminder that we need to actively engage with the biblical texts, the history of the church, the development of the canon, modern cultural frameworks, *and* the redemptive and eternal purposes of God. This does not make the task any easier but will alert us to possible blind spots or alternative perspectives, and hopefully encourage us to engage with each other and the tasks of the gospel with humility and hope.

Family Drama: The Household Codes in Narrative-Dramatic Perspective

David Starling

The process of interpreting and applying the NT household codes is a notoriously contested enterprise: no approach can eliminate altogether the responsibility of the interpreter to make complex judgements about the significance of context and culture for our understanding of the text and our obedience to its message, or insulate us against the clash between the wisdom of the gospel and the values of the culture we live in. Nevertheless, some approaches serve better than others in providing us with the categories and questions that we need for fulfilling our interpretive responsibilities fittingly and faithfully. My purpose in this paper is to argue that, in the case of the Ephesian household code, a narrative-dramatic approach fits well with the shape and purpose of the letter as a whole, and allows for faithful translation of the code's instructions into new social contexts without surrendering to the temptation to domesticate its message and conform it to the values of our own time. Within an age in which we have learnt to understand gender as a matter not of essence but of performance,[18] a perspective of this sort may prove to be particularly helpful as a framework for understanding and applying Paul's instructions.

Ethics, Accommodation, and the Household Codes in Evangelical Interpretation

Popular-level evangelical readings of Ephesians tend to follow one of two basic approaches to the interpretation and application of the letter. The first, typically more conservative, approach, reads Ephesians as being made up of a doctrinal first half (chs. 1–3) followed by an ethical second half (chs. 4–6), which spells out a timeless set of prescriptions for how Christians are to live in a way that pleases God.[19] The logic that connects the doctrine of the first half with the ethics of the second is generally spelt out in terms of the interplay between grace and gratitude: since God has been so gracious to us, as the first half of the letter affirms, we are to live good lives as an expression of our thankfulness to him.

The second approach has a great deal in common with the first, and typically replicates its account of the relationship between the doctrine of the first half and the ethics of the second. Where it differs is in the heavier emphasis that it places on the extent to which the ethics of the letter's second half is qualified by a pragmatic accommodation to the structures and values of the culture within which the letter's original readers lived. In cruder versions of this approach, the various injunctions of the letter's second half are simply divided up between the two categories: "Be kind and compassionate" is ethical; "Wives, submit . . . to your husbands" is cultural, and so on. More

---

18 See especially Butler, *Gender Trouble*. Butler's own use of the concept of "performativity" is a curious hybrid of theatrical metaphor and speech-act theory (understood in her own idiosyncratic manner); as she herself puts it in the preface to the 1990 edition of *Gender Trouble*, her theory "waffles between understanding performativity as linguistic and casting it as theatrical." Within this paper I will be using the language of "performance" in the theatrical sense of the word, and assuming a distinction between sex (as a term for the biological differentiation between male and female) and gender (as a term for the whole intricate construction of social roles and customs through which we collectively enact a performative interpretation of our bodily maleness and femaleness).

19 E.g., Foulkes, *The Letter of Paul to the Ephesians*, 20.

sophisticated versions of this approach acknowledge the overlap between the two categories, and explain the instructions Paul gives to his readers as a kind of amalgam of ethical principles and cultural accommodations.

The most obvious portion of the letter in which the difference between these two approaches can be seen is the household code in Eph 5:21—6:9. Under the first approach, the household code tends to be read and applied as a timeless template: God's design for the family and the workplace. Under the second, the code is read as an accommodation, to a greater or lesser degree, to the patriarchal power-structures of the Graeco-Roman social order and the pagan cultural norms that legitimated those structures. In his heart of hearts, according to the proponents of this approach, Paul was an egalitarian like us, but because the world was not yet ready for a community whose social practices enacted an understanding of this sort, he counselled a way of living within the Christian household that accorded more closely with the pagan social values of the time.

Neither approach is entirely convincing. The former approach, which assumes that the code is to be read as a timeless ethical template, struggles to maintain that assumption in dealing with the prescriptions for slaves and masters: for the vast majority of modern readers of the letter, who are neither slaves nor owners of slaves, the instructions in 6:5–9 are simply impossible to apply without at least some degree of translation and re-contextualisation. The latter approach struggles to offer a plausible explanation for why an inspired writer would advocate a morality that he considers to be sub-Christian in order to conform to the values of a pagan culture, why he would do so without any mention of this accommodationist rationale, and why he would locate the instructions urging a household morality of this sort within a section of the letter that is headed by a vigorous reminder that his readers "must no longer live as the Gentiles do, in the futility of their thinking" (4:17).

Clearly a better approach is needed. In this paper I explore one possible way forward, *via* a re-examination of the relationship between the instructions in the second half of the letter and the narratives, prayers, and doxologies of the first half.

Divine Drama: Ephesians as Mystery Play

One of the most stimulating studies of Ephesians to be published in recent years is Timothy Gombis's book, *The Drama of Ephesians*.[20] In it, he argues that the relationship between the first and second halves of the letter can best be understood within a narrative-dramatic framework. Ephesians, Gombis proposes, should be read as "a drama in which Paul portrays the powerful, reality-altering, cosmos-transforming acts of God in Christ to redeem God's world and save God's people for the glory of his name."[21]

Within a framework of that sort, the function of the instructions in the letter's second half is not merely to outline an *ethical* pattern of action that the readers are to offer up to God in gratitude for the salvation described in the first three chapters. It is also, and more basically, to offer direction to the church for its performance of a pattern of *communicative* action that faithfully corresponds to and displays the divine wisdom that has been made known in the story of salvation. According to Paul, the purpose of God for the church is that it should function as a display of his "manifold wisdom" (3:10); its members are called to a pattern of speech and action through which they are to embody and perform the saving truth that they have learned in Christ (4:15, 20–24).[22] Within a narrative-dramatic framework of this sort, the gospel story that Paul retells in chapters 1–3 functions not only as the *motivation* for the patterns of conduct that he instructs the Ephesians to follow in the second half of the letter, but also as the *message* that is to be communicated through them.

On this reading of Ephesians, the crucial question to be asked as we interpret and apply the instructions in the letter's second half is how they relate to the salvation history which Paul recounts in chapters 1–3, directing the conduct of the readers so that they faithfully perform that story in their own speech and action. In the remainder of this paper I will focus on the instructions that Paul gives to his readers within the household code of

---

20   Gombis, *The Drama of Ephesians*.
21   Ibid., 15.
22   Cf. ibid., 16.

5:21—6:9 and the ways in which Paul relates them to the narrative of God's saving acts, before offering some reflections on the implications of this reading for our own performance of the code within the context in which we find ourselves today.[23]

Family Drama: The Household Code and the Story of Salvation

"Be filled with the Spirit . . ." (5:18–21)

Whilst the Ephesian household code is comprised chiefly of the series of six paired paragraphs in 5:22—6:9 (addressed, respectively, to wives, husbands, children, fathers, slaves, and masters), the syntax of 5:21–22 inseparably links the beginning of the code to the participial clause in verse 21, "submit[ting] to one another out of reverence for Christ." This clause is itself the conclusion to a sequence of similar clauses in vv. 19–21, which describe the outworkings and manifestations of the command in verse 18 to "be filled with the Spirit."

Whatever answer we give to the notoriously contested question of how the words "submit" and "one another" in verse 21 are to be understood, the first and most obvious observation to be made is that the household-members addressed in the code are being encouraged to understand themselves first as members of the Spirit-filled community,[24] and to act within their household relationships in a manner that is continuous with the speaking, singing, and thanksgiving of vv. 19–20. In keeping with their election and inclusion "in Christ" (1:4, 11, 13) and the pattern of truth that they learned in him and are now to live out (4:20–24), the readers' lives of thankful response to God's grace are to be offered up "in the name of our Lord Jesus Christ" (5:20): whatever variegations there are between the particular roles and responsibilities of the different household-members addressed, they are

---

23   Cf. the sketches for a larger, theodramatic account of complementarian gender theology in Edwards and Paylor, "A Play for Harmony."

24   Cf. Gombis, "A Radically New Humanity," 323.

grounded first and most basically within this common calling and shared identity.

Nevertheless, the instructions in the paragraphs that follow are clearly differentiated and (in most cases) asymmetrical in the roles and responsibilities that they describe, and in the ways in which the various actions and dispositions they encourage are given a meaning in relation to the story of salvation.

"Wives . . . and husbands"

The first and longest set of instructions, in 5:22–33, is addressed to wives and husbands. Wives are urged to submit to their husbands "as you do to the Lord" (v. 22). The following verse supplies a reason for this exhortation: "For the husband is the head of the wife as Christ is the head of the church, his body, of which he is the Savior" (v. 23). Already, even before the husbands have been addressed, their role within the marriage has been constructed as analogous to Christ's role as head of the church.

The following paragraph continues and applies the analogy in a series of exhortations to husbands, beginning with a command that they should "love [their] wives, just as Christ loved the church and gave himself up for her" (v. 25). The analogy is further developed in verses 28–30 *via* a reflection on the care that a person takes for his or her own body, and the care that Christ takes for his body, the church. The threads are drawn together in verses 31–32, which appropriate the words of Gen 2:24 about the one-flesh unity of a husband and wife as a "mystery" pointing toward the unity of Christ and the church: the implication is that God the creator, who established the institution of marriage in the beginning, already had in mind its fittingness as an image for his own relationship with his people.[25]

"Children . . . and fathers"

The instructions to children and fathers in 6:1–4 are noticeably briefer than the preceding paragraphs. Children are urged to obey their parents "in the Lord"—i.e., as an expression of their own identity in Christ and their calling to speak and act as his people (cf. 4:17, 5:8).[26] The further warrant, "for this is right" (v. 1b), would probably have carried a certain self-evidentness within the moral consensus of the time, but its context here, sandwiched between the reminder that Christian obedience is to be rendered "in the Lord" and the quotation from the Decalogue in the following verse, suggests that the primary source for believers' knowledge of what is right is the will of God, not the values of the surrounding culture.[27] The quotation of the fifth commandment that follows (vv. 2–3) is interrupted by an editorial comment from Paul that focuses his readers' attention on the promise of blessing and inheritance that accompanied Moses's commandment to the Israelites, and invites them to identify their own situation as typologically equivalent to that of Moses's first hearers.[28]

Fathers, for their part, are told to bring their children up "in the training and instruction of the Lord" (v. 4). Given the background of Paul's language in Prov 3:11–12, the most likely intended sense is one in which he is reminding human fathers that their activity is meant to function as a vehicle

---

25 Paul's appeal to the creation story of Gen 2 in this context does not function as a philosophical argument, in Aristotelian fashion, to assert a particular view of the gendered roles of husbands and wives as a direct and necessary inference from the biological differences of nature. (Cf. the rationale Aristotle offers for the social roles that he prescribes in *Politics* 1260a, 9–14.) It does, however, suggest an understanding of the roles of husbands and wives in which they function as an expression of the communicative purpose of the God who created those differences.

26 See the discussion in Thielman, *Ephesians*, 397 in favour of this reading of "in the Lord."

27 Cf. the parallel exhortation in Col 3:20 ("Children, obey your parents in everything, for this pleases the Lord") and the brief comments in Arnold, *Ephesians*, 416.

28 For a brief discussion of the hermeneutical issues raised by Paul's use of Moses's commandment in Eph. 6:2–3, see Starling, "Ephesians and the Hermeneutics of the New Exodus," 155–58.

for the Lord's own fatherly training and instruction of his children,[29] with the implication that they should regulate the manner and conduct of their teaching accordingly.

"Slaves . . . and masters"

Finally, in 6:5–9, Paul turns to slaves and masters, urging the former to "obey [their] earthly masters with respect and fear, as [they] would Christ" (v. 5), and masters to "treat [their] slaves in the same way . . . not threaten[ing] them" but remembering that slave and master alike have a common master in heaven.

Two features of the word to masters in verse 9 stand out when it is compared with the comparable words to husbands and fathers. The first is the phrase "in the same way" (*ta auta*), that brackets the word to masters alongside the word to slaves in a relationship that is not only reciprocal (as are the wife/husband and child/father relationships) but also implicitly symmetrical or equivalent.

The second, reinforcing that implication, is the way in which Paul gives the actions of both slaves and masters the same meaning in relation to the story of salvation. Unlike husbands, who are to relate to their wives as Christ to the church, and fathers, whose training and instruction are represented as an extension or manifestation of the fatherly discipline of God, masters are *not* encouraged to interpret their role as a participation in or reflection of the Lordship of Christ; rather, they are to remember that they, like the slaves who work within their households, are subject to the judgement of the same master, and that "there is no favoritism with him."

---

29   I.e., reading the genitive "of the Lord" as a subjective genitive, with the same force as the equivalent expression in LXX Prov. 3:11. Cf. Thielman, *Ephesians*, 402; Arnold, *Ephesians*, 418.

Performing the Household Code Today: Translation, Staging, Theme, and Casting

What implications does a narrative-dramatic approach to the interpretation of the household code have for the way in which it might inform our performance of the relevant social roles today, within a context in which the relationships of which the code speaks are named with different names, embedded within a different set of political and economic arrangements, and evaluated according to a different set of cultural standards and assumptions? A narrative-dramatic approach to the Ephesian household code does not eliminate the complexities of the hermeneutical task, but it does suggest a better set of categories with which to approach that task.

Translation and Staging

On the one hand, a reading of the household code as a script for communicative action implies an approach to the letter's contemporary application that grants the legitimacy—indeed the necessity—of taking sufficient account of the differences of culture and context for the theme of the narrative and its dramatic effect to be faithfully conveyed within a changed set of circumstances. A play by Chekhov or Aristophanes can be meaningfully and powerfully performed in twenty-first century Australia, in faithful continuity with the intentions of the dramatist, but faithful performance is not the same thing as antiquarian mimicry of the language and theatrical conventions of fifth-century Greece or nineteenth-century Russia.

There may come a time, for example, in a culture that has learned the meaning of the word "submission" not from Ephesians but from *Fifty Shades of Grey*, when faithful translation will require a new form of words to articulate the intended meaning of Paul's call for Christian wives to honour and acknowledge the responsibility that God has given to their husbands. Similarly, when it comes to the patterns of action with which the household codes call on Christian slaves and masters to perform their parts in the theodrama, those who are cast to play the equivalent parts in our own context will need to give due consideration to the starkly different social and political conditions that constitute the metaphorical "stage" on which the roles are to be performed.[30]

Theme and Casting

The necessity of such translations and adaptations, however, does not imply the right of the modern interpreter to falsify the themes or bowdlerise the narrative. Faithful performance of the household codes requires a pattern of speech and action that represents the same motifs and themes within the story that Paul calls on the household-members of the first century to embody and enact: the shared identity of the church as the Spirit-filled community, offering up thanksgiving to God in the name of Jesus; the sacrificial, care-giving love of Christ for the church; the church's submission to the headship of Christ; the obedient faith of God's people as they look toward their promised inheritance; the fatherly training and instruction of God; and the impartial rule and judgment of the risen Christ over all, whatever their social position.

Nor are we at liberty to reassign the various roles through which those themes are conveyed, without reference to the casting decisions handed down to us in Scripture and the rationale that informs them.[31] In some instances, of course, there is a certain complexity to the judgements we are required to make regarding the casting of the parts for the drama. Within a context in which none of us is a slave or a master in a sense that corresponds precisely to the meaning of those terms within a first-century household, we are required to reassign those parts to their closest contemporary equivalents, adapting the performance of the roles accordingly, in order to convey the same theme

---

30   Cf. Gombis, *The Drama of Ephesians*, 18.

31   This is precisely the course of action that Andrew Lincoln recommends, when he advises that "it is best, then, to see this vision of marriage for what it is—conditioned by the cultural assumptions of its time—and to appreciate what it attempts to accomplish in its own setting . . . Instead of assigning love to the husband and submission to the wife, a contemporary appropriation of Ephesians will build on this passage's own introductory exhortation (v 21) and see a mutual loving submission as the way in which the unity of the marriage relationship is demonstrated." Lincoln, *Ephesians*, 392–93.

of Christ's impartial lordship over both those who exercise human power and authority and those who live under it.

In the other roles of the household code, however—wives and husbands, children and fathers—the casting decisions conveyed by Paul's instructions come with an embedded rationale that implies their permanence and non-transferability. Human fathers have a unique responsibility (in partnership with mothers) to represent and participate in the fatherly training and instruction of God; husbands are to exercise a headship that is patterned on the sacrificial care of Christ for the church—a casting decision that is informed not only by the way in which power was distributed within the Graeco-Roman household, but also, and more basically, by the "profound mystery" written into the purposes of God in creation:

> When viewed in theodramatic perspective, we see that we are but actors who have received divine casting calls . . . Our identities "are fundamentally determined, not by human social construction, but by the creative and redemptive activity of God." It is the producer's call. Our task is to respond to our vocation as embodied creatures and to play our parts as well as we can to God's glory.[32]

Conclusion

The Ephesian household code is not, of course, the only one in the New Testament, nor are the household codes the only biblical texts that ought to inform how we understand the roles of husbands and wives as followers of the Lord Jesus. Nevertheless, Paul's instructions to the husbands and wives of first-century Ephesus shed clear and indispensable light on one crucial dimension of how Christians are to perform those roles, summoning us to a pattern of relationship that faithfully imitates the relationship of Christ and

---

[32]   Vanhoozer, "A Drama-of-Redemption Model," 197, quoting from Harries et al., *Some Issues in Human Sexuality*, 183.

his church and fulfils the purposes of the God who made us male and female in the beginning. Our performances of the various social roles in which we play our parts as members of Christ's people are not reducible to a conformist mimicry of the patterns taught to us by the culture we live in, or (conversely) to an ironic parade of parodies aimed at subverting those traditional scripts.[33] Instead, our performances derive their meaning from the gospel narrative of the grace of God in Christ, and we enact the parts in that drama which we have been given by the wise and loving casting decisions of the God who created us to play those roles for his glory.

---

33   See especially Butler, *Gender Trouble*, 107–93, and the criticisms in Nussbaum, "Professor of Parody."

Response: Michael Bird

David Starling begins his presentation by juxtaposing two different interpretive strategies for understanding the Ephesian household code, one that is static, and another which views them as liberalised accommodations to cultural norms. David wisely rejects the former approach of treating the household codes as a "timeless ethical template," but also rejects anachronistic attempts to turn Paul into a modern egalitarian on the grounds that Paul seems to be unaware of making any accommodation. Instead, building on the work of Tim Gombis, David proposes a divine drama model where Christian praxis is to proclaim and embody the divine wisdom announced in the story of salvation. On the Ephesians household code, David shows how one can conceive of marriage as an institution that images God's own relationship with his people. One can identify fatherhood as a vehicle for the Lord's own fatherly instruction of his children. Also, masters are to treat slaves with similar concern as for wives and children and reminded that they too are subject to a master. David is also aware of the hermeneutical complexity in moving from ancient Ephesus to the Emerald City and that a faithful performance of the text does not require antiquarian mimicry, but rather, a careful re-staging of the narrative. In particular, I like how David says that the performance of our roles should be driven by the gospel of grace, which becomes enacted and lived out in our lives. But he warns against falsifying themes in the narrative, he cautions against re-assigning roles without reference to the narrative itself, and urges that Paul's instruction have a certain permanence and non-transferability. For all of David's caveats about hermeneutical complexity, he still argues (I think) for the widespread normativity of the household codes. And herein lies the heart of my two concerns. First, I found that David's presentation fails to grapple with the cultural contingency of the household codes. A suburban Christian father in twenty-first century Melbourne is not anything like a *paterfamilias* in first-century Ephesus. If you want to avoid problems, then before you explain what is permanent and transferable in the household codes, you should first set out what is contingent and culturally specific. Second, I wonder how David would go about creating a biblically based ethic to undermine a biblically sanctioned institution of slavery. You can argue against the practice of slavery *if* you recognise the culturally contingent nature of the household codes and *if* you have a hermeneutical approach that shows that some biblical motifs outrank others in a gradation of ethical absolutes. I would like to see an approach that yields the same emphasis on the power of the divine drama to shape the identity and behaviour of Christians, while recognising that the drama has to be performed differently because of cultural inadequacies, not just in our culture, but in Graeco-Roman culture too.

Response: Gayle Kent

David Starling's paper adroitly begins with an acknowledgment that any interpretation or application of the household codes is a "notoriously contested enterprise." David's approach is to apply the households codes for today within a narrative-dramatic framework; looking at the broader considerations of "translation and staging" and "theme and casting."

A major strength of David's paper is the way he seeks to find a possible middle ground between an overly simplistic and conservative standpoint on the household codes as ethical templates and a perspective that argues that the codes were a concessionary cultural construct. By placing the codes within the great drama of salvation history, David seeks to focus our attention on the specific responsive actions of men and women within a community *and* draw our attention to the grander narrative of the gospel. This approach provides a helpful reminder that our interpretation and application of the Bible must reflect our new identity and calling in Christ, and the call to demonstrably live out the purposes of God. David limits his discussion of the household codes to the passage in Ephesians 5 and more could be said about how this framework could reframe the other household codes in the New Testament or other passages often used in discussions of gender roles.

In his application of a narrative-dramatic perspective, David takes a more conservative stance on the household code, the tasks of a dramatic director, and gender roles of the "actors." In his section on translation he concedes that terminology, as well as actions, need to be considered in their cultural frameworks. As we seek to apply household codes today we grapple, for example, with the fact that "submission" is a culturally loaded word and that the actions of slaves and masters have no modern equivalent. While acknowledging the need for flexibility in some areas, in other aspects such as the "casting decisions" of gender roles in marriage and parenthood, David argues for a fixed and divinely "embedded" framework.

Finding a balance between flexible and rigid interpretations highlights a potential difficulty in approaching the household codes through a narrative-dramatic perspective. The post-postmodern world readily validates different readings or appropriations of texts and there is significant freedom to adapt them to speak to new audiences. While it is accepted by most that the modern interpreter or director does not have the freedom to adapt the "drama" beyond recognition, drama has always been designed to be adapted, abridged, and experimented with. Any modern production of Chekhov, Shakespeare, or Aristophanes will most likely, and possibly contentiously, manipulate the text, adapt the setting, or explore gender roles while maintaining the "same motifs and themes." Does a narrative-dramatic perspective of the household codes offer the same opportunity?

While helpfully reminding us of our need to place all passages of the Bible within the grand narrative of faith, David's paper highlights yet another layer of complexity to the enterprise of applying biblical texts about gender and family roles in today's world.

Adult, Single, and Christian: Exploring the Impact of Gender Expectations and Family Roles

Gayle Kent

In 2015, Proctor and Gamble's advertising campaign #LikeAGirl caught the world's attention, especially when one of its adverts was broadcast during the famous NFL Superbowl half-time commercials. This campaign compared how preteens and teenagers interpreted what it meant to throw, run, or fight "like a girl."[34] It invited a conversation about the ways that our Western culture conditions men and women to view gender roles; challenging stereotypical or biased views about femininity, strength, and confidence.[35]

Imagine a similar campaign with adult Christian men and women. What would the answers be if they were asked what it meant to love God and love others #LikeAWoman or #LikeAMan? Notwithstanding the clunkier

---

34   Procter & Gamble, "Our Epic Battle #Likeagirl."

35   Judkis, "Always Super Bowl 2015 Commercial: Redefining 'Throw Like a Girl'." Further campaigns have challenged the limitations society places on girls. The popularity of the #LikeAGirl campaign and others like it indicates that conversations about gender, equality, and society are ones we need to have.

hash tags, would additional qualifiers based on marital status or maturity of Christian faith change the conversation? This paper suggests that many of our conversations about adult single Christians[36] can too easily reflect stereotypical or conditioned responses about gender expectations and family roles. Instead of real dialogue "sides" talk "past one another,"[37] drifting towards what divides or marginalises.

There is, therefore, the need to have better conversations; ones that challenge, encourage, critique, enrich, and ultimately help all believers grow in faith. This paper therefore poses four "conversation starters" to help us explore gender expectations and family roles as they relate to adult single Christians:

1. Why do we need a conversation about adult singleness in the church?

2. Are the household codes of the New Testament relevant to adult single Christians?

3. How do perceived views of gender expectations and family roles impact our understanding of maturity?

4. How can the Bible enrich our understanding of relationships within the family and beyond?

Why Do We Need a Conversation about Adult Singleness in the Church?

As the church seeks to engage with a changing world, particularly in Australia, United Kingdom, and North America, it is important that conversations about gender, family, and relationships represent the views and experiences of adult single Christians. Such conversations will help churches better equip those already part of their faith community and also provide an added impetus to engage missionally.

---

36   I have consciously ordered these descriptors so that emphasis is given to the unity that people have as adults and also as believers in Christ. Our marital status is one subset of our lives.

37   Fulton, Gouldbourne, and James, "Biblical Truth and Biblical Equality."

In today's culture, the range of people who are single (whether by their own choice or the choice of others) reflects broader shifts in family and community life. Many factors have influenced the experience of singleness and marriage: the increasing median age of marriage, the prevalence of civil ceremonies over religious ones, the continuing high rate of co-habitation before marriage, steady divorce rates, and an aging population of widows and widowers to name a few.[38]

Similarly, the changing nature of what constitutes a family or household has impacted how we experience singleness. A model that is centred on a family unit of two parents and their children ignores the reality of those who live alone as well as those living in single-parent households.[39] The nuclear family, while it still may be the ideal for many, is no longer as dominant in broader Western culture. It too often remains, however, a normalised expectation in many Christian churches.

Despite the wealth of biblical teaching about the worth and benefits of singleness, for many adult Christian singles, their life and faith are exercised in a "couples' world"; within and outside of the church. A conversation is therefore needed if the church is going to genuinely engage with adult single Christians.

For women in particular, where society's expectations are increasingly diverse, rigid religious views about gender and family roles are being challenged. One study in Britain suggested that "adaptive" women, whether single or married, are less likely to be committed to faith communities which emphasise traditional gender roles.[40] Other research suggests that while there could be a rise of adult singles in congregations due to the aging population

---

38   Australian Bureau of Statistics, "3310.0 – Marriages and Divorces, Australia, 2013." In 1976, around two-thirds (67%) of 24 year olds in Australia were, or had been, married, compared with 14% of 24 year olds in 2011. "Young Adults Then and Now: 4102.0 – Australian Social Trends, April 2013."

39   Australian trends indicate that approximately 9% of adults live alone in single households, which is projected to rise in coming years. In the latest census, 19% of households are considered one-parent families. These statistics also reveal a noteworthy prevalence of one-parent households headed by a single mother (16%) over lone father families (3%). "3236.0 – Household and Family Projections, Australia, 2011 to 2036." ; "4442.0 – Family Characteristics and Transitions, Australia, 2012-13."

40   Aune, "Evangelical Christianity and Women's Changing Lives," 289.

of those who attend church, the Australian church is still not engaging with single or married young adults in their twenties and thirties.[41]

Models of Christian relationships that are tied to certain views of marriage or even the "traditional" family unit are no longer representative or adequate, if they ever were. While views on marriage and family remain important and valid, we have the opportunity, and the responsibility, to engage in a much broader discussion about our shared human experience.

Are the Household Codes of the New Testament Relevant to Adult Single Christians?

Any conversation about gender expectations and familial relationships explored within a Christian perspective will most likely include an assessment of how the early church sought to understand and apply the realities of their new community and unity in Christ. Believers were to be valued as brothers and sisters in Christ, and all were invited into a new way of living, regardless of status or gender. The household codes, found in passages such as Ephesians 5:21–26, Colossians 3:18—4:1, 1 Timothy 2: 9–15, Titus 2: 2–10 and 1 Peter 2:13—3:7, presented a new way of relating, and challenged old patterns of societal relationships.

These passages remain highly influential and are often, together with Jesus's own words in Matthew 19:1–12 and Matthew 22:23–3, focal points of discussion about gender roles within the family. They raise questions about headship and submission, about freedom and responsibility, and about family life. Historically they have led to views that overvalued or undervalued either singleness or marriage.

In the midst of academic debate about whether the actions of headship and submission are best understood through the lens of creation and the fall, or how to respond to the hermeneutical challenges of applying ancient household codes to today's society, issues specific to single life are

---

41   McCrindle Research, "A Demographic Snapshot."

too often neglected or sidelined. They are a small act in a much larger play about how husbands and wives should relate to one another or how the marriage relationship reveals biblical models of manhood or womanhood.[42]

Despite this marginalisation, adult single Christians should be cautious of dismissing these passages as irrelevant nor be limited by an overly literal interpretation or reductionist framework. To do so would fail to take into account their grander purposes as a starting point of a broader discussion of the church, its eschatological mission, and its new kingdom community.[43]

One flawed attempt to make these passages relevant to adult single Christians is to focus gender expectations and family roles through a lens of marriage; transposing certain expectations of husbands and wives onto all relationships. Piper, Grudem, Köstenberger, and Jones, for instance, argue that because gender expectations and family roles are, for the most degree, universal, single men and women should reflect gendered roles of leadership or submission as they interpret them within a marriage relationship.[44] At its worst, such views place unrealistic pressure on single men and women to fulfil certain expectations, and also lay a foundation for misaligned perspectives on authority, power, and influence.

Within this perspective, dating or engaged couples should especially foreshadow certain patterns of behaviour. [45] The imprecise and unique transition from singleness to a committed relationship highlights the complexity of such interpretations. If one holds to a view of clearly defined gender expectations within marriage, when and how does that shift occur? How should a couple transition from the "now and not yet" to the fully

---

42   An example of this is in Piper and Grudem's influential collation, *Recovering Biblical Manhood and Womanhood*, where adult singles are referred to in the Preface, but specific issues pertaining to singleness and gender are not discussed in depth.

43   Osiek, "Did Early Christians Teach, or Merely Assume, Male Headship?" 27; Witherington, *Women in the Earliest Churches*, 55–56; Barton, *Life Together*, 39–40.

44   Piper and Grudem, *Recovering Biblical Manhood and Womanhood*; Knight, *The Role Relationship of Men and Women*; Köstenberger and Jones, *God, Marriage & Family: Rebuilding the Biblical Foundation*.

45   Chandler, "Should a Boyfriend 'Lead' His Girlfriend?"; Köstenberger and Jones, *God, Marriage & Family: Rebuilding the Biblical Foundation*, 160.

fledged living out of certain roles? Does it happen when they are first sexually intimate, which might be before marriage, or only when the minister or celebrant pronounces a couple husband and wife? How is this explained to a de-facto couple who are committed to Christ but may still be technically seen as "single" or not "married" in the eyes of a faith community?

Whether intentionally or not, defining gender roles and relationships according to prescribed distinctions can also marginalise those who are single and childless. Some of those writing from a more traditionally hierarchical and static view suggest that adult singles should also adopt parent-like roles. Single women are encouraged to "bear, nurture and encourage spiritual children" as a sign of their "mature femininity."[46] Single men are challenged to adopt quasi-fathering roles so that the "millions of children who have no father present will have a chance of making it."[47] While the need for all to nurture future generations both in faith and life is valid, seeing this behaviour solely through a somewhat foggy lens of marriage or parenthood can exacerbate the differences between single and married adults. At its worst, such a view could reinforce the impression that adult singles are merely in the rehearsal stage of certain gender expectations and family roles, waiting to be called on stage only when marriage or biological parenthood occurs. The pressure for adult singles, especially women, to find a sense of fullness through marriage or childbirth establishes not only a distinction between single and married but also between those who have been able to have children and those who have not, whether by choice, circumstance, or physical ability.

If adult single Christians are not willing to be in "rehearsal" mode or choose to dismiss prescriptive frameworks, in what ways then can these household codes still be relevant? There is great benefit in reading beyond the directives to husbands and wives in these passages and to be shaped by the broader challenge to foster faithful Christian relationships. Gender expectations and family roles are reshaped around the life, death, resurrection,

---

46   James, *God's Design for Women*, 156.

47   Hardenbrook, "Where's Dad?"

and victory of Jesus and his kingdom.[48] Single Christians are also caught up in the mysterious metaphor of Christ's relationship with his bride, the church.

Much more can be said about our role as children and how we navigate adult relationships with parents and older generations of caregivers. Grappling with what it means to be obedient or respectful as an adult child, to establish healthy differentiation, to honestly share celebrations and hurts, and to respond to a parent's hopes and dreams, are tasks for married and single children alike. For adult singles, especially from cultures that have strong parental bonds and expectations, navigating this relationship is imperative.

While the context of masters and slaves is historically and socially distanced from our own circumstances, all people can be challenged about how the powerful and the powerless relate to one another. All believers also need to address injustice and the immoral use of power in our world. For adult single Christians, reactions to power and powerlessness could also be seen in the ways that they respond to their individual freedoms, or how they respond to situations where they are invisible or forgotten due to their lack of a partner.

Most importantly, the call to mutual submission in Ephesians 5:21 highlights an overarching identity as brothers and sisters in Christ called to live in community with one another. The household codes serve as a reminder of our interrelatedness and the gift of family, however we define it. This community, this identity, invites all believers into a rich, challenging, non-hierarchical, and inclusive view of relationships that echoes Galatians 3:26–29. The household codes are thus relevant but should not be read in isolation. To do so would be to neglect the other examples of relationships between men and women found in Scripture, and impoverish our imaginations of how we should live together as the community of God.

---

48   Loader, *Sexuality in the New Testament*, 397.

How Do Perceived Views of Gender Expectations and Family Roles Impact Our Understanding of Maturity?

Asking the question "What does it mean to be a grown-up?" can be the start of another conversation about gender expectations and family roles. Psychosocial theories of adulthood and transition, such as those posited by Erikson and Levinson in the 1960s and 1970s, still have influence despite the fact that they no longer adequately reflect our communities or our churches.[49] These theories suggest that normal, healthy, adult maturity involves completing certain psychosocial tasks or resolving developmental crises within one's lifespan. Both marriage and having children are typically included in a "normal" adult experience. These theories and structures do little to validate those who have not achieved these perceived markers of adulthood and can further marginalise adult singles.

Too often our church activities and organisational structures are categorised by similar markers. Whether psychosocial expectations are given a veneer of religiosity or views of Christian relationships are propped up by such theories, notions of maturity that are inherently connected to a set of pre-defined roles or tasks can create unnecessary and destructive stresses for adult single Christians.

An understanding of maturity that is based on respect, responsibility, tolerance, and flexibility as a measure of Christlikeness is far more inclusive.[50] Men and women, single and married, young and old, parents and the childless, able and less able are called to seek maturity in Christ. Viewing expectations of gender and Christian maturity through this lens places gender and relationships within the grand narrative of God's redemptive purposes for his people and the world. All followers of Christ are called to maturity; to be conformed to his image (Rom 12:1–2; Gal 3:27; Phil 2:5); to relate to one another through the fruit of the Holy Spirit (Gal 5:22–23); to reach unity in the faith, and together as God's people find maturity under Christ's

---

49   Erikson, *Identity, Youth, and Crisis*; Levinson, *The Seasons of a Man's Life*.
50   Cook and Frost, "Being Single in a Couples' World," 5.

headship (Eph 4:1–16). Such a framework does not deny that at times in our lives we might face certain psychosocial challenges but offers a significantly alternative way to discuss our common identity, purpose, and vision.

How Can the Bible Enrich Our Understanding of Relationships within the Family and Beyond?

Limiting our understanding of gender expectations and family relationships to precursors, expectations, and experiences of a marriage denies everyone from experiencing the expansive and rich diversity of relationships found in Scripture. It would be foolish to dismiss the examples of married and family life that we see in the grand narrative of Scripture but equally foolish to neglect the rich understanding to be gained through exploring broader examples of familial relationships in the Bible.

The friendship and family ties of Jonathan and David or the brotherly relationship of Jacob and Esau will challenge pre-conceived notions of masculinity and power. The interplay between Abraham and Lot, and their extended family, highlights the complexities of living and working with family members. The working out of leadership between Moses, Aaron, and Miriam highlights the giftedness of both men and women, and the challenges that all face when called to lead. The strength and determination of both Ruth and Naomi provides encouragement and challenge—especially when seen in the context of their broader patriarchal community. The relationship between Esther and her uncle Mordecai reveals how one's family can shape identity and expectations. The pairs of brothers, Simon Peter and Andrew, and James and John, amongst the disciples give us a glimpse of brotherly companionship and competition. The family bond of adult siblings, Mary, Martha, and Lazarus, enriches our experience of discipleship, grief, and celebration. The advocacy of Paul in relation to the slave Onesimus and his master Philemon reminds us of the new identity we have in Christ. These relationships, and many others, invite us to explore beyond narrow or pre-conceived views of gender expectations and family roles.

Continuing the Conversation

While this paper has focused on just a few possible conversations, further exploration about gender expectations and family roles as they relate to adult single Christians is needed. We will benefit from finding common ground, between genders as well as between those married and single, as people all created in the image of God and called to love him and others.[51] Exploring the implication that we are all "single people who are intended to be communal in nature" [52] will open up new ways of valuing extended family relationships and community. Affirming people's sexuality while advocating biblical ethics will protect us from overemphasising or devaluing sexual intimacy.

Our conversations should start and end with courageous humility and a desire to learn from each other's stories. We should not be afraid to speak about how history, class, power, economics, culture, biology, identity, and even biblical hermeneutics impact our understanding of gender and family.[53]

As followers of Christ, our common purpose and mission for women and for men, married or single, are much grander than those who created the #LikeAGirl campaign. Our quest for unity and community as the family of God and the bride of Christ demands that we pay attention to the ease with which our conversations stereotype or marginalise, especially in the areas of gender expectations and family roles. As we share our stories and our lives, we will be better able to see and affirm the work of God's Spirit and our identity in Christ. As we seek instead to build one another up in faith and knowledge, conversations such as this one, and ones to follow, will hopefully help the church grow to maturity under Christ.

---

51 Bilezikian, *Beyond Sex Roles*, 161; Grudem, *Evangelical Feminism & Biblical Truth*, 28; Morse, "Gender Wars," 6.

52 Spencer, "Marriage and Singleness," 7.

53 Aune, "Evangelical Christianity and Women's Changing Lives," 288.; Oakley, *Sex, Gender and Society*, 72; Nordling, "Gender," 498.

Response: David Starling

The question that Gayle addresses in her paper is one that is of vital importance for the formation of Christian disciples and Christian community today.

Gayle is rightly critical of versions of complementarianism that seek to discern an abstract, universal template of masculinity and femininity, derived from the teaching of the NT about the roles of husbands and wives, and apply it to all male-female relationships within the church and the world at large. However neat and orderly a vision of this sort may look from a distance, it is not the path that the NT writers model for us: nowhere in the NT am I exhorted to relate to women in general as if they were my wife, or Christian women exhorted to relate to me as if I were their husband.

How then does the NT encourage us to relate the categories of marriage, family, and household to the identity and experience of adult single Christians? As a contribution to the discussion Gayle has opened up in her paper, I would like to suggest half a dozen complementary ways in which the NT writers encourage us to draw connections of this sort.

The first three are ways in which the NT writers encourage single Christian men and women to understand their situation in relation to the blessings and burdens of marriage. Starting at what is perhaps the most obvious place, in 1 Corinthians 7, Paul encourages single Christian men and women like himself to understand themselves both as *free from marriage*, with its particular burdens and concerns (1 Cor 7:32) and *free to marry*, within certain constraints depending on their particular circumstances (1 Cor 7:35, 39). But these are not the only words the NT speaks about the experience of adult Christian singleness; balancing Paul's words in 1 Corinthians 7 about singleness as a situation of freedom are the words of Jesus in the gospels about singleness (whether chosen or unchosen) as a life-situation that involves cost and deprivation; single adult Christians are, very often, people who have "*left behind* [the reality or potential of] *home* or *wife* [or *husband*] . . . or *children for the sake of the kingdom*" (Luke 18:29; Mk 10:29; Matt 19:12).

Nor is the meaning of adult Christian singleness to be understood solely in terms of the absence of marriage. Three more NT categories suggest themselves as complementary ways in which household roles and images apply to single adult Christians, in common with married believers. Within the fictive kinship networks of the church, adult single Christians are to see themselves and be seen by others "as *mothers* . . . as *fathers* . . . [as *daughters* and as *sons*]"; such is the import of Paul's advice to Timothy in 1 Tim 5:1–2, and his reference to the mother of Rufus in Rom 16:14.[54] Fifthly, even more basically, believers are to regard themselves as *brothers and sisters* to one another within the household of the church.[55] And sixthly, most basically of all, believers are to regard themselves as *daughters and sons of God*, sharers together in the sonship of the Lord Jesus (Gal 3:28–29). A thoughtful and hermeneutically responsible appropriation of these six complementary perspectives would, I think, take us a long way toward answering the important questions that Gayle poses.

---

54   See also 1 Cor 4:14–17; Mark 10:30.

55   See especially Hellerman, *The Ancient Church as Family*, and *When the Church Was a Family*.

Response: Michael Bird

Gayle suggests four scintillating and challenging questions about Christians and family as it relates to adult singleness in the church. She rightfully puts out that the shape of family and marriage is changing in Australia within larger demographic movements. Gayle also raises the question of the relevance of the household codes to Christian singles. She remains concerned and confused about the teaching of conservative thinkers who compel singles to emulate, in some way, the roles and submissiveness in the household codes, something that adversely affects both single men and women. I very much share her concern in that regard, especially as I contemplate my own children growing into adult singleness. Our sense of being complete or mature is often determined by pre-defined roles, whereas Gayle urges us to consider maturity instead in terms of respect, responsibility, and Christ-likeness. When it comes to understanding appropriate relationships, she urges us to look beyond the nuclear family, to other relationships, friendships, colleagues, and ministry partners as both a source of wisdom and the place in which relational wisdom is lived. Probably the best part of her paper was that rather than conceive of singles as potentially marriageable persons, somehow lacking and defective, we think of them as persons in their own right, who are part of a network of meaningful relationships. The only thing I would add is perhaps on the virtues of singleness for things ranging from mission to holiness.

Part Three

Gender, Scripture, and Church

"Teaching" as Traditioning in 1 Timothy 2:12: An Historical Observation

John Dickson

Introduction

In its official report on women's ordination to the priesthood more than thirty years ago, the Doctrine Commission of the Anglican Diocese of Sydney, under the guidance of the Cambridge-trained New Testament scholar (and then Archbishop) Donald Robinson, concluded:

> In the Pastoral Epistles, teaching appears to be an authoritative function concerned with the faithful transmission of apostolic doctrine or tradition and committed to men specially chosen (e.g., 2 Timothy 1:13–14; 2:2; 1 Timothy 3:2; 5:17; Titus 1:9). It is within this context that the specific prohibition of 1 Timothy 2:12 must be understood. Women are not to assume the authoritative teaching office that properly belongs to men in the Christian congregation. In our own

context this would not appear to exclude absolutely the possibility of women preaching or teaching in church. It nevertheless appears to exclude the possibility of women exercising the role of teaching elder or "priest" as that term is defined by the Anglican Ordinal.[1]

In a follow-up report of 1987 (also under the direction of Robinson) the commissioners observed:

> Contemporary preaching is not identical with teaching in the NT. Preaching covers a whole range of activities, including teaching, evangelism, encouragement, exhortation, prophecy and testimony. Teaching in the NT refers to the faithful transmission and defence of apostolic doctrine or passing on the fundamental structures of the faith. Admonition, prophecy, exhortation and encouragement are derived from this teaching ministry.[2]

The concern of this paper is not to endorse a particular view of women's ordination, nor to defend the views of a former generation of Anglican scholars.[3] It is to lay out something of a history of "teaching," *didaskein*, in the Pauline corpus. In doing so, it will become clear that this relatively obscure doctrine report from the 1980s did hit upon a crucial aspect of Paul's idea of teaching: for Paul *didaskein*, "to teach," is fundamentally a *traditioning* activity. It is not about conveying Christian truth in all its forms. It is about transmitting and preserving for a congregation the apostolic traditions of the gospel. It certainly does not refer to all that one might include under the modern rubric of a "sermon."

The genealogy of Donald Robinson's idea is relatively easy to trace. His teacher at Cambridge was the famed C. F. D. Moule. In Moule's classic

---

1   Jensen et al., "9/84 Ordination of Women."

2   Knox et al., "8/87 Ministry of Women."

3   Robinson's direct thoughts on apostolic tradition may be found in two short books: Robinson, *Faith's Framework*, and *Ordination for What?*

The Birth of the New Testament (published in 1961), he stressed the way the New Testament betrays a deep concern for *fixing* the gospel traditions of the apostle. "A good deal of prominence," Moule observed, "is given in these [Pastoral] Epistles, to the need for careful transmission of the apostolic teaching; it is a precious deposit, entrusted by God to the apostle, and by the apostle to his chosen disciple."[4]

German scholarship noted the same pattern around the same time. In his 1962 *Das Verständnis der Tradition bei Paulus und in den Deuteropaulinen*,[5] Klaus Wegenast argued that we can see in the Pauline corpus an increasing concern for fixing traditions, from the earlier undisputed letters of Paul to the later disputed letters. In this entry on *didaskō* ("teach") in the *New International Dictionary of New Testament Theology* (NIDNTT), Wegenast remarks "'to be taught' no longer means 'to hear the message in a concrete situation', but 'to receive and keep the teaching handed down'—reminiscent of the teaching methods employed by the rabbis." Of the Pastoral Epistles specifically he says that "invariably 'to teach' involves passing on a tradition which is more or less fixed . . . The emphasis falls on handing it on."[6] More recent scholars, such as Thomas Schreiner, agree with Moule and Wegenast that the Pastoral Epistles lay great stress on the "fixed body" of apostolic teaching, but rightly insist that the same concern for a fixed tradition is already present in Paul's earlier, undisputed epistles: e.g., 1 Cor 11:2; 15:1–5; Romans 6:17, Phil 4:9.[7]

My contention is that *didaskein* in both the undisputed and disputed letters of Paul almost uniformly refers to the task of carefully transmitting the apostolic gospel tradition to a congregation so that believers learn it.[8] This is the function—and no other—that Paul reserves for certain men in 1 Tim 2:12.

---

4   Moule, *Birth of the New Testament*, 252–53.

5   Wegenast, *Das Verständnis der Tradition*.

6   Wegenast, "Teach," 765.

7   Schreiner, *Paul*, 388–99.

8   See the discussions of the technical quality of "teaching" vocabulary in Towner, *Timothy and Titus*, 129–31, and in the same author's *Goal of Our Instruction*, 215. See also Saucy, "Paul's Teaching on the Ministry of Women," 291–310. Saucy's account of the referent of *didaskein* in the Pastoral Epistles is almost identical to my own.

1. *"Teaching" Isn't Everything*

The exegetical argument begins with the observation that Paul distinguishes between various kinds of speaking. In Rom 12:4–8 "prophesying," "teaching," and "exhorting" are said to "differ" (*diaphoros*) from one another: "Having gifts that *differ* according to the grace given to us, let us use them: if prophecy (*prophēteia*), in proportion to our faith;[9] if service, in our serving; the one who teaches (*didaskō*), in his teaching (*didaskalia*);[10] the one who exhorts (*parakaleō*), in his exhortation (*paraklēsis*), the one who contributes, in generosity." We can no sooner collapse "prophesying" or "exhorting" into "teaching" than we can equate "service" with "contributing." Otherwise, Paul's "body" metaphor—not to mention the adjective *diaphoros*—means little. The distinction between "teaching" and "exhorting" in this passage is described well by Peter Stuhlmacher: "The teacher must adhere to the doctrine which has been prescribed to him and pass it on without falsifying it (cf. 6:17). The preacher who is called to exhort and comfort the church must say and do that which serves the building up of the church."[11] One is fundamentally about *educating in the traditions*, the other about spiritual and moral edification.

A similar distinction can be observed in 1 Corinthians 11 and 14. Famously, Paul assumes that Corinthian women will "pray" and "prophesy" in worship (1 Cor 11:5).[12] Yet, a few chapters later he remarks, "Women should keep silent in the churches. For they are not permitted to speak" (1 Cor. 14:34). Assuming the paragraph is original (which many have doubted),[13] Paul cannot be contradicting what he said about women just a few chapters earlier (11:5). One satisfactory solution is that "silence" here refers to nonparticipation in the activity Paul has just mentioned: *weighing* what is said in prophecy (14:29).

---

9   Schreiner, *Paul*, 388–99.

10   Towner, *Timothy and Titus*, 129–31.

11   Stuhlmacher, *Romans*, 193.

12   Given that prayer and prophecy in the church service are topics of extended discussion in 1 Corinthians 12–14, it is unlikely that Paul is referring to something different in chapter 11. So also Carson, "Silent in the Churches," 140–53.

13   "[T]he section is accordingly to be regarded as an interpolation." Conzelmann, 1 Corinthians, 246.

Following Carson,[14] I take this to refer to judging the content of prophecy against the apostolic teaching. Paul distinguishes between "prophesying" and other forms of congregational speaking.

In 1 Tim 4:13, three public speaking activities are distinguished: "Until I come, devote yourself to the public reading of Scripture, to exhortation, to teaching." The triple use of the definite article (*tē anagnōsei, tē paraklēsei, tē didaskalia*) indicates, as Howard Marshall notes, "that these are familiar, recognised activities in the congregational meeting."[15] As in Rom 12, a distinction is being drawn between "exhorting" and "teaching".

What then is "teaching"?

2. Teaching and Traditioning in Paul

Several texts in the Pauline corpus suggest a close parallel between *didaskein* ("to teach")—the word used in 1 Tim 2:12—and Paul's technical "traditioning" vocabulary, *paradidōmi* ("hand on") and *paralambanō* ("receive"). It is widely recognised that "hand on" and "receive" are activities derived from Paul's *Jewish* background, as already noted above by Wegenast.[16] The Pharisees had an ever-increasing body of legal, narrative, and liturgical material. Passing on these "traditions of the fathers" (mentioned by Paul in Gal 1:14 and by Jesus in Mark 7:4–9) was "the single most distinctive feature of Pharisaism," says Joachim Schaper in his chapter on the Pharisees for the Cambridge History of Judaism.[17] Josephus provides one piece of oft-quoted evidence:

---

14   So also Carson, "Silent in the Churches," 133–47.

15   Marshall and Towner, *Pastoral Epistles*, 562.

16   Important books on oral tradition in Judaism and early Christianity include Wansbrough, *Oral Gospel Tradition*; Gerhardsson, *Reliability of the Gospel*; Dunn, *Jesus Remembered* (esp. 173–254). For the fundamental importance of oral tradition in ancient Judaism, see the massive study by Hezser, *Jewish Literacy*. She is far more sceptical than I am about the accuracy of Jewish oral culture, but she lays out the compelling evidence that ancient Jews, despite having a book at the centre of their worship (the Torah or Old Testament), were profoundly oral, not literary, in their approach to culture and religion.

17   Schaper, "The Pharisees," 409.

> The Pharisees passed on [*paradidōmi*] to the people certain regulations handed down by a succession of fathers and not recorded in the Laws of Moses, for which reason they are rejected by the Sadducaean group, who hold that only those regulations should be considered valid which were written down, and that those derived from the traditions [*paradoseis*] of the fathers need not be observed.[18]

A concern for "'handing on' and 'receiving'" a relatively fixed Christian tradition is found frequently in the Pauline corpus (1 Cor 11:2, 23; 15:1–3; Gal 1:9, 12; Phil 4:9; Col 2:6; 1 Thess 4:1; 2 Thess 2:15; 3:6).[19] A particularly revealing example has Paul reciting a tradition about the Last Supper twenty or so years before a near-identical account would appear in Luke 22:

> For I received (*paralambanō*) from the Lord what I also passed on (*paradidōmi*) to you: The Lord Jesus, on the night he was betrayed, took bread, and when he had given thanks, he broke it and said, "This is my body, which is for you; do this in remembrance of me." In the same way, after supper he took the cup, saying, "This cup is the new covenant in my blood; do this, whenever you drink it, in remembrance of me." (1 Cor 11:23–25)

Of particular significance for my argument are those occasions when the technical "traditioning" language (*paradidōmi* and/or *paralambanō*) is employed alongside "teaching" and "learning" vocabulary. Three examples will suffice.

---

18   Josephus, *Antiquities of the Jews* 13.297. One is also reminded of the later famous description of Jewish tradition in the Mishnah: "Moses received the Law [i.e., the oral Torah] from Sinai and committed it to Joshua, and Joshua to the elders, and the elders to the Prophets; and the Prophets committed it to the men of the Great Synagogue . . . Simeon the Just [third century BC] was of the remnants of the Great Synagogue . . . Antigonus of Soko received the Law from Simeon the Just ... Hillel and Shammai received the Law from them . . . Raban Gamaliel said: Provide thyself with a teacher and remove thyself from doubt (Danby, "Abot 1.1–16," 446–47). The passage is frequently cited as something of a parallel to the Pauline model of tradition: O'Brien, *Colossians—Philemon*, 105; Bauckham, *Jesus and the Eyewitnesses*, 269–70; Martyn, *Galatians*, 143.

19   See also Bauckham, *Jesus and the Eyewitnesses*, 269–70.

In Gal 1:12 the apostle insists that he came to know the gospel not in the normal human way, as the Galatians did, but through a direct disclosure from Jesus: "I did not receive (*paralambanō*) it, nor was I taught (*didaskō*) it." Some scholars, like James Dunn, baulk at seeing these two verbs as synonyms. He nonetheless thinks that "teaching" here must refer to "the basic catechesis in which no doubt already all new converts to the new faith were instructed."[20] Others see little or no difference here between "receiving" and "being taught." J. Louis Martyn says that "taught" in Gal 1:12 is "the key expression of the traditioning process"; Paul is saying, "I did not receive the gospel in a line of tradition."[21] Ronald Fung likewise insists that "'to be taught' or 'to learn' (cf. Eph. 4:21; Col. 2:7; 2 Thess. 2:15), no less than "to receive" and "to deliver," are used in connection with Christian tradition."[22]

In Col 2:6–7 we read, "Therefore, as you *received* (*paralambanō*) Christ Jesus the Lord, so walk in him, rooted and built up in him and established in the faith, just as you were *taught* (*didaskō*)." Here, the expression "as you were taught" is, as Marcus Barth notes, "used in a parallel construction to 'as you received'."[23] Doug Moo offers the same insight.[24] The point is not that the two terms are synonyms, but simply that "teaching" and "learning" are how the apostolic deposit was "handed over" and "received."

In 2 Thess 2:15 we again find the combination of "hand over" and "teach": "So then, brothers, stand firm and hold to *the traditions* (*paradosis*) that you were *taught* (*didaskō*) by us." Again, "teaching" is the activity by which the apostolic traditions changed hands. *Didaskein* is formal Pauline *traditioning* language.[25]

But what of the Pastoral Epistles themselves?

---

20   Dunn, "Epistle to the Galatians," 53.

21   Martyn, *Galatians*, 143.

22   Fung, *Galatians*, 52.

23   Barth et al., *Colossians*, 306.

24   Moo, *Letters to the Colossians and to Philemon*, 182.

25   Morris, *1 and 2 Thessalonians*, 240–41.

3. Traditioning in the Pastoral Epistles

Strikingly for a group of letters so focused on preserving the apostolic traditions, the technical language of "handing over / receiving" (*paradidōmi* and/or *paralambanō*) does not appear at all in the three Pastoral Epistles. Instead, we find the same concept conveyed through the language of "entrust/deposit"—and, importantly, *didaskein*-language stands close by.

In the single longest discourse on "teaching" in the Pastorals (2 Tim 1:11—2:2) the connection between transmitting the fixed gospel traditions and "teaching" is explicit. There is a kind of inclusio in the passage, beginning with a reference to Paul as the *didaskalos* (1:11) and closing with a call for Timothy to appoint others who will *didaskein* (2:2); Timothy is the bridge between them. Another word play centres on the "deposit" language. Paul gave a "deposit" (*parathēkē*) to Timothy (1:14); now Timothy is to "deposit/ entrust" (*paratithēmi*) that same content to people who can teach others also, i.e., who can transmit this fixed content: "And the things you have heard me say in the presence of many witnesses entrust to reliable people who will also be qualified to teach others" (2 Tim 2:2). "*Teaching*" *is the activity by which the apostolic deposit is deposited.*

The use of the noun "teaching" is also instructive. There is a terrific increase of the noun "teaching" (*didaskalia*) in the Pastoral Epistles: fourteen of the seventeen uses across the Pauline corpus appear in these three letters, where, as Hans-Friedrich Weiss remarks, it is "a technical term for apostolic or Christian teaching as a whole"[26] (1 Tim 1:10; 4:6, 4:13, 4:16; 5:17; 6:1, 6:3; 2 Tim 3:10, 3:16; 4:3; Titus 1:9; 2:1, 2:7, 2:10).[27]

---

26   Weiss, "Didaskalia." 317. On a few occasions the noun *didaskalia* functions as a verb to describe the activity of "teaching" (1 Tim 4:13, 5:17; 2 Tim 3:16).

27   The cognate noun *didachē* ("teaching") appears just twice in the Pastoral Epistles, where it is a clear synonym of *didaskalia* (2 Tim 4:2; Titus 1:9). In his earlier letter to the Romans, Paul uses *didachē* in precisely this way, to refer to the basic deposit already delivered to the Roman Christians (Rom 6:17; 16:17).

It is true that cognate verbs don't always share precisely the same referent as their nouns, but they *frequently do*. And on at least three occasions in the Pastoral Epistles the verb and noun for "teaching" appear together in the same train of thought (1 Tim 4:11–16; 6:1–3; 2 Tim 1:11—2:2), suggesting that what is "taught" is (unsurprisingly) the fixed "teaching."

The context of the all-important 1 Tim 2:12 ("I do not permit a woman to teach") has three uses of teaching-vocabulary in close proximity: a noun, a verb, and an adjective. First, as in 2 Tim 1:11, 1 Tim 2:7 gives Paul the threefold designation: preacher/herald, apostle, teacher (*didaskalos*). Unlike in 2 Timothy, though, Paul does not immediately move on to the importance of appointing "faithful men who will be able to teach others also" (2 Tim 2:2). Instead, he offers a brief word about men lifting holy hands in prayer (1 Tim 2:8) and about women adorning themselves respectably (1 Tim 2:9–10). And then Paul issues instructions to Timothy about the appointment of teachers: first negatively ("I do not permit a woman to teach [*didaskein*] or to exercise authority over a man," 1 Tim 2:12), and then, a paragraph later, positively (an overseer must be *didaktikos*, "apt to teach," 3:2). As in 2 Tim 1:11—2:2, Timothy is portrayed in 1 Tim 2–3 as the bridge between Paul, the "teacher" *par excellence*, and those appointed to carry on the teaching.

To "teach" (*didaskō*) in the Pastoral Epistles refers not to instructing people in Christian truth generally, but to causing people to learn the apostolic traditions, the deposit of the faith, precisely what it connotes in the other Pauline examples already discussed (Gal 1:12; Col 2:6–7; 2 Thess 2:15; cf. Phil 4:9).

Conclusion: Contemporary Reflections

Numerous public speaking ministries are mentioned throughout the Pauline corpus: preaching, evangelising, prophesying, praying, reading, exhorting, and teaching. Whatever overlap there may be in these activities, especially in content, there is every reason to think that Paul viewed them as *diaphoros*, "different." He explicitly acknowledges the probity of women "praying" and "prophesying" in public worship (1 Cor 11:5), and yet he does *not* envisage women publicly "weighing" prophecy against the apostolic teaching (1 Cor 14:34). The thought of 1 Tim 2:12 is not far away from this. While all sorts of public speaking activities were presumably open to women at the time of the writing of the Pastoral Epistles—including prophesying, preaching, exhorting, reading, and so on—1 Tim 2:12 does not envisage women transmitting and preserving the apostolic deposit. Paul does not grant "teaching-authority" to anyone but certain trusted men.

What does this historical and exegetical conclusion mean for the modern debate about the ministry of women in our churches? I can imagine four different approaches.

1. *No sermons from women.* Those who reserve the pulpit only for transmitting and preserving the apostolic deposit will find good exegetical grounds for not inviting women to give any sermons in the weekly church service. One question confronting this interpretation, though, will be: What place is given to women in our modern context to "prophesy" or "exhort"?

2. *Sermons on a spectrum.* Some may conclude that, although the modern sermon is not always equated with what Paul calls "teaching," some sermons today will be close analogies to the careful transmission of the apostolic deposit. On this view, sermons are seen on a spectrum: some are more like prophesying and exhorting, aiming to urge obedience to Scripture or encourage confidence in God's truth; others function more as a focused mandating of apostolic doctrine. The former sermon type will be open to trusted men and women alike, the latter only to certain trusted men.[28] How such a view avoids arbitrariness, or even casuistry, is a question that will have to be faced. It is one that presents itself to most complementarian interpretations. A line is always drawn somewhere—whether at sermons, song leading, service hosting, or Bible reading.

---

28   I myself advocated for this view in my earlier *Hearing Her Voice*.

3. *Restricting the office of teacher.* A third response might focus on the *role* or *office* rather than the activity. This seems to be the course taken by the Anglican reports mentioned earlier. Though somewhat reserved in expression, the report affirms that 1 Tim 2:12 "would not appear to exclude absolutely the possibility of women preaching or teaching in church." It rather does "exclude the possibility of women exercising the role of teaching elder or 'priest'." Here the concern is not really about what kind of sermon is preached but *who* in the congregation bears ultimate responsibility for transmitting and preserving the apostolic deposit. In a paper published around the same time, J. I. Packer came to a similar conclusion.[29] By laying the emphasis on the office of "teacher" rather than the activity of teaching, this view perhaps avoids the problem of casuistry.

4. *The canon as teacher.* A fourth, more far-reaching, line of reasoning might observe that in a fully literate culture like ours, where everyone has a Bible on their laps, Paul's concern for securing the deposit of the faith is amply fulfilled by the canon of Scripture itself. All ministry roles in church life, therefore, are open to men and women alike, without any breach of the intention of 1 Tim 2:12.

Whichever of these four applications is appropriate, the key point of this paper is a simple historical one. "Teaching" in the Pauline corpus does not refer to any and every kind of public proclamation of Christian truth. It is part of Paul's all-important *traditioning* terminology. To quote Donald Robinson's commission once more, teaching "refers to the faithful transmission and defence of apostolic doctrine or passing on the fundamental structures of the faith." Whatever this means for contemporary church practice, I think this historical observation is sound.

---

29   Packer, "Challenge of Biblical Interpretation: Women," 114–15.

Response: Lyn Kidson

I would like to begin by saying that I appreciate John Dickson's efforts to bring a fresh insight to the interpretation of 1 Timothy chapter 2. In doing so he has reignited a discussion that needs to be had about the interpretation of the passage and its modern application. While I think that John has put his finger on a key problem, he unfortunately has missed the opportunity to hear the voice of the writer of 1 Timothy. As John observes, fourteen out of seventeen uses of *didaskalia* occur in the Pastoral Epistles. In 1 Timothy it occurs seven times, nine times if one includes its use in the compound word *heterodidaskaleō* (1 Tim 1:3; 6: 3). One could conclude that *didaskalia* is a major theme in this letter and warrants careful investigation. In my own research I have found that the word in general Greek usage means "instruction," which includes both the passing on of a body of traditional material as well as its application in the present day. For instance, in Hippocrates it means the passing on of the body of medical knowledge as well as the application of that knowledge.[30] Such an observation does not bode well for John's interpretation that *didaskalia* is equivalent to *paradidōmi* or the passing on of tradition.

---

30   Hippocrates, *Law* 2; also *Inscriptiones Graecae* IX,1 881.

It appears that *didaskalia* has a distinct sense from *paradidōmi* in that it involves the passing on of tradition as well as its application; a word most suited to Christian instruction in 1 Timothy. What is lacking in John's account, as well as Hefin's account, is how this command "I do not allow" relates to the overall purpose of the letter. The writer has made his purpose for writing quite clear in the opening body of the letter, "As I urged you upon my departure for Macedonia, remain on at Ephesus so that you may instruct certain men not to teach strange doctrines…" (1 Tim 1: 3). The key word here is the compounded verb *heterodidaskaleō*—"to teach the other [teaching]." This purpose is repeated in 1 Tim 3: 14–5 and 1 Tim 6: 3–5; 20–21. In my research into letter writing, I found that the repetition of the opening statement at the end of the letter signaled the writer's prime concern in writing. It is a clue to the writer's purpose. The big challenge for those studying 1 Timothy is how to relate the obvious purpose of the letter with the instructions that appear to be about church order. In other words how does the letter cohere? I would suggest that the command, "I do not allow a woman to teach" (1 Tim 2:12), actually relates to the overall purpose of the letter "so that you may instruct certain men (which could easily be translated as 'certain people') not to teach the other [teaching]."

Response: Hefin Jones

No-one has made me think harder about Scripture, gender, and church in recent years than John Dickson. It's a real pleasure to respond to his succinct account of teaching as fundamentally a traditioning activity in Paul.

John's paper echoes the Sydney Doctrine Commission's statement, "In the Pastoral Epistles, teaching appears to be an authoritative function concerned with the faithful transmission of apostolic doctrine or tradition and committed to men specially chosen," a statement that can hardly be improved on. While "transmission" featured in both editions of *Hearing Her Voice*, in his current paper it eclipses the previously prominent description of teaching as "laying down" the traditions.

Two sets of questions, and a comment about application are in order. First, to what extent is transmission a traditioning activity? Clearly traditioning is a kind of transmission. However, not all that could be covered by the rubric of transmission is traditioning. One wonders to what extent is the sense of *didaskō* (I teach) identical to the senses of *paralambanō* (I hand down) and *paratithēmi* (I entrust) in Paul? Are these terms essentially synonymous in Paul, or are they only partially synonymous? Might it not be the case that even in texts where synonymity is highly likely (e.g., Gal 1:12) the choice of two alternative terms to describe what might be one underlying activity points to the fact that the two terms describe different aspects of that one activity? And isn't it possible to read 2 Timothy 2:2 in such a way that *paratithēmi* and *didaskō* refer to distinctly different activities, the first to the training of the teachers and the second to their work in the congregation? John is, I'm sure, aware that not all of those he's cited as supporting the view that teaching is transmission of apostolic tradition would understand teaching to be traditioning in the way John has described it (e.g., Schreiner).

Second, isn't the nature of the prohibition in 1 Timothy 2:12 vital? Doesn't Paul prohibit women teaching *with authority*? Isn't that prohibition of women functioning as if they were overseers the key to understanding and applying 1 Timothy 2:12? In *Hearing Her Voice* John has defended the view that the prohibition is of women teaching with authority, and I suspect that it is still his view. However, little is made of that fact in his account. Paul is not prohibiting traditioning, but rather transmission of the apostolic deposit *with authority*. Curiously, in 1 Timothy, Paul *always* pairs *didaskō* with a verb of "suasive power" (2:12; 4:11; 6:2). What Paul calls upon Timothy to do, to teach with some form of suasive power (4:11; 6:2), he prohibits to women in 2:12.

While I agree with John's view—"Paul does not grant 'teaching-authority' to anyone but certain trusted men"[31]—I wonder if each of the four tentatively offered approaches to application adequately reflect that insight. I wonder if authority in the congregation is partly a function of *recognition by the congregation* as much as a function of the content or mode of speech employed. If someone speaks in such a way, often enough, that the congregation comes to regard them as one of their teacher-leaders then they have become an overseer/elder *in fact*, if not by *name* or *office*. It is this functioning as if an overseer/elder that Paul prohibits to women in 1 Timothy.

---

31   see page 118, above

"Teaching" and Other Persuasions: The Interpretation of *didaskein* "To Teach" in 1 Timothy 2:12

Lyn Kidson

Introduction

In the early two thousands I completed my Masters of Divinity by submitting a project on the concept of motherhood in the Bible. In this project I concluded that there was no reason not to translate *gynaiki* and *andros*[32] in 1 Timothy 2:12 as "a wife" and "a husband."[33] In fact there was every reason to do so as it made sense of the last verse in this difficult passage, "But women will be preserved through the bearing of children ..." (NASB).[34] The problems with interpreting this verse become insurmountable, in my

---

32   *Gunaiki* and *andros*.

33   Hugenberger, "Women in Church Office," 341–60.

34   Bible quotations within this chapter are from NASB, except where otherwise indicated; Note that *sōthēsetai* is in the singular "she will be saved" (NRSV) or "a woman will be saved" rather than the NASB's plural "women."

view, if the verses preceding it are about every woman and every man and not about couples. Later on in my Masters of Early Christian and Jewish Studies at Macquarie University, I argued that Eve in verses 13 and 14 is a negative example of a modest wife. In this paper I wish to demonstrate that the word rendered "to teach" (*didaskein*) has a much larger semantic range than it does in English and should be rendered "to persuade."[35]

Genre of 1 Timothy

For readers to grasp the intended meaning of a document they must first recognise the genre of the writing. This is the basic level of understanding.[36] It is the shared ground of communication between a writer and a reader. It is important to note in regard to the genre of 1 Timothy that there is evidence that philosophical letter writing traditions and topics were drawn on by the writer.[37]

The Exegesis of 1 Timothy 2: 8–12

1 Timothy 2:8

Verse 8 begins a new section with an indirect command, "I want therefore . . ." What is this command?: " . . . the men in every place to pray, lifting up holy hands, without wrath and dissension."

Most commentators see that this section relates principally to prayer, as it appears to be an expansion of the previous command.[38] However, I would argue that the writer is moving on in thought.[39] Dio Chrysostom, similarly, urges citizens not to go about their business with hatred or wrangling:

---

35   Carson observes that words have semantic ranges: *Exegetical Fallacies*, 49–50. It is not that a word has *a meaning* that can be slotted into a sentence, but that words take on nuances when used in certain contexts.

36   Rabinowitz, a literary critic, makes the point that genre comes before reading in *Before Reading*, 27.

37   Fiore argued persuasively that the principal hortatory technique used in 1 Timothy is the example of Paul, *The Function of Personal Example*, 22, 198–201, 232–36; Huizenga has shown that philosophical topics relating to women are used in 1 Timothy in *Moral Education for Women in the Pastoral and Pythagorean Letters*.

38   Towner, *Timothy and Titus*, 201–03; Marshall, *Pastoral Epistles*, 445; Guthrie, *The Pastoral Epistles*, 84.

39   Kelly argues that "the main point" is that men "must raise holy hands," *Pastoral Epistles*, 65–66.

> Do you imagine there is any advantage in market or
> theatre or gymnasia or colonnades or wealth for men
> who are at variance? These are not the things which make
> a city beautiful, but rather self-control (*sōphrosynē*),
> friendship, mutual trust … No one is suggesting that; on
> the contrary, you may rest assured that in all our cities
> there are public funds, and a few persons have these
> funds in their possession, some through ignorance and
> some otherwise; and it is necessary to take precautions
> and try to recover these funds, yet not with hatred or
> wrangling.[40]

Dio Chrysostom's comments suggest that prayer in 1 Timothy 2:8 is offered in the context of civil concord. This emphasis on the civic context is an extension of the prayers that are offered at the beginning of the chapter "on behalf of all men, for kings and all who are in authority, so that we may lead a tranquil and quiet life in all godliness and dignity" (2:1b–2). In the Roman Empire, good citizens prayed for their emperor and for peace and prosperity in their empire.[41]

Further, there was an intimate connection between the virtue *sōphrosynē*,[42] "modesty," and the ideal citizen worthy of imitation. In Plato's *Republic* Socrates and Glaucon are discussing the citizen worthy of being hymned, since he is being lifted up as a model to imitate,

> Again, leave out that other mode that a man uses in
> peaceful, voluntary activities that do not entail force
> when he is trying to persuade someone, or plead with

---

40   Dio Chrysostom, "Discourse," 48.9; Cf. Demosthenes, "Oration 42," 12, the moderate man does not rush to court and minds his own business; Aristotle takes it for granted that anger in the political sphere is harmful, *Politics* iii.10.1286a. 31–35; see Harris, *Restraining Rage*, 157–200 for a discussion on anger in the polis.

41   Augustus says that the citizens of the Empire prayed on his behalf in his *Res Gestae*, Cooley, *Res Gestae Divi Augusti*, 69; Cf. King Seleucus: I donated various items to the temple of Apollo at Miletus (288/7 BCE). The people of Miletus were to deposit them, "so that you may use them for libations and other uses in behalf of our health and fortune and the safety of the city, for which I wish and you pray." Welles, *Royal Correspondence*, letter No 5.

42   North, *Sophrosyne*.

him: a god by prayer, or another man he is teaching or advising; or the other way round, when he defers to someone else who is pleading with him, instructing him, or trying to make him change his mind, and as a result acting according to his judgment without behaving arrogantly, but in all these things proceeding with sound sense and moderation (*sōphronōs*), and ending up contented.[43]

In *The Laws*, Plato describes the connection between physical motion and *sōphrosynē*, "temperance": "there is the motion of a temperate (*sōphronos*) soul living in a state of prosperity and moderate pleasures."[44] As we can see in the quote from *The Republic*, *sōphrosynē* includes the right attitude and action in prayer. This was the case for both pagans and Christians.[45] Plutarch, in his biography of Marius, describes how Marius washed his hands and then both he and his companion prayed, "lifted them to heaven" while making vows to the gods.[46] Similarly, Clement of Rome urges the Corinthians: "Let us, therefore, approach him in holiness of soul, lifting up to him pure and undefiled hands, loving our gentle and compassionate Father who made us his own chosen portion."[47]

My main point here is that the men of verse 8 are to be men with correct deportment, which is closely associated with the virtue *sōphrosynē*. Importantly, in the context of our passage, it makes sense of the similarity being drawn between men and women. As men do, so do women.[48]

---

43   Plato, *Republic* 3.399 b–c; Cf. The ideal city in *The Republic*, 4.427e, is one that is "wise, courageous, temperate (*sōphrōn*) and just"; In Isocrates, *To Nicocles*, 31, the ideal king is an example of *sōphrosynē*: "on the contrary, let your own self-control stand as an example to the rest" (*alla tēn sautou sōphrosynēn paradeigma tois allois kathistē*).

44   Plato, *Laws* 7.814e; Cf. Cicero, de Officiis, 1.35.128.

45   Kelly notes the Christian frescos in the Roman catacombs illustrate men at prayer, *Pastoral Epistles*, 66.

46   Plutarch, "Caius Marius," 26.2.2-6; cf. 22.2.2-5; Dio Chrysostom, *Discourse* 32.82.

47   *1 Clement* 29:1.

48   See Cicero, *Topica*, X. 41-45 for use of similarity in developing an argument.

Verse 9

"Similarly, I want women to adorn (*kosmein*) themselves with proper clothing (*katastolē kosmiō*), modestly and discreetly (*sōphrosynēs*), not with braided hair and gold or pearls or costly garments . . . "

The emphasis here is on the woman's deportment.[49]

In the Graeco-Roman world the ideal woman was a woman with *sōphrosynē*.[50] It was a virtue closely associated with women, since it involved the idea of self-restraint.[51] As classicist Helen North describes, "[t]he general tendency of *sophrosyne* to suggest inhibition of some kind made it particularly suitable . . . as a *summa* of feminine virtue."[52] Sōphrosynē was commonly used on statue bases, public inscriptions, and gravestones as a way of summing up a woman's virtue.

Similar expressions of feminine *sōphrosynē* are found in the philosophical literature.[53] The letter of Melissa from the Pythagorean Epistles is a good example. This letter has a complicated textual history as it began life in Doric Greek[54] but at one point came to be translated and expanded in Koine Greek.[55] We will read the Koine translation by Professor Edwin Judge who notes the Koine expansions:

---

49 Pseudonymous Crates in a letter to Mnasos "but the one that decorates you most nobly is the one that makes you decorous and it is decorum that makes you most decorous," *kallista de kosmei ho kosmiōtatēn poiōn, kosmiōtatēn de poiei kosmiotēs*, Epistle 9.4–5 (1st –2nd Century CE).

50 Pomeroy, *Women in Hellenistic Egypt*, 70.

51 North, "The Mare," 35–48; She describes *sophrosyne* as "the most multifaceted of all the Greek virtues," 35; For a comprehensive discussion of the virtue see North, *Sophrosyne*.

52 "The Mare," 38.

53 The conduct of women/ wives was a well-known *topos* in philosophical literature and always discussed the woman's *sōphrosynē*, Thom, "The Mind Is Its Own Place," 555–73; On *sōphrosynē* in women's literature see Pomeroy's discussion of the Neopythagorean letter of Perictione in *Women in Hellenistic Egypt*, 68–71.

54 The earliest extant codex manuscript of the letter of Melissa to Kleareta is *Harleianus* 5610. This letter appears in a collection of Pythagorean women's letters. This manuscript is variously dated from 1200 to the early fourteenth century CE. See Huizenga, *Moral Education for Women in the Pastoral and Pythagorean Letters*, 32.

55 P.Haun. II.13 (3rd C CE.), see Judge, "A Woman's Behaviour," 365–67 for text.

For your zealous [wish] to listen to the topic of [women's adornment] offers fair hope [that you intend] to perfect yourself in virtue. [It is necessary then] for the moderate (*sōphrona*) and liberal woman to live [with] [her lawful] husband [adorned] with quietness (*hēsychia*), white and clean in her dress, plain and [not costly], simple and not elaborate [or excessive]. For she must reject […] and garments of purple or gold … but if she is to be [attractive] to one man, her own, a woman's ornament (*kosmos*) is her manners and not her clothing. A liberal and moderate woman (*sōphrona*) must seem good-looking to her own husband, but not to the man next door, having on her cheeks the blush of modesty rather than of rouge and powder, and good bearing and decency and moderation (*sōphrosynēn*) rather than gold and emerald. For it is not in expenditure on dress and looks that the moderate woman (*sōphrona*) should express her love of the good but in the management and maintenance of her household, and pleasing to her own husband, given that he is a moderated (*sōphronounti*) man, by fulfilling his wishes.[56]

The echoes of this advice in 1 Timothy 2: 9–10 are remarkable.[57] While the advice in Melissa's letter seems to relate only to the domestic sphere, there is a public dimension to the woman's adornment. In this letter it is assumed that the woman adorned in fine clothes and cosmetics is observed by her male neighbours. It is implied that she has dressed for their admiration not just her husband's pleasure.

---

56   The *koine* paraphrase from the Doric, translated by Judge, "A Woman's Behaviour," ll.5–31, 365–66; Huizenga, *Moral Education*, 40, "Yet, most importantly, P.Haun. II.13 reveals that Pythagorean women's letters, apparently from two different textual traditions (one Doricized and one not), were already being placed in a collection during the time of the Roman Empire."

57   Harding, *Tradition and Rhetoric*, 115.

Indeed, the inscriptions that publically laud a woman's *sōphrosynē* declare what was already known: her private *sōphrosynē*.[58]

Verse 10

Unfortunately, word limitations preclude a discussion of verse 10.

Verse 11

"A woman must quietly (*en hēsychia*) receive instruction with entire submissiveness."

I would like to make the case that verse 11 sums up verses 9–10. Most scholars see this verse as belonging to the next verse.[59] The instruction of verse 11, however, belongs in thought to the command of verse 8 because it falls under the rubric of a *sophrona* (a woman with *sōphrosynē*). As it does in the letter of Melissa, "for the moderate (*sōphrona*) and liberal woman to live [with] [her lawful] husband [adorned] with quietness (*hēsychia*)."

From the time of the Homeric poems, *sōphrosynē* was associated with silence or being briefly spoken; this silence was recognition of one's appropriate social status (e.g., *Odyssey*, IV.158–160). This was an important aspect of *sōphrosynē* for women throughout Greek literature.[60] Silence could be viewed as a strength giving the person dignity. Ignatius commends a bishop because his silence achieves more than those who speak in vain,

> I was impressed by his gentleness because when silent (*sigōn*) he can do more than those who speak in vain. For he is attuned to the commandments as a harp is to its strings. Therefore my soul blesses his godly mind recognising it as virtuous and perfect and his

---

58   Bremen, *The Limits of Participation*, 3; E.g., the people of Kyzikos (1 CE) honoured Apollonis for her moderation (*sōphrosynē*) and, " in order that the remembrance of her moderation (*tēs sōphrosynēs autēs*) may be visible to all the city, a statue of her is to be erected in one of the rooms of the Square Agora" (55). Translation by Horsley, *New Documents Illustrating Early Christianity*, Vol.4, 10–17.

59   Malherbe, "The Virtus Feminarumin 1 Timothy 2:9–15," in *Renewing Tradition*, 45–65; Towner, *Timothy and Titus*, 103; Scholer, "1Timothy 2:9–15," 193–224.

60   North, "The Mare," 37.

immovability and freedom from wrath all gentleness characteristic of the living God.[61]

A person of silence has freedom from wrath and a gentleness that is characteristic of God. In this sense silence is valued and stands in contrast to talkativeness, vain talking, quarrelling etc. In discussing the silence of the bishop in this passage, Harry Maier says,

> Silence here does not denote the absence of sound or the lack of speaking ability. It is the opposite of intemperate speech and as such connotes the well-deployed rhetorical ability of the virtuous who have trained themselves to use the right word at the right time to achieve the common good.[62]

Just as the silent bishop is one who knows when to use the right word at the right time, so a *sōphrōn* knows when to speak. Hence, Plutarch advises the bride to be ready to laugh and joke with her husband, but to know when and to whom to speak,

> Theano once exposed her hand as she was arranging her cloak. "What a beautiful arm," said someone. "But not public property," she replied. Not only the arms but the words of a modest woman must never be public property. She should be shy with her speech as with her body, and guard it against strangers. Feelings, character, and disposition can all be seen in a woman's talk.[63]

The instruction at verse 11, therefore, is that a woman learns, knowing when to speak and when not to. "In silence" (*en hēsychia*) here is in effect shorthand for temperate speech, which an ancient audience would understand to belong to a woman with *sōphrosynē*. As far back as Sophocles' Ajax it was a "hackneyed" expression that "silence makes a woman beautiful

---

61   Ignatius, "Philadelphians," 1:1–2; cf. Ignatius, "Ephesians," 6.1.

62   Maier, "The Politics of the Silent Bishop," 506.

63   Plutarch, "Advice to the Bride and Groom," lines 29–31.

(*kosmon*)."[64] Silence completes the command of verse 8 because it is an adornment.

Silence was believed to guard the educated woman against a loss of deportment and virtue. Plutarch wanted a woman to control her speech because he was aware of the concerns that educating women in philosophy and rhetoric could lead to immodest behaviour. Anxiety that a woman's learning may lead to her overstepping the bounds of propriety can be seen in Musonius Rufus' *That Women Too Should Study Philosophy*. He felt the need to defend his scheme to educate women in philosophy because there was a fear that they might become arrogant and engage in inappropriate speech:

> Yes, but I assure you, some will say, that women who associate with philosophers are bound to be arrogant for the most part and presumptuous, in that abandoning their own households and turning to the company of men they practice speeches, talk like sophists, and analyse syllogisms, when they ought to be sitting at home spinning. I should not expect the women who study philosophy to shirk their appointed tasks for mere talk any more than men, but I maintain that their discussions should be conducted for the sake of their practical application.[65]

Musonius' point is that philosophy would teach a woman modesty (*sōphronein*) and the virtue of managing her own home well, and therefore would dissuade her from engaging in "talk like sophists."[66] This brings us to the command of verse 12.

---

64   Sophocles, *Ajax*, 292–3: *gynaixi kosmon hē sigē pherei*, literally "for women silence produces an ornament" (see LSJ *kosmos* II. "esp. of women"); cf. "garments," Herodotus, *Histories*, 5.92 G.3; "she had decked her body" *Iliad* 14.187; "ornamentation" Hesiod, *Works and Days*, 76.

65   "That Women Too Should Study Philosophy," in *Musonius Rufus*, 43; Musonius is defending what Plato had argued in *The Republic* Book 5 that women (at least elite ones) should be trained just as the men.

66   "That Women Too Should Study Philosophy," 43.

Verse 12

"But I do not allow a woman to teach (*didaskein*) or exercise authority (*authentein*) over a man, but to remain silent (*hēsychia*)."

Verse 12 begins a sub-point to verses 9–11. Beginning a command with an infinitive with the indicative set back in the word order of the sentence is a technique for ordering commands in administrative letters.[67] I'd like to suggest that 1 Timothy is using a similar technique here to order the commands in expanding one from the other.

The infinitive, *didaskein*, in this word order, is in the emphatic position.[68] In the light of this, I would like to argue that this emphatic position combined with the negation "I do not allow," indicating a contrast with the woman with *sōphrosynē* of verses 9–11, would have alerted the ancient reader that *didaskein* was not to be taken in the sense "to teach." The verb *didaskō* has a much broader range of meaning than the verb "to teach" does in English. We will now canvass some of options for the meaning of *didaskein*.

1. The infinitive *didaskein* does regularly mean "to teach" in an educational setting: "When someone asked him if women too should study philosophy, he began to discourse (*didaskein*) on the theme that they should..."[69]

2. It varies from the English word "teach" in that it can be used to mean "to inform" or perhaps "to tell": Sextus, sword in hand, tries to persuade the Roman matron Lucretia to have intercourse with him, "For," he said "if you will consent to gratify me, I will make you my wife, and with me you shall reign ... for I know that I shall succeed to my father's kingdom, as is right, since I am his eldest son. But why need I inform (*didaskein*) you of the many advantages which attend royalty ... since you are well acquainted with them?"[70]

---

67   Kidson, "1 Timothy," 96–115.

68   Leiow, "Imperatives and Other Directives," 97–119.

69   Musonius Rufus, "That Women Too Should Study Philosophy," III.26, 38–39; Cf. Josephus, *Jewish Antiquities* XI.49.

70   Dionysius of Halicarnassus, *The Roman Antiquities*, IV.65.2.

3. It can be rendered "to show": "As for the king, Cassander tried to show (*didaskein*) Polyperchon that if the restoration should take place he would do what was ordered by others . . . "[71]

4. It can also introduce indirect speech:[72] "At an order so strange and unexpected all rapidly assembled, upon which Adeimantus, who disapproved of this proceeding, came forward and tried to address the people, pointing out that (*parakalein kai didaskein dioti*), "These proclamations and orders to assemble in arms should have been made of late when we heard that our enemies the Aetolians were near our frontier."[73]

5. Further, it can be used to mean "to persuade." There are three examples I would like to discuss:

6. The first example is from Polybius, *The Histories*. The context is the aftermath of the first Punic war. The Carthaginian mercenaries, after falling back to Tunis, found themselves with an upper hand over their masters. They made a number of demands including payment for pay in arrears and the loss of horses.[74] Gesco, the Cathaginian general, arrived at Tunis with the money. He held meetings with the officers and the troops:

> He rebuked them for their past conduct, attempted to enlighten (*didaskein*) them about the present, but most of all dwelt on the future, begging them to show
>
> themselves well-disposed to those in whose pay they had been from the outset.[75]

---

71 Diodorus of Sicily, Vol. 10. 20.28.2; Cf. Polybius, *The Histories*, XVI 34.5, "When Philip wished to prove (*didaskein*) that the Rhodians were the aggressors, Marcus interrupted him and asked, 'And what about the Athenians? What about the Cianians?'"

72 Kroeger and Kroeger's point in *I Suffer Not a Woman*, 190–92.

73 Polybius, *The Histories*, IV.22.9–10; Cf. Josephus, *Jewish Antiquities* IX.65 (LCL).

74 Polybius, *The Histories*, I.68.

75 Polybius, *The Histories*, I.69.2.

The sense here is that Gesco is attempting to convince the mercenaries that they should focus on the job at hand—defending Carthage—rather than extorting money from their masters. In an older translation, Shuckburgh translated *didaskein*, "to convince," which seems to capture the sense far more than Paton's "to enlighten."[76]

a. The second example is again from Polybius's *The Histories*. Here Hannibal contemplates marching on Italy from Spain with his army, but it was foreseen that it would be difficult to feed the troops on such a long march. Hannibal had discussed this with his generals a number of times, when Monomachus said he could see only one way to reach Italy: "When Hannibal asked to explain himself, he said [Hannibal] must teach (*didaxai*) his troops to eat human flesh . . . "[77] This use of the infinitive (although an aorist) clearly demonstrates the possible nuance *didaskein* can take. Hannibal is not merely to educate or inform his troops about cannibalism, but he is to persuade them that this course of action will give them success in their march.

b. The last example is from Josephus's *Jewish Antiquities*. The context here is that the young Herod has fled from the Synhedrion, being convinced by the High Priest Hyrcanus that they wanted to put him to death. Herod withdrew to Damascus and shored up his position with the governor: "Thereupon the members of the Synhedrion became indignant and attempted to persuade (*didaskein*) Hyrcanus that all these things were directed against him."[78] The Synhedrion is intent on persuading Hyrcanus to act but he refuses, because, Josephus says, "of his cowardice and folly."[79] It is clear in this example that the present infinitive has a nuance that means, "to persuade," rather than the English, "to teach."

---

76   Polybius, *The Histories*, I.69.2.
77   Polybius, *The Histories*, IX. 24.6.
78   Josephus, *Jewish Antiquities*, XIV.179 (LCL).
79   Ibid.

Implications for Interpreting *didaskein* in 1 Timothy 2:12

Summing up, it can be seen that *didaskein* has the nuance "to persuade." What does this mean for 1 Timothy 2:12? Andreas J. Köstenberger concluded that "or" (*oude*) coordinates the two infinitives *didaskein* and *authentein* and that these two activities can be viewed either positively or negatively.[80] Köstenberger assumed that *didaskein* was an inherently positive activity as this is the way it is often used in the Pastorals and the rest of the New Testament.[81] However, as has been argued, there is a negative contrast being drawn here between the positive behaviour of women of verses 9–11 and their possible negative behaviour in verses 12–14.[82] Although in the examples we have looked at *didaskein* does not have a negative connation in and of itself, when teamed with *authentein*, which can be translated "to domineer,"[83] the two words together make a distinctly negative picture. My conclusion is that this is not what the apostle Paul wants; he does not want, "a woman (a wife) to persuade and domineer." This interpretation is supported by Josephus, who in his *Antiquities of the Jews*, describes Eve as being persuaded (*anapeithei*) by the serpent and in turn persuades (*anepeisen*) Adam to eat the fruit.[84] Thus the apostle does not want a wife to be like Eve who, being deceived, persuaded and pressured her husband into the deception.[85] This then ties the command back into the purpose of the letter: "As I urged you . . . remain on at Ephesus so that you may instruct certain men not to teach strange doctrines" (1 Timothy 1:3).

---

80 Infinitives are often paired for emphasis, Polybius, *The Histories*, II.56.11; XXXVIII.9.4; Josephus, *Jewish Antiquities* IV.167; VIII. 128; Köstenberger makes the point that *oude* coordinates the two infinitives, "A Complex Sentence Structure in 1 Timothy 2:12"; Paired negative activities or concepts, Luke 3:14, 12: 33; Acts 2:27; 2 Corinthians 4:2, 7:12; Galatians 4:14; Philippians 2:16; 1 Timothy 1:3-4; 6:17.

81 Ibid., 105–54.

82 See the relationship between "queenly Persuasion" (*potnia Peithō*), the bedecking of Pandora in clothes and jewels, and the formation wrought "within her lies and crafty words and a deceitful nature," Hesiod, *Works and Days*, 70–79.

83 BGU, vol. 4, 1208.38 (26/27 BCE.); "dominates," Ptolemy, *Tetrabiblos*, III.13.157/158 (2nd CE); "They will lord it over," in Hippolytus, *On the End of the World*, 7.5. Baldwin, "αὐθεντέω in Ancient Greek Literature (Appendix 2)," 269–305, footnote 5, suggested translation "having compelled". However, his argument for translating the word as "have legal authority" in Hippolytus seems irrelevant given the context (activities that take place at the end of the world), "*authenteō* in Ancient Greek Literature," fn. 10.

84 Josephus, *Antiquity of the Jews*, I. 42 & 44; LSJ, *Greek-English Lexicon, anapeithō*: "persuade," "convince".

85 In Jewish works Eve is called Adam's wife, LXX, Genesis 4:1, 25; Tobit, 8:6; Josephus, *Antiquity of the Jews*, I. 40; *Jubilees*, 3:4-7; Eve as an example of deception, but for the whole congregation, 2 Cor 11:3.

Response: John Dickson

I appreciate Lyn Kidson's reminder to keep in mind the wider context when reading our New Testament documents. Social concepts such as "deportment" and "silence" were clearly part of the cultural context of Graeco-Roman antiquity and should inform our reading of letters such as 1 Timothy.

The value of historical-critical readings of the New Testament is clearly on display in Lyn's paper. Questions remain for me, however, about the pertinence of some of the ancient references, especially to the activity of "teaching." Lyn is correct to note, of course, that *didaskein* has a "broader range of meanings" than the typical English translation might imply: it can mean to *instruct, to inform, to tell*, etc. The particular sense recommended in the paper is "to persuade," and some valid examples are offered (two from Polybius and one from Josephus). This is all well and good if we are looking for a dictionary account of possible renderings of the term.

I wonder, though, whether it is appropriate to reach outside of the Pastoral Epistles for the sense of *didaskein* when this collection of writings— not to mention the broader Pauline corpus—offers such powerful testimony to a technical use of *didask*: vocabulary relating to the transmission of the apostolic deposit. The terms *didaskalos*, *didachē*, and *didaskalia* all have this technical sense. It would be surprising if the verb did not share in that meaning, especially given the use of the verb in the broader Pauline corpus and in 2 Timothy 2:2, as discussed in my paper, where our verb sits in parallel with "to entrust (a deposit)." The point has been emphasised recently in Moisés Silva in his article on the term: "The striking usage of this word group in the Pastorals shows that no tension was felt between (i) the gospel, constantly preached afresh, and (ii) doctrine to be learned, kept pure, and defended against heresies. Indeed, 'to teach' involves passing on a tradition that is more or less fixed, as is stressed also by the term *parathēkē*, 'that which is entrusted'."[86] When such a clear use of a term is on display in the very literature under discussion, one does not need to reach back to Polybius or forward to Josephus to understand Paul's reference to teaching-authority.

---

86   Silva, "διδάσκω," 715.

Response: Hefin Jones

Lyn's paper did what a good paper should do: it shed light and sparked the imagination. I found the material on the *topoi* of male and female deportment enlightening, enlarging my understanding of *sōphrosynē* in particular. The Letter of Melissa was a revelation! Lyn made a persuasive case for including "to persuade" within the semantic range of *didaskein*. She brings the perspective of the Graeco-Roman historian to bear on 1 Timothy 2:8–12, and as John Dickson has said, that perspective is vital to the New Testament specialist.

What then is Lyn's bottom line? If I read her aright, Paul wrote 1 Timothy 2:8–12 to express, in terms of Hellenistic pop-philosophy, a Christian view of the appropriate deportment of both men and women in which *sōphrosynē* was key. The virtuous first-century woman should conduct herself in such a way that she isn't known for her volubility, but rather her wise moderation in speech. In particular, the virtuous wife should not attempt to persuade and domineer her husband so as to lead them both astray.

Two questions remain: First, why should we select "to persuade" as the relevant sense within the semantic range of *didaskein* in 1 Timothy 2:12? Second, what exactly are we meant to conclude from the fact that Paul seems to speak the language of the first century and shares, maybe unconsciously, some of its presuppositions?

Lyn doesn't really present an argument for adopting "to persuade" as the relevant sense of *didaskein*, other than to venture a very brief criticism of Andreas Köstenberger's argument that both *didaskein* and *authentein* are positively encoded. I would suggest that Köstenberger's article in both its original and now revised forms does in fact present fairly compelling reasons for thinking that *didaskein* is positively teaching the truth rather than teaching "other doctrine." The argument has been made many times that in 1 Timothy prefixes, or other immediately apparent modifiers, are present whenever "other" or "false teaching" is meant, and that "teaching" vocabulary which has no such prefixes or modifiers invariably refers to teaching the apostolic deposit. Further, the relatively "known" element, *didaskein*, should determine the sense of the relatively "unknown" element, *authentein*, rather than vice versa as Lyn does. The combination of these infinitives is not negative but rather positively "teaching the apostolic deposit with authority."

As for the question about the cultural shift between the first and the twenty-first centuries, it is not at all clear to me that establishing the embeddedness of a text in its historical context in any way diminishes its current relevance. All biblical texts are thoroughly embedded in their linguistic, cultural, and social contexts. The possibility that Paul used Stoic vocabulary, and may have been familiar with a typical Hellenistic account of the virtuous woman is interesting, but in and of itself does not answer the question of how Paul's words might still function authoritatively for us today.

Lyn has given me reason to think harder about the relation of *sōphrosynē* to *en hēsychia*, but I remain convinced that Paul was applying his consistent theology to the particular contingencies of the disorder of the Ephesian church. Further, though I find it entirely plausible that "to teach" in 2:12 *included* the notion of persuasion (now positively encoded), I am not persuaded by her implicit claim that it *does not include* the notion of imparting the apostolic tradition.

Women, Teaching, and Authority: A Case for Understanding the Nature of Congregational Oversight as Underlying 1 Timothy 2:11–12

Hefin Jones

The last two generations have witnessed a sea change in the way women and men relate and work together within congregations. Part of this change has been the result of revisions, renewals, sometimes revolutions, in practical ecclesiology. The distinctions between those who hold office and the remainder of the body of Christ have either been redrawn or largely obliterated. Expectations about what gets done and who gets to do it when the saints gather have changed enormously. Even within congregations that have pursued what they might prefer to call "reformation" rather than revision or renewal, models of ministry are quite different from the norms of the early twentieth century. Our focus, however, is on the question of gender and the way we work together in congregations. While the renewal and reformation of "ministry" and "worship" have been far from uncontroversial, the sharpest divisions have been over whether women should be the, or among the, principal teachers and leaders in congregations. It is that issue which is the focus of this paper, and especially how 1 Timothy 2:11–12 contributes to it.

I will argue that 1 Timothy 2:12 prohibits women from authoritatively teaching men, and thus bars women functioning as overseers in congregations that include men. As such this is a non-egalitarian reading of 1 Timothy 2:12. It is certainly not a novel interpretation and application of that particular sentence, having explicit precursors that extend as far back as Calvin at the very least.[87] There are, however, "complementarian," "hierarchical," and "patriarchal" interpretations of 1 Timothy 2:12 that differ significantly from both the exegesis and application presented here. Further, this capsulation of 1 Timothy 2:12 is formally identical to one recently offered by John Dickson[88] but with one important distinction: while Dickson understands "teaching" as *always involving* the definitive preservation and laying down of the fixed apostolic tradition, I will claim that teaching may simply be instruction in, explanation of, and application of the apostolic tradition broadly considered.[89]

The limits of space require that only a sketch of this exegesis and application of 1 Timothy 2:12 be presented and I will not be able to deal with a number of issues which arise from it. However, in the interests of promoting conversation we will consider some summary objections against the interpretation offered from the work of a prominent evangelical egalitarian, Philip B. Payne. Further, given the formal similarity but substantive difference between John Dickson's view and the one offered here, I will attempt to interact very briefly with some of his specific arguments about the nature of "teaching" and how those arguments play out in the application of 1 Timothy 2:12 to churches today.

---

87   Calvin, *Epistles to Timothy*, 221. See also Hurley, Man and Woman in Biblical Perspective, & Blomberg's contribution in Belleville et al., *Two Views on Women in Ministry*, Revised Edition.

88   Dickson, *Hearing Her Voice*, 19.

89   Ibid, 27.

I. 1 Timothy 2:11–12 and the Nature of Congregational Oversight

First Timothy 2:12 occurs within a section that describes appropriate behaviour for men and women as they gather to pray, but that shifts into a broader consideration of female piety (1 Tim 2:8–15, esp. 2:8 and cf. 3:15). Men (2:8) and women (2:9–12) are instructed positively in behaviours and attitudes to adopt, and negatively in terms of behaviours and attitudes to avoid. The emphasis of 1 Timothy 2:11 is that the women learn "in quietness." The prepositional phrase *en hēsychia* ("in quietness") is placed in emphatic position prior to "should learn," the main verb of 1 Timothy 2:11, and is thus more prominent than the following "in full submission." This emphasis on "quietness" is confirmed by the repetition of the exact same phrase at the end of 2:12. "In quietness" then functions as a wrapper for the instruction for women to learn and the prohibition of them authoritatively teaching men.

The kind of "quietness" envisaged has been much discussed since both biblical and non-biblical usage suggests either a "silent attentiveness" or a "freedom from disturbance."[90] While neither necessarily implies absolute silence, and both imply that the function of quietness is to aid learning (2:11), the idea of "freedom from disturbance" chimes with the instruction to men to pray "without anger or disputing" (2:8). There is no reason to believe that the "full submission" of 2:11 is of women in general to men in general, but of the women learners to whomever is their instructor. Paul's instruction to Timothy is that women should learn without causing disturbance or turmoil, just like the men should avoid anger and disputing in their prayer. The wider context of 1 Timothy indicates that there is both false teaching and disorder in the Ephesian congregation(s) that are leading to controversy and friction (1:3–7; 4:1–4; 6:3–5). One can easily imagine the meetings of these congregations descending into angry confrontations and noisy debates. Paul's instruction, while quite general in application (cf. 3:14–15), is apposite.

---

90   Cf. BDAG 440 for the second gloss, the first gloss is my own. The noun *hēsychos* found in 1 Timothy 2:11 and 12 has a counterpart in the cognate adjective *hēsychios* found in verse 2 of the same chapter that BDAG 441 glosses as "without turmoil."

The prohibition in 1 Timothy 2:12 is framed, then, as a counterpart to the instruction of 2:11, and within the injunction not to cause disturbance. However, what does Paul prohibit? He prohibits *"didaskein . . . oude authentein andros"* (to teach . . . or have authority over a man). Again the sentence structure of 1 Timothy 2:12 attracts attention. The first of two infinitives, "to teach," has been detached from the rest of the phrase to which it belongs and moved to the front of the Greek sentence. This has been done to place emphasis on "to teach." Despite the oddness of this particular process of detachment and movement to us as English speakers, it is not especially unusual in Koinē, occurring throughout the New Testament. The coordinate phrase would have still been understood as a coordinate phrase, hence our English translations keep "to teach or to have authority" together. Following normal usage in Greek, the specification that this is with respect to men is equally true of the teaching and of the having authority. Syntactic and historical considerations also suggest that the two infinitives "to teach" and "to have authority" are intended to be understood as one composite activity, "to authoritatively teach."[91] Authoritative teaching in 2:12 is the counterpart of the "learn with full subjection" in 2:11. Thus, in 1 Timothy 2:12 Paul prohibits women from authoritatively teaching men.

I am unable in this current paper to discuss the detail of Paul's appeal to the creation and fall narrative of Genesis 2–3 in 1 Timothy 2:13–14 other than to note that it is given as a reason not only for the prohibition of women's authoritative teaching of men, but also for the women's learning without causing disturbance (1 Tim 2:11).[92]

Paul shifts from the discussion of propriety within the congregation in 1 Timothy 2:8–15 to what we might call congregational "office" in 1 Timothy 3:1–13. Note that Paul refers back to all the instructions of 1 Timothy 2:8ff (possibly 2:1ff) as being about how people should conduct themselves in God's household (3:14–15). First, Paul sets out qualifications for overseers

---

91   Payne, "1 Timothy 2.12 and the Use of Οὐδέ [*Oude*] to Combine Two Elements to Express a Single Idea," 244–46.

92   See Payne, "The Bible Teaches the Equal Standing of Man and Woman," 7; Dickson *Hearing Her Voice*, 132–33; Köstenberger and Schreiner, *Women in the Church*, 85.

(3:1–7), and then deacons (3:8–10, 12–13), including women deacons (3:11). While the list of overseer qualifications contains items that suggest men are intended (esp. vs. 4–5), the repeated "in the same way" (3:8 and 3:11; cf. Titus 2:3, 6) is rather more suggestive that male overseers *only*, and *both* male *and* female deacons are intended. Even more decisive is that the most stringent ("manage well" 3:4–5) and the most distinctive ("teachable" 3:2) elements in the list of overseer qualifications are related to the very activity of "authoritative teaching" that was prohibited in 2:12. Furthermore, when Paul returns to discuss elders later in 1 Timothy 5:17, "to direct" and "labouring in word and teaching" seem to be their key roles. Exactly the same Greek verb lies behind both "manage" (3:4) and "direct" (5:17). The office of overseer in 1 Timothy 3, who must be able to manage and teach, corresponds to the elder, who directs and teaches the church in 1 Timothy 5.[93]

Though many see a distinction in 5:17 between elders who *only* rule (or *manage* or *direct*), and elders who *both* rule *and* teach,[94] this is not the only way to understand the Greek. It could be translated as, "Those elders who rule well are worthy of double honour, namely those who labour in word and teaching." It's not so much that there are some elders who rule well and there are some who rule well and teach, but rather, that elders who rule well by their word and teaching should be doubly honoured.[95] As in 1 Timothy 2:12 teaching and authority are linked.

In Titus 1:5–9 we have the description of the qualifications and function of an elder/overseer (Titus 1:5, 7). The qualifications largely overlap with those of 1 Timothy 3:1–8, but the "managing"/"directing" and "teaching" functions are expressed differently: the office of the overseer should be to exhort people in the apostolic teaching and to convict or reprove those who contradict the apostolic teaching. In verses 11 and 13 the convicting/reproving ministry of verse 9 comes into play through "silencing" (*epistomizō*) and sharply rebuking false teachers. I would suggest that "exhorting through the

---

93   I will leave to one side the discussion whether overseers and elders are strictly or only partly synonymous.

94   Calvin, *Epistles of Timothy*, 261.

95   Mounce, *Pastoral Epistles*, 307.

teaching" and "rebuking" are Titus's functional equivalents to 1 Timothy's "authoritative teaching" and "rule well by word and teaching."

Despite the local and historically particular circumstances that led to the framing of the arguments of 1 Timothy and Titus, there seems to be no more reason to limit their present applicability than any of the other letters of Paul, which also exhibit local and historically particular circumstances. Paul prohibits women from authoritative teaching of men. Since authoritative teaching is of the essence of being an overseer/elder then it too is prohibited to women. Not only should women not occupy the office of "overseer" or "elder," but also women should not *function as if they are* authoritative teachers. Women should not be *de facto* elders any more than they should be *de jure* elders.[96]

II. Defending This Exegesis and Application of 1 Timothy 2:11–12

The exegetical sketch offered above leaves many unanswered questions. Evangelical egalitarians in particular would want to offer some criticisms of the position just outlined. Fortunately, Philip B. Payne, one of the doyens of evangelical egalitarian exegesis, has recently published a "state of the investigation" summary of the biblical case for egalitarianism.[97] In addition, John Dickson's exegesis of 1 Timothy and Titus suggests a key criticism of the position I've outlined.

(1) Doesn't Paul's use of the present indicative of *epitrepō* (I do not permit) in 1 Timothy 2:12 demonstrate that the prohibition only applied to that circumstance with no specification of universality?[98]

---

96 The exegesis offered here is largely compatible with Blomberg's in *Two Views on Women in Ministry*. Where we would differ is over what constitutes "authoritative teaching" today.

97 Payne, "The Bible Teaches the Equal Standing of Man and Woman." See also his, *Man and Woman, One in Christ*.

98 Ibid., 7.

No, not necessarily. The present indicative can be used in injunctions of both limited duration and of abiding validity.[99] Howard Marshall also points out examples from extra-biblical sources as well as Hebrews 6:3 where *epitrepō* is used in ways that do not indicate limited applicability.[100] To those we would add Paul's own usage of the same verb in 1 Corinthians 14:34 which is clearly of more than local applicability.[101]

(2) Shouldn't *authentein* be translated as "to *assume* authority" as the NIV 2011 has it rather than "to *have* authority" (NIV 1984), and further doesn't it refer to the *unauthorised* assumption of authority?[102]

Here Payne points out a debate that has played itself out repeatedly in English translations of the Bible since Wycliffe. Wycliffe had "to have lordship" and Tyndale followed with "to have authority," but the Authorised shifted it to "to usurp authority." The question is whether *authentein* has an inherently inceptive sense, and whether it is also negatively encoded: "domineer" or "unauthorised authority"? At this point Payne fails to interact with A. Wolters's important 2011 article demonstrating that secular Koinē texts previously misdated but now known to be virtually contemporaneous with the New Testament use *authentein* and its cognates without an inherent inceptive sense and with the meaning "to be superior to" or "to

---

99   Marshall, *Pastoral Epistles*, 454 n143 lists 1 Cor 7:10; 1 Thess 4:1, 10; 5:14.

100   Ibid., 455 n144.

101   Payne excludes 1 Corinthians 14:34–35 as being essentially non-Pauline, "The Bible Teaches the Equal Standing of Man and Woman," 8 & 10. His arguments for doing so are weak and somewhat misleading. Payne argues that the evidence of the transposition of 1 Corinthians 14:34–35 from its location after 1 Corinthians 14:33 to after 14:40 that is found in a small number of relatively late and Western manuscripts is tantamount to evidence of the non-originality of 1 Cor 14:34–35 altogether. He argues that D. A. Carson is inconsistent in discounting the originality of John 7:53—8:11 in his *John* commentary and then insisting on the originality and location of 1 Corinthians 14:34–35 in his essay critiquing Gordon Fee's exclusion of 1 Corinthians 14:34–35, Carson, "'Silent in the Churches' on the Role of Women in 1 Corinthians 14:33b–36." The problem with Payne's argument is that the relative weight of the evidence is reversed in the two cases. Many, early, and diverse witnesses, especially P[46] and both Codices Vaticanus and Sinaticus, have 1 Corinthians 14:34–35 *in situ* following 14:33 with no significant marginal annotations or the like. See now Shack, "A Text without 1 Corinthians 14:34–35?"

102   Payne, "The Bible Teaches the Equal Standing of Man and Woman," 7.

have authority over."[103] Since the aorist is used elsewhere with *authentein* to indicate an inceptive usage, the present infinitive in 1 Timothy 2:12 should not be understood as inceptive. The translation "have authority" has adequate warrant.

(3) Isn't it an error to read the overseer requirements in 1 Timothy 3 and Titus 1 as if men are implied?[104]

No. While I agree with Payne's observation about the use of masculine pronouns not precluding the applicability of these lists to women as well as men, and further, that the mention of "the-one-woman-man" need not imply that the overseer is a man any more than he is currently monogamously married, our argument is different. I note the strongly parallel grammatical structures of Titus 2 and 1 Timothy 3. In both cases Paul isolates different groups by gender and either age or office from one another by means of the repeated use of *hōsautōs* (1 Timothy 3:8; 11 and Titus 2:3, 6). Paul *explicitly* refers to women (deacons) at 1 Timothy 3:11 but does not mention women overseers.

(4) Doesn't Paul's repeated affirmation of women in ministry elsewhere in his letters indicate that 1 Timothy 2:12 must address a particular circumstance?[105]

Non-egalitarians must take seriously the evidence of Romans 16:1–16 for the highly valued, visible, and varied ministry of women and men: Phoebe the deacon; Prisca (Priscilla) Paul's fellow-worker; and Mary, Tryphaena, Tryphosa, and Persis, hard workers in the Lord. Certainly Romans 16, especially when coupled with further evidence from 1 Corinthians and elsewhere about women as the hosts of congregations, prophetesses,

---

103   Wolters, "An Early Parallel of αὐθεντεῖν [*authentein*] in 1 Tim 2:12." Since first writing this paper I have come across Westfall's important recent study, "The Meaning of αὐθεντέω [*authenteō*] in 1 Timothy 2:12". This is an especially fine work. However, her dependence on a not uncontroversial linguistic framework (Systemic Functional Linguistics, 147), her adoption of a very controversial presupposition (monosemy, 140), her exclusion of certain data because of her theoretical framework (register, 149–50), and her analysis of authority (167ff.) make her conclusions less persuasive.

104   Payne, "The Bible Teaches the Equal Standing of Man and Woman," 7.

105   Ibid., 6.

and praying in public, should function as a strong warning against overly narrowing women's congregational ministry.[106] However, one might not follow Payne in all the implications he sees flowing from Romans 16. That Phobe was the deacon of the church, officiating in the office whose qualifications are outlined in 1 Timothy 3:8–13 seems undeniable. Payne's and others' translation of *prostasis* (Romans 16:2) as "leader" need not be followed as "helper" is equally likely lexically.[107] That Junia was a woman is almost certain, but questions remain about both the reference of "apostle" and whether the prepositional phrase indicates the group she is *drawn from* or the group *among whom* she is esteemed (Romans 16:7). Payne attempts to directly connect cognate terms from Romans 16:3 to 1 Corinthians 16:16, and Romans 16:6 and 12 to 1 Thessalonians 5:12 without regard for the fact that there other qualifying terms in the Corinthian and Thessalonian contexts that further specify who these fellow-workers and hard workers are. Not all fellow-workers or hard workers have some kind of authority within the congregation.

(5) Don't Paul's explicit affirmations of the equality of women and men in Galatians 3:28 and 1 Corinthians 11:11 demonstrate that 1 Timothy 2:12 must be of only local significance?[108]

Payne is right to see an equality between men and women in 1 Corinthians 11:11 but it isn't a symmetrical equality, or an equality of equivalence, but rather an equality of interdependence. Paul had not abandoned that equality of interdependence when he penned 1 Timothy. Payne is also correct in claiming that Galatians 3:28 cannot be circumscribed to a narrowly soteriological significance. However, Paul makes nothing more of the male / female dimension in the argument of Galatians following 3:28. Paul's argument there had been triggered by the phenomenon of unequal treatment (Gal 2:11ff.), but we note it is unequal treatment of quite a particular sort: one in which the discriminating party was *explicitly* calling

---

106   To Payne's (p. 5) brief sketch one must also now add Mathew, *Women in the Greetings of Rom 16.1–16*.

107   Note Danker's comment, BDAG 885. Danker specialised in the inscriptional evidence regarding benefaction: *Benefactor: Epigraphic Study of a Graeco-Roman and New Testament Semantic Field*.

108   Payne, "The Bible Teaches the Equal Standing of Man and Woman," 5.

into question the salvific status of the people they were excluding (cf. 2:15). Various distinctions are necessarily made within the congregation without the salvific status of those distinguished being brought into question.

(6) Haven't you assumed without demonstration that "to teach" includes instruction, explanation, and application?

The key point of distinction between the view promoted in this paper and that argued by John Dickson in *Hearing Her Voice* is that I would adopt a more inclusive understanding of the verb "to teach" in the Pastorals and the rest of Paul than that put forward by Dickson. He proposes that "teaching" in Paul generally, and in the Pastorals in particular, is crucially the *preserving and laying down* of the fixed apostolic tradition, and is not instruction in general terms, or the exposition and application of Scripture, or even the exposition and application of the apostolic deposit. As he acknowledges, his proposal has precursors, but *Hearing Her Voice* represents the most sustained and well-informed version of this argument.[109] Crucial to his case are a number of lists of gifts, functions, and offices in the Pauline corpus that distinguish "teaching" from other speaking activities in the Pauline communities. Equally crucial is the strong degree of synonymy he sees between "teaching" and traditioning words like "received," "passed on," and "entrusted." The Pauline "teacher" "teaches" "the teaching" only if he preserves and lays down the apostolic traditions from and about Jesus in so doing. Consequently the modern male elder is defined by the tasks of ruling and of laying down the apostolic tradition now preserved in the New Testament canon. I can only briefly indicate my lines of response here: (i) Dickson is surely correct in saying that "teaching" was principally teaching the apostolic deposit. (ii) I would largely agree with his quite expansive account of what those apostolic traditions consisted of. (iii) It is also undeniable that preserving and transmitting that apostolic tradition was a *necessary* task of "teaching." (iv) However, the ordinary language character of the New Testament, the partial instability of the lists of speaking gifts, functions, and offices, and the occasional nature of the epistles all cast doubt on whether the fairly hard and fast distinctions

---

109   Dickson, *Hearing Her Voice*, 116.

between "teaching" and other speaking ministries is likely. (v) For example, when Paul speaks of the qualifications and work of an overseer-elder in Titus 1:9 and he describes them as able to "encourage others by sound teaching," it is doubtful that this is different from the qualification of "being able to teach" (1 Tim 3:2) or the work of those who "work . . . in teaching" (1 Tim 5:17). The passing on of the apostolic deposit is a constitutive activity, but teaching does not have to include the virtual rote repetition and authoritative "fixing" of the deposit "in the minds of churches"[110] on every occasion. This broader understanding of "teaching" is quite typical of teaching in the Bible (LXX) and in the Graeco-Roman context of explanation, persuasion, and drawing out the implications of the tradition handed on.[111]

III. Some Concluding Reflections

The account of 1 Timothy 2:11–12 given here is narrow almost to the point of "biblicism." It does, however, establish at least one parameter of the broader discussion of how women and men work together serving God in and through local congregations. It is the combination of authority with teaching that provides the key contextual indicator that Paul is prohibiting women from functioning as overseers. Further and deeper consideration of the way oversight/eldership relates to the body of Christ (1 Corinthians 11–14) and the evidence of Romans 16:1–16 might lead to the consideration of the following propositions:

- Women and men should be taught, trained, and encouraged in the loving full exercise of their God-given gifts within the God-given order of the congregation.

- Congregational overseers are responsible to promote the serving and speaking of both women and men within, and on behalf of, the congregation, including (maybe *especially*) those who are not themselves overseers.

---

110   Dickson, *Hearing Her Voice*, 51.

111   Cf. LSJ *didaskō* and cognates.

In addition:

- Under Christ, congregational oversight is restricted to some suitably qualified and recognised men, where congregations include both men and women.

- Male overseers are responsible to preserve, propagate, and defend the teaching given within Christian congregations that include men.

But that must await a further conversation.

Response: John Dickson

Hefin Jones and I agree on most of the exegetical issues, including the way to read the key expression "to teach or to have authority" in 1 Timothy 2:12 as a reference to one composite activity: the task of authoritatively teaching. He is right to observe that 1 Timothy 5:17 also appears to link teaching with authority. Hence, both of our readings are "complementarian" in the sense that we both judge that Paul is restricting some activity to certain authorised men. In this way, I agree with Hefin's criticisms of the arguments of evangelical egalitarian Philip B. Payne.

Hefin's description of our disagreement is straightforward: "while Dickson understands 'teaching' as always involving the definitive preservation and laying down of the fixed apostolic tradition, I will claim that teaching may simply be instruction in, explanation of, and application of the apostolic tradition broadly considered." Two responses to Hefin might progress the conversation. First, I am not entirely comfortable with words like "always" and "definitive" in the above sentence. I accept that sometimes *didaskein* may be used in a non-technical sense (e.g., Romans 2:21; 1 Corinthians 11:14), as indeed *euaggelizesthai*—Paul's most obvious technical terminology—may also be used for something other than preaching the gospel message (e.g., 1 Thessalonians 3:6). I also acknowledge that one must not make strict distinctions between "teaching" and other types of speaking. As I have previously explained, "I have no doubt that Timothy added to these apostolic teachings his own appeals, explanations, and applications, but these are not the constitutive or defining element of teaching . . . I am not creating a hard distinction between teaching and exhorting, but I am observing that, whereas teaching is principally about laying something down in fixed form, exhorting is more about urging people to obey and apply God's truth."[112]

Nevertheless, secondly, Hefin's argument (against me) seems to suggest that because teaching may involve, or morph into, more general instructions and exhortations, Paul's restriction of teaching in 1 Timothy 2:12 will mean that women may not engage in these various types of speech. This feels like a *non sequitur*, as if to suggest that if "teaching" can involve some exhortation and explanation, Paul's prohibition of women "teaching" necessarily involves a prohibition of women exhortation and explaining. But this doesn't follow. "Prophesying" must also have involved some exhorting and explaining, and yet Paul plainly approves of women prophesying (1 Corinthians 11:5). If it is important not to make hard distinctions between the terms, it is equally important not to flatten the distinctions Paul makes between "teaching" and "exhorting" and "prophesying" (Romans 12:4–8). There is both overlap and difference. The fact that "teaching" may involve exhortation does not make exhortation and teaching the same thing, anymore than the fact that "exhortation" may involve some teaching makes these two activities the same. Paul forbids women to "teach." This simply means that he does not permit women to function in the congregation as the person responsible for maintaining the apostolic traditions, the office of the teacher, regardless of whether this task shares some overlap with less authoritative forms of speech open to all trusted members of the Pauline congregations.

---

112   Dickson, *Hearing Her Voice*, 77–78.

Response: Lyn Kidson

Hefin Jones in his paper has reiterated a traditional interpretation of 1 Timothy 2:12. However, I was surprised to find that Hefin argues that the two infinitives *didaskein* and *authentein*, coordinated by the conjunction *oude*, should be taken to mean "authoritatively teaching." Köstenberger in his comprehensive and persuasive article argued that this phrase should not be rendered to "teach authoritatively," but should be kept semantically apart "to teach or to have authority."[113] Köstenberger quite rightly argues, in my opinion, that the phrase could be viewed positively or negatively by the author. He believed that the verb *didaskō* could only be taken positively, therefore the whole phrase must be viewed positively: the woman is not to teach or to have [legitimate] authority over a man. However, as I have demonstrated in my own paper, *didaskō* can have a negative connotation in this instance, since "to persuade" would be viewed as unbecoming for a woman.

I would like to take up Hefin's critique of the work done by Cynthia Westfall on *authenteō*.[114] His assessment that this is an important study is quite correct. Her systematic approach to studying the word is to be commended. It should be enough to do away with statements like Hefin's "since the aorist …" as if the nuance of the word would rest on the verb's aspect alone. Further,

---

113   Köstenberger, "A Complex Sentence Structure in 1 Timothy 2:12," 81–103.

114   Westfall, "The Meaning of αὐθεντέω [*authenteō*] in 1 Timothy 2:12," 138–173.

the nuance of the word must be judged on the context in which it is used. It is quite apparent from studies (listed by Hefin) that this word has a range of connotations from positive to negative. Saying that "the translation 'have authority' has adequate warrant" is reasonable, but leaves the question open, why this word in this command? If the writer of 1 Timothy meant ordinary authority, then one must wonder why he did not select the more common verb *exousiazō* (to exercise authority). It must be considered that the writer has selected this word because it suits his purpose. The main difficulty is that this verb arose during the Hellenistic period, and has few occurrences before the first century. Its use in 1 Timothy is one of its earliest occurrences that we have in the extant record. Westfall's observation that "the patterns of usage of the verb are quite consistent even through the Byzantine period" is very helpful in making judgements about the use of the word.[115] However, the main focus should be on its use, as scant as it is, in the first century BC through to the second century AD. If one applies this procedure to the evidence and combines this with Westfall's study the negative aspect of the verb predominates, "exceeding authority," which naturally fits with the negative command "I do not allow . . ." When combined with "persuasion" it becomes obvious that the writer doesn't allow what is unbecoming for a woman: "to persuade and to domineer."

---

115 Westfall, 141.

Part Four

Gender, Culture, and Context

Gender: Counter-Cultural Practice? Cultural Construct? New Creation?

Megan du Toit

In evangelical circles, the rhetoric around discussion of gender frequently invokes the need to be counter-cultural. In this language, there is an implicit assumption that gender roles are at least somewhat culturally constructed. On the other hand, there is often an appeal by evangelicals to the created intentions for gender, due to God's creation of two sexes, men and women.[1] If God had specific intentions for gender when he created the sexes, you would expect that either gender characteristics would be relatively fixed by the biological attributes of sex, or that God would have given careful instructions on gendered behaviour—that is, that either gender would be biologically determined, or, if it is culturally determined, that we would have some guidance from God in how to construct a healthy gender

---

1   As we discuss gender identity, we need to be careful about the use of these two terms, "gender" and "sex." "Gender" is the term for the social and cultural traits of men and women, while "sex" refers to their biological attributes. The term "gender" gained usage in the light of sociological studies, as a way to refer to the greater fluidity of cultural expression of gender, as opposed to the fixed nature of sexual physiology. See Storkey, "Evangelical Theology and Gender," 162.

culture. However, when we examine how Christians are constructing gender, the emphasis on counter-cultural gender practice seems to suggest that Christian gender understanding is deliberately constructed to be antithetical to that of the prevailing culture. Yet is a counter-cultural approach the most useful way to develop Christian gender identity?

This clarion call to counter-culturalism is present right across the evangelical spectrum. On the complementarian side, a recent example of counter-cultural language use is that of Bruce Ware. He sees gender as an important frontline in the culture wars. So, he states:

> I believe this doctrine is central strategically in upholding the Christian faith within a culture all too ready to adopt values and beliefs hostile to orthodox and evangelical conviction.[2]

It is due to their importance in upholding faith against invidious outside influences that Ware regards gender issues as primary. Yet, despite acknowledging then that current gender practice is culturally formed, Ware stands firm against this cultural practice because he views gender relationships as primarily designed by God rather than being culturally formed.[3] So then, for many complementarians who seek to be counter-cultural, the prevailing Western culture is one of gender difference erasure and unbiblical sameness of roles. On the other hand, many egalitarians who invoke counter-culturalism in regard to gender have a very different culture in mind. So, for instance, in Custis James's recent book *Malestrom*, she consistently declares her program is counter-cultural. In her conclusion, she states regarding Jesus:

> It was not his intention to offer men a kinder, gentler patriarch. His mission was to turn this fallen world right side up. The men whose stories we have considered demonstrate a robust countercultural way of life. To

2   Ware, "Gender Moves?"

3   Ibid.

bear God's image inevitably means going against the cultural grain.[4]

The culture she is invoking is patriarchy; the predominant understanding of gender in the West for millennia, and one that arguably still has great influence. Of course, Western culture contains both these cultures—one which upholds traditional different gender roles, and one which seeks to set aside these traditions in favour of high gender fluidity. And in the popular mind, gender practice is usually an inconsistent blend.[5]

This desire by evangelicals to claim the counter-cultural label is due to such language having powerful sway within evangelicalism. As Creegan and Pohl suggest, one attraction of evangelicalism is its counter-cultural stance, as embedded deep within evangelical discourse is an "us and them" dichotomy. [6] Gender is one of the current areas in which evangelicals seek to employ this language, because gender remains a contested field in Western society. Increasingly though, as Olson contends, one stream within evangelicalism is becoming more open to contemporary culture, while the other stream seeks to remain faithful to evangelical tradition.[7] Indeed, gender is a key area which groups use to signal their relationship towards culture. McKinney has utilised Weber's church-sect typology to explain differing Christian gender constructions. Sects are categorised as those groups which desire to exist in greater tension with cultural norms, while churches are those groups who are more accommodating of the norms of their society. She argues that American colonial Baptists and twentieth-century Southern American Baptists both used gender to stand in opposition to culture, but in the earlier case this resulted in egalitarianism, and in the latter case hierarchicalism.[8] McKinney notes that sects view themselves as counter-cultural. The problem as she sees it though is that both sects and churches in this theory are allowing their

---

4   James, *Malestrom*, 204.

5   For instance, those who justify the over-sexualisation of women as female empowerment might be viewed as one such inconsistent blend.

6   Creegan and Pohl, *Living on the Boundaries*, 66, 69.

7   Olson, "Tensions in Evangelical Theology," 78.

8   McKinney, "Sects and Gender," 2.

practice to be determined by culture. Thus, rather than one group possessing the evangelical high ground of biblically based gender practice, both groups are aligning themselves on gender due to their stance towards culture. My suspicion is, though, that progressive evangelicals are seeking on the one hand to present to the surrounding culture that they are culturally relevant and attuned, but on the other to their evangelical constituency, that they remain faithfully resistant to culture. Hence their use of counter-cultural language. Conservative evangelicals who resist the fundamentalist tag face a similar juggling act—to avoid the implication of sexism while still remaining resolute against the polluting influence of culture. Ironically, an analysis by Gallagher and Smith has shown that evangelicals in America are, for the most part, shown to be navigating the uncertain waters of gender in the same ways as the rest of the society around them—in both resistance and participation.[9]

Counter-culturalism, then, is of little help when it comes to understanding how we establish Christian gender practice. How then, are we to understand gender? The wider culture has been engaged in a long and fierce debate as to whether gender is rooted within biological difference, or is almost completely culturally constructed. Christians have entered this debate with fervour. For if gender can be shown to be biologically based, many reason, then the imprimatur of God's creative intent will be upon any gender differences revealed. One might imagine then, that those who seek to support distinct gender roles would be the most likely to try to find support within biology. Certainly, those of that mind have often been keen to cite scientific support for their position. So, for instance, Johnson's essay in *Recovering Biblical Manhood and Womanhood* examines the scientific evidence in order to support complementarianism. He bases his position of distinct gender roles and identities upon scientific studies which show what appear to be inbuilt differences.[10] He quickly dismisses studies to the contrary as having too many variables to produce reliable results.[11] However, it isn't only those of a complementarian mindset who attach importance to studies showing

---

9   Gallagher and Smith, "Symbolic Traditionalism and Pragmatic Egalitarianism," 230.

10   Johnson, "The Biological Basis for Gender-Specific Behaviour," 281.

11   Ibid., 281–82.

biologically based gender differences. Grenz, an egalitarian theologian, had an essentialist view of gender. Grenz cites studies which show hardwired differences, including some in anthropology and neuropsychology.[12] Grenz did recognise that there can be deviation from the typical gender patterns by individuals, and did not utilise sex difference to defend hierarchy.[13] However, he did see gender difference as created by God and therefore to be encouraged, while allowing flexibility. Grenz's essentialist view of gender has been based on the work of Gilligan, among others, but subsequent studies[14] have suggested since Gilligan that social context affects gender experience very early in life, quite possibly accounting for much of the difference between men and women that Gilligan observed. Indeed, studies that purportedly show inbuilt differences between men and women have come increasingly under scrutiny. While much has been made of brain differences between men and women, more recent research suggests that the brain is more plastic than was once thought, and thus experience shapes the brain.[15] DeFranza also cites evidence which shows few individuals conform to male or female average patterns.[16] Indeed, as van Leeuwen points out, the problem with nature versus nurture questions is that the variables are so confounded that, even with care taken to reduce this problem, the results remain open to interpretation. [17]

Apart from these issues of interpretation, there are other underlying questions about the usefulness of scientific studies in revealing the mind of God to us. Storkey takes issue with Christians who support distinct gender roles using scientific research, but would have difficulty with other conclusions arising from similar studies on other parts of human behaviour.[18] For example, if research shows human beings to be "naturally" violent due to evolutionary pressures, we would hardly accept this as a guide to Christian

---

12   Grenz, *Sexual Ethics*, 38–39.

13   Ibid., 40–41.This view has changed little in his later work *The Social God and the Relational Self*, 272–93.

14   See Neitz, "Gender and Culture," 394.

15   Eliot, "Girl Brain, Boy Brain?"

16   DeFranza, *Sex Difference in Christian Theology*, 270–71.

17   Van Leeuwen, *Gender and Grace*, 19.

18   Storkey, *Origins of Difference*, 31.

behaviour. As van Leeuwen argues, the biblical understanding of human beings as moral agents means that biology cannot be determinative of our behaviour.[19] We will each be held accountable for what we do (2 Cor 5:10). Biology, after all, is subject to the fallen nature of the world.

Thus, we turn instead to the special revelation of Scripture. Here we encounter a problem. I maintain, as others have, that the Bible is conspicuously silent on the content of masculinity and femininity.[20] The terms themselves do not occur, and there is little explicit teaching about gender attributes. The creation narrative contains both gender difference (the genders are created separately) and similarity (bone of my bone) but arguably the thrust of the narrative is an emphasis on human commonality (Gen 2). Piper is an influential conservative evangelical who has been an important voice in the call for distinct definitions of masculinity and femininity. Piper's book, *What's the Difference?*, attempts to define masculinity and femininity in biblical terms. Piper acknowledges that there is very little exegesis involved in this book, but says he addresses this in the more scholarly *Recovering Biblical Manhood and Womanhood*.[21] However, when one turns to Piper's chapter in that book, one finds passages extrapolated to produce general qualities of masculinity and femininity quite beyond the intent of such passages.[22] Passages about marriage, for instance, are mined for possible underlying gender attributes, but the purpose of these passages isn't to provide that information.[23] For Piper, masculinity is a benevolent leadership which provides for and protects women, while femininity affirms, receives, and strengthens leadership from men.[24] In giving content to masculinity and femininity he elaborates on the qualities his definitions require. The end result, in my view, is a construction of elaboration upon extrapolation—not really a firm foundation. Piper also runs into issues in applying these definitions to every man and woman. He attempts to include less able men by saying they can still exercise spiritual

---

19   Van Leeuwen, *My Brother's Keeper*, 247.

20   Examples: Tripp, "Man Does Not Live by Man Skills Alone"; Storkey, *Origins of Difference*, 101.

21   Piper, *What's the Difference?* 14, 65.

22   Piper, "A Vision of Complementarity," 36–49.

23   See for instance, ibid., 40–41.

24   *What's the Difference?*, 22.

leadership, if other kinds of leadership become impossible.[25] As Koks, a man with cerebral palsy, contends, this leaves disabled men with a lesser masculinity.[26] Piper also allows for women to take masculine roles within the family if no man is present,[27] putting such women in the precarious place of sacrificing their femininity to fulfil their God-given role of mothering.

Moreover, what Piper hasn't addressed is the cultural situatedness of the passages he examines. If gender is at least partially culturally constructed, then any biblical examples of gender role and identity need to be assessed for how much they are normative, and how much they are responses to the cultural context. This is why Volf dismisses the examples of gender identity in the Bible as culturally situated and of limited normative value.[28] One answer to this problem is to turn to the relationships within the Trinity to deduce how gender works. Yet Volf disallows this strategy. It is Volf's contention that masculinity and femininity are qualities we share with animals rather than God, who is non-gendered. Thus, gender is to be rooted in the sexed body. It isn't identical with it, but is culturally constructed upon the given of the sexed body. Gender identity thus can have a certain degree of fluidity.[29] So in Gal 3:28, the intent of Paul isn't to erase the sexed body but to remove the power of cultural codes.[30] While I would agree that the sexed body is the basis for any understanding of gender, I would be hesitant to claim that the sexed body is as stable or as easily described as might be thought. Koks, as a disabled man, takes issue with Volf's understanding of the sexed body as stable.[31] Volf does acknowledge that bodies are not as static as we might think—suggesting that women's bodies are shaped by culture.[32] Indeed, female bodies have often been modified to be more compliant with societal gender ideals—whether by foot binding, corsets, breast augmentation or hair removal. Male bodies have

---

25   Ibid., 25.

26   Koks, "Being Masculine in My Disabled Male Body." Koks reveals the problems with rigid gender roles in his reaction to them as a man with cerebral palsy.

27   Piper, *What's the Difference?* 35.

28   Volf, *Exclusion and Embrace*, 182.

29   Ibid., 170–75.

30   Ibid., 184.

31   Ibid., 185.

32   Ibid., 35.

not been exempt either.[33] Yet, Volf has still chosen to speak of the sexed body as stable. A further problem with this characterisation is the fallen nature of the sexed human body. Many conditions can disrupt the human experience of gender, causing an experience of the sexed body outside the norm. Yet another problem is the wide variation of the sexed body. The depictions of the sexed body in media often conform to a cultural idea of that body that ignores the natural variation.[34]

Volf's position is also predicated upon a certain interpretation of Gen 1:27, in which the *imago Dei* is present in both sexes, but not given content by their gender. Grenz takes issue with Volf's non-gendered understanding of the *imago Dei*, finding this understanding of the verse unconvincing.[35] Nevertheless, even if we can say something about the *imago Dei* on the basis of the two sexes,[36] the non-gendered nature of God defies using the Trinity to assign qualities to each gender. Coakley also questions those who attempt to find models within the Trinity for how the genders should relate, as the threeness of the Trinity prevents us from imposing twoness. The Trinity then, in Coakley's view, provides instead a model for transgressing twoness, suggesting not that gender is obliterated or a third gender required, but rather that gender can be transformed. [37]

The slipperiness of gender concepts might suggest we should give up and exit the conversation about gender. However, post-fall gender identities have created victims of both men and women. To be female is to be much more likely to be poor or oppressed or dead.[38] On the other hand, the statistics on men's life expectancies, health, crime rate, and educational success suggests that to be male is also dangerous.[39] Many of those who

---

33   "Six pack" surgery is a case in point.

34   I am often bemused by the number of people who comment on my son's long eyelashes as being unusual for a boy, when experience suggests, unlike our representations of eyes, eyelash length has little to do with gender.

35   Grenz, *The Social God and the Relational Self*, 271.

36   For instance, we might say that the fullness of human gender expression is found in God.

37   Coakley, *God, Sexuality and the Self*, 56–58.

38   Durber, *Of the Same Flesh*, 7; James, *Half the Church*, 29–35.

39   Quinn, "Dangerous Thinking," 17–18, Van Leeuwen, *My Brother's Keeper*, 18–21.

desire a return to traditional gender roles cite what they call a contemporary "masculine crisis." Custis James admits to a masculine crisis, but for her it dates not post feminism, but post fall. [40] The overwhelming gender problem for her is male violence (against both females and males), a problem that runs right throughout human history. [41] When we look at the global situation, it is evident that rather than just a masculine crisis there is a gender crisis that we must speak into as Christians. The crisis is not a modern result of feminism, but a universal human issue resulting from power imbalance and human sin. The God-given nature of humanity as male and female has been corrupted into gender pain (Genesis 3).

The answer is not to take a counter-cultural stance. Nor is it to produce rigid gender identities, whether based upon a selective understanding of science or a debatable reading of gender identity from Scripture. Rather, the answer lies within the gospel. Coakley proposes that we can cut through the impasse of cultural discussions by placing gender in a framework of salvation history. [42] The redemption of creation includes gender, since gender is part of human identity. When we seek to understand our human nature in Christ, we learn we are a new creation—2 Cor 5:16–17:

> From now on, therefore, we regard no one from a human point of view; even though we once knew Christ from a human point of view, we know him no longer in that way. So if anyone is in Christ, there is a new creation: everything old has passed away; see, everything has become new! (NRSV)

What is this new creation to be like? It is to be transformed by the Spirit, showing the fruit of the Spirit (Gal 5:13–26). As several writers have commented, the Bible puts much more emphasis on men and women displaying the fruit of the Spirit rather than specific gender identities. [43] What

---

40   James, *Malestrom*, 17.

41   Ibid., 19.

42   Coakley, *God, Sexuality and the Self*, 54.

43   Storkey, "Evangelical Theology and Gender," 166. Van Leeuwen, *My Brother's Keeper*, 34.

confounds human perception of gender is that many of these fruit, enjoined on both men and women, can appear more "feminine." Fruit such as those of peace, gentleness, and forbearance are more associated with femininity. [44] Our calling then, rather than to be counter-cultural, is to pursue the fruit of the Spirit regardless of whether those fruit align with cultural gender constructs or not. We need to break free from the church/sect typology in how we relate to gender. I would advocate a cultural positioning that Volf terms soft difference, a refusal to either affirm or deny the world.[45] Instead the church is to be positively created in Christ.[46] Our exemplar in gender—as both men and women—is Christ. Instead of the embodied maleness of Jesus being a barrier to women understanding how to enact their gender, as both Storkey and Custis James contend, in his very maleness, Jesus performed a new vision of gender for both sexes.[47]

The discussion about gender has stagnated, stymied by competing claims for counter-culturalism and the intractability of the nature/nurture debate. Efforts to uncover a biblical manhood and womanhood seem unattainable. Scripture seems to have little interest in specifying gender identities. And, as DeFranza maintains, while average differences between men and women can be identified, and are useful in analysis of gender performance, this doesn't provide a template for every individual experience of gender.[48] Instead, we are called to re-create ourselves in the image of Christ, to allow the Spirit to transform us into new creations—including how we enact our gender. In this transformation, we see women and men, instead of emphasising or prescribing their differences, seeking a common likeness: that of Christ.

---

44   *My Brother's Keeper*, 34; Storkey, *Origins of Difference*, 129.
45   Volf, "Soft Difference," 34–35.
46   Ibid., 20–21.
47   Storkey, "Evangelical Theology and Gender," 173; James, *Malestrom*, 151, 75.
48   DeFranza, *Sex Difference in Christian*, 270–71.

Response: John McClean

I agree that positioning any theology of gender (or any theology) as merely counter-cultural is problematic and it is interesting to see how both "sides" of the discussion have tended to do just that. One danger is that the espoused position is *merely* a denial of certain elements of culture. That model robs us of the chance to subvert culture by participating in it. I hope the integrated model that I am proposing does allow for such a subversion.

I agree that evangelical theology cannot ground its views of gender in biological or social scientific studies. That is the path of an invalid natural theology. I have always found Oliver O'Donovan very helpful in that regard. Much of the burden of his famous *Resurrection and Moral Order* is that evangelical ethics is grounded in a created order which is confirmed by Christ's resurrection and to that extent he shares significant ground with the natural law tradition. But when it comes to how we discern this order, he remains evangelical (in the best sense) asserting that knowledge of the created order comes *via* redemptive revelation in Christ.[49]

The key question raised by Megan's paper is whether revelation in Christ, as we receive it from Scripture, presents a worldview which includes two genders, with different roles in family and church. I agree "there is

---

49   O'Donovan, O., *Resurrection and Moral Order*, 85.

little explicit teaching about gender attributes" and the attempts to develop "biblical" descriptions of normative gender traits fail. But I can't agree that "the Bible is conspicuously silent on masculinity and femininity." Especially since the task of theology is, in part, to consider the questions of contemporary culture in the light of Scripture, and when we bring the question of gender to Scripture, there is a significant amount of material to consider.

A starting thesis of any theological anthropology *must* be that all humans share in a common humanity, to which differences of gender, race, or ability are secondary differences. Yet sexual and gender differences are not irrelevant. Christopher Roberts argues that the great tradition of orthodox theology has held that sexual difference is part of human identity. This has often been a latent or implicit conviction, because debate about gender differences have been rare prior to the twentieth century. Nevertheless, he shows the assumption running through the great tradition.[50]

That is, there is a biblical worldview which includes a normative view of sexual differentiation. That has to be understood on the basis of common humanity, and does not rule out a wide variety of cultural and personal expressions of gender identity. The discussion should be about what it looks like to live virtuously with the identity God has given us in the culture in which he has set us. Megan and I aren't entirely agreed on the answer, but we are both seeking to answer the same question.

---

50   Roberts, *Creation and Covenant*, 236.

"Do Not Conform": Thinking about Complementarianism as Contextualisation

John McClean

Introduction

Gender exists in culture; it is a social and cultural reality. Yet complementarians often speak as if gender roles are or should be settled. So it may seem rather optimistic to consider the movement as an exercise in contextualisation. My justification for considering it as such is two pronged. First, all theology and Christian practice is contextualisation—it may be unaware and unreflective, but it will contextualise. Second, there are points at which complementarianism is self-conscious of its relation to a cultural context.

When Claire Smith reflects on why Christians aren't able to agree about gender she suggests that "our own personalities and experiences provide the context for us hearing, understanding and accepting the truth and wisdom of God's word."[51] True. Is that something that we should overcome? No doubt "personalities and experiences" complicate the discussions, yet receiving God's word in our context and applying it there is exactly what we *need* to do in order to understand it. An abstract comprehension with no application is likely no understanding at all.

I will describe a three-fold pattern of contextualisation and then I will use this pattern to explore four areas of complementarianism. While I am a complementarian, my goal in this paper is primarily observation; in passing I will offer some assessment and suggest some defences.

1. Patterns of Contextualistion

Three of Stephen Bevans's models of contextualisation are particularly useful for evangelical theology: the translational, counter-cultural, and praxis-based approaches.[52] I will note something of the basis and risks of each approach.

Translational approaches seek to express the faith in a new setting by finding parallel expressions. By and large "translation" here is a metaphor; it extends far beyond translating Scripture and Christian literature to every aspect of the Christian faith.[53] It draws from past expressions and ultimately from Scripture, but involves genuine re-expression.

God's revelation is already enculturated; it is not delivered in a special revelation language or culture and the incarnation is the climactic expression

---

51   Smith, *God's Good Design*, 218. The other reasons are "human frailty and limitations" which mean that "our knowledge of God and his will is partial and provisional," and human sinfulness, which leads us to doubt the goodness of God's word and to reject its authority.

52   Bevans, *Models of Contextual Theology*. The others he discusses are anthropological approaches which expect to find the content and forms of the faith in the culture and produce an indigenised theology; synthetic approaches which hold that the culture and the faith connect in ways which allow fuller insight into both but in which both retain "integrity"; and transcendental approaches which seek to discover and express the common religious experiences of all humans.

53   "Contextualization is both verbal and nonverbal and has to do with theologizing, Bible translation, interpretation and application, incarnational lifestyle, evangelism, Christian instruction, church planting and growth, church organization, worship style"; Hesselgrave, "Contextualization," 115.

of God's accommodation to a culture. The Day of Pentecost shows that the gospel can and should be given in a variety of languages. The New Testament is built on the translation, since it largely uses the Septuagint as its Scriptures. Translation is in the DNA of Christianity.

Yet, much may be "lost in translation." There is a risk of subverting the message as it is accommodated to a new setting. For example, in 1 Corinthians Paul deals with an attempt to "translate" the practice of Christian preaching into patterns associated with sophistic tradition and declares that it destroys the gospel (1 Cor 1:17—2:5).

The *counter-cultural model* is suspicious and critical of the culture it addresses, presuming that divine revelation challenges all cultures. Paul in Athens offers a trenchant critique of idolatry and finishes announcing divine judgement and calling for repentance (Acts 17:30–31).

The counter-cultural model risks denying the goodness of creation and the doctrine of common grace.[54] Despite the breadth and depth of the effects of sin, human culture is not only evil and corrupted. There is a risk of being hypercritical of culture.

These two models, together, reflect the dynamics of evangelical theology. Both look beyond their own context for a norm. The gospel declares that we cannot save ourselves or know God from our situation—he must enter our world and redeem it. So the human situation is not the source of our knowledge of God, but he makes himself known in our situation. Translation stresses the capacity of God to make himself known by his word to humans. Counter-cultural approaches stress that need for repentance in order to know God. Barth's theology captures this dual relationship between God's truth and culture. Hunsinger summarises:

> Jesus Christ as the one Word of God is the truth in all fullness and perfection. His truth is original and sovereign; that of all other words, derivative and

---

54   See Mouw, *He Shines in All That's Fair.*

fiduciary. Their truth cannot complete, compete with, combine itself with, or transcend him. Yet his truth can do any of these things, as appropriate, with them: complete them, defeat them, combine itself with them, or transcend them.[55]

A third model of contextualisation stresses *praxis*, insisting that genuine contextualisation starts from a concrete identification with people. It asserts that we contextualise as we seek to work for God's kingdom and faithful action is the test of true understanding.

At the least, this approach recognises that "application" demands a concrete understanding of and commitment to a context. It goes further and says that we do not "understand" and then "apply"—rather we understand in action; and a reflective understanding comes *after* action. We must be "doers of the word" in order to understand it.

A praxis model can also reflect a strong doctrine of providence. Since God is present in and active in our circumstances, he leads his church into a fuller grasp of him and the implications of the gospel as we seek to obey him. There is genuine progress in theology as we confront new circumstances and seek to live faithfully in them and understand our faith in the light of that obedience.

The danger of a praxis-based contextualisation is that it lacks a critical element by which to test its actions. Rene Padilla comments on liberation theology, the obvious example of a praxis-based contextualisation, that it can be too pragmatic and use Scripture to justify practices (e.g., revolutionary war). It calls attention to the importance of the historical situation of the interpreter but risks treating the situation as "the text."[56]

---

55   Hunsinger, *How To Read Karl Barth*, 248. This is from his reflections on Barth's discussion of secular parables of the truth.

56   Padilla, "Liberation Theology," 42–46.

A praxis-based contextualisation is insufficient, by itself. An evangelical contextualisation has to affirm "Jesus Christ as the one Word of God is the truth in all fullness and perfection," and look to him as our norm. Yet translation and counter-cultural contextualisation must be grounded in concrete obedience, and worked out by the Christian community in action. So I propose an integrated model of contextualisation in which those seeking to follow the Lord in a particular setting bear the responsibility to express the faith in their context in ways which make it accessible but also show how it critiques their culture.

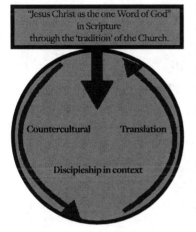

The rest of the paper uses this integrated model as a framework to examine complementarianism as an exercise in contextualisation.

2. Complementarianism and Contextualisation

a) Complementarianism as Counter-Culture

Complementarianism is decidedly, self-consciously, and boldly counter-cultural, especially against "feminism." Claire Smith opens *God's Good Design* setting her position against feminism which, she says, "is part of the cultural air we breathe."[57] She observes a "head-on confrontation of feminism with the Christian God and with his purposes for man and women as *men* and *women*."[58] While affirming good elements in feminism, Smith identifies the basic dynamic as one of conflict, since "the agenda of feminism is *different* from God's agenda ... most of the time."[59]

---

57   Smith, *God's Good Design*, 11.

58   Ibid., 12.

59   Ibid., 15. Grudem, *Biblical Foundations for Manhood and Womanhood*, a significant book defending complementarianism, includes a section on "Standing against culture." Jones, "Sexual Perversion," 273, positions complementarianism in a culture war of cosmic proportions: "the real opponent in the Sex Wars ... is not Christian feminism but the fiercely anti-Christian religious paganism that now surrounds us on every side."

This approach rests on a basic assumption of complementarianism—that biblical revelation offers not only a message of redemption but also a normative worldview which includes an understanding of differentiated gender. In contrast, egalitarians hold either that the biblical teaching is egalitarian or that the Bible has no direct implications for views of gender roles. Roger Nicole sets out the first position with the summary assertion that in the light of the gospel "sexual differentiation vanishes, and women have access to the three main human functions marked by God with a special unction."[60] Elaine Storkey expresses the second, arguing that one of the failings of complementarianism is that "it is trying to get from the biblical text something which the text is not trying to give."[61]

The construction of a worldview from Scripture and the articulation of views of gender within that worldview are complex interpretive exercises. Having made that admission, I hope you will excuse me for using the term biblical "teaching" as shorthand for this complementarian conviction. It avoids lengthy circumlocution.

With the conviction that there is a biblical "teaching" about gender, complementarianism sets this against three related elements of contemporary Western culture. First, it opposes androgyny, "unisex," and other trends which "blur" gender distinctions. It offers a distinctive construction of masculinity and femininity. Some US complementarians are explicit and prescriptive about this.[62] Australian complementarians tend, I think, to be more cautious in describing such gender types.

Second, and more centrally, complementarianism is counter-cultural by insisting on prescribed roles for men and women, at least in church and family. This is *more* counter-cultural than the idea that there are typical constructions of masculinity and femininity.

---

60   Nicole, "Biblical Egalitarianism," 7.

61   Storkey, "Evangelical Theology and Gender," 166.

62   Piper's definition may be the best known: "at the heart of mature masculinity is a sense of benevolent responsibility to lead, provide for, and protect women in ways appropriate to a man's differing relationships" and "at the heart of mature femininity is a freeing disposition to affirm, receive and nurture strength and leadership from worthy men in ways appropriate to a woman's differing relationships." Piper, *What's the Difference?* 22.

The most counter-cultural element of complementarianism is that it differentiates the roles of men and women in terms of authority. According to Smith, "women are not to be the authoritative teachers for the gathered household of God . . . they are to learn with quiet, willing and voluntary submissiveness" and "the husband is head of the wife as Christ is the head of the church, and the wife is to submit to her husband as the church submits to Christ."[63]

In contrast Hégy and Martos argue that gender roles should only be differentiated on the basis of sex-related physical attributes (such as reproduction) and only then "if they result in a balance of status and power between males and females." In this argument, they appeal to modern Western culture.

> Today, the unjust assignment of higher status and higher power roles to one gender . . . is understood sociologically as sexual discrimination or sexism. In the context of the Christian religion, it is becoming increasingly common to regard sexism as sinful and contrary to the will of God.[64]

If Hégy and Martos are correct about current culture, then complementarianism is decidedly counter-cultural.

Yet we shouldn't overstate how counter-cultural the position is. Australian popular culture often embraces highly differentiated constructions of masculinity and femininity. Anything approaching androgyny is limited to very small circles. What is more, recent work suggests that nearly 20 percent of Australians agree that "men should take control in relationships and be the head of the household" and almost 30 percent think "women prefer a man to be in charge of the relationship."[65] So, when complementarianism defines itself as primarily counter-cultural, it may misread the culture. The wider

---

63   Smith, *God's Good Design*, 35 and 115.

64   Hégy and Martos, "Understanding the Dynamics of Gender Roles," 181.

65   Webster, K., et al., *Australians' Attitudes to Violence against Women*, 62.

culture is not dominated by an undifferentiated "feminism"; things are far more complicated than that.

A more profoundly counter-cultural account of men and women which focuses on Christian virtues needs to be developed. Piper seeks to do this, to some extent. His "mature masculinity" is gentle and kind; he affirms strength as a masculine virtue, but urges men to use strength in service, not domination. This needs to be pursued far more fully, especially in the discussion of femininity, where Piper focuses primarily on the need to "affirm, receive and nurture strength and leadership from worthy men."[66]

b) *Translating Gender Theology*

There have been attempts within complementarian circles to strike a different note which is more accessible to contemporary culture. These stress freedom for men and women to "be themselves," rather than to satisfy set gender types. They explore ways in which men and women can work together, even with somewhat different roles; and seek to displace issues of power and authority in marriage and church from the centre of the discussion.[67] They view relationships as primarily mutual and co-operative. Headship and submission are not denied, but they are not treated as the central dynamic of the relationship. All of these can be seen as efforts to "translate" complementarianism for contemporary culture.

Padgett notes some of these trends when he argues that current complementarian teaching on gender roles is "revisionist." On his telling, the position only developed in the 1970s as it dropped what he terms the traditional Christian view that women are "inadequate" or inferior and instead taught "that men and women are *equal* in being but that their *roles* are different."[68] I am not convinced by his view which claims that complementarianism and egalitarianism are equally revisionist. Yet he notices a genuine development

---

66   Piper, *What's the Difference?* 54.

67   E.g., Alsup, "Practical Theology for Women"; Byrd, "John Piper's Advice"; Trueman, "An Accidental Feminist?"; Keller, *Jesus, Justice, and Gender Roles.*

68   Padgett, *As Christ Submits,* 10.

in complementarian theology as it is explained for contemporary culture. Translating convictions into a new idiom and dealing with new questions are the ways in which theology develops. Christians with convictions about differentiated roles of men and women have had to re-think how they explain those differences, and in the process have somewhat developed their position.

There is a growing emphasis on "servant leadership" for male leaders, rather than stressing headship and authority in ministry.[69] In a similar vein complementarian churches and ministries explore ways in which women can be involved in public ministry, leadership, and decision-making.[70] These are attempts to translate complementarian convictions for an inclusive culture. Of course, some who are more committed to a counter-cultural vision of complementarianism will view them as cultural accommodation.

c) Complementarianism as a Missional Obstacle

Complementarianism is often associated with churches which are active in evangelism, yet their position on gender can create an obstacle for mission. Kathy Keller recounts a woman who found that Redeemer church would not ordain women elders reacting that "it was like finding out that your fiancé was a child molester."[71] The Danvers statement asserts that complementarianism "should find an echo in every human heart"; but that is not the common experience. Claire Smith asks, "Who among us has not been the target of jokes and jibes about the church's view on women? It would be nice to have a way out!"[72] Roy Williams argues that views of sex and gender

---

69   Hammett, "Human Nature," 300 claims "the best contemporary expressions of complementarianism find a moderating position . . . that involves servant leadership . . . following the pattern of Christ, and full affirmation of the value and giftedness of women." See Frederick, "An Interpretation of Evangelical Gender Ideology," 184.

70   E.g., "The church must boldly articulate a robustly positive perspective of womanhood and of woman's role in the church. . . . If a local church remains silent on this issue, women will be unequipped to fulfill their covenantal calling. It is insufficient for churches that hold to male headship simply to compile a list of things that are permissible for women to do. We must go to the Scriptures and determine what is needful for women to do. Gender-aloneness was "not good" in the garden and the same is true in the church." Hunt, "Women's Ministry in the Local Church," 37–38.

71   Keller, *Jesus, Justice, and Gender Roles*, loc. 25.

72   Smith, *God's Good Design*, 17.

have been significant obstacles to Australian society accepting the church and its message.[73]

No doubt, these issues create an obstacle, though recent McCrindle research found that when non-Christians who would consider changing their view of Christianity were asked to list significant "blockers" only 13 percent reported that the role of women was a major issue.[74]

Smith engages the problem directly. She acknowledges that some people will think that complementarianism "is just too culturally abhorrent, too open to misunderstandings to do any good."[75] Her response is that human sin "is the rejection of the goodness and wisdom of God's word." If God has revealed a pattern for gender roles, she argues, then to suspect this of being abhorrent and unacceptable is simply to accept the sinful premise. "We cannot change the substance of God's truth to make the gospel more appealing. The gospel is more radical, more counter-cultural, more confronting than anything the Bible has to say about men and women, or wealth, or sex . . . it is entirely wrong-footed to think we can silence a 'difficult' part of God's word in order to win souls for Christ."[76]

Not only are complementarian views potential obstacles to bringing others into a church community, they can also be obstacles to involving women (and men) fully in the mission of the church. At least some women feel disconnected and unmotivated by a church environment with all male, or overwhelmingly male, leadership. I certainly know about this effect anecdotally, though I have not been able to find any research which investigates the issue.

I wonder how fully churches recognise these obstacles. Churches can consider how they can make their views of gender roles less of an obstacle—

---

73   Williams, *Post God Nation?*; Aune, "Evangelical Christianity" presents evidence from the UK that women who do not fit traditional roles or marriage and motherhood are likely to leave complementarian evangelical churches. Gayle Kent kindly supplied me with the reference to Aune's paper.

74   McCrindle Research, *Australian Communities Report.*

75   Smith, *God's Good Design*, 233.

76   Ibid., 233–34.

that is, how they can seek to translate. Yet if we do have convictions about gender roles and these convictions are biblical and theological and related to the gospel then they cannot be concealed. It will be better to teach on and advocate for them from time to time.

d) Complementarianism and Domestic Violence.

The most troubling aspect of complementarianism for me is the accusation that it allows or promotes domestic violence. Julia Baird raised this concern in a series of article in *The Sydney Morning Herald* recently.[77]

Domestic violence and abuse, and violence against women seem to be increasing in Australia, though accurate statistics are not available. Certainly many women are affected by such violence and abuse.[78] Some of the literature on domestic violence from the 1970s asserted or assumed a direct connection between patriarchy and abuse of women.[79] Recent Australian reports have continued this theme, noting a correlation between violence against women and views of gender roles.[80] Yet the picture is more complicated, since more recent research has identified several other likely causes and some significant analyses of the data suggest that adult male abusers "could not be differentiated from non-abusive men on the sole basis of traditional (patriarchal) gender attitudes."[81]

When regular church attendance is added to a patriarchal view, the picture changes further since "there is an inverse relationship between church

---

77   Baird, "Submission is a fraught mixed message" asks "if conservative churches preach the dominance of men, and submission of women, does this add weight to those who think men have a right—even a divine right—to control their partners?" In the following column, "Doctrine of headship a distortion," she writes of a flood of reports which came to her of just this kind of abuse: "my inbox filled with stories of assault, and ministers told me privately of colleagues who'd preached that women should stay with abusive men." A local Christian counsellor told her, "I have worked with numbers of women and children who have been the victims of a twisted view of male headship which gives men permission to do whatever they want in the family."

78   For a detailed examination of the statistics see Phillips and Vandenbroek, "Domestic, Family and Sexual Violence."

79   Tracy, "Patriarchy and Domestic Violence," 576–78.

80   For details see K. Webster, et al., *Australians' Attitudes to Violence against Women*, 40.

81   Tracy, "Patriarchy and Domestic Violence," 580.

attendance and domestic violence." Some studies suggest "conservative Protestant men who attend church regularly are . . . the least likely group to engage in domestic violence." Christian community with models of loving, non-dominating, masculinity and improved confidence from this community all serve to reduce abusive behaviour.[82]

Nevertheless, as Tracy suggests, patriarchal thinking is risk factor for abuse.[83] Complementarians must not simply protest the accusation; they must protect women in churches. This brings the "praxis" dimension of contextualisation most clearly into focus. The experience of women in complementarian churches must be taken seriously and complementarians have to take responsibility for the kind of church and family culture they are promoting.

It must be made patently clear that a Christian doctrine of headship is no pretext for abuse. There is no basis for a husband to force submission or to seek to control his wife, or to dominate her, or cause her to fear. It must be very clear that God is opposed to abuse and violence in marriage and in the family. He particularly warns husbands to be considerate to their wives and treat them with respect (Ephesians 5:28–30; 1 Peter 3:7). The model of love in the Bible, Jesus' suffering for others, is the very opposite of abuse.

Complementarian churches should recognise that all-male leadership can make it difficult for women facing abuse to find help and protection from the church. There is a tendency to protect men (especially church leaders) from accusations. So, churches must ensure that women who face abuse are confident they will be supported, identifying women to whom they can turn to report abuse and find help.

Approaches to complementarianism which do not view marriage as primarily a relationship of headship and submission go some way to ameliorate the risk of abuse.

---

82   Ibid., 581–84.
83   Ibid., 584.

Conclusion

I am only too aware that this paper is a brief study and has skated over serious issues, and probably skirted several as well. My goal was to show that viewing complementarianism as contextualisation may help those inside the movement and outside to understand it better. It helps to raise some of the hermeneutical issues involved and locates them, appropriately, in a cultural setting.

Complementarianism often presents itself as primarily counter-cultural. I have sought to show that the reality is more complex than that. Those of us who hold that the Bible offers a normative worldview which includes a view of gender roles in church and family must continue to think about how we express that in word and action in our cultural context.

Response: Megan du Toit

I am encouraged by John's thoughtful approach to counter-culturalism as a complementarian. His point that "The counter-cultural model risks denying the goodness of creation and the doctrine of common grace" is well made. In this he seeks to avoid the fortress mentality that evangelicals can display. I also wholeheartedly agree with him that "when complementarianism defines itself as primarily counter-cultural, it may misread the culture. The wider culture is not dominated by an undifferentiated 'feminism'; things are far more complicated than that." I would concede that egalitarianism at times also may misread the culture by assuming that it is patriarchy which has a stranglehold on society. John's humility in acknowledging the possibility that complementarian approaches may enable domestic violence is welcome. I would urge egalitarians to ensure that they do not just critique complementarians in this regard, but are actively part of a constructive answer to the open wound of our society that is domestic violence.

I find John's statement of his model of interacting with culture—"an integrated model of contextualisation in which those seeking to follow the Lord in a particular setting bear the responsibility to express the faith in their context in ways which make it accessible but also show how it critiques their culture"—one that is helpful in articulating a modified counter-culturalism.

I would further argue, though, that we can positively respond to culture not just by expressing ourselves accessibly but also by recognising that contemporary culture may give us the impetus to re-examine our theology and uncover past cultural accommodations.

I agree with John's point that complementarians in the US are more likely to set out prescriptive and highly defined lists of gender differences, and that Australians are more hesitant to do so. I think this probably reflects an American/Australian cultural difference. However, my own experience is that Australians still often refer to masculinity and femininity as if they are understood and agreed concepts. So for instance, former Anglican Archbishop of Sydney, Peter Jensen, in defending a revised marriage service in 2012, consistently used language about men being men and women being women. For instance, in a Sydney newspaper:

> When a husband promises to love his wife as Christ loved the church and give himself up for her, he is declaring his intention to be a man of strength and self-control for her benefit and for the benefit of any children born to them. Such qualities, properly exercised in the spirit of self-sacrifice, enhance the feminine and personal qualities of his wife. [84]

There is assumed content there as to what it is to be masculine and feminine and this presumed content is unhelpful in furthering the gender debate.

In conclusion, I found much to affirm in John's paper. Given the brevity of the paper though, I am still unsure as to how he sees male/female differences. I would like to see those who affirm the necessity of upholding different roles to more clearly articulate what those differences are and how they relate to the roles. It is only as we are open about our assumptions about gender that we can labour together in how to express gender as people in Christ.

---

[84]   Jensen, "Men and Women Are Different, and So Should Be Their Marriage Vows."

Response to Megan du Toit and John McClean: Miyon Chung

The papers presented in this section engage with some of the contemporary issues concerning gender identity and roles for the evangelical church to consider in its understanding and practice. They illustrate well how complex and complicated the subject matter of gender has become in many parts of the world. In so doing, both papers attempt to delineate hermeneutically and culturally what is involved in today's gender language and construct as well the ecclesial implications thereof. One of the important common features of the papers is that fluidity and variability exist in any given gender construct. In this aspect, the papers can open up the task of exploring God's prescriptions regarding gender identity and roles given to Israel and reiterated in the contexts of the New Testament church as heuristic tools in constructing our own re-contextualised gender construct.

Particularly, Megan du Toit's consideration of "new creation" as a proper and profitable vantage point from which to reflect on gender language and issues is helpful precisely because the ultimate goal of creation is not necessarily to return to the original creation but to conform to the image of Christ. John's McClean's paper reminds us that in the Triune God's eternal being and relationality, there is a sense of inherent alterity and otherness.

Not only does God create human beings in his image, "male and female," but also describes himself in feminine and masculine languages of fatherhood and motherhood. We should be cautious, however, of deducing God's own nature and relationality from that of the "image of God." Instead, we must leave the "image of" in Genesis 1 as a metaphorical tenor or paradigm wherein God's own personhood is concerned. Likewise, the church's cultivation of gender identity and roles should not lead to the hubristic assumption that human beings in their present lived experience concretely reflect the Triune God's relationality. I believe John McClean's paper at least has this in mind.

As an afterthought, I wonder if we can benefit from taking a detour in the trajectory of gender conversation only to reconfigure what might be a more sound or reconciliatory reflection on gender. My suspicion is that much of what has been presented in the present papers in terms of complementarianism and egalitarianism is lacking a more pronounced— perhaps even radical—and thematic consideration of the fact that the church now lives in the light of the resurrection of Jesus Christ and therefore in anticipation of his return and the ensuing consummation of creation. For instance, "male and female" clearly connote difference, not the sameness in God and with reference to human beings. For this reason, "male and female" will be taken into the consummation of creation, but not necessarily in terms of marriage and biological parenthood. In this light, what about Paul's eschatological woman in 1 Corinthians? In as much as God's eschatological presence is what transforms, equips, and missionally drives the church to its ultimate goal through Jesus Christ in the power of the Holy Spirit, is there not a scripturally legitimate basis for considering today's gender identity and roles in ways that transcend the dichotomy of "male and female" roles in societies? In other words, if Paul's eschatological woman is not simply an anomaly, can this serve as a paradigm for reconfiguring the evangelical church's gender questions as it lives in the "already and not yet" present?

The Late Nineteenth-Century Protestant Mission and Emergence of "the Bible Woman" in Korea

Miyon Chung

Late nineteenth-century Korea, which then called itself Joseon Kingdom and was known to the West as a Hermit Kingdom, was undergoing a phase of critical socio-political upheaval; it was by no means stable.[85] The old order was coming to a dead end due to excessive corruption and factionalism, and the ruling class was utterly unsuccessful in both national and international politics.[86] Actually, the struggle between those

---

85 Adams, "Church Growth in Korea," 16–17. The term Korea has been used by the West from around the tenth century by the Western merchants who travelled along the Silk Road. The nomenclature, Joseon or Chosun (조선), was made void from 29 August 1910, when Japan declared Korea as its annexed territory. After Korea regained its independence on 15 August 1945, South Korea adapted the nomenclature of Republic of Korea, otherwise called Dae-han-min-gook in Korean language.

86 For a brief historical background discussion on this topic, see Davies, "The Impact of Christianity upon Korea, 1884–1910," 795–99. Moreover, it is significant that Christianity (i.e., Roman Catholicism) was first brought into the Joseon Kingdom at the end of the sixteenth century by a group of scholars who were searching for a new philosophy or paradigm that could help them to institute reform and innovation into the nation. See Grayson, *Korea*, 140–46 and Moffett, *Christianity in Asia*, 2:146–47.

who wanted to preserve the old Neo-Confucian ethos—an ideology that governed all aspects of the nation's structure and customs—and those who sought innovation and reformation began as early as the seventeenth century. Identified as the "Shil-hak" or "Sirhak" Movement, many of the earliest Korean Catholic Christians were a part of this group of progressive scholars. One might say that Korean Christian faith from its incipience was interwoven with aspirations for renewal and progress. According to James Grayson, "in the altered political condition of the late nineteenth and early twentieth centuries, Korean Confucianism became an ally rather than an enemy of Protestant Christianity."[87]

There are three features important to discussing the initial Protestant missions in Joseon Kingdom. First, unlike many nations in Asia which first encountered Christian missionaries through Western colonialism, both Roman Catholicism and Protestantism were brought in by indigenous evangelistic endeavours. [88] The gospel reached Joseon Kingdom through self-propagation. For this reason, Archibald Campbell famously states that the Korean church "has always been one jump ahead of the missionaries."[89] Likewise, Samuel H. Moffett also notes: "In Korea it was the Koreans themselves, not foreign missionaries, who first brought the Christian faith to their own people from across its guarded borders."[90] Secondly, Korean converts also translated the Bible into Korean vernacular and planted churches in Joseon Kingdom before the arrival of foreign missionaries. These observations are meaningful because the Korean church did not encounter Christianity via Western colonialism. Thirdly, Protestant missionaries provided many social and medical services and established

---

87 Grayson, *Early Buddhism and Christianity in Korea*, 139.

88 Grayson, *Korea*, 245–62.

89 Moffett, *Christianity in Asia*, 1:528, see especially the footnote reference 1. Initially, Roman Catholicism was embraced as "Cheonjugyo" ("Religion of the Lord of Heaven"). This nomenclature was given at the end of the eighteenth century by the Joseon's delegates to China who brought Christian books written in Chinese language by Jesuit missionaries. Evangelism, church planting, appointment of leaders, and administration of sacraments were done by indigenous converts' initiative and Catholic faith survived through years of intense and widespread persecution, especially the great persecution of 1866–67. See Ibid., 309–21.

90 Moffett, *Christianity in Asia*, 2:309.

systematic educational venues for the non-elite class and women.[91] One might say that medical work provided an entry point of Protestant mission, but it blossomed by a conjoined success of conducting regular Bible study, achieving high literacy, and establishing systematic education for all people. Eventually, Protestant mission influenced Korea's rigidly structured social patterns and paved ways for transformation into a modern society.

Therefore, without detouring from the priority of evangelism, and even at the risk of challenging their Western compatriot's trade interests to open a new market in Joseon Kingdom, the missionaries continuously introduced Western industrial and technological progress.[92] Social progress was used in ways that "augmented and supported evangelism, making the faith easier to believe."[93] Medical work was particularly vital to the early Protestant mission efforts.[94] For example, William B. Scranton (1856–1922) began evangelistic work in the hospital. Patients were brought into his Sunday services regularly. In his mission, medicine and Christian books were sold simultaneously.

Among numerous remarkable changes Protestant mission accomplished, perhaps the most radical was its impact on women's identity and their public participation and mobilisation. When Lilias Horton Underwood (1851–1921) arrived in Korea after she married one of the two earliest Protestant missionaries to land in Korea, Horace Grant Underwood (1859–1916), women in Joseon were not perceived as unique persons.[95] Without having her own identity, a woman was regarded by others as her father's daughter, husband's wife, children's mother, or by her hometown or village. The majority of women in Joseon Kingdom were uneducated

---

91   Moffett, *Christianity in Asia*, 2:532. The first Protestant missionary to enter Joseon Kingdom was Horace Newton Allen, a medical doctor. In fact, three of the first five Protestant missionaries were medical doctors. Ibid., 535.

92   Moffett, *Christianity in Asia*, 2:535.

93   Moffett, *Christianity in Asia*, 2:535.

94   Hunt, *Korea*, 76–77.

95   Henry G. Appenzellar, one of the two first Protestant missionaries to arrive in Chosen in 1885, was a married clergy. But he and his wife were temporarily sent back to Japan until Chosen allowed Western women to enter. See Moffett, *Christianity in Asia*, 2:532.

and marginalised from social participation. Even the royals and upper class women were systemically subjugated by men in the society. Protestant mission efforts challenged this very bleak social system into which women were locked in from birth and contributed indisputably and irreversibly to the formation of Korean women's modern identity and lifestyle through formal education and the creation of professional careers. As Moffett notes, "Most revolutionary of the Protestant educational innovations, however, was not a boy's school, but a school for girls."[96] Furthermore, the fact that the pioneering missionary of women's education was Mary F. Scranton (1832–1909), the first woman missionary to arrive in Joseon and the mother William B. Scranton, foreshadows the remarkable relationship forged between the early Protestant women missionaries and the women converts in Joseon Kingdom.

The purpose of this chapter, therefore, is to delineate how the early Protestant mission work has contributed decisively in creating a modern womanhood for Korean women. Surprisingly, although Protestant mission endeavours in the nineteenth-century Joseon Kingdom were holistic, the change was undoubtedly instigated and flourished because of the Bible conferences uniquely designed as Sah-gyung-whe and the ensuing creating of "the Bible woman," who functioned as catalytic agents and role models of so-called "the new women" of Joseon Kingdom. Although the more radical, dramatic, and significant influences were produced in the twentieth century and on, this chapter will focus on the initial Protestant mission work in the nineteenth century. In terms of delivery, the context of the mission work and its impact will be highlighted. Unfortunately, limits of space prevent this chapter from providing critical evaluations.

---

96   Moffett, *Christianity in Asia*, 535.

Identity and Place of Women in Joseon Society

Two words are sufficient to sum up the living condition of women in Joseon Kingdom: seclusion and obedience.[97] Although women were divided according to their class, seclusion and obedience applied to them all irrespective of their birth or social status. As such, unwelcomed from birth as the unfavoured gender, women found that both their proper place and role in Joseon society were strictly restricted to the domestic sphere of life. From a very young age, females in general had little or no freedom of movement or public access, forbidden or rarely allowed to have social interactions with people outside of their family, close relatives, and household servants and slaves. They were also taught to obey their fathers when young and their husbands and parents-in-law after marriage. Women's vulnerable social position was reinforced by Joseon's marriage principles and customs. For example, the society laid out seven cardinal evils for married women: 1) not serving and honouring the parents-in-law properly; 2) not being able to produce a son; 3) immoral conduct (broadly connoting dishonesty, corruption, or illegality); 4) jealousy; 5) carrying contagious diseases; 6) talking too much (especially talking back to her husband or parents-in-law); 7) stealing. Among these rules, only the acts of immorality and stealing were applied equally to men. Should a married woman be accused of having committed one of the seven cardinal evils, she would be expelled from her husband's household without a prospect of returning to her father's household. For no father would risk his family's reputation by accepting an ostracised, shameful daughter. As Ellasue Wagner, a Southern Methodist missionary in Korea from 1904 to 1940, succinctly described, a woman in Joseon society had "no home, only a house."[98] In other words, she had no family, only obligations.

Given this social system, it is not surprising that the general population was outraged by the "immorality" of Christian women and men worshipping together in the same room. In fact, from the time when the Roman Catholic

---

97   Rhie, "Early Korean Christian Women," 13–24. See also, Kyung-ran Kim, "'Jikyok' (Occupational Classification) and Its Meaning of Women in Chosun Dynasty," 39–68; Hyo-Chae Lee, "Protestant Missionary Work and Enlightenment of Korean Women," 37.

98   Wagner, "A Korean Home," 90.

faith was first introduced in Joseon centuries ago, Christianity presented at least two unthinkably perverse ideas and practices that no proper person in Joseon could accept. One was the staunch refusal to participate in ancestral veneration, which was vital to preserving Joseon's social, moral, and religious ethos and order.[99] The other was the belief and practice of equality for all people, regardless of gender or class. In terms of observing religious rituals, Confucianism excluded women from participating in religious rites. The rituals held by shamans and Buddhists were either individualistic or did not involve personal interactions. Christianity, however, not only propagated the belief that all human beings are created equal in God's image but also held corporate worship regularly. In the eyes of Joseon society, that Christian women and men worshipped in the same room with only a partition between them was indeed scandalously immoral. [100]

Neo-Confucianism and Christianity: Sacred Texts, Enlightenment, and Virtue

Despite extreme hostility and impediments against Christianity on political, religious, and cultural grounds, in addition to the past persecutions against Catholic Christianity, Protestant missionaries began to see the fruit of their work in a relatively short period of time. In this section, representative sympathetic background elements from Neo-Confucianism that were conducive to Protestant missional endeavours will be traced in brevity. The most basic preparatory common grace for the reception of the gospel was the admiration of and zeal for learning and scholarship. Joseon society valued books and literati above all else and as such had a high regard for teachers. Although not nearly as revered now in contemporary Korean

---

99 Bae, "Ancestor Worship." For background on Korean religiosity and ancestral veneration and worship, see 69–85. The early Korean Catholics in Joseon Kingdom rejected ancestral worship, which caused a severe persecution by the establishment. In recent times, however, Pope Pius XII "declared that the Chinese custom of ancestor worship should be considered a civil rite as a means of expressing filial affection towards their ancestors." Consequently, the Korean Catholic Church also adopted this tolerant attitude and reinstated a modified version of ancestral worship in 1940. This stance was reaffirmed by the Second Vatican Council (1962–65). Some liberal Protestants likewise hold a similar position on the practice. Ibid., 88.

100 Moffett, *Christianity in Asia*, 2:533.

life, teachers were regarded on par with parents in terms of influence and authority.[101] Whereas Joseon operated under the authority of the Neo-Confucian teacher, Chu Hsi, Protestant missionaries presented Paul as the supreme expositor of God's truth (or the heavenly truth).[102]

Another important connection came from the theological conservatism of the early Protestant missionaries who came to Joseon.[103] As the official philosophical and religious system of the Joseon Dynasty (1392–1910), Neo-Confucianism was the basis on which the educational and examination systems were established and operated, and Joseon's elite had a strong "predilection for ideological orthodoxy."[104] Because this attitude had degenerated into a stifling narrow-mindedness, an increasing number of people for centuries searched for a paradigm shift, or a replacement ideology or belief system. The Confucian proclivity toward orthodoxy, however, was retained as a general culture, which some people carried onto their reception of the Christian faith.

Specifically, Neo-Confucianism taught acceptance of the authority of sacred texts *prima facie* and emphasised rote memorisation as the highest mode of learning.[105] Likewise, the first generation of Protestant missionaries who were from conservative Presbyterian and Wesleyan revivalist backgrounds presented the Christian Scriptures as the supremely authoritative text of God's special revelation. The earliest Protestant catechisms written in Korean phonetic form, *Hangeul*, emphasised the Bible as the unique, unmatched, right foundation of human thought and actions— the most sacred text of all sacred texts.[106] The missionaries also emphasised the importance of memorising portions of Scripture, which suited well with the already established learning system of Joseon Kingdom. In fact, many among the initial converts and leaders were from the elite class who had

---

101   For a basic historical discussion on Confucianism's influence on Korean people, see Seth, "Korean Education," 5–16.
102   Adams, "Church Growth in Korea," 18.
103   Adams, "Church Growth in Korea," 17–18.
104   Hahm, *The Korean Political Tradition and Law*, 84.
105   Young Mee Lee, "Biblical Interpretation in the Early Korean Christianity," 48.
106   Ibid., 45–46.

mastered Confucian classics through memorisation and comprehension. For example, Sun-choo Kil (1869–1935) after his conversion to Christianity is known to have devoted himself to an intense study of the Bible and served as one of the most effective Bible teachers in the kingdom.[107] During the time of imprisonment for his part in the 1 March 1919 Independency Movement against Japanese annexation, he is said to have memorised the entire book of Revelation.

Moreover, according to Neo-Confucianism, sacred texts were to be accepted as guides to truths and enlightenment.[108] The proper attitude toward sacred texts was one of listening attentively in order to gain understanding or to be enlightened. The ultimate goal of understanding, however, was not merely to be enlightened but to embrace and practise the realised truths life and thereby live virtuously. The basic belief was that the right knowledge leads to the right action. The early Christian converts in Joseon therefore carried this attitude and practice to the Christian Scripture. Neo-Confucian belief created room to ascertain the possibility that Christian Scripture contained the ultimate right knowledge from above and that the established orthodoxy (i.e., Neo-Confucianism) could be set aside in favour of a higher or the highest knowledge from above. It also served to communicate the Christian teaching about the relationship between the power of the word of God and personal transformation. Most importantly, the greatest significance of Christianity was in extending access to "the right knowledge" in anticipation of enlightenment and transformation to all people, irrespective of class or gender. The remaining portion of the essay, therefore, will delineate how out of this cultural ethos Christianity gave birth to a new way of constructing women's identity and place in Joseon society overall.

---

107   Clark, *Church in Korea*, 175.

108   Young Mee Lee, "Biblical Interpretation in the Early Korean Christianity," 48. See also Adam, "Church Growth in Korea," 17–18. For a superb example of a Korean Confucian scholar's adaptation of the Protestant faith, see Yohan Bae's presentation and analysis of Soo-jeong Y's (alternatively spelled as Su-Jeong Lee) testimony given from 1884. Full information is provided in the bibliography.

Christianity for Women in Joseon

Despite the opposition from the establishment, various venues to educate girls and women were formed almost from the beginning of Protestant mission and soon paved a pathway that would change the identity and role of Korean women irreversibly. Remarkably, just as the first instances of Protestant Christian conversions in Joseon Kingdom had occurred without the presence of foreign missionaries in the land, the first Protestant Christian's prophetic call for social reform concerning women's status also came from a native convert, Soo-jeong Yi.[109] The initial call for reformation of Joseon society, especially regarding women's place, was an indigenous one, not forced on it by Westerners. An esteemed scholar of Neo-Confucianism, Yi was a part of Joseon's short-term emissary to Japan. Shortly after his arrival in 1882, Soo-jeong Yi became converted through the evangelistic work of a Christian from Joseon.[110] Putting his Confucian background to good use, he quickly acted on the new-found truth (Christian faith).[111] Consequently, while in Japan, he worked with Henry Looms of the American Bible Society and contributed to translating the four gospels into Korean. This is the precise Bible that the pioneering missionaries Underwood and Henry G. Appenzeller (1858–1902) had brought with them when they landed in Joseon in 1884.[112]

Yi further implored the Presbyterians in the USA to send missionaries to Joseon Kingdom, specifically denoting the need for women's

---

109   This does not necessarily mean that the call was initiated in isolation from any Christian community around him but that his was the first registered appeal made to Christians in the United States of America.

110   Bae, "A Confucian Analysis of Lee Su-Jeong's Confessional Essay," 484–87.

111   Soo-jeong Yi's testimony presented on 13 May 1883 at Japanese Christian Fellowship shows his understanding of John 14 against the backdrop of a core Neo-Confucian thought, "There is no distance between heaven and me" or "mutual correspondence between God and humanity." The testimony was written in classical Chinese in a highly fluid style. In it, he clearly articulates that he has embraced the basic Christian doctrine that truth is not to be discovered but that which the Holy Spirit reveals to an individual for salvation. More relevantly for this chapter, he uses several analogies to denote the need to live in accordance with the truth gained.

112   Grayson, *Korea*, 104.

transformation.[113] He "strongly advocated women's education as part of Korea's [Joseon] enlightenment project, and he felt that American missionary women would provide invaluable support in the initial changes."[114] Under the pen name of Rijutei, Soo-jeong Yi's letter was published under the title of "A Call from Corea," in *Heathen Women's Friend*.[115] In it, he explained in detail how the political climate in Joseon was favourable to receiving Western missionaries and pleaded for women missionaries to be sent who could work with women in Joseon so that these women in turn could "elevate and reform people, to educate children, to lead their husbands to virtue."[116] He further wrote:

> On the other hand, though the husband be ever so ill mannered, if he has a good wife he will become a better man. For though he be ever so bad . . . she must ever exert a correcting influence on his life.

Although the Roman Catholic converts had already rejected Joseon's social stratification, Soo-jeong Yi was the first person to actually identify women as the key driving force to reforming the entire people and nation.

Likewise, other Christian men in Joseon also engaged themselves to improve women's lives. Often the converted husbands brought their wives, daughters, and relatives to the church.[117] These men also pressed missionaries to hold Sah-gyung-whe (SGH) for their wives, through which the Korean

---

113   Actually, his letter was instrumental to the arrival of the first Protestant missionaries in Joseon Kingdom. The Board of Foreign Missions of the Presbyterian Church USA recorded: "About 1880, Rijutei, a Korean of high rank, was sent to represent his government in Japan. Here he was led to accept Christ, and begged earnestly that missionaries should be sent to Korea. In answer to this appeal the Presbyterian Board sent Dr. H. N. Allen, then working as a medical missionary in China. He arrived in Korea, September 1884. General Foote at once appointed him physician to the United States Legation, which assured his safety and favourable reception."

114   Choi, "The Visual Embodiment of Women," 94.

115   His first letter was sent in 1883. This letter also appears as "Tokio, August 8, 1884" for he sent it while in Japan.

116   "A Call from Corea," *Heathen Women's Friend*, 16:7 (January 1885) 158-59 cited in Choi, "The Visual Embodiment of Women," 94.

117   Rhie, "Early Korean Christian Women," 24.

Protestant Church grew in maturity and numbers.[118] In addition to weekly Bible study classes, SGH or Bible conferences were started for Korean converts. The term was created by conjoining the terms "study or research," "sacred text," and "gathering."[119] The root of the term can be traced back to the Sah-gyung-ban ("ban" meaning a "class") when Underwood in 1890 gathered seven Joseon converts for a Bible study at his home.[120] In June of the same year, Underwood invited John Livingston Nevius (1829–1893) from China to speak at the first Christian seminar organised in Joseon. After consulting with Nevius, SGH was devised as a missional strategy in view of creating a self-motivated Bible study movement among Joseon Christian converts. It was a blend of intense biblical and theological studies and revivals. The result was a great success. Even the Great Revival of Pyungyang which began in Wonsan was kindled by SGH.[121]

Most significantly, revival experiences such as the famous Pyungyang Great Revival "changed the consciousness of the Korean Church toward gender, family, society and nation at the days of beginning." [122] For example, Mary Scranton's reports reveal that women's SGH would not have been organised so quickly if it had not been for the constant pressure and demands made by the local male converts who were awakened to the implications of the gospel for women in Joseon.[123] Whereas the missionaries felt more time was needed to prepare for women's SGH, the local Christian men repeatedly insisted on it: "We are now receiving this teaching. What reason can there be for our wives to not be learning these doctrines?" Consequently, cities

---

118   Moffett, *Christianity in Asia*, 2: 545.

119   Young Mee Lee, "Biblical Interpretation in the Early Korean Christianity," 43.

120   Cf. "The Academy of Korean Studies." Underwood's first training sessions for Korean Christian leaders from throughout the peninsula were held in August 1888 in Seoul. The sessions were held for a month with emphasis on the basic Christian doctrines. See Hunt, *Korea*, 77.

121   Young Mee Lee, "Biblical Interpretation in the Early Korean Christianity," 43. Furthermore, Sah-gyung-whe's organisation reflected the levels of biblical knowledge of its participants, distance people had to travel, and the time available to attend. It was used to train lay leaders, and topics ranged from biblical studies to applications such as the four Gospels, exposition of the Lord's Prayer and the Apostle's Creeds, catechisms, methods of evangelism, and pastoral counselling. A day's conference began from a dawn prayer meeting until evening, whereas some conferences last for days. See *The Academy of Korean Studies* available at http://terms.naver.com/entry.nhn?docId=578314&cid=46647&categoryId=46647.

122   Rhie, "Religious Experience and Formation of Feministic Consciousness of Church Women," 73.

123   Rhie, "Early Korean Christian Women," 38.

such as Pyungyang held Married Women's Sah-gyung-whe twice a year.[124] The first was held in 1901 January 7 to 20 (according to the lunar calendar) in which fifty women attended. At that meeting, the participants completed Bible study material made for women leaders and moved onto studying from the evangelistic materials which had been originally written for American Christians.

Not all women were supported by their husbands but many were eager to learn from Christian missionaries once the revival broke out. Historically, SGH was the first public opportunity for women to learn the truth. Samuel Moffett's letters mention two among many other women who sat patiently waiting for someone to teach them the Bible.[125] An elderly woman came and sat in the men's quarter, which was simply not done in Joseon society, perchance that someone might teach her. A young girl trained as a dancer—a rather disreputable occupation—was regularly attending Christian gatherings dressed as a man. After receiving the gospel, she no longer wanted to live as a dancer/artisan and instead was eager to learn the truth taught by Christians.

Records such as those submitted by Mattie Noble (1872–1956), a Presbyterian missionary in Pyungyang (1892–1934) who served with her husband William Arthur Noble (1866–1945), indicate how some women walked for days to attend Sah-gyung-whe.[126]

> Two hundred and fifteen earnest women and girls attended the ten day's session of this Bible Institute. One hundred and eight women walked in from the country, a half to four days' traveling. In the group, which presents only a small part of the company, are a few Bible women and teachers, who toil day by day spreading the light

---

124   Young Mee Lee, "Biblical Interpretation in the Early Korean Christianity," 43.

125   Young Mee Lee, "Biblical Interpretation of Korean Early Church and Its Ripple Effect," 521. She cites from Samuel A. Moffett's letters translated into Korean by In-soo Kim, *Missionary Samuel Moffett's Missionary Letters: 1890–1904*, 388.

126   Noble, "A Bible Institute in Korea," 399–400.

of truth; old women, who love to sound the praises of God, but who never can really sing until their voices are attuned to the music of heaven; young women, who have endured persecutions for Jesus' sake . . .

In the same excerpt, she makes a note of a woman "who carried her baby on her back forty miles hither and forty miles home again." This woman experienced the death of her child afterwards but remained in faith and continued to teach other local women the Bible for she trusted in God's love for her and her child.[127] The missionary records from the late 1800s to early 1900s are filled with proud reports of how Joseon women converts enthusiastically responded to Christianity.

Quickly, SGH gatherings produced dramatic changes in relation to Joseon's rules of social conduct; the converts began to break away from the traditional rules of segregation between gender and classes.[128] According to Mary Scranton's report, in an SGH held in 1888, a male evangelist for the first time taught Christian women doctrine and expounded the Scriptures. He crossed over the wall that had divided men from women to preach and teach women in a public setting. Moreover, male converts from the upper class were also found to be willing to interact with and share the same space with women and people from lower classes. These changes gave the missionaries confidence that Joseon converts were beginning to internalise their faith and that the church in Joseon would continuously grow.[129] As the converts' attitudes toward each other began to change, missionaries built churches without the dividing walls so that everyone could worship together as a unified congregation. On 26 December 1897, Scranton's church building was completed and people for the first time worshipped together. One would expect that everyone will have felt certain elation over the enlarged space. Testimonies from women converts converged on how they were deeply moved by the experience of worshipping in the same room with men ("at the

---

127   For a fuller account of Mattie Noble's missionary record, see Noble, *The Journal of Mattie Wilcox Noble, 1892-1934*.

128   Rhie, "Early Korean Christian Women," 42–43.

129   Ibid., 39.

same time under one roof") after ten years of having worshipped separately with a partition that divided them. Another record shows that on 8 April 1898, women finally took a role during a worship service in a Methodist church; they together with men gave their testimonies.[130]

"The Bible Woman" as the Catalyst for "the New Women" in Joseon

Sah-gyung-whe gave rise to the creation of "the Bible Woman." They were instrumental to the evangelism and education of women in Joseon and contributed vitally to creating a new brand of women in Joseon, "the new woman," who challenged and reformed Joseon women's identity, lifestyle, and status. This section will discuss, therefore, the synergistic relationship between Protestant women missionaries and Joseon women in evangelism, and how this relationship contributed directly to modifying the male chauvinist social conventions of Joseon society. Mary Scranton, two years after her arrival in 1886, obtained permission to build a "Girls' School and Home" from Queen Min.[131] Although it was difficult to find men who would send their daughters and wives to a public school, her school quickly filled up and has become today the largest women's university in the world, Ewha Women's University. As exemplified by her, more women missionaries arrived in Joseon either with their husbands or as singles with professional skills.[132] The primary ministries of the women missionaries were evangelism and education of all women, which they carried out in conjunction and without discrimination. Their strategy was "evangelism for unbelievers and education for believers."

In the beginning, however, evangelising women in Joseon was tremendously challenging because of the rule of seclusion and the impediment of illiteracy. When women were allowed to come to church, men and woman sat apart from each other with a curtain drawn in the centre

---

130   Ibid., 48.
131   Liptak, "Bible Women," 54; Moffett, *Christianity in Asia*, 2:535.
132   Liptak, "Bible Women," 54, 56.

of the room.[133] Classes for men were naturally more readily available than for women. When William B. Scranton baptised the first woman convert in 1886, he had to "cut a hole in the curtain and asked the woman to put her head against the hole, and baptized the top of her head, thankful that she was not a Baptist."[134] Also, for many women the reason for the initial attraction to Christianity was not purely one of religious interest; their interests ranged from curiosity toward Western women, culture, technological equipment, and expectations that Christianity would reform their husbands to be monogamous.[135] It was in this circumstance that "the Bible Woman" was created. The English term, "the Bible Woman," in Korean is *Jeon-doe-boo-in* ("the lady of evangelism").[136] The precise dating of the first appearance of the Bible woman is disputable, but assumed to be late 1880s or early 1890s.[137] From the beginning, they took an active role in the church and served as assistants and interpreters for foreign missionaries, Bible distributors, and itinerant evangelists and teachers.[138] Because the male missionaries in Joseon were forbidden to evangelise women and Western women missionaries were faced with much difficulty in travelling to the country side, the Bible women proved to be essential and effective. The goal was to commission the trained Bible women to share the gospel and thereby enhance the quality of life for the rest of the women in Joseon.[139]

---

133   Moffett, *Christianity in Asia*, 2: 533.

134   Ibid.

135   Choi, "The Visual Embodiment of Women in the Korea Mission Field," 91. See also Rhie, "Early Korean Christian Women," 25–26, 39.

136   Joo, *Korean Presbyterian Women*, 54. Sun Ae Joo's family was one of the earliest converts in the northern part of Joseon. Her book provides the details of women's training and education in the early period with reflection over the reports and records composed by Western missionaries. Incidentally, the term *joeondoebooin* is no longer used today. Instead, *jeondoesah*, which means evangelist, is used to refer to unordained men or women ministers. Most frequently, the term is used to refer to seminary students who are not yet ordained to be pastors.

137   Jang, "Education of Korean Bible Women and Their Missionary Work," 221–22.

138   Ibid., 221–44. See also Chou, "Bible Women and the Development of Education in the Korean Church," 30–45. One of the most important records of the personalities and activities of the Bible women from early Protestant mission work is *The Journals of Mattie Wilcox Noble (1892-1934)*. As mentioned above, she and her husband, William Arthur Noble (1866-1945), served as Presbyterian missionaries in Pyungyang during the period of 1892–1934.

139   Jang, "Education of Korean Bible Women and Their Missionary Work," 224.

The Bible women, then, emerged as the first reputable, modern career for women.[140] They were among the first to receive a formal education and training outside of the home and in turn served as itinerant evangelists, preachers, counsellors, educators, and role models for modern women, "the new women."[141] Because Protestants used *Hangeul* to translate the Bible and to write study materials, they contributed significantly to the rapid increase of literacy rates of Joseon people.[142] In fact, the adult converts were required to be able to read the Bible before baptism. As noted, "The simple Korean phonetic script, which even the most ignorant women are almost all capable of learning, has been a great boon" in evangelising and teaching women.[143] Although missionaries did not have a unified consensus on the level of education of the Bible women, they unanimously supported their role and education.[144] They established varieties of educational venues for them to target and long-term goals of evangelism and women's education.[145] The content and level also varied depending on each woman's previous learning, travelling distance, and time available. A comprehensive curriculum included biblical, doctrinal, ethical, and social areas of learning.

Most of the early Bible women were impoverished widows or women who were neglected or abandoned by their husbands.[146] Although divorce was practically non-existent in Joseon society, it was not uncommon for husbands to take in concubines or to establish separate households with their concubines. It was easier, consequently, for Western missionaries to approach these women who were detached from male authority figures.

---

140   During the Joseon period, women had only a few career opportunities. Some women's domestic labour went beyond the household economy and extended to the commercial economy. Also, there were a few occupational options for women which included serving as medical assistants, gisaeng or ginyeo, or palace staff. See Kyung-Mi Kim, "Women's Labor and Economic Activities in the Late Chosŏn," 85–116. Kyung-ran Kim, "Jikyok," 39–66.

141   Frey, "The Bible Woman," 42. See also Cooper, "The Bible Woman," 6–10, and Jang, "Education of Korean Bible Women and Their Missionary Work," 227–35.

142   *Hangeul* is the simple Korean phonetic script invented in 1443 by King Sejong and his team of scholars.

143   Soltau, *Korea: The Hermit Nation and Its Response to Christianity*, 39.

144   For instance, Ella Appenzeller and Mary Scranton disagreed about the readiness of the Bible woman before she could be commissioned to evangelise others. See Jang's account of the missionary reports from this period in "Education of Korean Bible Women and Their Missionary Work," 228.

145   Ibid., 228–332.

146   Liptak, "Bible Women," 75. See also Yi, "Early Korean Christian Women (1887–1920)," 13–25.

Ironically, precisely because of their abandonment, they were accessible to missionaries and were free to travel to evangelise others. In fact, some of them, mostly the widows who did not have family obligations, served full-time and were given a regular salary.[147] The full-time Bible women were crucial to evangelism, especially in countryside villages, far from the city centres where missionaries resided.

For instance, as Mattie Noble's SGH gatherings became more organised into four times a year in Pyungyang, nearly three hundred women came to be trained. Some of them returned to their villages and took initiatives to organise village-based SGH gatherings. Furthermore, while evangelism was their primary and explicit work, the Bible women also impacted the moral transformation of other women.[148] Specifically, Circus Kim, a Bible woman trained and named by Mattie Noble, travelled to several northern provinces in Joseon for evangelism, while another woman is recorded to have met in a year's period 6,730 people for evangelism and sold 4,491 Bibles.[149] As such, the role of the Bible woman provided occupationally legitimate reasons to break away from the centuries-old custom of female immobility.[150]

Moreover, the Bible women were among the first to have articulated women's emancipation and the recovery of the right to exist as a woman.[151] Married women in Joseon typically were never addressed by their given names; they were poignantly described as the "nameless people."[152] When Mattie Noble baptised these women, however, she gave them baptismal names which functioned decisively in creating a personal identity.[153] Dorcas Kim's testimony echoes this remarkable experience:[154]

---

147 Choi, "The Visual Embodiment of Women in the Korea Mission Field," 110–11; and Cho, "The Missionary work and Social Network of Mattie Wilcox Noble," 53.

148 For specific cases, see A. F. Robb's report in *Korean Mission Field,* 8, no. 7 (July 1912).

149 Jang, "Education of Korean Bible Women and Their Missionary Work," 226.

150 Ibid., 224–27.

151 Rhie, "Early Korean Christian Women," 34.

152 Ibid., 31–34.

153 Choi, "The Visual Embodiment of Women in the Korea Mission Field," 111. See also Liptak, "Bible Women," 72–73.

154 Kang, "Mrs. Dorcas Kim Kang," 82.

Of course I rejoiced most that I was acknowledging the Lord as my Saviour. I also rejoiced that freedom had come to me, a woman. The day that Jesus Christ was preached in Korea began the emancipation of women from the bondage of thousands of years. Since my childhood name was, according to custom, discontinued when I was about eight years old, I had never had a name. Think of it—for nearly fifty years without a name. On my baptismal day I received a name, all my own—"Dorcas!" Yes, it was the happiest day of my life.

Furthermore, the Bible women went beyond self-actualising experiences by devoting themselves to educating others; they virtually became the incipient women leadership in Joseon. They also served as counsellors to Christian women in place of shamans who gave spiritual guidance and remedies to troubled women.[155] For instance, Sejee Kim, also Mattie Noble's disciple, was the first Bible woman to have received regular stipends from the Methodist Women's Society (USA).[156] She learned the Korean script after conversion and eventually became a Bible woman, after which she was charged with the task of selling the Bibles, preaching, comforting other women, and organising Bible and literacy classes. An excerpt from her memoir illustrates the gospel's illuminating power to liberate women from the bondage of sin and from a male-dominated, oppressive society and to empower them to lead others into God's presence:[157]

Even though I am over sixty years old, I hardly have any stories to boast about to the people in the world. It is much more so before God. I can only thank God for his immense grace. Though I was but a lowly creature, God thought of me and led my teacher and benefactor, Mrs. Noble, to come to our nation, Joseon, in which

---

155   Chou, "Bible Women," 34.
156   Rhie, "Early Korean Christian Women," 10.
157   Ibid.. The translation from Korean to English is mine.

women like us for several thousand years have lived without freedom, under the oppression of men, and without personal names. She spread the bright light of the gospel profoundly and taught women to realise their freedom and purpose in life. Likewise, God broke my ignorance and granted me to know the saving truth about salvation so that I could be saved from eternal death due to my sin. And not only was I saved but also I worked to spread the truth about Christ Jesus to many men and women that several thousand have committed to become children [of God] by believing in the Lord's Word. For all this, I, first of all, offer praises of thanksgiving to God; secondly, I do not think it is excessive to boast about this to the people in the world.

In 1919, Sejee Kim was elected as President of the National Association of Patriotic Women in the Methodist Church and joined other Christian women leaders who were instrumental in mobilising Christians to stand up under Japanese oppression against Christians.[158] Her testimony exemplifies how the leading Bible women along with other likewise educated Christian women served as the catalytic agents of bringing about women's human rights, modern education, and culture.[159]

In conclusion, Protestant missions made lasting contributions to transforming the old Joseon society into what Korea is today by introducing critical medical, educational, and cultural innovations and enhancements. Even though the outcome was not without some negative consequences, the emergence and fostering of modern womanhood in Korean history is unquestionably one of its greatest impacts. Unfortunately, the Bible women were never fully given the equal authority and position of their male counterparts, although their functions and capacity were often equally

---

158   Rhie, "Early Korean Christian Women," 10.
159   Ibid., 35.

matched.[160] Even so, after the turn of the century, especially during the Japanese annexation of Korea (1910–1945), the Bible women's roles along with other educated Christian women were extended to covering for many pastors who were imprisoned, tortured, and/or executed by the Japanese governing authority in Korea.[161] Joseon Kingdom was no longer, but the harshness of colonial rule ironically contributed to Christian men and women working alongside each other toward protecting the church and regaining Joseon's independence. Furthermore, by 1901, Christian newspapers such as "Christ Daily" and magazines such as *Shin Hak Walbo* (*A Biblical and Church Monthly*) were created and, along with the regularly published Bible study materials, both Protestant women and men wrote editorials that consistently called for social reformation based on the doctrine of the image of God.[162] At a time when Japan's imperial enforcement of "the comfort women" was ravaging the sanctity of womanhood, the Korean Protestant Church, particularly the Bible women, stood out as a brilliant and hopeful contrast.

---

160   Chou, "Bible Women," 38–40. It has been argued that Protestant missionaries of the nineteenth century were responsible for transmitting not only the gospel but also their own patriarchal culture. Since the early Protestant missionaries who came to Joseon Kingdom were predominantly from the American middle-class, they were delimited by their own cultural standards and shortcomings. See Ryu, "Understanding Early American Missionaries in Korea."

161   Chou, "Bible Women," 34–36.

162   See, for instance, the following editorial article, which argued that the equality between women and men was not only God's creative intention but also in accordance with right reason:

> When the highest Lord created the heaven and earth and everything in it, the most precious of all was human beings . . . That [the Lord] created male and female as free beings, without discrimination, should come as natural to anyone with reason, why is it that we have come to regard women to be of lowly beings and shackled them to men that they are never given freedom in their entire life, never allowing them to be independent? In doing this we have not only gone against the ways of heaven but also we have done many things that are not in accordance with compassion . . . On the whole, the highest Lord created all human beings to be equal, without dividing them into high or low, male or female. This therefore is the way of the heaven that all must follow . . . To set women free [from male domination] is not only to acknowledge the compassionate way of heaven but also by this many outstanding individuals will be produced in the world.

"Christ Daily," (1 May 1901) quoted in Young Mee Lee, "Biblical Interpretation in the Early Korean Christianity and Its Influence on Women's Status," 57.

Response: Megan du Toit

It is a privilege to read Miyon's insight into the impact of Christianity on gender relationships in Korea, since Miyon speaks as a Korean American now teaching in Australia, and thus she brings her experience of several different cultures to bear on her research. As someone who has spent the majority of her ministry years so far within a Chinese-Australian context, though myself of Anglo-Australian heritage, I appreciate the insight experience within different cultures brings, and also the benefit of bringing this insight to gender issues.

It is particularly encouraging to read the positive impact that the gospel had in breaking down gender barriers in Korea. The encouragement of women to learn brought to my mind the story of Mary and Martha, and Jesus' own revolutionary encouragement for women to learn within a culture that didn't value the role of learner for women (Luke 10:38–42).

It is also inspiring to read the transformation that *imago Dei* theology brought to the status of women and those of lower class. I think that the full implications of humanity as bearing the image of God are still to be worked through globally. This also reveals the close connection between the status of women and others deemed to be inferior. Christian responses to other human inequities, such as slavery, poverty, and institutionalised racism, cannot ignore the way that these inequities interact with gender inequity.

Miyon's focus was a historical one, and such studies are needed as we bring insights from history to bear on our current context. I would love though, to read more on how this initial freedom for Christian Korean women developed as Christianity became more established in the Korean context. When we look at Western Christian history, we see contradictory impulses at work—Christianity both acting to raise the status and increase the freedom of women, but also to restrict them or justify their oppression.

Miyon has given us a case study in the social implications of the gospel. This argues against those who frame gospel implications in purely spiritual terms. I think most Christians would want to celebrate the impact of the gospel that she describes. I believe most would also acknowledge the direct connection between the gospel and the transformed understanding of gender that occurred in Korea. This transformation Miyon records is the redemption of gender that I urge in the conclusion to my paper. When people argue that progressive understandings of gender have ruined Western society, I think it would behove them to look back to the previous conceptions of gender and their results within Western culture, and also to look at how understandings of gender impact the lives of women globally. We in the West speak from a context in which the gospel has already had a transforming effect on gender, and we are often unaware of how deeply grateful for that we should be. Miyon's paper should be a spur to us to bring the gospel to all the women in the world—they are desperately in need of its transformative powers.

Response: John McClean

Miyon's paper introduced me to an area of history about which I knew very little beyond the basic story of the gospel coming to Korea in the late nineteenth century. The details of how that occurred are fascinating.

God in his providence had brought some disappointment with Neo-Confucianism so there was a search "for a paradigm shift, or a replacement ideology or belief system." Yet, respect for ancient texts and patterns of memorisation provided a channel for introducing Christian Scripture and the gospel. As Miyon highlights, there are aspects of common grace which God uses to bring the gospel into any culture. "Christ against culture" is not the only stance which Christians should take.

The Christian gospel will also challenge aspects of every culture, and that challenge has to be expressed in actions, not only in words. Miyon highlights how the gospel challenged ancestor worship and gender roles in Joseon society. Christian worship was shockingly immoral as men and women sat in the same room, albeit with a partition. (I suspect the refusal to worship ancestors was equally immoral, since it was a familial obligation.) There must have been a temptation to move worship into gender-segregated settings. How good it is that the indigenous church leadership and the missionaries seem not to have succumbed to that pressure. Given the setting, such a change would surely have signalled the acceptance of the view that women were less than men, and denied Gal. 3:28: "you are all one in Christ Jesus." In fact, the opposite happened and, quite literally, men and women crossed the "dividing wall of hostility," already destroyed in Christ (Eph. 2:14).

Miyon does not suggest any ways in which the Christian view of women (and men) could be allied with a traditional Korean view. The Christian view had to largely demolish the traditional view and its practices, and construct something new. Miyon's account traces the development of patterns of worship and ministry which were increasingly liberated from the assumptions of Confucianism.

Is it truly "surprising" that it is "Bible women" who were the key agents for change? I expect that the ministry of the word will transform thinking and lead to changed actions (Rom. 12:1–2). Many women devoted themselves to learning and sharing Scripture, and then helped to lead the church in faithfulness when persecuted. They are a great testimony to the transforming power of God's word and the courage he gives to his people.

In my chapter I suggest that proper "contextualisation" has to be grounded in Scripture and always involves affirmation and challenge in the context of active Christian discipleship and mission. The story of the gospel and gender in the early Korean church seems to fit that pattern well.

Part Five

Gender, History, and Hermeneutics

The Servant and Zion in Isaiah

Caroline Batchelder

Introduction

Many Bible readers are familiar with the poems in Isaiah 40–55 traditionally known as the "Servant Songs."[1] Jesus drew on these, with their masculine figure of the Servant, to speak of himself and of those whom he called as disciples,[2] and Paul used them to speak of his ministry and the churches' ministry.[3] For Christians, they are among the most familiar parts of the Old Testament.

Part of this paper's purpose is to foster an awareness of factors such as historical tradition and situation, which (often unconsciously) govern our reading and practice of Scripture. I well remember a moment of heightened awareness when I encountered John Sawyer's article about poetry involving

---

1   The "Servant Songs" are generally considered to be Isaiah 42:1–4(or 9); 49:1–6 (or 12, or 13); 50:4–9 (or 10, or 11), and 52:13–53:12.
2   Blocher, *Songs*, 14–18.
3   Ibid. 11–14, also Stuhlmacher, "Gospels and Acts," Hofius, "NT Letters."

a *female* figure in Isaiah 40–55.[4] Sawyer calls this poetry the "Zion Songs,"[5] and explores their relation to the more famous Servant Songs, with which they are interwoven. He asks: "Is it possible that that same male, Christian bias that had for a century preoccupied readers and commentators with the identity and role of the man in the 'Servant Songs', had prevented us from taking seriously the woman in the 'Zion Songs'?"[6] One, he observes, has been "studied almost to the point of idolatry by Christian exegetes, while the other" is "almost totally ignored." In encountering this neglect of Isaiah's Zion poetry, I had encountered the effect on my reading of something called "nominative determinism"; literally, "name-driven outcome."

Nominative determinism is usually applied to the idea that someone's name may influence their future. Would Usain Bolt have run as swiftly with the name "Usain Plod"?[7] In the case of the Servant Songs—the name given to a series of poems "identified" within the text of Isaiah by Bernhard Duhm in his 1892 commentary—this naming has strongly influenced their interpretation future.[8] Both their naming and the intensive scholarship addressing them are relatively recent phenomena, but although their existence is widely considered to have been refuted by Mettinger in his oft-cited (but more rarely quoted) 1983 essay, "A Farewell to the Servant Songs," the name "Servant Songs" still influences readings of Isaiah today.

The Christian significance of the Servant poetry surely began with Jesus himself,[9] and has persisted because it enables Christians to understand the person of Jesus as fulfilling the mission of Israel to the earth.[10] A better understanding of the feminine Zion Songs, and the nature of their relation to the masculine Servant Songs, will undoubtedly enhance this understanding.

---

4   Sawyer, "Daughter and Servant."

5   These should not be confused with the psalms called "Songs of Zion," Psalms 46, 48, and 76 (von Rad, *OT Theology 2*, 157).

6   Sawyer, "Daughter and Servant," 233. See also Quinn-Miscall, *Reading Isaiah*, 195.

7   Alter, *Drunk Tank Pink*, 10. For a broader use of "nominative determinism" (as here), see Harrison, *Incessant Theology*, 98, and McKean, *Hundred Dresses*, 53.

8   Duhm, *Jesaia*. Mettinger, *Farewell*, 9–15.

9   Stuhlmacher, "Gospels and Acts," 149.

10   As argued by Wright, "Jesus, Israel, Cross," and elsewhere.

To this end, I will survey some of the literature dealing with the Servant and Zion, consider grammatical issues, and finally, investigate the poetry itself.[11]

The Literature

Sawyer is not the only writer concerned with Zion's significance in Isaiah 40–66, though he was one of the first to explore it in relation to gender and the Servant. In 1965, von Rad had suggested that the two focal interests of the prophet Isaiah are the election traditions of Zion and of David.[12] Engaging the tradition of the inviolability of Zion as well as the need for a faithful response to Yahweh,[13] von Rad argued that Yahweh's plans within history were plans "for the deliverance of Zion," in which Israel would be implicated.[14] While von Rad did not address the feminine image of Zion,[15] he argued that the Zion and David traditions underlie and inform the poetry of Isaiah.

Dumbrell's 1985 essay on the purpose of Isaiah argues that the "*overmastering* theme which may be said effectively to unite the whole . . . is the theme of Yahweh's . . . devotion to the city of Jerusalem."[16] Linking the salvation of Zion and the salvation of Israel (as von Rad does), Dumbrell concludes: "Jerusalem becomes a major biblical symbol uniting city and saved community, *combining sacred space and sanctified people*. Isaiah makes it clear that there can be no thought of a restored Israel without the *prior restoration* of Zion."[17]

Explicitly building on Dumbrell's work, Webb's essay, "Zion in Transformation," describes the "theological cohesion" provided by Isaiah's "sustained focus on Jerusalem/Zion." Isaiah moves "from the historical

---

11   Zion and Jerusalem are more or less interchangeable in Isaiah, though "Zion" perhaps more often evokes the eschatological city.

12   von Rad, *OT Theology 2*, 165–66, 169.

13   Ibid. 156–60.

14   Ibid. 162.

15   Schmitt, "City as Woman," 95–96.

16   Dumbrell, "Purpose of Isaiah," 112, Dumbrell's emphasis.

17   Ibid. 128, my emphasis.

Jerusalem of the eighth century, which is under judgement, to the new Jerusalem of the eschaton . . . symbol of the new age." Focus on Zion is apparent in the "structurally pivotal" chapters 36–39, with their "fine interplay . . . between the certainty of Yahweh's commitment to Zion on the one hand . . . and the very real consequences of human faith . . . or faithlessness . . . [one might say servanthood or rebellion] on the other."[18]

Seitz's 1991 book, *Zion's Final Destiny*, inquires into Isaiah's "pivotal" chapters, 36–39,[19] tracing the connection between the sickness and deliverance of the king (Hezekiah, the Davidic servant), and the sickness and deliverance of the city (Zion).[20] Seitz concludes with a proposal that despite "the masculine language of the songs," Zion *is* the Servant, and that the final Servant poem may been composed for Zion "on analogy" with King Hezekiah's psalm, written after his deliverance from sickness and death (38:10–20).[21] The Servant as a personification of Zion had earlier been suggested by Wilshire in his essay, "Servant City,"[22] and developed by Korpel in "The Female Servant of the Lord," who finally draws back from "full identification" of the Servant with Zion.[23]

The Grammar of Gender

Unlike English, Hebrew is a gendered language. Most Hebrew verb-forms are gendered, keeping gender continually before the Hebrew reader.[24] The names of people-groups are grammatically masculine, after the name of the man who "fathers" them; thus the people Israel is grammatically masculine.[25] For example, in Exodus 4:22, Pharaoh must release God's "first born son," or God will slay Pharaoh's first born son.[26]

---

18   Webb, "Transformation," 71.

19   Seitz, *Final Destiny*, 208. Seitz does not engage with either Webb's or Dumbrell's essays.

20   Ibid., 171.

21   Ibid., 203–5.

22   Wilshire, "Servant City," 367.

23   Korpel, "Female Servant," 161, 66–67. Brenner, "Identifying the Speaker," 148 also suggests this. See also Low, *Mother Zion*, 155, Maier, *Daughter Zion*.

24   Schmitt, "Two Gendered Images," 19.

25   Ibid.

26   "Ancient Israel," 117.

Not only is Israel consistently masculine in the Old Testament, but the images used for Israel are—possibly without exception—masculine.[27] This is in contrast to English, where people-groups, including Israel, are often referred to with the pronoun "she," which has caused some confusion in biblical studies.[28] Schmitt demonstrates that even the images of unfaithfulness to God, repeatedly misunderstood as feminine images (often using the Hebrew verb *zônāh*[29]) are masculine. While "Israel" in the Old Testament may take either a masculine singular or masculine plural verb, and use either the pronoun "he" or "they" without any particular significance being attached,[30] Israel is "consistently masculine."[31] Isaiah opens with a lament over Yahweh's rebellious sons, Israel.[32] Yahweh is Israel's parent (notably, Isaiah pictures Yahweh as both father and mother[33]), and Israel is Yahweh's male child, or children.

On the other hand, names of cities are always feminine, along with land, earth, and countries.[34] "Zion" and "Jerusalem" are feminine throughout Isaiah. One of the ways of navigating as a reader through the complex poetry of Isaiah 48–54, where Zion poetry and Servant poetry intermingles, is by awareness of the gender of the verbs, and thus of their subject. Zion is always grammatically feminine. Going beyond this, the poet sometimes develops Zion's gender to personify her as a woman in varied roles.[35]

---

27   So claims Schmitt, "Two Gendered Images," 19. Schmitt explains Hosea's "wife" imagery in "Ancient Israel," 119–21, and "Wife," 5–16.
       Feminine images often taken for Israel's (e.g. in Brenner, "Identifying the Speaker," 137) are in fact Zion's, or Jerusalem's (e.g. Isaiah 1:25, 30).

28   Schmitt, "Ancient Israel," 115–16, "Two Gendered Images," 31.

29   Koehler and Baumgartner, "HALOT," 1:275: "to *be unfaithful* in a relationship with God." In Deuteronomy 31:16, the verb-form is *qal* perfect, 3rd masculine singular, but often translated as 'play the harlot' (NAS), 'prostitute themselves' (NET, NIV, NRSV), suggesting a feminine subject.

30   See details in Schmitt, "Two Gendered Images," 19.

31   Ibid. Schmitt remarks that only twice in 2,507 occurrences does "Israel" take a feminine singular verb (1 Sam 17:21 and 2 Sam 24:9), which exceptions he considers to be mistakes. *Pace* Brenner, "Identifying the Speaker," 147, 48: "'Israel' is the wife / mother . . ."

32   *Pace* Maier, *Daughter Zion*, 99, who describes Isaiah's opening "woe-cry over the city."

33   Maternal images of God in 42:14, 45:10, 49:15, 66:13.

34   Isa 3:8a: "For Jerusalem (f) has stumbled, / and Judah (m) has fallen."

35   Schmitt, "City as Woman," 97.

One conclusion from this grammatical enquiry is that when a city is used in Scripture to represent her inhabitants,[36] both male and female people may be included in the grammatically feminine noun.[37] Conversely, when the figure of the Servant is used to represent Yahweh's servants, both male and female people may be included in the grammatically masculine noun.[38]

It is important to remember that in the ANE and so in the related Old Testament literature, the city is thought of as the wife of the principle god.[39] So culturally, Zion has a spousal-type relation to Yahweh, and Zion's true sons are "sons of Yahweh," demonstrating this by obedience to Yahweh (54:5–8, 13). In contrast, Israel by *dis*obedience showed themselves to be sons who "do not know" (1:3). What is not known is unspecified, but is clearly basic to Israel's self-understanding and wellbeing, and seems to be the loss of wisdom to live well in the world that comes from knowing Yahweh.[40]

Feminine Experience in Isaiah

It has occasionally been suggested that the author of Isaiah 40–55 might have been a woman.[41] Reasons tendered include the poet's distinctive use of feminine metaphors for God,[42] and the portrayal of the community's experience in terms of a woman's experience: of being a bride, "a wife and a mother, of rape, divorce and widowhood" (49:14, 18, 20–23; 50:1, 54:6), and of the community's restoration in those same terms: as reconciliation with her husband, "surrounded by children . . . enjoying a woman's finery" (54:1–12).[43] Only in Isaiah 40–55 are both sons *and* daughters addressed by God (43:6;

---

36   Isa 48:2. "Two Gendered Images," 29, footnote 39, also Goldingay, "Theology of Isaiah," 176.

37   *Pace* Brenner, "Identifying the Speaker," 137, who considers Isaiah 1–4 to be offensive to women.

38   See "corporate personality" in Korpel, "Female Servant," 166; also Beuken, "Isaiah LIV," and North, *Suffering Servant*, 103–10.

39   Dobbs-Allsopp, "Syntagma of *Bat*"; Sloane, "Aberrant Textuality?" 67, Walton, *ANE Thought and the OT*, 276–78.

40   Childs, *Isaiah*, 17.

41   Isbell, "Limmûdîm," 108, fn 25, Stone, "Prophet to Patriarchy," and Goldingay and Payne, *Isaiah 40–55, vol 1*, 47–48. Brenner, "Identifying the Speaker," 147–49 proposes as a solution to "the problem of literary structure" in 50:1–11that "a [metaphorical] *female* speaking voice" is recognised in the third Servant Song. She neither mentions nor explains the pulling-out of the speaker's beard in 50:6.

42   42:14; 45:10; 46:3; 49:15 (cf. 66:13).

43   Goldingay and Payne, *Isaiah 40–55, vol 1*, 48.

49:22–23 [56:5]),[44] and apart from the book of Genesis, Sarah is mentioned only in Isaiah (51:2).[45]

While this conjecture about Isaiah's authorship must remain unresolved, it seems likely that Isaian reflection about the relation of Zion to her inhabitants, and to Yahweh, and about the relation of these to the earth, has heightened the poet's awareness of feminine experience and its significance for the future of the earth.[46]

Zion and the Servant

Zion emerges early in Isaiah as "daughter Zion." Isaiah opens with Yahweh's lament over his sons' rebellion (1:2–4), which affects land and cities, "devastated" and "burned" because of it (1:7, 8). "Daughter Zion" is pictured as "left behind" [*yātar*],[47]

like a hut in a vineyard,

like a shelter in a field of cucumbers . . .

It becomes apparent that those whom the poetry addresses as "you," i.e., the "nation who sins, people heavy with iniquity," over whom "woe" is pronounced in 1:4, are the *cause* of Zion's distress. Verse 9 affirms this with its reference to the "small remnant" that Yahweh has left behind [*yātar*], already signalling the idea of the faithful remnant that persists throughout Isaiah, and which the figure of the faithful Servant takes up in chapters 40–55.[48] Zion is pictured as suffering because she is acted upon. Zion is the *place* where the sons' rebellions are enacted. What is done in her desecrates her.[49] A kind of "balancing" passage in 3:16—4:1 pictures the rebellious and desecrated "daughters of Zion." 1:21 bewails the city's condition:

---

44   Ibid., Korpel, "Female Servant," 165 (though cf. Jer 48:46).

45   Goldingay and Payne, *Isaiah 40–55, vol 1*, 48.

46   See also Schmitt, "Motherhood," 560–61.

47   Koehler and Baumgartner, "HALOT," 2:452: nip'al, "to be l=eft over . . . survived."

48   Childs, *Isaiah*, 19 discusses this hint of "remnant theology."

49   Thomas, "Zion," 909.

How has she become a harlot [zônāh]?

The faithful city!

Full of justice,

righteousness lodged in her,

but now murderers . . .

The word for "harlot" in the first line, zônāh, plays upon "Zion." The name of the once-faithful city may not be *mentioned* in connection with the horror of the deeds done in her, but the sound-play subtly implicates her.

Fullness with what is good or what is not good is another emerging Isaian theme.[50] Fullness that glorifies Yahweh is the earth's destiny, crystallised in the seraphim's words in 6:3: "the fullness of the whole earth is [Yahweh's] glory" (cf. 11:9). Zion's "fullness" in 1:21 is clearly *not* the justice and righteousness that Yahweh plans to be done in her,[51] and indeed which must be done, in order for Zion to be Yahweh's dwelling-place.

As well as the dwelling-place of Yahweh's people, Zion is *Yahweh's* dwelling-place, "the mountain of Yahweh's house" (2:2),[52] so the deeds done in Zion must be consistent with Yahweh's character. Right from the beginning, Isaiah evokes Zion's destiny with a series of significant verbs (2:2–3): Zion is to be *established* as Yahweh's dwelling-place,[53] *raised up* above the hills,[54] where justice and righteousness is *done*,[55] from which torah and Yahweh's word *go out*,[56] to which all the nations stream.[57] The *deeds* of Zion's inhabitants are key to Zion's restoration.

---

50   See wordplay on "full" in 2:6, 7, 8.

51   See 1:17, 1:27, 3:13–14; 5:7, 16; 26:8, 9; 28:16–17 etc.

52   See also 8:18, 12:6, 18:7, 24:23, 33:5.

53   *kûn.*

54   *nāśā'.*

55   *hālak.*

56   *yāṣā'.*

57   Cf. 65:17–25; 66:10–13, 22–23.

This dependence of Zion on Israel—sons *and* daughters—for her wellbeing is part of a major theme in Isaiah linking the actions of Yahweh's people to the earth's wellbeing. This is particularly clear in chapters 40–55, where the earth's rejoicing consistently follows human obedience to Yahweh,[58] and where, after the Servant's self-offering in the final Servant Song, rejoicing breaks out and is sustained until the end of the section in chapter 55.

Just as Zion is *desecrated* by deeds done in her in Isaiah 1:1—2:3, so Zion may be *redeemed* by deeds done in her (1:27). Isaiah 40–55 develops this idea through the figure of the Servant in the Servant Songs. Named for his utter obedience to and dependence on Yahweh, the Servant's deeds align with Yahweh's character *by* his obedience: they are exactly the kind of righteous deeds needed for the redemption of Zion. We hear of the Servant's deeds of justice and righteousness in the first Servant Song (42:1–7). In the second Song the Servant realises the implications of his obedience for his people Israel and for the earth (49:5–6); in the third Song he models obedience in persecution and darkness (50:4–11); and in the fourth Song he exchanges his righteous obedience for the disobedience of Israel (53:2b–6), in order to produce righteous offspring who will also do the deeds the Servant does (53:10). Thus Zion may again be "full of justice and righteousness," a fitting dwelling-place for Yahweh.

Parallel Stories

The parallels between the Servant and Zion in Isaiah 49–54 are often noted.[59] Both are pictured firstly as barren (53:8/54:1), then with offspring (53:10/54:1b–3). Both are often unnamed.[60] Both are notable for their suffering, and both are finally vindicated. The stories of both unfold in instalments, but are recognisable as continuing characters in a larger narrative.[61] Both have

---

58   Israel's obedience, or the Servant's, or even the pagan emperor Cyrus's; 42:10–12, 44:23, 45:8, 49:13.

59   Jeppesen, "Mother Zion, Father Servant"; Korpel, "Female Servant," 163–65, Sawyer, "Daughter and Servant," 243–45, Willey, *Former Things*, 222–26.

60   Miscall, *Isaiah*, 125.

61   Sawyer, "Daughter and Servant," 243.

implications for the nations (52:15/54:3).[62] Brenner notes further important parallels between a servant and a wife: both are contractual, subordinate, dependent legally and economically (and so vulnerable), and their position may be terminated by their lord or husband.[63] Although Brenner finds this offensive for women, it may instead illustrate essential *human* dependence on God: masculine servant and feminine wife.[64] Indeed, "lord" and "husband" are the same word in Hebrew [bā'al].

Zion and the Servant are paralleled, entwined, compared, contrasted, but not identified. Indeed, in view of their interdependent significance throughout Isaiah (sketched above), it is essential to keep them separate. We have seen that Yahweh's dwelling-place is dependent on her *human* inhabitants for the nature of the deeds done in her. Isaiah 51:17 and 52:1–2 depict Zion/Jerusalem as helpless to answer the prophet's exhortations to "rouse up" and to "rise up"; to shake off her chains, and to put on "garments of glory." Her sons, drunk and faint, cannot help (51:17, 20), but as the poetry urges response, *the Servant* (instead) answers Yahweh *by his obedience* in the fourth Servant Song. The results are immediate for the formerly barren woman, who becomes a city filled with children taught by Yahweh; clearly (given the context) Zion, in chapter 54.

When Isaiah finally brings Zion and the Servant together at the end of this chapter (54:17),[65] the "heritage of the servants of Yahweh" *is* the restoration of the woman-city. The servants' righteous deeds, enabled by the faithful Servant's obedience,[66] will restore the city. This is Dumbrell's "sacred space *and* sanctified people," but the sanctified people—the servant(s)— *sanctify the space* by their righteousness, fitting it as Yahweh's dwelling-place again.

---

62   Ibid. 244.
63   Brenner, "Identifying the Speaker," 146.
64   Ibid.
65   For Korpel, "Female Servant," 161, 54:17b *identifies* Zion with "the famous servant of YHWH."
66   This faithful individual may be aligned with the "small remnant" of 1:9.

This demonstrates a further parallel between the Servant and Zion. Just as the Servant, through his obedience to Yahweh, does the deeds of Yahweh (justice and righteousness), and so is sanctified and restored as Yahweh's true son, so the city, through the deeds done in her by the Servant (justice and righteousness), is sanctified and restored as Yahweh's true dwelling-place. All this is brought about by the obedience and self-giving of Yahweh's Servant.

Isaiah offers this story of the Servant, Zion, and Yahweh as a pattern for the earth. As we have seen, the Servant is instrumental in Zion's story, both doing and enabling others to do the righteous deeds by which Zion will be redeemed. But this is part of a much larger story, suggested at the beginning of Isaiah, when the prophet calls "heavens and earth" to hear Yahweh "speak," signalling that the impending word will continue the story of creation begun in Genesis 1.[67] Yahweh's sons' rebellion that led to Zion's desecration in Isaiah is told against the background of the first humans' rebellion that led to the earth's desecration, and to their exile from their dwelling-place with Yahweh (Gen 3:1–22).[68] The redemption of Zion by the deeds of a righteous Servant is told against the prophetically-seen future of the whole earth as Yahweh's dwelling-place (66:1), filled with the glory of Yahweh, when all are servants of Yahweh.[69]

Conclusions

The Servant Songs and the Zion Songs in Isaiah 40–55 are indispensable to one another, and indispensable for understanding Yahweh's work *through* humanity *in* the world. While the significance of Zion's feminine gender within Isaiah has been more fully realised in recent research, there is much to be learned about the interplay of masculine and feminine language and images, and their significance for meaning in Isaiah's complex poetry.

---

67   See the creation of Zion, set in the new heavens and the new earth in 65:17–18, full of good things (19–25). Miscall, "New Heavens," 47–53.

68   Walton, *Lost World*, 84–85 proposes that Genesis pictures the cosmos as a temple where God may dwell with humanity.

69   Except for the final provision for refusal, 66:24. Cf. Psalm 29.

i) Becoming Aware

Isaiah's poetry is always about more than geographical Zion and national Israel. It is about *the whole earth* (feminine) as the place of Yahweh's glory, and *all peoples* (masculine) as enactors of Yahweh's justice and righteousness. In Isaiah, Zion is desolate, and beyond Zion, the earth is estranged from Yahweh. Only the faithful Servant, and Israel restored as Yahweh's servants, may fill the city with justice and righteousness, fitting it for Yahweh. Beyond the city, only Yahweh's servants may, by justice and righteousness, fit the whole earth for Yahweh's dwelling, and for the "fullness" of Yahweh's glory (6:3). This "way back" to Yahweh for Yahweh's rebellious sons (resolving Isaiah's opening dissonance) is given in the pattern of sanctified humanity enacted in the Servant Songs.

Equally, "righteousness" is inseparable from acts of righteousness,[70] and Zion, redeemed by the righteous acts of the Servant(s), is the place to which all nations will come to learn Yahweh's ways (2:2–4), i.e., to become servants of Yahweh, and so to enact Yahweh's deeds to fill the earth with Yahweh's glory. Zion is the pattern of sacred space for the earth.

For native speakers of an ungendered language, it is important to keep the gendered nature of the Hebrew text in mind, along with cultural differences between perceptions of gender in different eras. Isaiah is a text about blindness and seeing again, and not only *again*, but *differently*; seeing the heavens and the earth as Yahweh intends them, "the fullness of Yahweh's glory" (6:3). Recovering these aspects of the text will open our eyes and ears to hear it newly, going beyond our unconscious, gender-determined learning difficulties.

ii) Becoming for the Other

As mentioned, the images of both the masculine Servant and the feminine Zion include both males and females. Unlike being female and being male, "[t]he feminine and the masculine are not the exclusive property

---

70   Goldingay, "Justice and Salvation," 174–75 notes that *mišpāṭ ûṣĕdāqâ* ['justice and righteousness'] are not abstract nouns in Hebrew as they are in English.

of women and men—they are modes of being-in-the-world that each may participate in."[71] As such, women and men who fail to understand and participate in the mode of being which is other than their physical gender, are to that extent less able to see, and so less able to fully enact Yahweh's justice and righteousness.

Additionally, in the interplay of person and place that the Servant and Zion demonstrate, *each is for the other*. Humankind are called as servants of Yahweh, doing deeds that sanctify and restore their cities and the earth for Yahweh's dwelling. Equally, humankind are to be *recipients of* and *sanctified by* the righteous deeds of others; ourselves, our habitations, and our communities made fit for Yahweh's dwelling by righteousness that is not our own. Seeing ourselves like Zion-Jerusalem in Isaiah, incapacitated by rebellion, our own sons "lying senseless" (51:17–20), we know ourselves in need of the Servant's (and the servants') righteousness.

iii) Becoming Open

Isaiah's texts are characteristically open, seeking fulfilment in their audience's response.[72] They work to raise up servants, to bring dulled sensory perceptions alive to the future glory of the earth and her inhabitants under Yahweh's lordship: they are rhetorical and persuasive texts whose work is not done until action is accomplished in their audience.

Our response to the poetry of Isaiah will determine whether our eyes are opened, or not; whether we are raised up as servants, or not. Part of awakening to the fullness of sensory perception and servanthood is awakening to the significance of masculine and feminine gender and their interplay in Isaiah's poetry; to a kind of "gender communion" played out between the Servant and Zion. This opens our eyes to the significance of person *and* place for a nuanced understanding of our discipleship as enacted righteousness, and of obedience that is transformative for the earth.

---

71   Barnes, "Masculine and Feminine Time." See also Quinn-Miscall, *Reading Isaiah*, 195–96, "they present patterns for God's ways with the world." Sloane, "Gender, Biology, Identity," discusses difficulties of binary categories, and the cultural shaping of gender.

72   Woude, "Zion, Servant," 115.

Response: Edwina Murphy

Caroline makes a good point about the way things are named affecting how we perceive them. The Servant Songs thereby exist in a way that Songs of Zion do not—or at least, did not, until she revealed them to us, with help from Sawyer. Her work sparked my curiosity and sent me back to some long-neglected Hebrew and to Schmitt's article, "The Gender of Ancient Israel." Schmitt reminds us of the care that needs to be taken in reading the Bible. Israel is indeed masculine and his unfaithfulness should not be imposed onto negative stereotypes of women. But the feminine in relation to God is not absent. Even if the city Jerusalem is the referent in Hosea 2, the adulterous wife—who in future "shall respond as in the days of her youth, as at the time when she came out of the land of Egypt," (Hos 2:15, NRSV)—parallels the male child, Israel: "Out of Egypt I called my son." (Hos 11:1, NRSV) The feminine city Zion can stand for or represent the masculine Israel as a whole.

This opens up the intriguing interplay between Zion and the Servant, an image fulfilled in Rev 21:2 (NRSV): "And I saw the holy city, the new Jerusalem, coming down out of heaven from God, prepared as a bride adorned for her husband," the Lamb. In Rev 19:8, the bride wears fine linen, the righteous deeds of the saints—the sanctification of Zion is realised. Back on more familiar ground, I find the imaginative potential of these gendered texts exploited by Cyprian. He uses the above verses, among others, to demonstrate that, "He (Christ) is the bridegroom with his bride the church from which spiritual children would be born."[73] In light of this metaphor, Cyprian's famous dictum makes sense: "You cannot have God for your father unless you have the Church for your mother."[74]

Furthermore, Cyprian often uses women of the Old Testament as types of the church (men are typically types of Christ). To support the testimony, "That the Church which had been barren would have more children from among the Gentiles than the synagogue had before,"[75] he cites Isa 54:1–4 before illustrating with Sarah and the slave woman (Hagar), Rachel and Leah, and Hannah and Peninnah. In this elaboration of Gal 4:21–31, the first of the pair is the church; the second, the synagogue. Hannah, the mother of Samuel, is also a type of the church in that she models the prayer which should characterise it.[76] Rahab is as well—only the family members brought within the one house are saved.[77] However, neither Eve nor Mary is used as a type.

Just as Caroline has shown in the case of Isaiah's gendered language, Cyprian's use of gendered typology does not restrict participation in these modes of being to one gender or the other. The church includes both men and women; both women and men are called to imitate Christ. In Isaiah's vision, righteousness is both received from the Servant and enacted by his servants. As Cyprian says, "New-created and newborn of the Spirit by the mercy of God, let us imitate what we shall one day be."[78]

---

73   Cyprian, *Testimonies*, 2.19. *Translations from this work are my own.*

74   Cyprian, *The Unity of the Catholic Church*, 6.

75   Cyprian, *Testimonies*, 1.20.

76   Cyprian, *On the Lord's Prayer*, 5.

77   Cyprian, *The Unity of the Catholic Church*, 8; *Epistle* 69.4.

78   Cyprian, *On the Lord's Prayer*, 36.

Response: Nicole Starling

Caroline's paper provides an illuminating diagnosis of the Zion-blindness that has characterised much modern scholarship on Isaiah, and some powerfully suggestive ideas for how it might be remedied.

As I reflected on her paper from a church historian's vantage point, it occurred to me that the church has not always been as Zion-blind as the modern Isaiah scholarship that Caroline describes in her paper. From the very earliest days, Christian readers of Isaiah have seen in Isaiah's Zion-songs a figure who is to be understand allegorically as "our mother."

Paul the apostle famously draws this conclusion in Galatians 4. Paul's image of Zion as the mother of believers (and Sarah before her as a figure of the covenant that believers belong to) is preceded within the same chapter by his depiction of the church as a child in the process of being born and himself as "again in the pain of childbirth until Christ is formed in you" (Gal. 4:19).[79] Here, it seems, is an apostolic example of a reader of Isaiah who is "aware," "open," and "for the other."

---

79   See especially the discussion of Paul's use of mother-imagery in Susan Grove Eastman, *Recovering Paul's Mother Tongue*, 89–160.

In subsequent centuries, too, Christian readers from Cyprian to Calvin found in Isaiah's Zion language and imagery the inspiration for their claim that a person who wants to have God for their father needs to have the church for their mother. Calvin, for example, writes:

> But because it is now our intention to discuss the visible church, let us learn even from the simple title "mother" how useful, indeed how necessary, it is that we should know her. For there is no other way to enter into life unless this mother conceive us in her womb, give us birth, nourish us at her breast, and lastly, unless she keep us under her care and guidance until, putting off mortal flesh, we become like the angels.[80]

In the early evangelical hymns of the eighteenth and nineteenth centuries, too, believers were still depicted typologically as "Zion's children."

This longstanding tradition, inspired by the language and imagery of Isaiah, is an important corrective to the individualism that is so widely prevalent in more recent evangelical piety, and the one-dimensional missional emphases of some contemporary ecclesiologies. There is something profoundly important in the biblical and traditional image of the church as Mother Zion—a nurturing community for men and women who need formation, care and sustenance, not just an army that needs to be recruited and mobilised for mission, or a loose aggregation of individuals each pursuing a private spiritual relationship with their own personal Jesus. Caroline's paper is a beautiful and powerful reminder of this.

---

80   *Institutes* IV.1.4. Cf. Cyprian: "You cannot have God for your father unless you have the Church for your mother" (*The Unity of the Catholic Church*, 6).

Martyrdom, Gender, and Authority: Female Martyrs as Representatives of Christ

Edwina Murphy

All Christians are identified with Christ in baptism and, as Cyprian wrote, "We who desire to be Christians ought to imitate what Christ said and did."[81] There were, however, two groups in the early church which were understood to represent Christ in a special way: bishops and martyrs. As Ferguson states, "Martyrdom was an imitation of Christ, in which one shared in the sufferings of Christ and was brought into direct contact with the Lord, and the glory of Christ himself was manifested in the martyr."[82] Those who confessed but did not actually die also shared in this identification, Cyprian affirming that "Among the confessors of Christ the fact that their martyrdom has been deferred does not detract from the merits of their confession; rather, it serves to make manifest the marvellous works of our divine Protector."[83] For practical purposes, however, martyrs were honoured

---

81   Cyprian, *On the Dress of Virgins*, 7.
82   Ferguson, "Early Christian Martyrdom," 75.
83   Cyprian, *Ep.* 61.2.

in the liturgy, but their ongoing role in the life of the church was controlled by others; confessors awaiting martyrdom, or those who lived to fight another day, could themselves play an active part. I want to consider the way women martyrs were understood to be imitating Christ, the authority they were perceived to have, and how this authority was integrated with the emerging church order. I will explore these questions with reference to two prominent martyrs, Blandina and Perpetua, before drawing some conclusions on how gender and authority were negotiated in the early church.

Blandina

The martyrs who suffered in Lyons in 177AD were praised as being eager to imitate Christ, the "true and faithful witness," not only in his suffering, but also in his humility.[84] Vettius Epagathus was identified as "a true disciple of Christ, following the Lamb wherever he goes."[85] Of the torture of Sanctus it was written: "But Christ suffering in him achieved great glory, overwhelming the Adversary."[86] The most vivid account of a martyr identified with Christ in this account, however, is that of the slave Blandina. In the first round of the battle:

> She seemed to hang there in the form of a cross, and by her fervent prayer she aroused intense enthusiasm in those who were undergoing their ordeal, for in their torment with their physical eyes they saw in the person of their sister him who was crucified for them .. . tiny, weak, and insignificant as she was she would give inspiration to her brothers, for she had put on Christ, that mighty and invincible athlete, and had overcome the Adversary in many contests, and through her conflict had won the crown of immortality.[87]

---

84   *Martyrs of Lyons*, 2.2–5. The source of the work known as *The Martyrs of Lyons* is Eusebius, *Historia Ecclesia*, 5.1.3—5.2.8.

85   *Martyrs of Lyons*, 1.10.

86   Ibid., 1.23.

87   Ibid.,1.41–42.

Blandina's identification with Christ is closely linked to her effective prayer for her fellow martyrs. This intercessory power is also evident elsewhere in the *Martyrs of Lyons*. Those who had confessed and were awaiting execution are depicted as midwives in the rebirthing process of those Christians who had denied the faith, restoring them to the church by their prayers.[88] As intermediaries, they loosed all, but bound none.[89] Whilst prayer for those involved in transgression had always been encouraged,[90] in the *Martyrs of Lyons*, a developing role for martyrs in the economy of salvation is apparent. By interceding before the Father for those who were lost, and being the channel through which they were restored, they are in depicted a priestly role. Furthermore, great significance is attributed to the final testimony of martyrs. Christ had promised that the Holy Spirit would give them the words to speak when they were called to witness.[91] The church therefore carefully recorded them as utterances of the Holy Spirit.

How was this authority of the martyrs, stemming from their imitation of Christ, to be harmonised with that of the bishops and clergy? It appears that for Irenaeus, there is no conflict—both are a natural and integral part of the whole. The correct transmission of the doctrine of the apostles through the succession of the bishops sits comfortably with the declaration that the true church sends forward "a multitude of martyrs."[92] Conflicts were bound to come, however, as the church grew as an institution, and a natural way in which to synthesise these realms of authority would be to bring confessors into the official structure of the church. The well-known *Apostolic Tradition*, traditionally attributed to Hippolytus,[93] provides for this:

---

88   Ibid.,1.45–46.

89   Ibid.,2.5 [cf. Matt 16:19].

90   See, for example, *1 Clement* 56.1.

91   Acts 1:14.

92   Irenaeus, *Against Heresies*, 4.33.8–9. Frend is not so comfortable with Irenaeus' lack of explanation of how these different kinds of authority are to be harmonised. Frend, *Early Church*, 70, 349.

93   For discussion, see Stewart-Sykes, "Introduction," 11–50. Bradshaw, Johnson, and Phillips, *Apostolic Tradition*, 1–17.

Now if a confessor is in chains for the sake of the name of the Lord, a hand is not laid on him for the diaconate or for presbyterate. For he has the honor (τιμή) of the presbyterate on account of his confession. If he is to be installed as bishop, then is the hand to be laid upon him.[94]

The ordination prayer for presbyters preceding this statement indicates that the gifts required for such a position are the "Spirit of grace and counsel of presbyterate so that he might assist and guide [the] people with a pure heart."[95] As Hardy notes, since the saints (martyrs) reign with Christ, who "can more naturally occupy this position than those who have had the grace to confess Christ to the end, and only by accident as it were are still alive on earth?"[96]

But what of women confessors? Hall considers this situation in his discussion of Blandina.

Suppose she had survived and turned up in Hippolytus' congregation in Rome as a confessor, would she have been seated with the presbyters? Presumably not, since the sexes were normally sharply separated. She could be given the same portion of the offerings, the same τιμή. She might have sat with the official Widows. Clearly the charisma she is endowed with does not match the rising codes of ecclesial order, of which Hippolytus' is the best early example.[97]

---

94   Hippolytus, *Apostolic Tradition*, 9(10).1.

95   Hippolytus, *Apostolic Tradition*, 7(8).2. For more detail on presbyters and government, see Dix, *Jurisdiction in the Early Church*, 26–27.

96   Hardy, "Decline and Fall," 221.

97   Hall, "Women among the Early Martyrs," 15. *The Shepherd of Hermas* provides an early example of a woman, Grapte, carrying out a teaching ministry to widows and orphans. *Shepherd of Hermas*, 8.3. For more on the role of widows in the early church, see Thurston, *Widows*. Osiek, "Widow as Altar," 159–69.

It is true that we have no explicit record in the catholic church of the ordination of female confessors. However, there was more to church life than the clerical hierarchy. In the Rome of that time, for example, most catechumens received their preparation for baptism in private lecture-rooms from teachers who were only sometimes clerics.[98] It is very unlikely that a female slave of little education would open such a school, but as a confessor she may well find others willing to support her and learn from her.

In fact, we may have a hint that Blandina exercised a prominent role in the Christian community in Lyons even prior to her confession. Despite the presence of Roman citizens, physicians, merchants, and her own mistress among the confessors, she "stands out in the role of a heroine from the start of the persecution."[99] Irenaeus quotes God's promise that "in the last times he would pour [the Spirit] upon [his] servants and handmaids, that they might prophesy,"[100] and it is possible that women such as Blandina exercised a leadership role, albeit without a clerical title.

Perpetua

The other work I want to consider is the *Martyrdom of Perpetua and Felicitas*, set in c.203AD, which includes the first writing we have by a Christian woman.[101] The importance of prophetic authority, Spirit-inspired visions, and a perceived hostility to the church hierarchy have led some scholars to conclude that the martyrdom is Montanist, its protagonists members of the New Prophecy. However, since "the Montanist aspect of the work seems to have escaped the notice of Augustine and many of the early Fathers"[102] it at

---

98   Dix, "Introduction," xxvii.

99   Frend, *Rise of Christianity*, 183. See also Lang, *Ministers of Grace*, 51.

100   Irenaeus, *Against Heresies*, 4.17.1.

101   I agree with Heffernan that the weight of evidence supports the conclusion that Perpetua and Saturus wrote the sections attributed to them, and that the work as a whole was edited early in the third century. Heffernan, *Passion of Perpetua*, 5.

102   Musurillo, "Introduction," xxvi.

least largely reflects catholic tradition.[103] In addition, as Trigg has shown, two martyr acts from the Valerian persecution, the *Martyrdom of Montanus* and the *Martyrdom of Marianus* demonstrate that the catholic church also had the characteristics of the church of the Spirit which is supposedly in view in the *Martyrdom of Perpetua and Felicitas.*[104]

The understanding that Christ suffered in the martyrs, evident in the *Martyrs of Lyons*, is further illustrated by Felicitas.[105] When provoked by the guard who, seeing her suffer in childbirth, doubted her ability to withstand the beasts of the arena, she replied, "What I am suffering now . . . I suffer by myself. But then another will be inside me who will suffer for me, just as I shall be suffering for him."[106] While, as Pettersen notes, her fellow-martyr Perpetua was not as strikingly identified with Christ as Blandina, she too became an "*alter Christus.*"[107] Thus, in Jensen's words, "the salvation event continued to be written dynamically in the witness of the martyrs and martyresses . . . both sexes identify with Jesus, who withstood Satan and thus trod on the snake's head."[108]

Directly linked to her impending martyrdom was Perpetua's intercessory power. As those imprisoned were praying together, the name Dinocrates came to her lips. She realised she "was privileged to pray for him," and that night she had a vision in which Dinocrates, her biological brother who had died of cancer when he was seven, was suffering.[109] However, she was "confident [she] could help him in his trouble" and prayed for him every day.[110] Later, she had another vision in which Dinocrates was clean, refreshed,

---

103   This is now the general consensus, although an attempt was made by Butler to defend the Montanism of the work. Even so, he believes that a schism from the catholics did not occur until the mid-third century. Butler, *New Prophecy*, 129. Markschies further suggests that what we can know about so-called "North African Montanism," as opposed to the groups in Asia Minor, is quite limited. Markschies, "*Passio*," 277–90.

104   Trigg, "Martyrs and Churchmen," 245–46.

105   On the question of whether Felicitas was a slave, see Poirier, "Note sur la *Passio*," 306–09.

106   *Martyrdom of Perpetua and Felicitas*, 15.

107   Pettersen, "Perpetua," 140.

108   Jensen, *God's Self-Confident Daughters*, 106–7.

109   *Martyrdom of Perpetua*, 7.

110   Ibid., 7–8.

and healed. When she awoke, she "realised that he had been delivered from his suffering."[111] Perpetua's prayer was believed to be extraordinarily effective, able to reach even the dead.

As in earlier periods, the words of martyrs, including those of women, were highly prized. Perpetua felt it proper to record the visions granted her by the Lord when she knew she was to suffer, and these were preserved by the church, becoming a text referred to in theological discussions of the afterlife.[112] Augustine's interpretation of Perpetua's vision shows how seriously it was treated in the life of the church—he even had to point out that the text was not canonical.[113]

In terms of the interaction between martyrs and members of the clergy in the *Martyrdom*, the first thing to note is that Pomponius the deacon is viewed positively. Most likely, he was present at their baptism as in Perpetua's vision he calls her to a baptism of blood.[114] It is, however, the part of Saturus's vision in which he and Perpetua come into contact with the bishop Optatus and Aspasius the presbyter and teacher that has gained the most attention. Optatus and Aspasius appear divided from one another, and throw themselves at the feet of Saturus and Perpetua, begging them to make peace between them. The martyrs are taken aback by this behaviour, but embrace them and Perpetua talks with them in Greek. The angels direct the bishop and presbyter to allow the martyrs to rest and settle their own quarrels, telling Optatus, "You must scold your flock. They approach you as though they had come from the games, quarrelling about the different teams."[115]

Frend takes this to mean that while bishops are in some sense the martyrs' superiors, they are in an auxiliary role to that of the martyrs—administrators tasked with disciplining the congregation to maintain its

---

111   Ibid., 7–8.

112   Augustine, *On the Soul and its Origin*, 1.12. For the reception and early interpretation of the *Martyrdom of Perpetua*, see Kitzler, *From Passio Perpetuae*, 56–116.

113   Amat, *Passion de Perpétue*, 81.

114   *Martyrdom of Perpetua*, 10. See Jensen, *God's Self-Confident Daughters*, 98.

115   *Martyrdom of Perpetua*, 13.

purity.[116] But this is not the case. Perpetua and Saturus, far from expecting the bishop and presbyter to humble themselves before them, are surprised by their display.[117] The angels command the clerics not to rely on the martyrs and remind the bishop of his responsibility to act as a shepherd and discipline his flock. He is shown to be in a pastoral role—since when is church discipline simply an administrative matter? Still, in Saturus's dream, "Perpetua—a woman—appears naturally as the mediator of reconciliation."[118]

What role would a woman such as Perpetua have possessed as an imitator of Christ if she had managed to survive the persecution? Much of the discussion has been confused by attempting to make distinctions between the role of women in the New Prophecy and their place in the catholic church. Klawiter believes that with regard to the relationship of persecution and martyrdom to Christian authority, both catholics and adherents of the New Prophecy "probably agreed that Christ communicates his priestly authority through wom[e]n."[119] He thought, however, that women who had confessed and survived in the New Prophecy retained their authority, indeed, that was the source of their authority, whereas women in the catholic church reverted to their subordinate role when released. However, the only confessors mentioned in connection with the leadership of the movement are male. Similarly, Hall believes Perpetua "could have taken the place of honour without difficulty . . . In a church where the judgement of bishops is subordinate to the prophecies of assembled prophets of either sex, we may suppose that, if Perpetua had survived, she might have been found a place of honour."[120]

The main problem in making such distinctions in light of the New Prophecy is that Tertullian, supposedly of the same North African circle, was outspoken against women in clerical positions.[121] As Osiek notes, his "esteem

---

116   Frend, *Donatist Church*, 117.

117   See also Trevett, *Montanism*, 189.

118   Jensen, *God's Self-Confident Daughters*, 119.

119   Klawiter, "Role of Martyrdom," 261.

120   Hall, "Women among the Early Martyrs," 20. Similarly, Steinhauser: "Female authority on a par with male authority is a characteristic of Montanism." Steinhauser, "Augustine's Reading," 244–45.

121   Tertullian, *On Prescription against Heretics*, 41.5; *On Baptism*, 17.

for prophecy kept him from denying to women that spiritual gift . . . [and he] in fact knew of female prophets and visionaries from his own experience but tried rather unconvincingly to distinguish the exercise of prophecy by women from their speaking for the sake of their own instruction or imparting it to others."[122] This means that, associated with the New Prophecy or not, Perpetua is in the same position as the clearly catholic Blandina. Both are depicted as leaders and both, if they had survived, would have found a "place of honour," but it remains difficult to see what that place would have been in the context of the clerical orders.

If we examine the issue from a different perspective, we find that Perpetua was part of a group of catechumens taught by Saturus, a man of no known clerical rank. While members of the clergy are very visible in this martyrdom, teachers still have a significant role, and it is likely that a woman such as Perpetua would have been able to take on such a position herself. In fact, as Heffernan says, "Her status as a figure of authority and power must have been well established in the community before her arrest. The highest-ranking members of the church, all male, recognise her elevated spiritual rank from the beginning."[123] This is surprising given that she was still only a catechumen at the beginning of the account. Her high social status and devotion may have marked her out, however, as it did Cyprian after her. It may be that in the cases of both Blandina and Perpetua, the privilege of martyrdom was the suitable crowning of their role in the Christian community. Just as Polycarp's martyrdom was a culmination of his holy life as "an apostolic and prophetic teacher in our own time, bishop of the holy church in Smyrna,"[124] so too their faithful Christian witness was fulfilled by "follow[ing] the footprints of the Lord's passion."[125]

But perhaps Blandina and Perpetua were only granted such authority at the expense of their identity as women? Perpetua's visions, particularly

---

122   Osiek, "Ministry," 62.

123   Heffernan, *Passion of Perpetua*, 43.

124   *Martyrdom of Polycarp*, 16.2.

125   Irenaeus, *Against Heresies*, 3.18.5.

their gender implications, have spawned a cottage industry of their own.[126] The one in which she reports her transformation into a man in order to battle the Egyptian has led some, like Witherington, to conclude that "her femaleness was seen as an obstacle to her becoming a true martyr."[127] Yet even in this episode, Perpetua is referred to as a woman and greeted after her victory as "daughter."[128] In fact, the *Martyrdom* overall is notable for the way it alternates culturally male behaviour (bravery, direct gaze, authority) with laudable feminine interests (concern for breast-feeding her child, modesty in hair and clothing).[129] The male designations could hardly be otherwise in a martyr, since courage and self-control were understood to be the province of men.[130] Yet throughout the account, Perpetua is evidently very comfortable with herself as a woman.

Blandina, too, whilst her body seems to be in the image of Christ, is still called a "sister" to Ponticus, the young man executed with her.[131] She is also presented as a mother to the group as a whole with an allusion to the Maccabean martyrs: "The blessed Blandina was last of all: like a noble mother encouraging her children, she sent them before her in triumph to the King, and then, after duplicating in her own body all her children's sufferings, she hastened to rejoin them."[132] As Cobb puts it, "the narratives both highlight the women's masculine fortitude and underscore their femininity."[133] She sees this as due to two competing rhetorical goals: masculinisation bolstered the claims of Christians against their opponents, whereas feminisation served the purpose of how women should act within the Christian community.[134] I accept her first point, and Augustine certainly provides evidence for the *Martyrdom of Perpetua and Felicitas* being interpreted as she suggests in

---

126   For example, Lefkowitz understands them to "reveal a concern with destroying threatening male figures." Lefkowitz, "Motivations," 419.

127   Witherington III, *Women in the Earliest Churches*, 198.

128   *Martyrdom of Perpetua*, 10.

129   For a literary analysis, see Williams, "Perpetua's Gender," 54–77.

130   In the interactions between Perpetua and her father, he is consistently portrayed as demasculinised. For discussion, see Cobb, *Dying To Be Men*, 97–102.

131   *Martyrs of Lyons*, 1.54.

132   Ibid.,1.55 See Moss, *Ancient Christian Martyrdom*, 112.

133   Cobb, *Dying to be Men*, 92.

134   Ibid., 121–22.

the second.[135] In the context of the work itself, however, I take Perpetua's feminine concerns to be quite natural—she is, and remains, a woman. Neither Blandina nor Perpetua have to relinquish their identities as women in order to be faithful disciples of Christ. They are not presented as male or androgenised figures, but as women who, in placing their allegiance to their Saviour above all else, are honoured for their imitation of him.

Blandina and Perpetua are portrayed as imitating Christ and therefore representing him. They are depicted in a priestly role, interceding for sinners, and as leaders, even of their fellow martyrs. In addition, Perpetua's visions were taken seriously in theological debates. If these women had survived, they may not have been incorporated into the clerical hierarchy as presbyters, as was often the case with male confessors. Given that teachers were still somewhat independent of the clergy at this time, and that teaching was aimed at forming disciples of Jesus, this may have been their role. They would certainly have continued as important figures in their communities, with the added lustre of their confession. But then we would almost certainly never have heard of them.

---

135   Augustine, *Sermon* 281.2.

Response: Caroline Batchelder

Edwina, thank you for your paper. I found your discussion of martyrdom as imitation of Christ very engaging. The idea of Christ suffering *in* the martyr, and the startling contemporary description of Blandina as "*crucified for them*" are radical in their implications. Equally radical are the descriptions of the role of martyrs "in the economy of salvation": interceding as Christ intercedes, indeed as "another Christ"; their masculine, intermediary, priestly role; the feminine image of a midwife (also "intermediary"), bringing to birth those who failed to confess Christ, and so compensating for the sins of others; the significance of the martyrs' final words as "utterances of the Holy Spirit."

Suffering was clearly one way of imitating Christ in which men and women could indisputably share equally. You observe that the authority of the martyrs *stemmed from* their imitation of Christ, and you outline a trajectory, whereby if Blandina and Perpetua had somehow survived their martyrdom, by the authority gained by their imitation they might have functioned in the role of teachers, even though Perpetua was a woman and a young Christian, and even though Blandina was a woman and a slave (doubly disqualified according to the cultural values of the time).

This leads me to enquire whether there were other forms of the imitation of Christ in which women shared equally with men, and which also might lead to their recognition and authority? Or was it the case that martyrdom was such an extreme event, and so clearly an imitation of Christ's self-giving, that it simply *could not be denied* as an imitation of Christ; i.e., it was stronger than cultural preconceptions of gender roles, which in other less extreme situations must have had a hold on the perceptions of Christians.

To put this another way, if the imitation of Christ is the paradigm that goes beyond binary gender divisions, it would be interesting to investigate it as a force for change of all cultural paradigms, including gender roles, in the early church. For Paul, imitation of Christ certainly seems to have been a dynamic for change; e.g., Paul urging Philemon in a slavery-based society to accept Onesimus as "no longer a slave but a beloved brother in Christ." It would be interesting to make a comparison with male and female Christian slaves in non-martyrdom situations in the early church, as to whether the radical Christian equality similarly overcame their inequality of status.

I found it amusing that Tertullian (who, as you note, was against the priestly role of women in the church), made a similar move to one still made today: to distinguish women's exercise of the gift of prophecy from their exercise of the gift of speaking for instruction or impartation.

I appreciated your discussion and dismissal of the possibility that Blandina and Perpetua's authority came at the cost of renouncing their gender. I did wonder if it might be that becoming like a man might be the image that a profoundly patriarchal society *had* to use when grappling with the radical implications of Christian faith for gender equality. Perhaps Perpetua's "transformation into a man" might be a picture of her transcending gender rather than denying gender in a patriarchal society.

A closing question: was there a radical newness of Christian faith (including a radical gender equality) in the early church that gradually abated as people conformed it to their previous paradigms, or was there a growing realisation of the radical nature of Christian faith, and a wider application of it as its liberty was discovered? The recognition of female martyrs as the true likeness of Christ seems to suggest that the realisation of radical equality was still able to break in.

Response: Nicole Starling

Edwina's paper offers a fascinating glimpse into the complexities of how the early church understood the relationship between the vocation of all believers to "put on Christ," acting, speaking, and (when called upon) suffering in his name, and the differences of gender that were reflected in the modes and roles within which they did so.

As Edwina rightly stresses, the surviving accounts of the martyrdoms of Perpetua and Blandina depict them *both* as representatives of Christ, speaking and suffering in his name, *and* as "sisters" and "mothers" within the Christian community. The stereotypically "masculine" virtues of courage and fortitude displayed in their martyrdoms are honoured in a manner that does not dissolve the distinctive shape of the gendered social relationships within which their lives before their arrest and martyrdom had been configured.

By depicting Blandina in her martyrdom as one who had "put on Christ, that mighty and invincible athlete," the Christians of Lyons were making a pointed allusion to the words of Paul in Galatians 3: "putting on Christ," according to Paul, is not a privilege reserved for martyrs; *all* of us clothed ourselves with Christ when we believed and were baptised into him. The final victory won by Blandina in her death was one of "many contests" in which she had already overcome the adversary.

Although the letter of the churches narrating her martyrdom tells us little beyond this about her life before she was arrested, it is reasonable to infer, as Edwina does, that her role within the Christian community must have been of sufficient prominence that the authorities considered it worth their while to include her in the group rounded up for martyrdom. Although there is no suggestion in the surviving sources that the churches to which they belonged ordained women like Perpetua and Blandina as presbyters, the evidence does suggest that (in life as well as in death) they occupied a place of honour and influence among their fellow-believers.

Our own cultural context today is obviously vastly different from that of the early church, and the church order within most contemporary evangelical denominations contrasts starkly with the understanding and practice of the early Christian centuries. Nonetheless, there are some important ways in which the stories of women such as Blandina and Perpetua ought to prompt reflection and self-examination for modern evangelicals.

For those of us who hold to an egalitarian understanding of gender, Blandina and Perpetua offer a reminder that official structures such as clerical ordination are not the only form that honour and influence can take, and a spur to reflection on whether gender-blind, equal-opportunity ministry structures take sufficient account of what is unique and distinctive about serving Christ as "sisters" and "mothers" within the family of the church. For those of us with complementarian views, stories such as those of Blandina and Perpetua ought to provoke thought about whether the culture of our churches constructs roles for women that offer scope for similar honour and influence, and a similar expectation that female disciples of Jesus put on the might and invincibility of Christ the athlete in their baptism.

Angels, Helpmeets, and Mothers in Israel: Biblical Imagery and Patterns of Practice among the Earliest Australian Female Preachers

Nicole Starling

Introduction

In the accounts of women's involvement in nineteenth-century Australian church life that have so far been written, almost nothing is said about female preaching in the Australian colonies in the first half of the century. The large-scale studies by Janet West and Anne O'Brien both comment extensively on the philanthropic, educational, and missionary activities of women in this period, but neither offers any suggestion that

Australian women in the first half of the century were active as preachers.[136] A shorter study by Shurlee Swain examines the topic of women's preaching, but limits its scope to the second half of the nineteenth century,[137] and Hilary Carey's careful study of nineteenth-century missionary wives includes the passing comment that early nineteenth-century women were "not allowed" to preach, adding that what happened in practice reflected this prohibition.[138]

This absence of comment can leave readers with the impression that there is only one story worth telling about female preaching in colonial-era Australia: the story of the women in the second half of the nineteenth century whose path into the pulpit was impelled by a sense of prophetic calling and accompanied by vigorous public debates with the guardians of traditional gender roles. Stories of this sort are not hard to come by in the second half of the century, and they neatly echo the reported experiences of women in British Wesleyan Methodist circles after the official ban on female preaching imposed in 1803.

The female preachers of early Methodism typically described their ministry in prophetic categories, as a response to an irresistible call of God that compelled them into the pulpit. The most celebrated among them came to be known within the movement as "mothers in Israel"—a title borrowed from the biblical depiction of the prophetess Deborah in the song of Judges 5.[139] Among the Wesleyan Methodists of Britain, convictions of this sort continued to lead women into public preaching well into the nineteenth century, despite the increasing resistance that they experienced.[140] For these women, a conviction that God had called them to preach meant they felt compelled to choose between obedience to God and conformity to earthly convention. Sarah Boyce, for example, wrote to Mary Tooth in 1841:

---

136   Cf. West, *Daughters of Freedom*, 41–70; O'Brien, *God's Willing Workers*, 16–32. In a more recent, smaller-scale contribution, O'Brien includes a brief reference to the story of Ann Watson's activities in Wellington Valley (discussed below) and offers the comment that her case "may not have been uncommon." O'Brien, "Women in the Churches before 1992," 37.

137   Swain, "Female Evangelists and Hallelujah Lasses."

138   Carey, "Companions in the Wilderness," 240–41.

139   Cf. the early Methodist allusions to biblical prophetesses such as Deborah, Priscilla, Anna, and Huldah recounted in Krueger, *The Reader's Repentance*, 61, and the discussion of the category of "mothers in Israel" in Valenze, *Prophetic Sons and Daughters*, 37.

140   Cruickshank, "'If God ... See Fit to Call You Out," 74.

They own they cannot hinder me from public speaking because Mr Wesley took me in as a preacher, but I am denied the pulpit, I may exhort in the meetings but take no text . . . If the Lord see good to spare me a little longer on earth and strengthen my tottering frame I will go on as I have done and speak good of the name of the Lord where ever I go and if I am denied the use of chapels or pulpits I do not trouble at that, while there is a barn, or a wagon in our land, neither earth, nor hell, shall shut my mouth till the Lord shut my mouth, if I was near you gladly would I join you, and we would fight the Lord's battles together.[141]

In the Australian colonies, however, within the first half of the nineteenth century, no trace survives of any battles of this sort associated with the public preaching of women. It is understandable, therefore that the histories of female preaching in nineteenth-century Australia tend to approach the topic as if the century's first half was simply a blank stretch on the line between the "prophetesses" and "mothers in Israel" who fought the Lord's battles in the chapels and barns of early British Methodism and the colonial women and high-profile visitors whose preaching was the stuff of public *controversy* in the nineteenth century's second half. But to follow this approach is not to tell the whole story.

What histories of that sort omit is the more complex (and arguably more interesting) stories of those women in the first half of the century, whose preaching appears from the surviving accounts to have been understood in terms of a somewhat different set of biblical images, driven by a somewhat different set of motivations, and received with a somewhat different pattern of responses. It is the activity of those first Australian female preachers—the patterns of action in which it took place and the biblical paradigms within which it was understood—that will be the focus of this paper.

---

141   Quoted in Mack, *Heart Religion in the British Enlightenment*, 300.

Female Preaching in Early Nineteenth-Century Australia

Within the Anglican and Roman Catholic churches in early nineteenth-century Australia, the established hierarchical structures did not offer any official opportunity for women to preach. While women had been active as preachers in the early years of the Methodist movement in Britain, this was officially prohibited from 1803, before the first Wesleyan Methodists started arriving in the Australian colonies as missionaries in 1815. The sects that broke away from the Wesleyan Methodists such as the Bible Christians and Primitive Methodists continued to embrace women's preaching,[142] but they did not feature in any large-scale or organised way in early Australian church history, and no record survives of any female preaching within such circles in the first half of the century.[143]

Nonetheless, on a number of recorded occasions within this period, women within both Anglican and Wesleyan Methodist contexts were involved in preaching (or, in some instances, giving sermon-like addresses within the context of gathered worship, without using the word "preaching" to characterise their activities). Three instances of this sort are worth describing at some length.

The earliest of the three is described in the diary of Deborah Carvosso, who was married to the Wesleyan Methodist missionary Benjamin Carvosso. In an entry from the late 1820s she describes an occasion when she found herself leading a Chapel service in Windsor on a Sunday when her husband was called away to conduct a funeral during an influenza epidemic:

> I was therefore obliged to do my best to fill his place this morning at Chapel. The two or three persons who are

---

142   O'Brien, "Women in the Churches before 1992," 36.

143   The first officially constituted Primitive Methodist society was formed in 1840 in South Australia; cf. Petty, *The History of the Primitive Methodist Connexion*, 377. The Bible Christian church was established in Australia in 1850. There were certainly individuals from Primitive Methodist and Bible Christian backgrounds present in the colonies earlier than this, and it is possible that less formal meetings were occurring but these are not documented (cf. O'Brien, "Women in the Churches before 1992," 36–37; *God's Willing Workers*, 21).

accustomed to assist in prayer meeting are also ill. The congregation consisted of thirty persons. I commenced the meeting with singing the 44th hymn. Then made a few remarks on the awful visitations of providence; read one of Mr Wesley's sermons. I then concluded with singing and prayer. The Lord was my helper and guide and the people appeared anxious and devout. May the inhabitants learn wisdom in these afflictions.[144]

A similar incident, a decade later, is described in the journals of the Church Missionary Society's Wellington Valley Mission. William Watson, one of the CMS missionaries, describes in an entry from 1836 an occasion on which his wife Ann, after stepping into the breach to conduct a morning service in the mission-house while he was away, found herself faced by a congregation "apparently expecting a Sermon":

A short time ago I was from home on the Lord's day: Mrs Watson afraid that the natives would wander about all the day told them in the morning that they should have a church to themselves in the house. Accordingly the young men washed and dressed themselves and, at the hour of worship came into the house. Mrs Watson read through the morning service, the natives regularly responding. This was all Mrs Watson had intended to do; but to her great surprise when the prayers were finished, all the natives sat down apparently expecting a Sermon. She felt at a loss how to proceed. However, her mind was directed to some anecdotes of pious youths and children; and some accounts of happy deaths of several who had served the Lord in their early years. Having read several of these, and made occasional remarks, as how happy we should be in seeing this native, and that native in heaven &c she thought they

---

144   Diary reproduced in Stansall, *Alive to the Great Work*, 45.

would be tired, and enquired shall I give over now? Are you tired of hearing these? Kabbarrin said go on, go on. Gungin with his face literally bathed in tears, with difficulty articulated, no, read more, we are not tired.[145]

Over the next ten years Ann Watson went on to lead services and deliver addresses of this sort whenever her husband was away. William Watson reported to the Colonial Secretary that during his many absences his wife continued to lead services and guide the congregation through Scripture, hymns, and prayers.[146]

A third example (and arguably the earliest instance in which the address was understood unambiguously as "preaching") arose within the church-planting ministry of Jesse and Harriet Pullen in Brown's River, Tasmania, in the 1830s. Harriet and Jesse had emigrated to Van Diemen's Land in 1822, probably in response to a letter written by Benjamin Carvosso and published in the *Wesleyan Methodist Magazine* which outlined the need for people to assist with the work in Hobart.[147] In 1834, after a series of financial difficulties, Harriet and Jesse moved to Brown's River, a small settlement a few hours from Hobart.

A surviving memoir, passed down through a family diary, includes a description of the planting of a church in the tiny community and of Harriet's preaching there on a number of occasions between 1836 and 1838. While no authorship is assigned to the account in its surviving form, it is likely that it was written by Harriet and Jesse's eldest son George.[148]

---

145 Carey and Roberts (eds.). *The Wellington Valley Project.* Diary 4: July–September 1836, p. 10.

146 Jessie Mitchell, "The Nucleus of Civilisation," 106–07. A strikingly similar example from just outside our period is recounted by George Taplin, a missionary for the Aborigines Friends Association in Point Macleay from 1853, whose wife also found herself in a situation in which she was prevailed upon to preach on an occasion when Taplin was away from the mission station. She "took a volume of Line upon Line, selected a chapter and made it the foundation of an address upon the subject contained therein, and kept their attention the usual time." Taplin concluded: "I don't suppose my wife seriously infringed any law of the New Testament by acting thus in such very exceptional circumstances." Quoted in Carey, "Companions in the Wilderness," 241.

147 Benjamin Carvosso, "Methodism in Van Diemen's Land," 245.

148 Cf. the arguments in favour of this theory in Nicole Starling, "Between Two Paradigms."

It was during a time when Jesse Pullen was away in Sydney that Harriet first preached for the group. The fact that she was going to preach at the meeting was announced during the writer of the memoir's usual Sunday morning visits to invite the local residents to the gathering. The room that afternoon was unusually full of people. The writer says this sudden increase in attendance was mainly prompted by "curiosity to see how a woman would conduct a religious service," but goes on to describe the listeners as having been "earnest and astonished."

At the first meeting, Harriet opened the service "in the usual way"; a portion of Scripture was read and "seated behind the table she paraphrased and expounded the portion she read to the audience." Her voice "would rise to passionate and eloquent entreaty, the listeners sitting apparently awed and spellbound." It seems she preached again the following Sunday—once more to a crowded room of listeners—this time asking those who wanted to live a new life to stay behind and "talk freely about spiritual things" and "come to a decision in the great matter that concerned their soul's salvation." To her surprise nearly the whole audience of ten to twelve people stayed behind, and "on that night the first class meeting was formed." The diary goes on to describe the building of the chapel and its opening in late 1838. Jesse Pullen had been away in Sydney while these events took place, and the writer explains that Harriet continued the Sunday services and preached each week during this absence, until she died during childbirth on December 17th, 1838. It was at this point that the Brown's River preaching station was officially added to the Hobart circuit's preaching plan; when Jesse left to go to Sydney again, the local preachers organised a roster so that a preacher would be supplied every week.[149]

Early Female Preaching and the Helpmeet Paradigm

When the surviving accounts of the earliest instances of female preaching in the Australian colonies are compared with one another, a common pattern emerges.

---

149   Cf. Wesley Church, Hobart, "Minute Book of Local Preachers Meetings 1830–1874," 22 June 1839.

Common to all three accounts is a statement about the wife's desire, in each case, not to abandon the Sunday services her husband usually conducted.

Also common to the three accounts is the absence of any indication that the preaching was a matter of conflict or controversy. While the *official* records contain no evidence of these women leading services or delivering addresses of this sort, their husbands and sons were happy to record this involvement and imply their approval and support. William Watson, for example, recounts the example of his wife speaking within the Sunday service not primarily as an instance of problematic gender issues (though his account does suggest that his wife—"at a loss how to proceed"—was deeply aware of these), but as an encouraging evidence of the extent to which the minds of the local Aboriginal people were "susceptible of religious impressions."[150]

In all three instances, judging from both the language used in the surviving accounts and the pattern of activity that they record, the principal paradigm within which the speaking activity of these women appears to have been understood and justified was not as a response to the irresistible impulse of a prophetic call, but as an extension of their role as "helpmeet" to their husbands. The "helpmeet" language of Genesis 2:18, part of the traditional biblical vocabulary for describing the roles of married women, was used with particular frequency in the pioneering context of the early colonies, especially with reference to the wives of missionaries. According to Hilary Carey, "all Australian wives in the colonial period could occasionally be considered as helpmates and partners, but for the missionary wives this was their dominant representation."[151]

While the role of "helpmeet" was sometimes described in fairly narrow terms, in reality the missionary wives carried out a wide range of activities. In Sydney, for example, wives were involved in work such as teaching Sunday school and training women and children in craft and domestic work,

---

150   Carey and Roberts, eds. *"The Wellington Valley Project."* Diary 4: July–September 1836, p. 10.
151   Carey, "Companions," 230.

teaching in institutions such as the Parramatta Native Institution, as well as corresponding with a vast network of female supporters.[152] In the more rural missions, the role was interpreted even more broadly, especially in situations that required the extended absence of the husband.[153]

In the three examples of early colonial female preaching discussed above, there is no suggestion in any of the surviving accounts that the women understood themselves, or were understood by their husbands, as intending to challenge the accepted gender roles of the society to which they belonged.[154] Judging from the evidence that survives, their inclination to step in seems to have come from a desire to continue and uphold the work they were involved in with their husbands. In the situation in which they found themselves, being a helpmeet to their husbands happened to involve leading services and giving public (or semi-public), sermon-like addresses.

Of the three examples, the account of Harriet Pullen's labours in Brown's River is the one that suggests the strongest affinities to the "prophetic" preachers of early Methodism (the biographies of at least three of whom were held within the library of the Hobart Wesleyan Methodist Church)[155] and the female preachers and evangelists of the later nineteenth century. The content of Harriet's preaching (a reading from the Scriptures, which she then expounded to the congregation) followed the same pattern that a local preacher would follow in the public worship of a Methodist congregation.[156] The pattern also accords with the description that the celebrated eighteenth-century Methodist preacher, Mary Bosanquet

---

152   Carey, "Companions," 232.

153   See especially Carey, "Companions," 234, and "Conversion," 268–9.

154   Cf. Carey's comment, in relation to the Watsons, that they "embraced the full ideal of a mission marriage as a partnership with complementary roles for wife and husband." "Conversion," 262.

155   The library was established by the church in 1825 and was the first of its kind in Australia. A record of the books held by the library in 1830 reveals that the biography of Mrs Fletcher was part of their collection. The minute book of the library committee also shows that a number of other biographies of Methodist women preachers were purchased, including those of Fanny Newell and Hester Ann Rogers. Jesse Pullen was a member of the library committee and was involved in decisions relating to the purchase of these books. Cf. Wesley Church, Hobart, "Minute Book of Leaders' Meetings"; "Minute Book of the Wesleyan Library Committee"; *Rules and Regulations of the Wesleyan Library*.

156   Hempton, *Methodism*, 74.

Fletcher, gave of the format and content of her own preaching: "expounding, taking a part or whole of a chapter & speaking on it."[157] Fletcher's description, as Cruickshank points out, makes it clear that "she was not simply telling the story of her own experience or urging spiritual change . . . but preaching in the sense considered most authoritative, explaining and applying Scripture."[158]

The rhetorical style with which Harriet's sermon was delivered also had similarities to the earnest and impassioned mode of delivery characteristic of early Methodist women preachers such as Mary Bosanquet Fletcher, Sarah Crosby, and Anne Cutler.[159] The description of one of her later sermons is particularly redolent of the descriptions of early Methodist women preachers:

> In the last meeting before the opening of the chapel she was carried away by the intensity of her feeling; and her earnest appeals, exhortations and entreaties made a deep and lasting impression on the minds of her hearers. Her soul rose into a state of rapt ecstasy as she gave out the concluding hymn "My soul from out the body torn shall bless the day that, I was born" and all who sat there looking steadfastly on her face saw it as if it had been the face of an angel.[160]

The angelic image conjured up in the final line not only implies a perspective in which the preaching is viewed as having been empowered and legitimated by a special work of the Spirit; it also evokes an echo of the biblical account of the Spirit-filled preaching of Stephen (cf. Acts 6:15).

Despite these traces of the prophetic paradigm of early Methodism, however, there is nothing in the account of Harriet Pullen's preaching to suggest that it was motivated and understood in terms of an irresistible inward

---

157   Mary Bosanquet Fletcher, letter to Mary Taft, 28 November 1803, quoted in Cruickshank, "If God . . . See Fit," 66.

158   Cruickshank, "If God . . . .See Fit," 66.

159   Krueger, *Reader's Repentance*, 64.

160   Imms, *Methodist Cemetery*, 24.

call to preach, that it was exercised independently of Harriet's joint labours with her husband, or that it became a matter of private or public controversy. According to the writer of the memoir, her preaching was motivated by a desire to "carry on the work that had been so long and perseveringly maintained amidst much discouragement." The writer also makes a point of emphasising her husband Jesse's approval;[161] the fact that she preached again on a number of subsequent occasions supports this claim.[162]

Conclusions

What implications might these stories from early colonial Australia have for the discussion about ministry and gender roles among Australian Christians in our own time? At one level of course, the answer is probably "very few." The fact that women in an earlier century did or didn't minister in a particular way does not determine what our own convictions and practices ought to be. Nevertheless, the history of the church in previous generations can still be deeply instructive for us as we seek wisdom to interpret and apply the Scriptures in our own time. Two lessons in particular stand out from the stories of Deborah Carvosso, Ann Watson, and Harriet Pullen.

The first is a lesson about the inadequacy of the conflict-narrative within which the history of women's roles within the church is frequently narrated. It is certainly possible to find numerous stories from across the centuries of women impelled by strongly held convictions into fierce conflict with the guardians of the traditional order of gender relations; it is possible, too, to arrange such stories (within the last several centuries of the Western church, at any rate) into a trajectory that resembles the broader cultural movement toward a more liberal-democratic set of social arrangements. But the women of the past—including those whose actions might seem, on the surface at least, to have been at the vanguard of a movement of that sort—cannot always be readily conscripted into that cause. As far as we can discern from the surviving evidence, the women who were the first female

---

161   Imms, *Methodist Cemetery*, 22.

162   Ibid., 24.

preachers in colonial Australia did not see themselves (and were not seen by those around them) as striking a blow for the emancipation of women, but as attempting to serve the cause of the gospel in partnership with their husbands, as "helpmeets" and fellow-missionaries.

The second, closely related lesson has to do with the irreducible complexity of Christian experience (and of human motivation more generally). Debates such as the modern evangelical disagreement between complementarians and egalitarians can frequently give rise to polarised categories and attempts to sort people out onto one side or another of a neatly drawn line. History (including the history of Australia's first female preachers) reminds us that where human beings are involved the lines cannot always be drawn quite that neatly; taking the time to understand the men and women of the past in all their difference and complexity can help us learn the grace and patience that we need to understand our brothers and sisters today.

Response: Caroline Batchelder

Thank you for your paper, Nicole. It's good to have something written about this neglected subject. I appreciate your detective work in piecing together a history from the clues available; reading between the lines, as it were.

As a member of a housechurch-style church myself, I'm guessing that the household nature of Christian gatherings in early rural Australia would have some typical consequences. While records were probably *not* kept (as you observe) in the less-structured, church-planting environment, women would surely be *more* likely preach or teach; indeed to do whatever was needed. Additionally, while the lack of records of women preachers may demonstrate the church's restrictions on women preaching, it is also possible that these restrictions *led* to the lack of records when women did preach. I note the sense of obligation to preach described by Deborah Carvosso, and George Taplin's conciliatory tone in describing his wife's ministry. They feel they need some justification for preaching, implying that the situation required it. In the Pullens' case, the embryo church was outside the preaching circuit, and the account of Harriet's preaching survived through a family diary, rather than an official record. These things suggest unexpected demands, and people rising to the occasion, indeed the Spirit supplying what was needed for the occasion.

It interests me that the Methodists, against Wesley's own practice, banned women from preaching in 1803. Did this reflect their development from a missionary church (perhaps more able to be responsive to the Spirit) into a more institutional church? If so, one would expect that in the reverse situation women would be *more* likely to preach, as in these church-planting histories. You mention that "no record survives" of women preaching, even in groups which permitted it, which suggests that "no record" may be evidence of things other than non-occurrence.

Your third example is striking. After her initial sermon, Harriet Pullen preached again the following week, and later almost weekly. Obviously gifted, her preaching moved the entire congregation, leading to faith or renewed faith, and seems to have been more effective than her husband's. Her son's account of it seems likely to have been written in order that his mother's outstanding gifts were not forgotten.

I question the lack of evidence of calling, especially in this account. The description of the way Harriet preached suggests a calling being realised. The language of Stephen's martyrdom is surely the language of calling, given added poignancy because of Harriet's untimely death. More broadly, all three women and their husbands answered "a prophetic call" to plant churches. Perhaps this is more properly the prophetic calling within which their activities (including preaching) may be understood.

I suspect that the interpretive paradigm of women as their husband's helpmeet has influenced the way you read the histories. You write that all three women desire "not to abandon the Sunday services her husband usually conducted." A fuller appreciation of the women's contribution might render this as "*they* usually conducted." This is not to deny that the husband did the preaching or leading, but to underline the couple's joint responsibility for the work: so much so that in each account it continued relatively unchanged when the husband was away. The accounts do not themselves use the language of helpmeet.[163]

---

163   It would be interesting (if it were possible) to explore any limits of the "helpmeet paradigm." Are there some things a husband would do in missionary service which a wife *absolutely* would not?

I wholly concur with your comment that the gender "conflict-narrative" is inadequate. We need a more biblical narrative with its spectrum of images; of co-workership, of the body of Christ working together, of the servant willing to do something in which they find themselves "at a loss," as well as to be raised up by the Spirit in preaching.

Your paper is about much more than who preaches in conservative and missionary churches, but is about the fullness of the Spirit in women and men, surprising them, and liberating them to fulfil their missionary task.

Response: Edwina Murphy

Nicole's paper reminds us of how reliant we are on the chance survival of sources. We make pronouncements about what people thought and did based on those documents that have survived. Even though we acknowledge that the elite sources that have been preserved can only provide a partial picture, and from a particular perspective at that, it can be difficult to know what really went on. Nicole has done us a great service in uncovering this material. How much of women's activity in the church remains unknown because the records—journals, letters, personal notes—have not survived?

I love the natural accounts of Carvosso and Watson—they are just what one might expect in such a situation. I am reminded of Susanna Wesley's evening family devotions in her husband's absence, with more and more in attendance until the "family" reached almost two hundred people at times. Could it be wrong to teach Scripture to the people in the village, when only a dozen or two were attending the curate's morning sermons? I also think of Elisabeth Elliot teaching a sermon to an Auca man so that he could then preach it to the congregation, not wanting, as a woman, to preach herself. Two different ways women responded to their circumstances, with the same goal of sharing God's word with those who needed to hear it.

Nicole presents the accounts as being without controversy, at least on the part of their male relatives. I think she would also agree that the Anglican Watson, at least, is concerned to present the situation favourably to others. And as Taplin concluded: "I don't suppose my wife seriously infringed any law of the New Testament by acting thus in such very exceptional circumstances." If there is approval on behalf of husbands and sons, there is also an attempt to pre-empt criticism by others.

There are a number of themes that Nicole's paper has in common with my own. Firstly, she emphasises the priority of the gospel in the women's preaching—not the challenging of gender roles, but the carrying out of necessary work for the sake of Christ. I think we see the same intent in the case of the female martyrs—commitment to Christ led them to suffer for him, but they were not seeking glory for its own sake. Nicole also highlights partnership, rather than conflict. Again, although tension between martyrs and the clergy may have been present on a broader scale, just as there was controversy over women preaching in the early nineteenth century, the concern of the actors in the accounts themselves is for harmony and unity. Another point of similarity is that, although doing something normally reserved for men, the early female preachers, like the martyrs before them, do not renounce their gender. In the Australian context, it is precisely as married women that they carry out their ministry. Finally, and perhaps most importantly, the ministry of the gospel is not restricted to ordained clergy and neatly hierarchical structures but belongs to the wider body of Christ.

Part Six

Gender, Power, and Politics

Desire Chastened

Matthew Andrew

Introduction

When gender relationship crumbled after the fall, God's curse—or codification of an already present consequence—was that Eve's desire would be for her husband, whilst he would rule over her. Whatever form this desiring actually takes, I would suggest that it—and the interplay with the husband's ruling—is *disordered*. At the heart of broken gender relationships is the interplay of misshapen desires.

This malformation is often opaque to us: we misread our desires. If we consider the example of Amnon and Tamar we can see quite plainly that the moment a desire is realised we often discover that it was disastrously *not* what we actually wanted.[1] We want what we cannot have and consistently fail to realise both the true object of, and the destruction wrought by, our desires. An older tradition called this "concupiscence."

---

1   1 Sam 13. I am grateful to Oliver O'Donovan for this example. See chapter 7 of O'Donovan, *Church in Crisis*.

Yet there is an important current in contemporary theology that sees precisely the *evocation* of desire by the beauty of the Christian message as central to all forms of Christian proclamation, and particularly as a counter to what have been called the "ontologies of violence" (what we might call "reductive concupiscence"):[2] a vision of the world as irreducibly competing desires.

My project in this paper is to ask what this theological tradition—with its language of beauty and desire—might offer as we consider Christian witness on the questions of gender in the public realm. In order to answer this question we will begin with one important way of understanding our contemporary public sphere: the so-called "ontologies of violence."

Ontologies of Violence

Allow me to get a piece of philosophical technicalia out of the way by defining "ontology." All that need concern us here is that ontology is the enterprise of trying to reflect rationally on the world around us, particularly as a means of discovering what all things have in common. Thus an ontology of violence is one that sees all things in the world as irreducibly in competition, a game of power.

This view of the world is found in the work of Friedrich Nietzsche and has found its way into many contemporary thinkers, perhaps most strongly influencing the tradition of thought generally called "postmodern." Particularly important for our question is how Nietzsche's thought has been pressed into service in the development of *ethics*.

A significant example of this is the work of Emmanuel Levinas, a twentieth-century ethical thinker—one with no small influence on feminist thought—who, in the light of his experiences as a Jew during World War Two and his conviction about the death of ontology, was trying to figure out

---

2   See the chapter entitled "Ontological Violence" in Milbank, *Theology*, 278–326.

how to ground ethics.[3] Levinas has a problem with ontology: that, because it is interested in what is common to all things, it reduces otherness to the "same." For Levinas this means that the true ethical interval is closed.[4] Our actual ethical interval—not reducible to knowledge—is a relation: one of infinite responsibility before the *other*.[5]

The "other" is not simply our being confronted with another human being. It is most tellingly described as the "being that appears, but remains absent."[6] The most important thing to pick up here is that ethics depends on something that is *unrepresentable*. So form—whether in the guise of a political order, or cultural conventions—is always betrayal. The result of this is that ethics "becomes critique."[7] If established norms are always an imperfect representation of an unrepresentable relation, then morality loses its authority as anything but calling into question.[8]

Given that our project is concerned with desire, it is well to ask where it fits in a scheme of thought like this. Here desire—particularly love—is a movement-towards the "never completely, yet nearly reached."[9] While this sounds frustrating, Levinas argues that desire is neither satisfied nor unsatisfied, but rather is "accomplished" in the relationship with the other.[10] This means that once desire is directed to the unrepresentable it is fulfilled.

Desire is disordered insofar as it seeks to *overcome* the alienness of the other, as that—as we have just seen—is the context of its "accomplishment." We can put this together with the conclusion we reached above about form and the unrepresentable. To call the other from their otherness to a definite

---

3   I acknowledge that Husserl and Heidegger played perhaps the more important role in Levinas's thought, but Nietzsche's influence on the latter and the similarity of their projects at critical points means that I would argue that Levinas belongs in a genealogy of Nietzsche's influence.

4   Levinas, *Totality*, 42.

5   Levinas, *Totality*, 49–52.

6   Levinas, *Totality*, 181.

7   Or, perhaps, ethics could be conceived as judgement without (bodily) resurrection. On ethics as critique see Critchley, "Introduction,",15.

8   On this as a wider phenomenon see: O'Donovan, *Desire*, 10. See also Cavanaugh and his discussion of Maritian, Aquinas, and MacIntyre in this context: Cavanaugh *Torture and Eucharist*, 188–91.

9   Waldenfels, "Levinas and the Face of the Other," 77–78.

10   Levinas, *Totality*, 179.

form is an illegitimate "totalisation" or "forming" of the "infinite."[11] Here we see how beauty, how the *aesthetic* features in this thought. Form is betrayal, and thus beauty—which is linked to form—is also betrayal. The true object of desire is the unrepresentable, also known as the sublime.[12]

Let me summarise then: Levinas privileges the other *qua* other. We might call this an ethic of the unrepresentable. It is this kind of thinking that characterises the public realm and its rhetoric of tolerance.

Beauty

We have now examined at least one important kind of thinking that we see in the public realm insofar as it relates to desire and beauty. We have also seen how closely questions of form relate to ethics and are perhaps beginning to see how this line of aesthetic inquiry might be fruitful. So let us now turn our attention to how the language of beauty and desire is understood in the theological tradition invoked above.

The fundamental thought is that Christianity always presents "a rhetoric of conversion . . . it proclaims a certain form."[13] That form is beautiful, one that evokes desire. To understand how "beauty" is being used here, we will look at David Bentley Hart's project.[14]

If you will forgive my indulging in another piece of philosophical technicalia, beauty is understood as one of the "transcendentals." This is a concept that builds on ontology, and refers to those things which can be predicated of all beings, and is understood as belonging to them in a mode appropriate to what they are. An example of a transcendental is that all beings are *one*, a unity. If it were not so "there would be no way to distinguish

---

11   Though Levinas acknowledges that all translations of this relation into philosophical language are a betrayal (see his notion of the "saying" and the "said") it is also a painful necessity. Levinas, *Otherwise*, 43–45.

12   See the introduction to Hart, *Beauty*.

13   Hart, *Beauty*, 415.

14   I am thinking particularly of *The Beauty of the Infinite*, but Hart's concern is present throughout his major works.

this being from a collection of *these* beings."[15] All beings are similarly said to be *true*. God created things so that they are able to be known: our minds can be conformed to them, though not exhaustively. And all beings are *good* insofar as they are intrinsically valuable in their own way as God's creation.[16] In Christian thought these transcendentals belong to all things because they are ultimately grounded in the good and gracious God. All things also show us dimly—or analogically—what God himself is like.

What, then, does *beauty* mean as a transcendental? It is most properly "a relationship of donation and transfiguration, a handing over and return of the riches of being."[17] To put it less abstractly, it is the relationship that is embodied in Jesus Christ as the fullness of God dwelling bodily. Or to put it differently again, it is God's glory.[18]

This means that beauty is *objective*: it has a priority over our subjective experience. And it is objectively *desirable*: it evokes our desire. But beauty can only be received as a *gift*; its very core is as a movement of donation. A desirable form shares its beauty, evoking our delight in that which has shared its beauty with us. This helps us to see that the ground of beauty is distance, for it is the good gift possessed and given by another. This consecrates distance—otherness—as a genuine good.[19]

This consecration of otherness looks, at first glance, rather like Levinas's project. But there is a crucial difference. Beauty is given a *definite form*. Christian religion does not oppose form to infinity. The infinite God, the infinite other, is not unrepresentable, but has definitively revealed himself in the *form* of Christ and adorned creation with his glory. Thus "Christianity becomes *the* aesthetic religion *par excellence*."[20] There is a radical difference from Levinas's project. The other is not an absent presence but a present form. Christian ethics is not an ethic of the unrepresentable but an ethic of *form*.

---

15   With a subsequent regress to the limits of our knowledge of physics. Clarke, *One and the Many*, 293.

16   Clarke, *One and the Many*, 297.

17   Hart, *Beauty*, 18.

18   Hart, *Beauty*, 18–21.

19   Indeed distance is what beauty gives, beauty is the *ground* of distance. Hart, *Beauty*, 18.

20   Balthasar, *Glory*, 210. Emphasis original.

This shows us two important things. The first is that reality is not ontologically violent: the form of God is a movement of self-giving love. The heart of reality is love and peace. The second thing we see is that the desire of another can be directed to this definite form, not in violation of their otherness, but as a summons to mutual delight in the very ground of their otherness: distance. To call another to the form of Christ is not to reduce the other to the same, but to their own inhabitation of the interval of distance that is the ground of beauty. To put this less densely, if we remember that the possibility of beauty is distance—delight in the form of another—then we see that to call another to *this* form is not a call to surrender all otherness.

We are now in a position to see the shape of Hart's project. If we live in a world where form, where intelligibility has been rejected in favour of the unrepresentable as a means of preserving otherness, we can proclaim a *form* that is the ground of both otherness and peace.

Intervals

With this theoretical groundwork laid, I want to ask what this framework shows us about our public witness as Christians. As I do this it is important to remember that I am looking at church, witness, and scriptural passages *through* this lens. It will foreground certain things and push others to the background.

Hiddenness

We proclaim a form then, but where does it lie? Both Christian and Platonic thought have recognised the public realm as one in which only appearances can be judged—including patterns of life together—not hidden realities.[21] There is, therefore, a lamentable interval between the hidden truth of Christianity and the public realm. This interval is only fully closed with the return of Jesus, and is given its most horrifying expression—both in itself and in our call to imitation—in the crucifixion. Consequently it is often "the

---

21   O'Donovan, *Principles*, 3.

Christian sense that the most authentic relation of truth to the public realm is that which issues in martyrdom."[22]

Is beauty like this hidden truth? Is Christian form somehow hidden? Sarah Coakley has recently written a work outlining a new theological method, one cast particularly in the context of the debate on gender. A key argument of her project is that certain *hidden* practices are a *prerequisite* to gaining a particular kind of theological insight, thus opening the door to a particular type of public (in this case pastoral) practice. She foregrounds "deep" or silent prayer in particular, which inflames our desire for God by allowing God to chasten and reform our desires (particularly sexual) and our vision.[23] Our participating in the Spirit's love for the Father is, as it were, the hidden wellspring from which our practice in the world flows.[24]

We can think of these hidden practices as shaping our form of life according to the form of God's life. Our form of life *in the world* is shaped by God's hidden work of forming us according to his own form. While Coakley's particular Platonisation of desire is not a project everyone can accept, I would argue that she has articulated an important hiddenness which should underlie all Christian attempts to engage the public realm: the work of the Spirit in shaping our external actions. Our private experience of the desirability of God in the power of the Spirit shapes and checks our own concupiscence. Coakley acknowledges the importance of the context of the individual in this process, but other traditions have spoken more articulately of formation of the person through the process of being *in* community.[25] Whichever pole is emphasised, there is a strong link in the New Testament between inner transformation and outward practice.[26]

---

22   Though we more often find that the interval is traversed by patient endurance. O'Donovan, *Principles*, 4–5.

23   This is understood as recovering an emphasis on the Spirit, which by its very nature tends to threaten settled ecclesial order. Coakley, *God, Sexuality, and the Self*, 110–44.

24   Coakley, *God, Sexuality, and the Self*, 315–16.

25   See Coakley's fieldwork on the context of prayer and desire: Coakley, *God, Sexuality, and the Self*, 163–81. Perhaps the most obvious proponent of this tradition is Stanley Hauerwas, e.g., in *After Christendom?* See also the discussion in Volf, "Soft Difference."

26   Rom 12:1–2 is a paradigmatic example of this.

But there is a doubleness to this talk of transformation and form. The hiddenness of the work of transformation does not entail that the form undergoing the transforming is hidden. Our changing form is *public*. Beyond even this there is always something greater than *our* fidelity to the form of God at work in the public sphere. Paul's reaction to those preaching the gospel as a pretence in order to—amongst other things—make his life a misery is instructive: "What does it matter? Just this, that Christ is proclaimed in every way, whether out of false motives or true; and in that I rejoice."[27] Paul is confident in the gospel's proclamation *despite* hidden realities, despite a deceptive—or perhaps overtly antithetical—form. Yet we are reminded time and again in the New Testament that the public form of Christian practice can—depending on its fidelity to the form of the gospel—function as clearing ground for, or occlusion of, the gospel. 1 Corinthians 12–14 serves as a dramatic example.

So the faithfulness of our form both does and does not matter, and inward realities as form-shaping both do and do not matter. There is an *instability* here. I think this teaches us something important. There is a power of form above both church order and gospel proclamation. The power of beauty is, therefore, not its hiddenness but its objectivity. Beauty can be *obscured* or *mis-seen* but never hidden. It is always already in the public realm.

Form

We have been referring to beauty in terms of "form," "relation," and "gospel." How exactly do these realities fit together? I think beauty here both shows and reminds us that God's being is irreducibly formed in the manner we encounter in the gospel. In theological terms we need to remember that the three "persons" (hypostases) of the Trinity are not reducible to God's essence. God's life is the mutuality of the three *particular* relations we see revealed in the gospel.[28] God's infinite life is *formed*. This formed infinity

---

27   Philippians 1:18, NRSV.
28   The *ousia* is the infinity of the "mutual action of Father, Son, and Spirit." Jenson, *Systematic Theology*, 215.

means that predicates applied to God, such as "beauty," are not shapeless.[29] Beauty is not, therefore, the merely pretty but must be understood in terms of what happened in the life, death, and resurrection of Jesus Christ.[30] Above all I believe that beauty teaches us here that in our public speech we should never refer to God in the abstract. As Robert Jenson writes, "God is whoever raised Christ Jesus from the dead having before raised Israel from Egypt."[31]

We see, therefore, that our proclamations—including those about gender—will always point to a beauty that can only be seen on the other side of death, a peace available only in an objective form that is the story of the Son of God bearing our sins. It can be experienced as beauty only as our desires are re-ordered. This proclamation of a desirability we no longer trust or want will always precipitate war, as well as make peace.[32]

Yet it should be emphasised once again that this is not an ontology of violence. We stand in the public realm as those related to an objective beauty, the proclamation that the heart of all reality takes the form of an act of self-giving love. We seek to call others to this peace. But the desirability of the beautiful is obscured because the peace offered must be accepted as judgement on our desires—our concupiscence—and accepted as a gift. Form, however wonderful, is limitation. Christianity must talk not only of *desire* but of *misdirected desires*.

---

29   They must, as Stephen Wright provocatively phrases it, be "run across the three." This line of thought quickly takes on an arbitrary hue when attempts are made in the abstract to articulate these relations. Wright suggests, for example, that beauty might be understood as "God as artist, God as art, and God as beauty." Wright is self-consciously drawing on Augustine's notion of the lover, beloved, and love as model for the Trinity. Yet Augustine's project was to use such images as a means of understanding how the ontology of the Trinity works. Wright is using the ontology of the Trinity as a means of grounding concepts. Wright, *Dogmatic Aesthetics*, 84. See books XIV and XV of Augustine, *Trinity*. For an excellent criticism of contemporary Trinitarian theology because of its projection/retrojection shape see Kilby, "Perichoresis."

30   Hart, *Beauty*, 414.

31   Jenson, *Systematic Theology*, 63.

32   Hart, *Beauty*, 415.

Conversation

Beauty directs our attention to the fact that our standing in the public realm is as those related to an objective beauty. We relate to a particular *story*.[33] As argued above, our communal witness both is and is not important: we are imperfect mirrors. We imitate, stand as an object of desire (or repulsion) ourselves, but always in a relationship of imperfection to the gospel story. Those outside of the Christian community are also related to this objective beauty by a relation of imperfection: that of imperfect sight. True beauty is always objectively present but obscured both within, and outside of, the Christian community.

We obscure and reveal, they see and do not see, we see and do not see: beauty shows us the instability of ourselves and our communities. We must submit ourselves to the instability and the sight of the other. 1 Peter tells us to "conduct yourselves honorably among the Gentiles, so that, though they malign you as evildoers, they may see your honorable deeds and glorify God when he comes to judge."[34] In this instability lies the hope that our offensive practices surrounding gender might come to be glorified as good. But surely here is also the threat that there are practices which are *not* honourable, the threat that we might also be wrong. Because their sight is *unstable* the other might clearly see our brokenness. In a conversation about gender we must be open to the possibility that the other will expose our own broken desires.

But what does this talk of "directing another's gaze" to the object of beauty mean? We see here that conversation is *rhetoric*.[35] We are engaging in an enterprise of persuasion. To a world that will encounter this only as one more story vying for power, what form should our persuasion take that could display itself as beautiful? The only possible answer would be that kind which accords with the form of the story itself: self-giving love. We come to martyrdom. When power opposes the evocation of the form of the gospel it deconstructs itself, as the form of the gospel can be suppressed "only

---

33   Hart, *Beauty*, 428.

34   1 Peter 2:11 NRSV.

35   Hart, *Beauty*, 441.

through a violence that creates martyrs, and so confirms—contrary to all intends[*sic*]—the witness of a peace that is infinite."[36]

Conclusion

Let me bring these threads together. Beauty consecrates the otherness of gender as good. The *difference* of form is a gift to me, freely given, and in this movement of donation and delight the very form of God is displayed. The giftedness of the beauty that adorns genderedness serves as a guard against exploitation. For the correct standing towards a genuinely good gift is delight.[37]

Beauty is not abstracted from the particularity of the forms we see in world: beauty is the interval of difference. The gospel makes peaceful room for the otherness of sex and gender. The church's public witness must be as one that *norms* the various shapes and forms (phenotypes) of maleness and femaleness, against a culture that idealises certain physical traits. It must also *norm* as legitimate those expressions of *gender* which in wider society might be taken as inadequately "male" or "female" in an individual.

Beauty encourages us to seek form, against an ethic of the formless. It is directed to all the ethical content of the gospel story that grounds all form, all beauty, as a movement of donation and reception. The ethics of gender must always be sought by carefully examining the relationship between the affirmation of the goodness of creation and its structures in the incarnation, and the transformation of those structures in the resurrection.[38] In an age of formlessness, where technological innovation is allowing the breach of what was once called "natural," Christians are bound—by the doctrine of creation—to say that there are transhistorical goods which exist despite our apparent power to breach them. This includes our being sexed and gendered. The church's witness here must be a call to the *redirection* of desire.

---

36   Hart, *Beauty*, 442.

37   For a discussion of gift-giving as something that can be genuinely good, and not a power gambit, see Milbank, "Can a Gift Be Given?"

38   See part 1 of O'Donovan, *Resurrection*.

Once again we see the centrality of beauty's celebration of difference as *gift*. In the same way that giftedness guards against the exploitation of otherness, it also guards against resentment towards the limits of the form of the self.[39] What beauty teaches us is that a chastened desire is free to truly enjoy the differences of creation, because it recognises the good in both comeliness and limitation.

---

39   For reasons of space I cannot address the difficult work of trying to discern what part of our form is gifted and what part is simply broken. Nonetheless the affirmation of transhistorical goods in a Christian discussion of beauty means that we cannot simply abandon the struggle: we must recognise the presence form and brokenness.

Response: Beth Jackson

This paper raises a number of interesting points philosophically about the relation of gender to public discourse. Matt employs a lengthy critical engagement with philosopher and ethicist Emmanuel Levinas. In my response, I think it would be a helpful exercise to bring Levinas and Gayatri Spivak into conversation, though it certainly wouldn't be for the first time. Spivak was heavily influenced by Levinas, yet remained very critical of his approach. She views Levinas's gender-biased discourse "of ethics [as being] always certainly male" and therefore, finds it "difficult to take [his] prurient, heterosexist, male-identified ethics seriously."[40] Spivak offers a rather scathing review of Levinas, perhaps, but she illuminates the fact that Levinas's sense of otherness served to accentuate the alterity of the subaltern.

Perhaps Spivak has something to offer to this conversation on misshapen desire. Matt, in his critique of Levinas, argues for form. This argument is not dissimilar to Spivak who also argues for form, in particular gendered form, and this is perhaps her unique contribution to this discussion. For Spivak, "the call of the other and the response to that call is what shapes the ethical encounter."[41] The "other" to which she consistently refers is distinctively subaltern, with particular reference to the female form. Perhaps

---

40   Spivak, *Outside In,* 166–67.
41   Ray, *Spivak,* 90.

beauty, in this instance, is then found in that response of the call to the other, through self-giving love. Beauty, as the interval of difference—or, in Spivakian terms, the response of the call—plays an important part in Matt's theoretical groundwork. Beauty takes form, a distinctly gendered form, in the person of Christ who is, as Hebrews 1:3 states, "the radiance of God's glory and the exact representation of his being."

However, I think we can take Matt's work one step further drawing on the work of Parker Palmer. Palmer suggests that "the way we interact with the world in knowing it becomes the way we interact with the world as we live in it . . . Our epistemology is quietly transformed into our ethic."[42] If beauty, even in its gendered form, shapes our epistemology, then we understand the world through the embodied person of Jesus Christ and our ethic becomes cruciform. As we engage in public discourse, it will be through a cruciform ethic that eschews power and position, and values self-giving love above all else.

---

42 Palmer, *To Know As We Are Known*, 21.

Response: Michael Jensen

I think the recovery of a theology of beauty in the form of Christ—especially via martyrdom—is one of the richest veins to open for contemporary public theology. The themes of desire, beauty, peace, and love are precisely the things we should be talking about in the public square, since we see these themes being played out all around us, and with much pain and confusion. Debates as apparently as diverse as marriage redefinition and border protection can be understood and addressed through these lenses.

I was interested in hearing more from Matt as to how the subject of the day—gender—is addressed by his themes. He set up a sophisticated and indispensable theological structure but my impression was that the relation of that structure to the issue of gender was under-explored. There were some teasing moments: "in a conversation about gender we must be open to the possibility that the other will expose our own broken desires"—yes, I think I see that. But it would be interesting to know what that might mean for the Christian community.

Likewise: "Gender is not formless." That seems to me a very strong statement about gender, which needs exploring if it is going to be meaningful. Matt helps us by telling us what to avoid here. The notion of gift guards, he claims, against exploitation, because we delight in rather than make use of gifts, I take it. We are also always coming to the objects of our desire as broken and sinful creatures ready to be remade and renewed, calling ourselves into question.

That's helpful, but if gender finds a form, how is that form to be discerned? And—given the recent very public attention focused on the transgender appropriation of the genderedness of the other as a role to be taken up—what can we helpfully and specifically say about the form of gender? Given the roles that the doctrine of creation and the fall need to play here, too, what can be said? Form, after all, is limitation. So: what are the limits to this form?

Become Like This Child: The Girl Child and the Kingdom at the Margins

Beth Jackson

Each year, October 11th marks the United Nations' International Day of the Girl Child. It's a day of highlighting the situation of girls and young women around the globe, promoting their human rights, and addressing issues of sustained discrimination, inequality, and abuse.[43] As we have just celebrated the twenty-fifth anniversary of the United Nations Convention on the Rights of the Child (UNCRC 1989)[44], it is acknowledged that much has improved for young people in the last quarter of a century. The UNCRC is the most ratified treaty in history with only two countries, USA and South Sudan, having yet to ratify this document. It is the widespread adoption of this treaty that has been credited with the vast improvement in the welfare of children globally.

---

43   For more information, see UN Women, "International Day of the Girl Child."
44   For the full text, see United Nations, "Convention on the Rights of the Child."

However, there is more work to be done. Much international attention has been given to improving the situation of female children around the world. A targeted millennium development goal in improving gender equality, particularly with regards to education, was identified. Whilst much progress has been seen at the primary level, girls are still far under-represented at secondary and tertiary educational institutions.

The UN's Beijing Declaration and Plan for Action also identified the girl child as one of their twelve critical areas of concern, stating, "Girls are often treated as inferior and are socialized to put themselves last, thus undermining their self-esteem. Discrimination and neglect in childhood can initiate a lifelong downward spiral of deprivation and exclusion from the social mainstream. Initiatives should be taken to prepare girls to participate actively, effectively and equally with boys at all levels of social, economic, political and cultural leadership."[45]

UNICEF reports that as children begin the second decade of their lives, gender begins to play a role in shaping mortality patterns.[46] Several studies have demonstrated that rates of violence against girls and women are "higher in societies characterized by unequal gender roles, where 'manhood' is defined in terms of dominance and 'womanhood' is constrained by the fulfilment of certain rigid codes of conduct."[47] To this, one could also add child trafficking, forced child labour, child marriage, female genital mutilation, the effect of HIV/AIDS, sex-selective abortions, and infanticide amongst other significant global issues whose effect is greatest on the world's poor, 70 percent of whom are women and girls. We need not labour the point longer, as the plight of the girl child in our contemporary context is well documented and widely recognised.

---

45   UN Women, "The United Nations Fourth World Conference on Women," point 260.
46   UNICEF, "A Statistical Snapshot of Violence Against Girls," 3.
47   Ibid., 17.

The Universality of Childhood

One may ask why a close examination of the girl child is an important aspect of understanding gender discourse. However, to overlook the child, or even to assume the girl child as part of the larger female population, would be to miss an important distinction that has sociological, but perhaps more importantly, theological, significance.

Whilst there is no universal experience of "the child," and there are those who suggest that childhood is merely a cultural construct,[48] few could dispute the observation that childhood is a universal experience. Childhood is universally normative; over a third of the global population is under the age of fifteen. According to the UN, nearly 6.3 million children under the age of five died in 2013 alone, predominantly in sub-Saharan Africa and the Indian subcontinent.[49] With infant mortality so high, reaching adulthood in some parts of our world can be considered a privilege. However, rarely in our theological thinking is the child, in particular the girl child, considered normative.

Yet, even with the universality of childhood, an inequality exists between male and female children. In addition to the situations previously mentioned, in Chad, for example, for every one hundred boys who gain entry to secondary school, only forty-four girls receive a place.[50] This is not an isolated statistic. The inequality gap between the genders only widens as the young people grow and reach adulthood, where the young men often assume positions of authority, thus perpetuating the cycle. Therefore, as we further examine children in theological discourse, the girl child offers a distinct and important perspective.

---

48   The focus of this particular paper is not around the construct of childhood. However, for a more sustained discussion see James and Prout, *Constructing and Reconstructing Childhood*.

49   UNICEF, "Under-Five Mortality."

50   UNICEF, "State of the World's Children 2015."

Power and Agency

As feminist theologian Kate Ott argues, "children by virtue of age and ability as well as socio-economic position globally reside in tenuous space of non-agency, in many cases not counted as fully human in social practice and theoretically removed from the possibility of having agency in theological discourse."[51] Whilst I find Ott's argument compelling, I don't find it entirely convincing. Children are certainly disadvantaged by virtue of their age, ability, and socioeconomic and political positions, but whilst they may lack power, they don't entirely occupy a space of non-agency. Children have vast potential for social, political, and theological agency. One of the key words within childhood studies in the last twenty years has been "participation." Children act as participants, or social actors, within their communities through their participation in the political process in appropriate ways and using their voices in addressing issues of their concern. This increased participation has been a key outcome of the UNCRC. However, as with any context, "how, where, and when children should participate is a cultural construction"[52] and more appropriate in some contexts than others.

The Birmingham Children's Crusade

One very notable example historically of the political, social, and theological agency of children comes from my own cultural background. With thanks to director Spike Lee and his Academy-award-nominated documentary, many of us are very familiar with the tragic story of the "4 Little Girls" and the Sixteenth Street Baptist Church bombing in Birmingham, Alabama, in September, 1963. However, even as a university student living in Birmingham three decades later, I was less aware of another significant event involving young people in the civil rights movement: The Birmingham Children's Crusade. In May of 1963, just four months before the infamous bombing, over a thousand children, some as young as six, walked out of school and joined a non-violent protest march from Sixteenth Street Baptist

---

51   Ott, "Children as An/other Subject," 2.

52   Skelton, "Children, Young People, Unicef and Participation," 169.

Church onto the streets of Birmingham towards City Hall where their plan was to kneel and pray for a more inclusive community. Most were arrested upon arrival; the jails were overflowing with young people without hope for bail. However, it didn't deter the movement and the next day another 900 young women and men joined the protest march. Unfortunately, as they left the church, they were met with police dogs, high pressure fire hoses, and police with batons. As the images of that day were shown through the media around the globe, there was, understandably, a public outcry. Even some within the movement questioned the ethics of allowing children to face known violence, most notably Malcolm X. Anecdotally, it is recorded that most parents discouraged their children from joining, and yet, this large group of young people had a vested interest in securing a just and equitable future for themselves and following generations. As Martin Luther King, Jr. himself said, these "disinherited children of God" had "a sense of their own stake in freedom and justice."[53] They could not vote, they had no jobs or money, by all other accounts they were powerless. However, they were not without social and political agency. Their actions have oft been heralded as the turning point in the civil rights movement, mobilising a groundswell of support around the country and throughout the world.

The political agency of these young women and men was largely unrecognised by those holding power, including King himself. Due to an unequal distribution of power, we often read history from a King-centric perspective of the civil rights movement. According to Hasan Jeffries, "the King-centric perspective . . . deemphasizes the importance of grass-roots organizing, the slow and hard work of getting ordinary people to act on their deeply held desire to change the status quo."[54]

It is precisely this unequal distribution of power which enables us to overlook the political and social agency of the subaltern voice. This is precisely why child theology is such a crucial lens through which to examine gender as it gives voice to the subaltern girl child.

---

53   Burrow and Long, *A Child Shall Lead Them*, 113.

54   Crosby, *Civil Rights History from the Ground Up*, 262.

Child Theology and the Girl Child

The voice of the child in serious theological enquiry has been largely absent throughout history. Marcia Bunge's 2001 book, *The Child in Christian Thought*, highlights that whilst "there has been a groundswell in new scholarship on children from psychologists, sociologists, historians and philosophers, contemporary theologians have, on the whole, neglected childhood as a serious intellectual or moral concern."[55] Therefore, not a great deal of sustained thinking has been done on the contribution of the child in theological inquiry.

However, in the past decade, the intersection of children and theology has found a renewed energy. An emergent area of theology, child theology, has sought to address this significant gap and converge the world of the child with theological thought. The term, child theology, was coined only in 2001 in a forum of mission practitioners working with children at risk around the globe. There was considered a need for a more engaged theological reflection around mission practice. The central motif of The Child Theology Movement is "no child-related activity without theological reflection; no theology without the child in the midst."[56] The defining text of some of those engaged in child theology is found in Matthew 18, where Jesus placed a child in the midst of a conversation around the themes of power and politics. The disciples were arguing about who was the greatest in the kingdom of God when Jesus takes intentional and deliberate action.

> He called a child, whom he put among them, and said, "Truly I tell you, unless you change and become like children, you will never enter the kingdom of heaven. Whoever becomes humble like this child is the greatest in the kingdom of heaven. Whoever welcomes one such child in my name welcomes me." (Matthew 18:1–4)

---

55   Bunge, *The Child in Christian Thought*, xi.
56   Willmer and White, *Entry Point*, 13.

Jesus takes this unnamed and ungendered child and declares them a sign of God's kingdom. This child, who could have been male or female, points those seeking power and position to a new sign of the kingdom of God. The child Jesus placed in the midst becomes the lens for us in understanding God's kingdom. For as Judith Gundry-Volf highlights, "Jesus did not just teach how to make an adult world kinder and more just for children; he taught the arrival of a social world in part defined by and organized around children."[57]

We must be careful not to take a romanticised or idealised view of this child that Jesus placed in the midst of the disciples. Children, as with all of humanity, are wonderfully complex and not unambiguous. We hold in tension that children are simultaneously human "beings" and human "becomings," a parallel tension, one could argue, to the kingdom of God. The UNCRC is heralded for highlighting this emphasis in its document, but it has been a theological truth long held well before the UN's inception. Children, both male and female, are bearers of the *imago Dei*, created in the image of God as fully human and of intrinsic worth and value. Yet, children are still in a place of physical, moral, and psychosocial development and need the presence of others to guide and direct that growth.

Power, Normativity, and the Kingdom of God

This kingdom of God, as demonstrated in Matthew 18, offers an alternative narrative to the dominant one played out in our world and seen through the grim statistics. As a sign of this kingdom, we see all conceptions of power through the lens of the child Jesus placed in the midst. What if in our theological enquiry the girl child becomes normative? How do our conceptions of gender, power, and politics change? What if it was an eleven-year-old Cambodian sex slave placed in the midst of the disciples' conversation? What if we place an eight-year-old AIDS orphan who is looking after her five-year-old brother in the discussion on who is the greatest in the kingdom of God? Does this shape our understanding of power within God's economy? How might a child theology reading, with particular reference to

---

57 Bunge, *The Child in Christian Thought*, 60.

the girl child, help us shape a more constructive understanding of power in the public square and our kingdom response?

Kingdom Call To Relocate Power

A child theology reading is a kingdom call to eschew worldly power, in all its various forms. The kingdom call, seen through the lens of the girl child, is a counter-intuitive call to transform and relocate power. It is precisely this counter-narrative that we, as followers of Jesus, are called to model. Redefining power by relocating the source is timely and necessary. What is power within the kingdom of God and in whom does it truly reside?

The UNCRC has at its essence a desire to *empower* children to be participants in shaping their communities and the world. Empowering others who otherwise don't hold power in any given situation requires the powerful to willingly give away power to those without. How much, how often, and in what way they give away this power is controlled by those who hold the power. Therefore, ultimately, they still hold the power.

However, at the heart of the gospel is the notion of kenosis. Jesus's kenotic act—his incarnation in the form of an infant and his cruciform life—reveals God's willingness to completely eschew worldly notions of power. Rather than empowering his people, God surrendered his own power to become powerless in the incarnation, for there is nothing more powerless than a newborn child. In Christ, God redefined and transformed power, and as followers committed to living this alternate narrative, surely this reading points us to a similar cruciform and kenotic life.

However, some feminist theologians find this idea problematic. Daphne Hampson argues that "given women's oppressed state in human history, notions of self-sacrifice, self-abnegation, and service to others may only undercut women's struggle for full humanity and further justify oppressive structures."[58] I have some sympathy with Hampson's view as too often women, including young women, are expected to sacrifice for their

---

58   Papanikolaou, "Person, Kenosis and Abuse," 43.

male counterparts. We see this ultimately in sex-selective abortions. As noted previously, the Beijing Declaration highlighted the fact that girls are socialised to count themselves as least.

However, I have more resonance with Sarah Coakley who sees "a defence of some version of kenosis as not only compatible with feminism, but vital to a distinctively Christian manifestation of it."[59] She prefers to speak of a "power-in-vulnerability" that redefines power in a cruciform way.

I would like to recommend a third way which recognises the integral agency of the subaltern, in this case, the girl child, without the pursuit of power. Whilst Coakley's redefinition is helpful, I think a relocation is vital. Gayatri Spivak, a postcolonial critic, does offer a helpful contribution as we begin to construct an argument for the voice of the subaltern girl child in theological discourse. Spivak, herself not a theologian, examines "the margins at which disciplinary discourses break down and enter the world of political agency."[60] Spivak begins to develop the idea of turning the dominant narratives inside out. She recognises that she, an Indian women of affluence and influence in the American academy, possesses the unique opportunity to bring the outside into the centre as she resides in that space of being both "in" and "out." In her book, *Outside in the Teaching Machine*, Spivak addresses this apparent contradiction by seeking to re-centre the margins in arguing that the centre is also a margin. She correlates this centre to a centre line on a road, as opposed to the idea of a centre of a town or a hub. This "reconfiguring of the 'centre' (or re-centring, perhaps) also changes the position and status of the margins: no longer outside looking in, but an integral, if minor, language."[61] This classic deconstruction position places the margins in clear view of the centre.

Spivak's theory of re-centring the margins offers rich possibilities for the understanding of the agency of the girl child in political, social, moral, and theological discourse without seeking worldly notions of power

---

59   Hampson, *Swallowing a Fishbone*, 83.
60   Landry and MacLean, *The Spivak Reader*, 3.
61   "Gayatri Chakravorty Spivak," Postcolonial Studies at Emory.

or *empowerment*. In Jesus's act of placing a child in the midst, he re-centred the margins, the space girl children naturally occupy, and relocated power outside the centre. Power located in the margins is not so readily recognised as power but is properly understood as social, political, and theological agency in the way of the kingdom.

The hundreds of children arrested during The Birmingham Children's Crusade always remained on the margins, never gaining power in the way of Martin Luther King, Jr, but their action and presence had a significant impact on a nation and, indeed, the world.

Conclusion

In the action of Jesus placing a child in the midst of a theological discussion on power, he transformed and relocated the disciples' understanding of power within the kingdom of God. Jesus foregrounded the child as a sign of God's kingdom which offers Christians an alternate narrative for understanding the exercise of power. Engaging our theological imagination, we have placed a contemporary girl child in the midst in order to examine notions of power and agency with reference to the gendered child. Jesus's call for the kingdom requires a re-centring of the margins, such that the subaltern girl child and indeed all voices from the margins, young or old, male or female, black or white, find voice in the public square.

Response: Matthew Andrew

Let me begin by thanking Beth for a stimulating and enlightening paper. Not only was it interesting to discover parts of history such as the Birmingham Children's Crusade, but it was also challenging to be forced to think through what it means for Jesus to have foregrounded the place of children in the kingdom. I am both deeply interested in, and sympathetic to, Beth's examination of what this means for our understanding of power. It is here that I have two questions.

My first question relates to how Beth understands non-worldly power, or what she calls "social, political, and theological agency in the way of the kingdom." In Beth's conclusion she wants to avoid speaking of empowerment or worldly power, and uses Spivak's work to help articulate a different vision of power. Beth returns, however, to the illustration of the Birmingham Children's Crusade as—if I read her correctly—a non-worldly exercise of power. My question is this: how it is non-worldly? Is it non-worldly because it didn't gain the children further power and recognition in the way of Martin Luther King, Jr? Their failure to achieve this—their marginality—seems accidental to the enterprise. What distinguishes the children's crusade from other movements of activism such a King's?

My second question is whether the definition of a child that Beth seems to use in her piece is granular enough. The definition seems to come from the United Nations Convention on the Rights of the Child whereby a child is anyone under the age of eighteen. Does this give us a clear enough vision if we are trying to understand what it means for Jesus to be empowering children as social actors?

Rowan Williams—persuasively to my mind—locates as one of the key conditions of childhood the ability for children to try out language and other aspects of their agency without fear of consequences.[62] My five-year-old daughter, after picking up the language from a book we were reading, called my wife an "ugly witch." My wife had to suppress a smile as she responded. I would not get the same reaction.

In the same way, were my daughter to be seventeen, her maturity earns her the dubious privilege of being fully accountable for her words. No doubt we are coming up against the "being" and "becoming" of children that Beth highlights in her piece. This "agency of play"—if we can call it that—imparts a fragility to the actions of a young child that is not true of a seventeen-year-old.

Let us take the Birmingham Children's Crusade as an instructive instance of the exercise of child power. Sending a five-year-old to face violence seems an affront to this fragility, a sense that too harsh a clash with non-benevolent power will damage something irreplaceable. Is Jesus imbuing children with a power which might cost them one of the very things that marks them out as children? In contrast, sending a seventeen-year-old could be seen as a difficult assumption of adult responsibility. So, is the UN definition granular enough?

These questions aside, let me once more thank Beth for the chance to hear and interact with her work.

---

62   Williams, *Lost Icons*.

Response: Michael Jensen

In most churches I have been in, we have customarily sent children out to a different building when it came time for the serious theological business of the reading of Scripture and the sermon. Now there are good reasons for it, and I am sure if we took a snap poll of the kids on a Sunday morning, they'd vote for going out to their age-appropriate programs! Nevertheless, there's a powerful symbolic message in the exclusion of children from our worship, if we don't do it carefully—that children are tolerable for about ten minutes, and that God likes quiet.

And that's where it would be interesting to ask: what could churches do, week by week, to signal the remarkable centring of children that the gospel invites?

I was interested to reflect, in the first instance, that a lot of Beth's examples came from the experience of children in the two-thirds world. If anything, the child in the rich West is thoroughly centred and included, given extraordinary toys and pampered with luxurious experiences. The middle-class children in my area of Sydney are chauffeured around in SUVs as they go from private school to flute lessons to maths coaching to a playdate at Cynthia's. What might child theology have to say to the idolisation of the child as a symbol of prosperity?

It is interesting also to note that Jesus, while bringing the child into the centre, both uses the child as a lesson for adults—it is child-like-ness in humility that he is teaching them—and also doesn't give the child in question a voice. We don't hear from the child in the story. In fact, as Beth points out herself, we don't even know what age or gender the child is. She, or he, remains a parable for adult behaviour. I wonder if Gundry-Volf's comment about "the arrival of a social world in part defined by and organized around children" is thus an overstatement. Is the text of Matthew 18:1–4 being squeezed for more than it will actually give?

I think it is important that a description of *kenosis* be done in a very careful way, as well. Does God himself "surrender his own power to become powerless"? I hesitate here, because, while it is true that what is true of one of the persons of the Trinity is true of the others, it was only the Son who became incarnate and died on the cross. The self-emptying of the Son is not the same as the self-emptying of God. God remains sovereign and almighty, even as he displays that sovereignty through the work of the Son. The Scriptures depict the vindication, ascension, and exaltation of the Son. *Kenosis* undermines worldly notions of power—and I think we could have heard about that from 1 Corinthians rather than from Spivak—but it does not undermine power itself. The story of divine power is not just about *kenosis*—*kenosis* is but one act in the drama.

Gender, Politics, and Power

Michael Jensen

"He Will Rule over You"

I begin with the recent words of Justice Harrison, at the sentencing of Christopher Cullen to a thirty-year prison term for the murder of his wife Comrie in January 2014:

> Mr Cullen callously decided to kill the deceased for his own selfish and personal reasons. Her death was unnecessary, unwarranted, unfair and inexcusable. The death of the deceased is another example of the extremely prevalent violence perpetrated by men in our society against women to whom they are married or with whom they share a relationship of domestic intimacy.[63]

Cullen drove his estranged wife to a secluded fishing club, where he launched a savage attack on her with knives he had bought on the journey.

---

63   ABC News, "Christopher Cullen sentenced."

Let's not beat around the bush: this is where the issue of gender, power, and politics really lives. How human beings understand and experience the relationship of gender to power and power to gender is not simply theoretical. The blood of Comrie Cullen cries out from the ground. Her terrible wounds are a terrible inscription of the ancient judgement on Eve: *Your desire will be for your husband, and he will rule over you.*[64]

For many women, even sadly in the church, the reality is that the intervention of the *polis* into the domestic world comes too late.

How is the gospel of Jesus Christ good news for the world of the Cullen family? What can it say about the practice of power by men over women? In this paper I will try to show that the Christian church is invited into a radically different practice of common living—a politics in other words—in which those with supposedly natural advantages of power, including men, are to express their advantage in loving and costly service, inviting those who are apparently weaker into relationships of profound mutuality. The complication is that the church itself is not as yet a fulfilment of the promise it has received. The invitation in many respects lies on the church table, unopened.

Hannah Arendt: Public and Private Life

In order to provide some back-story for the discussion, I should like to enlist the help of the German-born political theorist Hannah Arendt (1906–1975). In Arendt's landmark work *The Human Condition,* first published in 1958, she argues that Western philosophy since Plato has denigrated the world of human action, or the *vita activa*, and has subordinated it to the contemplative life (the *vita contemplativa*).[65]

In her second chapter, "The Public and Private Realm," Arendt explains how we moderns find it difficult to understand the sharp division

---

64   I am aware of the ambiguity of this verse. Wenham is undecided as to whether Eve's "desire" is an urge to dominate or a sexual desire. Wenham, *Genesis*, 81.

65   Arendt, *The Human Condition.*

in the world of the Greeks between the public and private realms, "a division," she says "upon which all ancient thought rested as self-evident and axiomatic."[66] The loss of that division is symbolised by the use of the word "economy" to describe the very public monetary affairs of the nation, and yet which takes its heritage from the Greek word *oikonomos*, or "house-keeper."

The private realm was the sphere of "natural" community, and driven by the bodily necessities of survival. In this sphere, the tasks of man and woman were divided: to one was given the duty of the provision of food, to the other was given the task of giving birth. For the Greek philosophers, because the domestic sphere was pre-political, and driven by necessity, force and violence were justified within it. If you owned slaves, for example, it was necessary to master them, with violence if necessary.

Mastery of the private sphere meant that one could enter the sphere of the political, and therefore exercise freedom. Indeed, to liberate oneself from the necessities needed for survival meant true freedom. The Greek *polis* was a sphere in which men could interact as equals, to put aside violence, and to persuade others with words instead. The household, on the other hand, was the realm of strict and unequal hierarchy. So, as Arendt describes it: "Within the realm of the household, freedom did not exist, for the household head, its ruler, was considered to be free only in so far as he had the power to leave the household and enter the political realm, where all were equals."[67]

Private and public named those things that should be hidden and those things which could be shown. Things connected with the necessity of bodily survival were the business of slaves and women. Women did not belong to someone else like slaves, but their lives were, like that of the slave, devoted to matters of the body. They were, as Aristotle would explain in his *Politics,* expected to act virtuously, but their virtue was relative to the obedience. As he says: "The courage of a man is shown in commanding, of a woman in obeying."[68]

---

66   Arendt, *The Human Condition*, 28.
67   Arendt, *The Human Condition*, 32.
68   Aristotle, *Politics*, 51.

On Arendt's account, things become complicated when the boundary between public and private sphere, between the *polis* and the *oikos*, became blurred by what she calls "the rise of the social." That is, the formerly concealed activities of the private sphere—what we might call "housekeeping"—emerged into the sphere of public concern. We got for ourselves an economy; and true political activity, instead of focusing on the discussion of noble ideas and virtuous free action, became a matter of bureaucracy and banality driven by necessity. The private world likewise shrank, and became a "shelter of the intimate."[69] Matters of bodily concern, like health and welfare, became public concerns rather than private matters.

It is not my purpose here to give a critical exposition of Hannah Arendt, interesting though that may be, but rather to pick up her description of the ancient distinction between the private and public spheres as the starting point for my consideration of the theme of gender, power, and politics. Arendt has been criticised by some feminists, in fact, for being too nostalgic about the division between private and public;[70] for we can readily see that the hiddenness of the operations of power in the private world leave women open to the kind of abuse that Comrie Cullen suffered. Arendt's longing was for a revitalisation of the old idea of the public sphere.

The domestic world, even today, is shaped by the necessities of bodily life: of sex, reproduction, food, and shelter. How does power then operate in the domestic world? It has a tendency always to exist in a structured and hierarchical form because of the presence of children who are not equal but dependent on the labour of the parents for survival and flourishing. A brute fact of the domestic environment, of which we are continually reminded by painful experience, is that between male and female there is, ordinarily, a disparity at the level of physical power. That disparity becomes,

---

69   Arendt, *The Human Condition*, 38.

70   In partially defending Arendt, Seyla Benhabib writes: "It is thus hard to avoid the impression that in these early passages of *The Human Condition*, Arendt ontologizes the division of labor between the sexes, and those biological presuppositions which have historically confined women to the household and to the sphere of reproduction alone." Benhabib, "Feminist Theory and Hannah Arendt's Concept of Public Space," 98.

in a percentage of cases which is hideous to imagine, not just a difference of strength in theory. The hiddenness of the private sphere is a shadow world from which we, the public, sometimes hear vague reports. There, the public, democratic, peaceable man, the doer of public goods and the possessor of visible virtues, can become a vicious tyrant of the hearth.

As with so many things in the modern world, this is where the "social" (in Arendt's terms) seeks to make its intervention into the private realm. It seeks to make inquiry by means of statistical analysis; to attempt healing by providing social work and psychiatry; and to make judgement through the process of family and sometimes criminal law. You can see how these are necessary; but also how they are ill-designed to "redress the wounds of individuals whose 'home' has been their 'hell'" (in feminist philosopher Seyla Benhabib's words).[71] Peering voyeuristically through the windows of Australian homes we have started to grasp a terrible truth: that the home is still oftentimes, as in the days of Aristotle, a scene for the exercise of the absolute and unchecked power of male over female.

As a generalisation, the contemporary discourses surrounding gender, power, and politics tend to focus on women's access to the freedoms of public life. When we ask "what can we do?" we think immediately of what can be done by governments or their agencies, who ultimately have coercive power. Is this not the problem simply displaced? This situation poses a familiar dilemma for liberal societies, who both celebrate human freedom and cannot abide what it turns out people do with it.

The Christian Home

There are points at which Jesus of Nazareth preached such an unsettling of the private realm that we can scarcely believe what he is saying. We hear this shocking pronouncement in Matthew 10, for example:

---

71   Benhabib, "Feminist Theory and Hannah Arendt's Concept of Public Space," 111.

Do not suppose that I have come to bring peace to the earth. I did not come to bring peace, but a sword. For I have come to turn

"a man against his father,

a daughter against her mother,

a daughter-in-law against her mother-in-law—

a man's enemies will be the members of his own household."

Anyone who loves their father or mother more than me is not worthy of me; anyone who loves their son or daughter more than me is not worthy of me. (Matt 10:34–7)

The turmoil Jesus brings is not simply to the public but also to the private world. The "natural" order of things is about to be overthrown, and violently so. But one has to keep a careful eye on this. Jesus is not inviting his followers to revolutionary action, but describing rather the conditions under which they will have to live. In this apocalyptic picture, survival is not guaranteed by the ordinary family structure, just as it is not guaranteed by membership of a particular *polis*. A Roman citizen may find himself betrayed by his kinsmen and rejected by the state.

Thus in the New Testament epistles we get a picture of a new set of relationships which are analogous to both public and private spheres, but fully neither, and, indeed, something else again. In Ephesians 2:19 we find the private and the public strikingly overlaid: "you are no longer foreigners and strangers, but fellow citizens with God's people and also members of his household . . . "

Christians have been called into a new household. It is a place of the provision of what is necessary for spiritual survival, and because of the practice of having things in common, a place for the provision of bodily necessities as well. But it is also a new public sphere, where full and equal citizenship is granted to members so that they may interact with one another in freedom.

The constitution of this new form of community is not the determination of its members to love one another. It is not a "voluntary" society in that sense. It is formed by God in Jesus Christ by the Holy Spirit, and given as a gift. Grace is its constitution. But love is its ethos. The members of this household, the citizens of this kingdom, have an eschatological and spiritual unity which they are to receive and to realise in this present evil age. Because of this, the love which is standing orders of the Christian community is cruciform. It is of necessity sacrificial and forbearing, lived out in acts of service for the other.

Strikingly, citizenship and full membership are given to Jew and Gentile, slave and free, male and female. There is no sense in which the labour of slaves and women in the private sphere enables a man to enter into public life. On the contrary, the means of survival having been provided from above, the liberty of full citizenship is given to all.

But it is also the case that the Christian maintains a dual citizenship, and with it an ongoing loyalty to those earthly ways of life. The emperor is still to be honoured. National identities are not dissolved but rather included. Slaves and masters, husbands and wives, children and parents—these household relationships are still operational, even as they are relativised. They are among the "human institutions," the *ktiseis* of 1 Peter 2:13, which are to be recognised and honoured, even as their limitations and their temporality is exposed by the gospel of Christ.

What this means is that those ordinarily in power in the household sphere are invited in the Christian community not to lay down their authority or to pursue a kind of anarchy. The Christian community as it seeks to live under the rule of Christ will not lapse into anarchy either. The gospel is not the declaration of the disappearance of authority and power in human life. Rather, those to whom power has been given are called on to exercise that advantage in a way that imitates the cross of Jesus Christ.

This is what we see in the so-called *haustelfen*, the household codes, in the New Testament—and why they are so annoying to contemporary commentators.[72] The resemblance of these passages to passages in Aristotle's *Politics* does not escape notice. For Aristotle, the household head had complete (and sometimes violent) mastery of the private world, and this stemmed from the superior rationality of the male. He addresses husbands and wives, slaves and masters, parents and children.

And yet, there are several crucial differences. For a start, the New Testament makes no appeal to a superior rational capacity in males. Secondly, the invitation in Ephesians 5:20 to "submit to one another" as a kind of heading for the exposition of the household code signals that a shared reverence for Jesus Christ permeates all relationships in the new community. He is its true head. The fundamental basis for the relationships that follow was not "nature," or something that was universally true of men as men and women as women, but the sacrificial love of Jesus Christ. It is to this sacrificial love that Paul appeals when he describes the essence of true husbandly behaviour. If there is any thought that the masculine body gives to the husband a "natural" advantage of power and authority, it is given no chance for anything other than expression through humble service—which would have been a humiliating thought for the Graeco-Roman male.

Thirdly, it would also have been unthinkable for Aristotle to urge husbands by saying, as Paul does in Eph 5:28: "In the same way, husbands should love their wives as they do their own bodies. He who loves his wife loves himself."

The husband is not called to dominate so that he can free himself for political action. He is rather called into mutuality—to give and receive the necessities of bodily life and share in a mutual liberty in the Spirit. This is the direction of another controversial passage as well: in 1 Corinthians 11, the "headship" of the husband is only the start of Paul's logic, which ends in the mutual interdependence of husband and wife: "in the Lord woman is

---

72   Colossians 3:18–25, Ephesians 5:20–33, 1 Peter 3:1–7.

not independent of man or man independent of woman" (1 Cor 11:10). Paul would also direct the husband to his wife not just as labourer in the fields of child-bearing, but as his partner in sexual pleasure. The husband still has authority over the wife's body, but his body is likewise not his own: *she* has authority over *his* body (1 Cor 7:4).

Thus, co-membership in the household of God is to be transformative of natural family life. The experience of being a spiritual equal enjoying the liberty of Christ with his wife is to effect a transformation of husbandly masculinity—which is still recognisably husbandly and masculine.

A Gift Not Yet Opened

Yet it would be insulting to the experience of many women in the church to hold up this revamped vision of marriage as mutual and reciprocal as an ideal that has been successfully realised. The early Christian treatment of women did have a marked impact on ancient society.[73] Graeco-Roman women would find in lifelong, exclusive Christian marriages a better flourishing than they did in the pagan equivalent. It was not surprising that Christianity was attractive to many women. For both men and women, the freedom of the *polis* was not to be found in the suppressing of the domestic, but rather in the cultivation of a deeper companionship within the home. Service and freedom were not now opposites; they belonged together.

Nevertheless, the evidence sadly shows that, even in the church, many men and women are living out an untransformed version of gender roles, with coercive power, whether real or implied, as the constitutive force. Sadly, we have also to admit that theological reasoning and biblical texts have been too often deployed as a nuclear-grade weapon by husbands seeking the means to master their wives.

The failure of the church to embody the vision of loving community to which it witnesses should neither lead us to complacency nor despair,

---

73   Stark, *The Rise of Christianity*.

however. The lessons of recent experience remind us that the church is not yet a perfected community. The church should remember, as it confesses its sins each week, that it is a gathering of the forgiven and eminently fallible. It will contain among its members the abused, and their abusers. It should not be blind to this reality. It was never constituted to point to its own perfection, but rather as an unfinished work of the Holy Spirit it points to its heavenly future—a future for which it should yearn, and seek to trace into the present age.

That possibility is a source of real hope, because it is an invitation to embrace the identity and purpose we have been called to as men and women in full humility and without denying the need for ongoing transformation. It opens us to the work of the Holy Spirit—and who knows what miracles the Spirit might perform?

Response: Matthew Andrew

I first want to thank Michael for a fascinating paper. Being reminded of the way in which Christian household ethics differed from that of wider Graeco-Roman society is both helpful and timely. His argument that the Graeco-Roman notion of the private sphere was upended by the Christian household as a new public sphere where *God* is provider is deeply illuminating. It is something I will no doubt carry into my own understanding of our ecclesial and political situation.

Michael's piece did leave me with a question. He built on the apocalyptic pronouncements of Jesus and on Ephesians 2:19 to argue for the church as a new form of life which is both public and private, and yet neither. Michael then argued that there is a kind of dual citizenship for church members as old structures are not erased but are transformed. It is the church as "household" which is given particular attention within this framework.

There is an equivocation, however, in the use of "household" which conceals an important ethical question. This equivocation is, as Michael demonstrated, a New Testament one: "household" is applied both to the church and family unit within that church. Yet the very fact that individual households are regulated separately from the life of the church more broadly—though with a common ethos—leaves me wondering how the sub-relationship between *church* as household and *individual* households works. Do individual households—as one of the old structures that were not erased—share in the ambiguity of public and private that the broader church does? Or it is just that the use of power within them has been changed?

Abuse is more often than not a hidden phenomenon. Michael's piece has made me wonder whether the individual family unit's relationship to the broader church reconfigures our ethics relating to privacy, and if so, in what way this might help us discern and confront violence in families within the church. This is beyond the scope of what Michael was trying to accomplish, but I think it is a question that his work has helpfully raised. So once again my thanks to Michael for a thought-provoking piece.

Response: Beth Jackson

I appreciate Michael's opening assertion that "how human beings understand and experience the relationship of gender to power and power to gender is not simply theoretical." For all of us, this is a lived experience and often times that lived experience is painful. Yes, as he rightly states, "even sadly in the church." However, perhaps we should take that one step further and assert, "particularly in the church," as the church has, albeit inadvertently, sanctioned this behaviour through its long-held theological assertions for far too long. We all were shaken and distressed by the painfully revealing article in the Sydney Morning Herald in March of this year detailing one woman's traumatic experience at the hands of her reportedly "Christian" husband, *Abuse inside Christian marriages—a personal story*.[74] We know this is not an isolated experience.

As concerned and engaged followers of Christ, we recognise a need to articulate a different response and I am intrigued by Michael's assertion that Christ effects "a transformation of husbandly masculinity—which is still recognisably husbandly and masculine." I find it hard to define what is recognisably masculine. As Jennifer Glancy highlights in her chapter on New Testament masculinities, "in the Pastoral Epistles we find such a specification

---

74   Young, "Abuse inside Christian Marriages."

of what constitutes legitimate masculinity, ranging from a valorisation of self-control as the epitome of virtue to an insistence that Christian men should exert a controlling influence over their wives and offspring."[75] I'm not entirely convinced that we can claim a single definition of "biblical" masculinity or indeed what a transformation of that might resemble. I think close examination of the text doesn't allow us to make such sweeping generalisations. Otherwise, as Michael is careful to avoid, we could easily find ourselves once again in the place of legitimising gender-based violence. My hope is that the church is earnestly seeking to articulate a different response.

As a missiologist, my primary concern is that the kingdom of God is good news for women and men, old and young, Indigenous and non-Indigenous. I would like to go further than Michael in his call to strive for a vision that can't be realised this side of the eschaton. I would hope that Christian communities could model the kingdom vision here and now of a "profound mutuality" in our relationships with one another, male and female, young and old, Indigenous and non-Indigenous. I think this would require a new way of thinking that extends beyond our public/private binaries and indeed beyond the Graeco-Roman household code. It requires us to advocate for faith communities who intentionally exercise "profound mutuality" in the lived experience, who are marked by an inclusivity that fosters this mutuality, and who demonstrate a new way of relating to one another and those in the public square.

---

75   Glancy, *Protocols*, 237.

Part Seven

Gender, Biology, and Identity

The Biology of Sex and Gender

Patricia Weerakoon and Kamal Weerakoon

Introduction: Gender Complexity Today

Traditionally, a person identifies as being either "male" or "female." In Genesis 1:26–27, God creates humanity in his image, indicating that to be a human is to be either a male or a female, ruling out androgyny. In Genesis 2, the man fulfils his function of tending the garden complemented by woman, who is the same "kind" of being as him—his own "flesh and bone." Not a mere clone but a "helper suitable."[1]

Humanity's dimorphic gendered nature is affirmed throughout the biblical record. Characters are unambiguously stated as being either man or woman. Jesus was a man—the angel Gabriel announces to Mary that she will bear a son (Luke 1:31); the New Testament uses the male pronoun for Jesus;

---

1   This paper makes no comment on whether gender "complementarity" necessarily involves a "hierarchy" of male "headship." For this paper, the "complementarity" of male and female means simply that the two genders "fit" harmoniously together by divine creational intent. We hope this can be affirmed by both traditional "complementarians" and "egalitarians" who hold to complementarity without hierarchy.

he is son of God-David-Man. Jesus affirms the creation accounts of Genesis 1 and 2 (Matt 19:4). When marriage is used as a metaphor for the relationship between God and his people, Yahweh or Christ is unambiguously a male husband, and Israel or the church, a female bride.

This binary definition of gender is challenged by two developments. Medically, we now understand the complexities of gender and sexual development. More significantly, popular anthropology espoused by contemporary Western society is characterised by individualism, autonomy, and hedonism. Social assumptions prejudice people towards interpreting the medical data as creating a positive obligation to permit, even "celebrate," gender fluidity, and a parallel obligation to censure any ethical system which restricts gender identification to binary categories—like the Bible. But gender science is not against the Bible—this paper will interpret the scientific results in a manner consistent with biblical anthropology, including binary gender.

Defining the Terms "Sex" and "Gender"

Historically, *sex* has been considered a binary, biologically determined, category determined at birth, associated primarily with the physical attributes:

- chromosomes—XX female or XY male;

- gonads—ovaries or testes;

- hormones—testosterone or oestrogen; and

- matching external and internal anatomy.

Gender has referred to socially constructed roles, behaviours, and attributes that a given society considers appropriate for men and women.[2] In this view, it was assumed that:[3]

---

2 Money and Ehrhardt, *Man & Woman, Boy & Girl.*
3 West and Zimmerman, "Doing Gender," 125–151.

- What can be seen and demonstrated (i.e., chromosomes, gonads, hormones, genitals, and reproductive potential) is innate—biological or "natural";

- All individuals are psychosexually neutral at birth;

- A person's gender self-identification (i.e., male or female), the role they play (i.e., masculine or feminine) and erotic attraction (to men or women) are determined by external factors of environment and nurture, and under a person's volitional control and choice.

This nature–nurture dichotomy was called into question in the 1980s, and culminated with a debate on the sexual reassignment of one of twin boys as a girl following surgical misadventure at birth. Known as the "John/Joan" case, the infant's penis and testis were removed and the child reared as a girl. After years of problems, "she" committed suicide.[4]

The detachment of gender from any form of biological determination, and maximisation of individualistic, autonomous volition, has led to gender being considered a "spectrum." Facebook has increased its options for gender self-identification—in June 2014 the UK site had seventy-one options.[5]

Interplay of Nature and Nurture

Two current areas of research suggest that gender and sexuality are constructed by both nature *and* nurture.

First, techniques for *brain imaging* and mapping (like functional magnetic resonance imaging) and neurochemical studies enable the study of brain activity, changes, and differences in male and female brains. For instance, total brain volume, like body size, is larger in males than females. The amygdala is larger in males, whereas the hippocampus is larger in

---

4   Colapinto, "John/Joan," 54–97; Diamond, "Sexual Identity," 181–186; Diamond, "Sex and Gender Are Different," 320–334; Diamond and Sigmundson, "Sex Reassignment At Birth," 298–304.

5   Williams, Rhiannon, "Facebook's 71 gender options come to UK users."

females.[6] There is also some research on neural differences related to sexual orientation, particularly in men.[7]

Neuroplasticity is the process in which your brain's neural synapses and pathways are altered as an effect of environmental or behavioural factors, and adaptations to trauma. It takes place throughout life and involves changes to neurons, vascular cells, and connective and nutritive cells. Neuroplasticity occurs in tandem with synaptic pruning, where the brain deletes neural connections that are not useful and strengthens necessary ones.[8] Nurture and environment can therefore impact brain wiring, especially in childhood and adolescence when neuroplasticity is maximally active.

Second, *epigenetics* is the study of external or environmental factors which turn genes on and off, affecting how cells read genes. Epigenetics describes the dynamic alterations in the transcriptional potential of cells— how hereditary traits carried in the genes are expressed. Lifestyle factors, traumas, and even environmental factors of parents and grandparents could affect genetic expression. The role of epigenetics in sexual differentiation of the brain has recently become an active line of research.[9]

Gendered behaviour results from this complex interplay of genes, gonadal hormones, socialisation, and cognitive development. Current thinking on the determinants of sex, gender identity, sexual orientation, and gender roles therefore include both:

- biological "nature" factors of genetic influences, and prenatal hormone levels; *and*

- social "nurture" factors—environmental and sociocultural, family and peer influence throughout life.

The rest of this paper will explore the current scientific study of sex and gender and discuss their social expression.

---

6   Goldstein, "Normal Sexual Dimorphism," 490–497.

7   Hines, "Prenatal Endocrine Influences," 170–182.

8   Davidson and McEwen, "Social Influences on Neuroplasticity," 689–695.

9   Shen et al., "Epigenetics and Sex Differences," 21–29.

Complexity and Categorisation

This interplay of nature and nurture has led to sex and gender being described in four interrelated and interlinked categories.

1. Biological Sex has itself been demonstrated to be complex;

2. Gender Identity has to do with a person's core identity as either male or female;

3. Sexual Orientation describes erotic attraction identity and sexual behaviour as towards male, female or both; and

4. Gender Expression—the communication of gender identity to others through behaviour, clothing, hairstyles, and body characteristics.

1. Biological Sex

Medical research demonstrates that biological sex is formed through a complex, multi-stage development in the mother's womb. Aberrations at any stage in the development can lead to a person's biological sex not aligning to the traditional biological binary categories.

Biological sex is initially patterned by the *chromosomal combination* which occurs at fertilisation. The meeting of a "Y" chromosome-carrying sperm with an ovum results in a male embryo with "XY" sex chromosomes. Fertilisation with an "X" carrying-sperm results in a female embryo with "XX" composition. The developing embryo has the *potential* to develop either male or female gonads, genitals, and brain. The chromosomal combination does not itself *guarantee* binary biological development—the other stages of development have to occur as well.

Within a few weeks (six–seven) the Y chromosome directs the production of the testis-determining factor (TDF or SrY protein). This directs the formation of a *testis* in the undifferentiated gonadal cells. This is currently considered too simple by researchers who claim a multifactorial epigenetic influence on gonadal development.[10]

A few weeks later (eight–twelve) in the uterus, hormones in the developing testes (testosterone and *mullerian inhibitor substance*) result in male internal genitalia. In the presence of the *5-alpha-reductase* enzyme, these hormones also cause the development of male external genitalia. If these hormones are absent, or tissues cannot respond, the foetus will develop female genitalia.

Defective operation of these hormones could result in misalignment between a person's chromosomal sex, gonads, and internal and/or external genitalia. For example, *Androgen Insensitivity Syndrome* (AIS) occurs in genetic males (XY) where all tissues, including the brain, are insensitive to the hormone testosterone. They identify as female, are sexually attracted towards males, and have female external genitalia, appearing to be "normal" "heterosexual" women. But, they have undescended testes; testosterone levels are more male-normal than female-normal; and they have undeveloped internal genitals (neither male nor female).

In *congenital adrenal hyperplasia* (CAH), genetic women (XX) exposed in the mother's womb to excessive androgens, in addition to some degree of defective genital development, exhibit increased male-typical behaviour, and report an increased incidence of bisexual orientation and gender dysphoria. This masculinisation extends to all domains of gendered behaviour where males and females typically differ.[11]

The research on *brain sexual differentiation* is still in its infancy. Most clinical evidence suggests that testosterone induces typical "masculine" psychosexual differentiation in men prenatally.[12] Based on animal experiments and clinical evidence, sexual differentiation of the genitals has been found to take place much earlier in development (i.e., in the first two–three

---

10   Tachibana, "Epigenetic regulation," 19–23.

11   Meyer-Bahlburg, "Sex Steroids and Variants," 435–452.

12   Boa and Swaab, "Sexual differentiation," 214–226.

months of pregnancy) than sexual differentiation of the brain (the second half of pregnancy). They may therefore be influenced independently. It is conceivable that a person's genitals develop in one sexual direction, and that the same person's brain develops in the opposite sexual direction, because of some yet-undocumented misalignment of biological development in utero.

Brain sexual development is further complicated by neurological development at puberty. During puberty, the brain circuits that have been organised in the womb will be activated by sex hormones. For the vast majority of young people, this burst of sexual development will confirm the existing sexual pattern of their brain and body. But if the young person's sex organs were ambiguous at birth, the degree of masculinisation of the genitals may not always reflect the degree of masculinisation of the brain.[13] It is also conceivable that a young person's brain and genital development may, for some yet undocumented reason, become "unlinked," so that their brain develops in one direction while their genitals develop in the other, potentially leading to gender dysphoria or same-sex orientation.

2. Gender Identity

Gender identity is one's basic conviction of being a man or woman. In some rare instances, this core identity may not be congruent with biological sex. This is known as gender dysphoria (originally gender identity disorder, also transsexualism). Others express an identity that is not strongly one or the other and identify as "genderqueer." DSM-5 defines gender dysphoria to be:

> A marked incongruence between one's experienced/ expressed gender and assigned gender, of at least 6 months duration and associated with clinically significant distress or impairment in social, school/ occupational, or other important areas of functioning.[14]

---

13   Kreukels et al., *Gender Dysphoria*.

14   American Psychiatric Association, *Diagnostic and Statistical Manual of Mental Disorders* (5th ed.), 452.

A recent systematic review reported the prevalence of transsexualism as 4.6 in 100,000 individuals; 6.8 for trans-women (MF-male assigned at birth, female gender identity and pursuing physical feminisation) and 2.6 for trans-men (FM-female assigned at birth, male gender identity and pursuing physical masculinisation).[15] Time analysis found an increase in reported prevalence over the last fifty years.

It is important to differentiate three different manifestations of gender identity disorders:

- Those who exhibit a range of *transgender* behaviour;

- The narrower group of *transsexuals* who experience gender dysphoria severe enough for medical and surgical management;

- Children who exhibit *gender non-conforming* (or "gender variant") behaviour.

Transgender is an umbrella term for a diverse group of individuals (transsexual, cross dresser, she-males, queer, questioning, third sex, two-spirits, drag queen, transvestite . . .) whose gender identity varies significantly from their sex assigned at birth, and who cross or transcend culturally defined categories of gender. Some intersex persons identify as transgender. The prevalence of transgendered persons is said to be from 1:200 to 1:500.[16]

Gender nonconformity refers to the extent to which a person's (usually a child) gender identity, role, or expression differs from the cultural norms for people of a particular sex. Only some gender-nonconforming children and adults experience gender dysphoria at some point in their lives. Across all studies, the persistence rate of gender dysphoria is approximately 16 percent.[17] Of the larger group of children who do not continue to have persistent gender dysphoria in adolescence and adulthood, it is reported

15   Van Caenegem et al., "Prevalence of Gender Nonconformity," 1281–87.

16   Conron et al., "Transgender Health," 118– 122.

17   Steensma and Cohen-Kettenis, "More Than Two Developmental Pathways?" 147–148.

that 42 percent eventually identify as homosexual or bisexual.[18] Many adult transgender or transsexual individuals do not report a history of childhood gender role nonconformity,[19] although many men report fetishistic cross-dressing in adolescence and sexual arousal associated with seeing or imagining themselves dressed as a woman.[20]

Therefore, gender nonconforming behaviour, especially among children, does not necessarily indicate an established gender disorder. Parents should observe their children's development (called "watchful waiting"). If the child's behaviour persists for an extended period of time, and/or is accompanied by a degree of emotional torment which fits the DSM definition of gender dysphoria, they may require professional investigation.

As noted above, the aetiology of transgender or transsexual identity development remains largely unknown. It is most likely the result of a complex interaction between biological (intrauterine hormone environment, genetics) factors and environmental (social milieu of childhood and adolescence) factors.

3. Sexual Orientation

Sexual orientation is an enduring pattern of, or disposition to experience, sexual or romantic desires for, and relationships with, people of one's same sex, the other sex, or both sexes. Unlike biological sex and gender identity which are personal attributes, sexual orientation is mainly expressed in relation to others.

Same-sex sexuality has multiple manifestations, which might occur entirely on their own or in combination with one another.

- Same-sex *attraction* refers to sexual desire. It answers the question, "what or whom do I *crave*?"

18   Wallien and Cohen-Kettenis, "Psychosexual Outcome," 1413–23.
19   Zucker and Lawrence, "Epidemiology of Gender Identity Disorder," 8–18.
20   Blanchard, "Autogynephilia and Typology," 616–23.

- Same-sex *identity* is a response to both a sense of personal sexuality as well as a community belonging. It answers the question, "whom do I *identify* with?"

- Same-sex *sexual contact/behaviour* denotes sexual contact and intimacy. It is the response to the question, "whom do I *have sex* with?"

Other categories used in describing same-sex sexuality include:

- Same-sex *love/romance*—an emotional connection and is the response to the question, "whom am I *in love* with?"

- Same-sex *fantasies*—"whom do I *lust* after?"

- Same sex *arousability*, a laboratory term to describe "to what does my body *respond*?"

An Australia-wide study conducted in 2014 demonstrated the following results:[21]

- The majority of participants identified as heterosexual (97% men, 96% women);

- Women (2.2%) were more likely than men (1.3%) to identify as bisexual;

- Women were less likely than men to report exclusively other-sex (women 84.8% and men 92.8%) or same-sex (women 0.5% and men 1.1%) attraction and experience;

- Nine percent of men and 19% of women had some history of same-sex attraction and/or experience. It is unknown whether this significant variance stems from female sexuality being more plastic than male, or is due to the social effect of women facing less social stigma for displaying same-sex affection than men.

---

21   Richters et al., "Second Australian Study," 451–60.

- Sexual attraction, experience, and identity did not necessarily correspond: 22% of people who reported any form of non-heterosexual sexuality reported same-sex attraction *without* any same-sex experience or gay/bisexual identity.

A frequently asked question about same-sex sexuality is "is it biological?" or is a person "born that way?" The answer is complex.

- Genetic twin studies are not conclusive, and molecular genetic research in the area is relatively new;[22]

- Clinical studies, birth cohort studies, and studies of brain structural differences have shown that hormones, especially testosterone, could influence sexual orientation prenatally;[23]

- In terms of environment and nurture: men who have sex with men (MSM) report rates of childhood sexual abuse that are approximately three times higher than that of the general male population.[24] Men with histories of childhood sexual abuse had 6.75 times greater odds of reporting ever having same-sex sexual partners.[25]

It is likely that there is some biological predisposition, which becomes reflected in same-sex desire, and subsequently is experienced and understood by individuals, as influenced by their sociocultural positioning.[26] This pre-*disposition* is not pre-*determination*—one is not simply "born gay." But neither is it merely a personal choice, nor is it always a result of childhood trauma. Again, as mentioned previously in this paper, "nature" and "nurture" are intertwined in potentially mutually reinforcing manners.

---

22   Mustanski, Kuper, and Greene, "Development of Sexual Orientation and Identity," 597–628.

23   Hines, "Prenatal Endocrine Influences," 170–182.

24   Purcell, Patterson, and Spikes, "Childhood Sexual Abuse," 72–96.

25   Wilson and Widom, "Physical Abuse, Sexual Abuse, or Neglect," 63–74.

26   Whiteway and Alexander, "Understanding the Causes," 17–40.

4. Gender Expression

Particular cultures designate particular characteristics of personality, appearance, and behaviour to be "masculine" or "feminine." These characteristics depend on the social norms which dictate different interests, responsibilities, opportunities, limitations, and behaviours for men and women in that society.

Parenting and social influence undoubtedly have effects on gender expression. However, studies indicate that there is a biological basis for at least some variations in the way men and women think and behave. Different types of studies provide convergent evidence that testosterone concentrations prenatally influence children's subsequent sex-typed toy, playmate, and activity preferences.[27] As noted above, CAH girls, who have been exposed to abnormally high testosterone in the uterus, show increased male-typical play and reduced female-typical play. This is unlikely to be due to parental encouragement—researchers report that parents of CAH girls generally encourage more female-type behaviour in their children.[28] Similar effects are seen in girls whose mothers took androgenic drugs during pregnancy.

There are personality characteristics which show sex differences related to prenatal testosterone exposure. For instance, empathy, which is higher on average in females than in males, appears to be reduced in females with CAH.[29] And physical aggression, which is higher on average in males than in females, increased.

There are also important sex differences in cognitive and emotional responses related to learning and memory, language, fear, anxiety, and nociception, as well as risk taking and a range of diseases both psychological and neural.[30]

---

27   Hines, "Prenatal Endocrine Influences," 170–182.

28   Ibid.

29   Mathews et al., "Personality," 285–91.

30   McCarthy et al., "Sex Differences in the Brain," 2241–47.

A Possible Christian Response to Gender Complexity

The above data demonstrates that the way a person experiences their gender may be more complex than the traditional, biblical, binary model. The question still remains, though—how do we *respond* to the reality of this variation?

One's response depends upon a previous judgement on the relative goodness of the traditional binary model over against the possibility of a fluid, varied "spectrum." The Bible presents binary gender as an aspect of the divine image in human beings. It is good and healthy to know oneself as either a male or female, and be attracted to the other gender.

Therefore, from a Christian perspective, such gender variation is *not good*. It is a tragic declension from God's purposes for human flourishing. It is an involuntary effect of sin, an aspect of our bodies "groaning" as we long for full redemption and "healing" in the eschaton. We hope this actually validates the sense of grief and loss which many gender-variant people experience.

But note—it is *involuntary*. The book of Job shows how a "righteous" person may suffer "irrationally"—without fault, and without God revealing the reason for their suffering. Jesus rebuked his disciples for trying to rationalise "why" the man was born blind; Jesus simply saw it as an opportunity to display God's work in his life (John 9:1–3).

Following the biblical pattern, we encourage people not to remain gender indeterminate, but to identify as *a* gender—either a man *or* a woman. Secular counsellors are equipped to assist people through the process of working out who they really are.

There are numerous possible medical responses to gender variation, from hormone treatment to gender reassignment surgery. We do not completely dismiss gender reassignment surgery, but encourage it to be left for an absolute last resort. Consistent with the biblical principle of contentment, we encourage people to inhabit and enjoy, as best they're able, the body they currently have. This is, in principle, no different from what we would say to people who are not gender conflicted but are, say, obsessed with the "body beautiful."

The Christian response to gender variation will take into account the relationships the person is in—parents, spouse, and children. This differs from the secular approach of therapeutic naturalism. The secular approach tends to view persons as a-relational bodies, and therefore prioritises the satisfaction of biological needs. If the person's body "tells" them that they are the wrong gender, the secular approach would prioritise satisfying that need. Any relationships the person is in become a hindrance to the satisfaction of their biological urge.

In contrast, the Christian approach, while certainly not denying our embodied reality, views relationships as central to wellbeing—including physical wellbeing. We encourage people who experience gender variance to share their journey with those who are in relationship with them—their parents, spouse, friends, and church family. We hope that decisions that are made for the wellbeing of the gender-variant person, in light of everyone else who loves them, is genuinely good for everyone—the gender-variant person included.

Response: Justine Toh

I really appreciated hearing Patricia and Kamal's clear and comprehensive paper outlining the complexities involved in the biology of sex and gender. I found particularly useful the breaking down of concepts that we usually take for granted and treat as unified wholes—like sexuality. We often use "sexuality" to simply refer to our sexual orientation but being able to treat sexuality as an overarching category that can be divided into attraction (whom do I sexually desire?), identity (whom do I identify with?), sexual contact/behaviour (whom do I have sex with?), sexual fantasies (whom do I lust after?), sexual arousability (to what does my body respond?), and love-romance (whom am I in love with?) seems to be truer to the mysteries of our sexual desires and experiences—especially given the results of that 2014 Australia-wide study which found that, while people largely identified as heterosexual, this didn't mean they didn't experience some form of same-sex attraction.

Patricia and Kamal applied this useful breakdown to same-sex sexuality but is there any reason we can't similarly apply such a schema to heterosexuality? Such a segmenting out of the different dimensions of sexuality is humbling and democratising inasmuch as it reveals that even the most heternormative among us experience our sexuality in complex ways that often fall short of God's good purposes for sex. Such acknowledgement prompts heterosexual Christians (like me) to acknowledge their (my) own sexual brokenness, and moves them (us) to stand in solidarity alongside other people struggling with matters of sexuality and identity, rather than keeping them at a distance—whether out of fear, wariness, or just a general sense that these matters are all "too hard" to deal with.

There is one thing that I'd like to quiz Patricia and Kamal about further. They state that "following the biblical pattern, we would encourage people not to remain gender indeterminate, but to identify as a gender— either a man or a woman. Secular counsellors are equipped to assist people through the process of working out who they really are."

If the biblical pattern is God's best for everyone (notwithstanding the variations that can occur), then why entrust secular counsellors with the task of helping people work out "who they really are" when a Christian approach is more in tune with the way that things really are—and should be? And if, as Patricia and Kamal go on to say, the secular approach views the person as "an a-relational body, and therefore prioritises the satisfaction of biological needs," and we live in a culture that encourages individual self-realisation, then wouldn't this mean that people are heavily influenced to make a decision in line with a secular position? What unique insights might a Christian perspective have to offer to the individual that secular counsellors are profoundly ill-equipped to provide—and shouldn't we be making a case for the life-affirming nature of those resources?

All in all, however, that's a minor point to quibble on. Thanks Patricia and Kamal for a thought-provoking paper.

Response: Andrew Sloane

It is lovely to sit in on such a challenging and informative paper. Patricia's work in the biology and psychology of sex and gender has been very helpful in shaping my thinking in the area—as is obvious in my paper. I'm not convinced on every point, and I'll note a couple of disagreements. But there is much more that I found very helpful indeed, so let me begin there.

1. Biological sex and the experience of gender are complex phenomena. The development of sex and its dependence on genetics, epigenetics, and hormonal environment, indicate that the biology is much more complicated—and even fraught—than we might at first think. As, of course, is the relationship between gender (and sexual orientation and desire) and biology. Once again, gender and sexual orientation are complexly determined by genetics, epigenetics, hormonal environment (especially in utero and in early childhood), and environmental factors. We must remember that we are not dealing with simple matters that demand or allow for simple answers—lest we become dangerously simplistic in our response to these issues and the people who are affected by them.

2. Gender dysphoria (and related matters) are both distressing and are not simple volitional phenomena. The realisation that most people who struggle with gender and their bodily experience of the world do not choose this, and that it interferes with their ability to live well in the world must give us pause. Indeed, it must silence the easy condemnation of such people and their experience that we often hear from Christian people. And it requires of us nuanced responses that focus on helping them to live as well as they can in the world.

3. It was helpful to see the connection between completely fluid approaches to gender and sex and autonomous individualism.

There is also much of value on homosexuality, sexual orientation, etc., but that is of less interest to me than the questions of gender and sex. Let me note a couple of matters where I have issues with either what Patricia and Kamal say or how they say it.

1. Patricia and Kamal seem to tie together binary sex and gender behaviour, and see that as arising out of the biblical picture. I'm not quite sure how that works in light of the complexity of the issues—and the distinction between biological sex and gender identity that they clearly establish.

2. They also seem to see particular expressions of gender as more fixed and important than I think is warranted. I'm not sure, for instance, that we need to identify as a gender; nor do we need to see taking the lead or initiative in relationships as a primarily masculine quality. I believe that we must allow for fluidity of gender expression and allow gender to transcend (perhaps even transgress) particular conservative cultural patterns.

On those matters I'd be interested in taking the conversation further. But do note: theirs is an important and valuable paper, and it raises important theological questions (as I try to explore in my paper—from my own theological perspective, of course).

Enculturated or Created? Gender and Sex in the Context of Caitlyn Jenner's "New Normal"

Justine Toh

"I am the new normal," said Caitlyn Jenner in her reality TV show documenting the aftermath of her sex reassignment surgery. Perhaps she's right. In Australia, the *Safe Schools* program aims to educate students about gender and sexual diversity to combat bullying and prejudice.[31] The *No Gender December* campaign encouraged parents to stuff their children's Christmas stockings with gender neutral toys: no trucks for boys or dolls for girls.[32] And OxfordDictionaries.com has now added the title "Mx" to offer people an alternative to Ms, Mr, or Mrs.[33]

What stories are today being told about gender and sexuality in the West? That gender has no necessary connection to the sexed body, and that "gender and sexual diversity" are to be unilaterally affirmed. The sexual

---

31 See Safe Schools Coalition, "What we do."

32 See Ireland, "'No Gender December.'"

33 See Tobia, "I am neither Mr, Mrs nor Ms but Mx."

paradigm of this "new normal," strangely enough, parallels Charles Taylor's account of what it means to live in "a secular age" where belief in God, once unchallenged, is now "one option among others, and frequently not the easiest to embrace."[34] That is, once taken-for-granted gendered identities (male and female) and sexualities (more precisely, heterosexuality) are now understood to be one option among many. The result? We've all been queered. The old binaries of straight/gay, male/female are blurred; we've all become, as Peter Sanlon says, "plastic people."[35] Not only can our bodies be remoulded, but our very conceptions about sex and gender are flexible and up for discussion.

According to Jeffrey Weeks, sexuality is a "'fictional unity' that once did not exist and at some time in the future may not exist again."[36] He means that the meanings and values we attach to sexual acts, sexed bodies (the biological differences between men and women), gender (the culturally acquired sense of being "male", "female", or other), reproductive capacities, sexual identities, and so on are historically and culturally specific articulations of sexuality. In drawing attention to the constructed nature of sexuality, Weeks seeks to denaturalise (to make strange, to question) common sense notions of sexuality as a natural phenomenon, and something universally understood and lived in particular ways.[37]

Judith Butler similarly denaturalises gender as a cultural fiction. She is sceptical of gender essentialism, the notion that there is "an inner truth or essence" that outwardly expresses itself in "feminine" or "masculine" ways depending on whether one is a woman or a man.[38] Nor does she consider gender to be rooted in physiological sex differences for this would constitute biological determinism, the belief that biology dictates one's roles and capacities, that "biology is destiny." Feminists have long resisted attempts to

---

34   Taylor, *A Secular Age*, 3.

35   Sanlon, *Plastic People*, 4.

36   Weeks, *Sexuality*, loc 386.

37   This definition of "denaturalisation" is taken from Anderson and Schlunke, *Cultural Theory in Everyday Practice*, 301.

38   Weeks, *Sexuality*, loc 406.

read the social order off of the natural order since this entrenches existing inequalities as the natural order of things.

Instead, through the notion of gender performativity, Butler argues that gender is a social construction that "has no ontological status apart from the various acts which constitute its reality."[39] For Butler, not even the sexed body grounds gender. In fact, she holds that the sex/gender distinction is no distinction at all; sex is always already gender.[40] This doesn't mean that we simply ignore the biological reality of sexed difference. But Butler, along with other post-structuralist theorists, maintains that all reality is discursive, which means that we never access the materiality of the body without culturally constructed notions that are specific to a particular time and place.[41] As Gayle Rubin says, "we never encounter the body unmediated by the meanings that cultures give to it."[42]

For example, imagine a baby newly born. We immediately want to know its sex. But for Butler, the declaration "it's a girl!" is less a neutral description of the baby's sex and more a *performative* utterance: words that don't simply describe a state of affairs but in fact bring it about; such words *do something*. According to Butler, "it's a girl!" decodes the material reality of the body as a sign of femaleness and kicks off the lifelong process of being "girled": of being enculturated, disciplined, and habituated into dominant understandings and practices of what it means to be a girl.[43]

Consequently, cultural values of femininity will affect how the girl conceives of herself (as nurturing, maternal, non-aggressive, emotional, etc.) and how she lives her body (does she "throw like a girl"?[44] What does it mean to be ladylike?).[45] According to Butler, gender will solidify in the

---

39   Butler, *Gender Trouble*, 136.
40   Ibid., 7.
41   Salih, *Judith Butler*, 89.
42   Rubin, "Thinking Sex," 276–77.
43   Butler, *Bodies That Matter*, 7–8.
44   Young, "Throwing Like A Girl."
45   Sandra Lee Bartky offers a detailed account of the ways in which disciplinary practices produce femininity. See Bartky, "Foucault, Femininity."

body via repeated, stylised acts that so skilfully imitate recognisable forms of masculinity and femininity that they produce "the illusion of an abiding gendered self."[46] As Sarah Salih explains, "Gender does not happen once and for all when we are born, but is a sequence of repeated acts that harden into the appearance of something that's been there all along."[47] Butler's point is that such gender performativity *constructs* or brings the subject (the self) into being—rather than our common sense notions that the subject is merely expressing his or her internal gendered essence.[48]

Being "girled" will also affect who the girl desires. For gender, according to Butler, is part of a regulatory frame of "compulsory heterosexuality" that relies on the interconnection of sex, gender, and desire so that biological females will display "feminine" traits and grow up to sexually desire men.[49] This is "heteronormativity" where heterosexuality acts as the normative standard against which all other sexualities and gender identities are measured—and often found wanting. Gender performativity, that is, both produces and regulates us as desiring, heterosexual subjects—and failure to conform to gendered expectations carries harsh penalties.

But Butler says it need not be this way. She has in mind the cohort of LGBTIQQA people whose gender identities and sexual desires do not conform to the heteronormative order. Then there are those who are intersex: whose bodies, through a variety of chromosomal or genital variations, flout the neat binary classification of the sexes. Faced with such variety, Butler asks, why do we impose an artificial conformity on such bodies by assigning them as male or female?[50] In fact, feminist biologist Anne Fausto-Sterling claims that intersex conditions are found in sufficient number and variety to make the case for "at least five genders."[51] The hope of these theorists is that by loosening our attachment to sex and gender dimorphism we will no longer seek to discipline and stigmatise those who desire and identify differently.

---

46   Butler, *Gender Trouble*, 140–41.

47   Salih, *Judith Butler*, 66.

48   This definition of "subject/subjectivity" is taken from Anderson and Schlunke, *Cultural Theory in Everyday Practice*, 318.

49   Butler, *Gender Trouble*, 17–19.

50   Ibid., 109.

51   Fausto-Sterling, *Sexing the Body*.

That's a potted account of the post-structuralist story of sex and gender that underpins the "new normal" announced by Caitlyn Jenner. What of the Christian account?

The classical Christian understanding has been that God made humankind male and female so that together they can exercise responsible dominion over God's creation. It is in this context of this God-given task, Christopher Ash maintains, that the male and female are blessed with procreative ability so that others will also share in this work.[52] Since God ordains marriage as the appropriate state in which man and woman are to bear children, Oliver O'Donovan considers marriage the teleological fulfilment of sexual difference since it discloses the inherent meaning and purpose of the sexual union of male and female.[53]

Such a "creation ethic" outrages post-structuralist theorists for a number of reasons: it insists upon the uniformity of sexual dimorphism and the basic complementarity of the sexes and it is heteronormative in its privileging of heterosexuality. Moreover, it promotes biological determinism that definitively links women (in particular) to their reproductive capacities. This "grand narrative" of human sexuality, furthermore, is not historically and culturally specific but applies across all times and places. As Ash writes, "Christian sexual ethics addresses the world. It is public ethics."[54] That is, the traditional Christian vision that humans are fundamentally male and female, and that the sexual union of male and female produces children, is a bold proclamation that this is the way things *are*, and exactly how they *should be*. "It is not possible to negotiate this fact about our common humanity," O'Donovan says, "it can only be either welcomed or resented."[55]

And many do resent it. But some might find a slight silver lining in the fact that, while people often assume that the creation account institutes specific gender differences between the sexes, the biblical text is agnostic on this issue. While Ash maintains that our gender perceptions "ought to be

---

52   Ash, *Marriage*, 113–114.
53   O'Donovan, "Transsexualism and Christian Marriage," 141.
54   Ash, *Marriage*, 76.
55   O'Donovan, "Transsexualism and Christian Marriage," 141.

grounded in our bodily existence," he refrains from outlining just how exactly we will know whether our gender expressions align with our physiology.[56] His overall point, however, is that since the Bible is far from prescriptive on this matter, Christians shouldn't be either.[57]

Yet it is clear that Christians tend to promote absolute gender differences; what Michael Kimmel calls the "interplanetary theory of gender" in reference to John Gray's relationship bestseller *Men Are from Mars, Women Are from Venus*.[58] In recent years, we've seen the hyperbolic masculinity of Mark Driscoll, John and Stasi Eldredge's vision of Christian women as damsels in distress awaiting rescue by Christ the white knight, and John Piper's declarations that female police officers flout male authority inherent in the creational order.[59] Our men's and women's church events are prescriptive too: the former invariably involving craft and food (conveniently combined in gingerbread-house-making events at Christmastime), while men's events cover car restoration, the copious consumption of red meat, or watching *Courageous*.

Such events may appeal, broadly, to men and women, but perhaps this merely confirms Butler's point that gender is habituated and internalised so deeply it appears to express the inner gendered self. The problem with perpetuating such an "interplanetary" account of gender is that certain qualities become affixed to Christian ideas of masculinity and femininity when, surely, the fruit of the Spirit is not divided up into male and female responsibilities.

Another issue is that on this matter the church, as God's people, winds up uncritically reaffirming dominant notions of gender when masculinity and femininity need to be redeemed. Then there is the plain fact that gendered differences between men and women are dwarfed by differences *among* men

---

56   Ash, *Marriage*, 275–6. Even Oliver O'Donovan is frustratingly vague about what "masculinity" and "femininity" might entail. See O'Donovan, "Transsexualism and Christian Marriage," 143.

57   Ash, *Marriage*, 276.

58   Kimmel, *The Gendered Society*, 4.

59   On Driscoll, see Bruenig, "The Failure of Macho Christianity"; on Eldredge, see *Captivating*; on Piper, see "Should Women Be Police Officers?"

and *among* women. Ultimately, men and women share more than talk of their differences would give us reason to expect.[60] Which doesn't mean, of course, that men and women are interchangeable—just that churches should reconsider their often "interplanetary" account of gender.

Heather Looy and Hessel Bouma note that since Christians believe sex is fundamentally dichotomous, it is easy to imagine gender is as well, that essential masculine and feminine identities exist.[61] To counter the inflexibility of such a framework, and vast differences among men and women, they suggest the notion of "gender polarity" rather than "gender dichotomy." In this scheme, most people will tend to cluster at the "male" and "female" poles but others—for example, transgender, intersex, and/or gender non-conforming individuals—can plot themselves somewhere in between rather than being simply shut out of the orthodox categories.[62]

Gender polarity is appealing inasmuch as it strikes a balance between flexibility and stability concerning gender differences. Perhaps in concession to our "plastic" predicament where, recalling Sanlon, formerly given categories are now negotiable, flexibility serves to remind us that a measure of human freedom is available—for instance, there is no prescriptive way to be male or female. And yet this freedom is limited (or stabilised) by various checks on human freedom like sexual difference given by God, which in some way grounds our gendered identities, and the human body, which O'Donovan reminds us is good, not something debased. This latter point particularly reminds us that our bodies possess an integrity worth respecting. We should recognise in our bodies, O'Donovan says, "not only a vehicle for the free expression of our spirits, but also a given structure and meaning which limits that freedom."[63]

---

60 We should not be surprised at this. The creation account stresses not simply the complementarity of Adam and Eve, but also their likeness. See Ash, *Marriage*, 121.

61 Looy and Bouma, "The Nature of Gender," 166.

62 Ibid., 175.

63 O'Donovan, "Transsexualism and Christian Marriage," 151.

Post-structuralists will object that the body only comes to have meaning within social relations, that bodily structure and meaning are not self-evident but produced discursively.[64] That may be so but it's hard to see how such theorising avoids being a dead end, because if the body has no apparent integrity then there can be no rational objection to, for example, the transabled individual's request for doctors to amputate healthy and functional limbs that they, nonetheless, experience as alien and other to themselves. This condition, known as "body integrity identity disorder," involves an individual's "persistent desire to have their body match the idealised image they have of themselves" and poses a seeming paradox "of losing body parts in order to become whole."[65] If the transabled or transgendered individual is found to be of sound mind, then what can reasonably thwart their autonomous will for their bodies?

There are two points to make here. First, transgenderism and transableism appear to be forms of modern Gnosticism that elevate the spiritual above the physical, the mind or the inner self above its fleshly dwelling—conveyed in the sense of being "in the wrong body."[66] Such Gnosticism is also evident in, for example, an earlier version of the *Safe Schools* resource *OMG: My Friend's Queer*, particularly in relation to its definition of "pansexual" as those who "are generally attracted to the person inside."[67] Such a definition articulates gendered embodiment as incidental to the "person inside." The Christian affirmation of creation and the body acts as a necessary check on such Gnosticism and is why, as a general principle, Christian psychologist Mark Yarhouse recommends minimal surgical intervention for transgendered individuals.[68]

---

64 Nikki Sullivan and Susan Stryker, for example, suggest that bodily integrity is not premised on organic integrity but the body's incorporability: "the body's suitability for integration, its ability to be integrated as a biopolitical resource into a larger sociotechnical field, or into an apparatus such as the State." See Stryker and Sullivan, "King's Member," 51.

65 Ibid., 53; see www.biid.org (accessed September 5, 2015).

66 Crouch, "Sex Without Bodies," 74.

67 Safe Schools Coalition, "OMG My Friend's Queer," 6. This definition appears to have been updated in the 2015 publication "OMG I'm Queer" to remove references to the "person inside."

68 Yarhouse, *Understanding Gender Dysphoria*, loc 2595.

My second point relates to the first. In a Western culture that has given up talk of ends to which our choices must be directed if we are to flourish, freedom has come to mean the freedom to determine our own individual good; in this case, to bring our bodies into conformity with our inner sense of ourselves—even if post-structuralists dispute that such an essential self exists.[69] But a theology of creation that suggests that we are made—and do not, ultimately, make ourselves—means that we cannot simply choose our own good. We may bristle at such a limitation on our freedom but we also accept it implicitly. We acknowledge that the human body needs oxygen and food to thrive, and that developing a taste for, say, plastic, is a distortion of what it means to eat well—and will not ultimately serve one's good.

That we are created and do not freely determine our own ends is a necessary reminder in an age that risks instrumentalising the body in the quest for new forms of subjectivity (selfhood). Transsexual theorist Susan Stryker, for example, has written of her "transgender rage" at being locked out of the available, "compulsorily assigned," gendered categories.[70] Consequently, she calls for a transsexual embodiment that does not aim to reaffirm gender binaries but attain a "monstrous" subjectivity, since she recognises herself in Frankenstein's monster, who also exceeded the purposes of its maker: "As we rise up from the operating tables of our rebirth, we transsexuals are something more, and something other, than the creatures our makers intended us to be."[71]

But once Shelley's creature has murdered its maker it is not at peace. It will never feel "at home." Is this also the fate awaiting "monstrous" subjects whose gender and sexual identities fail to conform—some defiantly, as in Stryker's case? If so, it is a lonely one, which explains why there is a determined push—evident in the *Safe Schools* program, *No Gender December* campaign, and so on—to establish the "new normal" so that no one will be discriminated against and rejected.

---

69   Hart, *Atheist Delusions*, 22.

70   Stryker, "My Words to Victor Frankenstein," 252–253.

71   Stryker, "My Words to Victor Frankenstein," 248.

But it is questionable whether this "new normal" will usher in a utopian society of universal acceptance.[72] What if sex reassignment surgery, hormonal treatments, and campaigns to normalise diverse gender and sexual identities cannot actually work because they attempt to solve—through science and medicine, politics and ideology—a fundamentally *spiritual* problem? The issue is that people, for whatever reason, do not feel at home in their bodies, or in the gendered options their culture offers them. The gospel addresses this fundamental alienation in its proclamation that there is something acutely not right—both in the world and in ourselves.

So how might Christians respond? Yarhouse challenges us to be a "redemptive community" that journeys with people struggling with gender identity.[73] This is a community that remains committed both to traditional Christian sexual ethics and to the person alienated from their gender or sex—without imposing limits on the way that that individual manages their condition.[74] "In an atmosphere of grace," he asks, "can we come alongside people who are navigating this difficult terrain?"[75]

It is difficult to clarify what this means practically, and there are valid concerns that a biblical sexual ethic may be sacrificed in the process. But Yarhouse is rightly concerned that Christians operating exclusively out of what he calls the "integrity framework" (the "creation ethic" outlined earlier) risk promoting rigid gender norms and alienating gender non-conforming individuals—both in the church and in secular society.[76] We should reflect on Yarhouse's challenge. For, as Christians, we need to welcome those not at home in the sex and gender identities on offer in the world—and in doing so, point them to Jesus in the hope that they will find their true home in him.

---

72   It was on the basis of studies showing that post-surgical transsexuals did not experience vastly improved mental health outcomes after their sex reassignments that Paul McHugh, Johns Hopkins University former psychiatrist-in-chief, discontinued that institution's sex change surgeries. He concluded that performing such operations effectively colluded with mental illness, and that treatment would be better off addressing, to put it crudely, the matter between someone's ears rather than between their legs. See McHugh, "Surgical Sex."

73   Yarhouse, *Understanding Gender Dysphoria*, loc 2932.

74   Ibid., loc 2840.

75   Ibid., loc 3021.

76   Ibid., loc 895.

Response: Andrew Sloane

Again, this was a paper that taught me much and prompted interesting reflections. Let me note some of the key positives, before I note a couple of questions.

Justine clearly articulated the almost deliberately transgressive nature of fluid sex and gender in contemporary culture and the way that ties into broader cultural shifts. This raises important questions about the extent to which we want to identify some of the categories people now resist as true expressions of a Christian ethos.

She also very helpfully (and accessibly) articulated some of the more radical social theorists—especially Butler. This helped me see a number of things:

These are *post-structuralist* theories—and so, in order to come to grips with them, we need to have some idea of contemporary critical theory and the ways it challenges more traditional understandings of culture, knowledge, reality, and language.

In relation to that, Butler's understanding of language is both interesting and deeply flawed. Philosophy of language reminds us that the "direction of fit" of words and world is important; Butler seems not to allow for reality constraining our language usage at all—at least, not in matters relating to sex, biology, and gender.

On the other hand, Butler's criticism of gender essentialism seems sound—and something we as Christians need to think about a lot more. So too, it is very important to note that heteronormativity can be an oppressive phenomenon. How do we affirm some notion of creational sex and gender in non-oppressive ways?

I appreciated her point that while gender may be grounded in sex/biology, there is no prescription as to what gendered behaviour, etc., looks like. I think I would loosen the ties a little here; but the fundamental point seems right. It is deeply problematic that "the church, as God's people, reaffirms dominant cultural notions of gender when it should be more focused on being 'in' the world but not 'of' it—perhaps by challenging cultural notions of masculinity and femininity that burden both men and women." We need a polarity of gender rather than a binary. Indeed!

Also her discussion of Yarhouse was very helpful. I think we all agree that he's someone we need to listen to. There are, however, some points where I would either take issue, or invite further reflection.

Is it true that "the creation ethic insists upon the *uniformity* of sexual dimorphism and the basic complementarity of the sexes"? What does that uniformity mean? That sexual dimorphism has a standard or normative form? Furthermore, while marriage is the context for which sexual intercourse is designed, is it the *telos* of sexuality? Or does the "otherness" of female and male speak (also) of community as a *telos* of the diversity of embodiments and experiences that we find in humans as God's creatures?

I'd be interested to explore how we can talk to post-structuralist sex-and-gender constructivists. Is it, perhaps, that there might be other conversations that give us analogies to play with?

Again, on those matters I'd be interested in taking the conversation further, and I thank Justine for a very stimulating paper.

"Male and Female He Created Them"? Theological Reflections on Gender, Biology, and Identity

Andrew Sloane

Introduction

"Gender bending" as it was once called, has gone from the titillating sideshows of cabaret to mainstream social phenomenon.[77] What are we to do with that? Some, clearly, want to stick to their guns (so to speak, all Freudian allusions intended). Sex and gender are binary categories, established by God in creation, and only ever disrupted, questioned, or complicated by sinful will.[78] Others want to redraw the boundaries of embodiment and gender,

---

77   See, for instance, the prominence of related issues on the Australian Broadcasting Commission's news website: e.g., Reinfrank, "Transgender, intersex people"; Burin, "'I am not a man or a woman'"; and, of course, the innumerable news stories, blog posts, and so on, in response to Caitlyn Jenner's transition from male to female.

78   Colson, "Blurred Biology"; EFCA Spiritual Heritage Committee, "A Church Statement on Human Sexuality," 3-4.

and follow Facebook in theologically justifying the proliferation of gender categories.[79] I'm not satisfied that either of these options is *theologically* satisfactory. But in order to figure out a more faithful way of engaging these issues, we need to be clear about what questions need to be answered (or if not definitively answered, at least faithfully addressed), what resources we can mobilise in this engagement, and what strategies we might use in seeking to navigate our way through them.

I will begin by briefly rehearsing the evidence that has been used to render problematic traditional notions of fixed, binary categories of male and female, and masculinity and femininity, paying particular attention to gender dysphoria and indeterminate biological sex (intersex). Important methodological questions regarding how theology should deal with the "data" generated by scientific and sociological research must be addressed before substantive issues relating to a theology of embodied human identity can be explored. Having made a case for the mutual interrogation of theology and other disciplines, I will suggest that while our bodies are fundamental to our being in the world and crucially shape our understanding and engagement with it, both what we are (ontology) and who we are (identity) are primarily determined by the relationships we form and in which we find ourselves. And at the heart of those relationships is the one we enjoy with God in Christ which affirms our creation in God's image, redeems the brokenness of creation, calls us into new patterns of social relationship, and promises our full restoration and glorification in a transformed physical order.

Orientation—Data and Questions

Drs Weerakoon and Toh have helpfully engaged with the worlds of medicine and social theory and the complex pictures of sex and gender and their interrelationships.[80] Let me focus on two elements of those pictures that generate painful questions both for those who have to deal with them

---

79   Cornwall, "Transgender and Intersex"; Sheffield, "Performing Jesus." For the Facebook categories, see Williams, "Facebook's 71 gender options come to UK users."

80   Weerakoon and Weerakoon, "Biology"; Toh, "Enculturated or Created?"

and for those who seek to reflect on gender and sex theologically: namely, gender dysphoria and ambiguous physical sex (intersex).[81]

Intersex takes a number of forms, ranging from those whose bodily form does not match their genetic sex (Androgen Insensitivity Syndrome, in which a person with a male genotype has a female phenotype), through those with ambiguous genitalia (such as people with Congenital Adrenal Hyperplasia), to those who demonstrate "true" hermaphroditism (in which they have more-or-less well-formed male and female genitalia and secondary sex characteristics).[82] How do such people relate to our binary categories of sex? How do we understand them in light of God creating humanity as male and female when they fall neatly into neither category? The history of "assigning" such people a definitive sex (and gender) at birth, often accompanied with a regimen of complex and invasive surgery, is fraught with pain and tragedy.[83] It seems as though our binary categories serve such people poorly.[84]

Gender dysphoria, on the other hand, is a little simpler to understand. People with gender dysphoria generally have a fairly clear biological sex, but they do not identify with that sex or the gendered behaviours that go with it. Their experience is one in which they are alienated from their bodies; they are at home neither in their bodies nor in the social worlds in which they find themselves. And this causes them significant distress—hence gender *dysphoria*.[85] For some of them the distress is so great that they feel they must change their bodies in order to match their experienced gender identity if they are to have any hope of feeling at home in the world. How do such people relate to our binary categories of gender? How do we understand the connection (and disconnect) between bodily sex and cultural expressions of gender, and how fluid can they be?

---

81   Looy and Bouma, "Nature of Gender."

82   Ainsworth, "Sex Redefined"; DeFranza, *Sex Difference in Christian Theology*, Ch.1; Looy and Bouma, "Nature of Gender," 166–71.

83   See the accounts in DeFranza, *Sex Difference in Christian Theology*, Ch.1; and Dumas, "The In-Betweeners"; Looy and Bouma, "Nature of Gender," 171–73.

84   DeFranza, *Sex Difference in Christian Theology*, esp. chs.4 and 6.

85   Yarhouse, *Understanding Gender Dysphoria*, ch.1. The disturbingly high incidence of depression and suicide amongst people with gender dysphoria in itself warrants the term *dysphoria*.

In light of such phenomena, it is not surprising that the categories of sex (male and female) and gender (feminine and masculine) have been rendered problematic in recent discourse.[86] These are questions to which theology needs to give an answer—both in order that we might speak meaningfully in our cultural context, but also so that our theology can encompass the complex realities of the world in which we live. How to do this is a vexed theological question. But in order to address it, we need to deal with an important question of theological method: what role should the deliverances of science and sociology play in theological reflection? To this we now turn.

Strategies of (Dis-)Engagement

There are many approaches to the relationship between theology and science (including the social sciences), and a number of different taxonomies have been proposed. For our purposes three general categories will suffice: conflict, conformity, and conversation.[87]

The first sees science and theology as being in *conflict*: while they lay claim to the same conceptual territory, they make fundamentally incompatible claims and as such one or the other must give way. This is the line adopted by many conservative Christian groups. "In the beginning," they say, "God created them male and female." Any departure from that is a sinful expression of innate human rebellion against God and his ordering of the world. Some see the experiences of a person with gender dysphoria as the result of directly willed sinful choices; others do not.[88] Regardless of

---

86   Huston, "None of the Above"; Cornwall, "Transgender and Intersex"; Sheffield, "Performing Jesus."

87   For alternative taxonomies and discussions of relevant issues, see Carlson, *Science and Christianity: Four Views*; Jeeves and Berry, *Science, Life and Christian Belief*, esp. chs 3 and 13.

88   These discussions generally relate to questions of sexual orientation (and gender dysphoria is often conflated with or discussed mainly in relation to them). See Gagnon, *The Bible and Homosexual Practice*; and Gagnon's chapter (and response) in Gagnon and Via, *Homosexuality and the Bible: Two Views*, 40–92, 99–105. See also the public statements and policy documents of the (Australian) Christian Democratic Party: Christian Democratic Party. "All Australian Schools Must Stop Teaching 'Queer Sex'"; "2015 NSW Election Policy Snapshot"; "CDP National Charter." Such views are also reflected (with more or less vitriol) on news sites and blogs, such as: Walsh, "Bruce Jenner Is Not a Woman"; Moore, "What Should the Church Say to Bruce Jenner?"

aetiology, they cannot be allowed to determine the patterns of their gendered relationships in the world, let alone the form of their bodies. Their bodily form is a given of creation, and comes with prescribed patterns of gendered behaviour; non-conforming gender *behaviour* is an expression of a sinful will. While such views may account for the sociology of gender (by way of rejection of its claims), it is hard to see how they give any account of intersex. If the only categories we have are the binary ones of "male" and "female," how do we categorise those with ambiguous genitalia or a mismatch between their "genetic sex" and the form of their bodies? Are they male or female, and how do we decide? People who are intersex seem to be effectively excluded from theological anthropology, unless they are or subjected to (almost arbitrary) surgical assignment of sex. Furthermore, this strategy assumes that the Bible addresses the kinds of questions we are asking in the ways we are now asking them, and that our interpretations of Scripture and theological formulations cannot be modified in light of our developing knowledge of the world. Such an approach cannot provide adequate answers to questions such as these.[89]

This brings us naturally to our next strategy, in which science (broadly understood) dictates the terms to which theology must now conform. Old understandings of humanity as created male and female, and the associated idea that human sexuality is ordered towards either heterosexual marriage or singleness, are obsolete. We need to allow for a plurality of genders and sexes, and corresponding expressions of sex and gender in social relationships, bodily form, and sexual expression. Such views are seen in a number of "queer" theologies.[90] There are a number of problems with such strategies, including their tendency to adopt theologies of Scripture and interpretive

---

89   It is both ironic and suggestive that many LGBTQIA activists adopt a similar understanding of the conflict between theology and science; but in their case, theology must give way to science. See, for instance, an example of public statements and policy documents of the Australian Greens: "Scripture Books Promote Dangerous Messages"; "Equality for LGBTI Australians"; "Sexual Orientation and Gender Identity." Such views are also reflected (with more or less vitriol) on news sites and blogs, such as Green, "The Real Christian Debate on Transgender Identity."

90   Bohache, *Christology from the Margins*; Cornwall, "Transgender and Intersex"; Sheffield, "Performing Jesus." See also Via's chapter (and response) in Gagnon and Via, *Homosexuality and the Bible: Two Views*, 1–39, 93–98, and numerous web pages and blog posts, such as: Schultz, "Transitions"; Believe Out Loud, "Christianity and LGBT Equality"; Gay Christian Network, "The Great Debate."

strategies antithetical to the evangelical tradition.[91] While they may be able to address questions of intersex and gender dysphoria, they do not do so in fidelity to the Christian tradition or its Scriptures.

Thankfully, we are not bound by the options of conflict and rejection (of either science or theology) or conformity and accommodation to the dictates of "secular" reason. There is a third option in which science and theology are allowed to mutually interrogate each other.[92] This strategy has been adopted by Mark Yarhouse and Megan DeFranza in their work on gender dysphoria and intersex respectively.[93] Yarhouse outlines a threefold framework for understanding and dealing with the phenomenon of gender dysphoria: the *integrity* framework (male-female bodily distinctions are sacred); the *disability* framework (gender dysphoria is a non-culpable reality deserving compassion), and the *diversity* framework (transgender experiences are to be celebrated as part of diverse humanity), and suggests that each should inform our theology and practice where appropriate.[94] DeFranza recognises that the phenomenon of intersex renders problematic a simple binary opposition of male and female. Furthermore, she notes the way that maleness and femaleness have been seen as essential to our being created in the image of God generates problems for our theology of God as well as our concepts of sex, sexuality, and gender in creation and the *eschaton*.[95] I'm not convinced of the ways in which she ties together the image of God, social Trinitarian thought, and human bodily existence in light of the incarnation of Christ. Nonetheless, she rightly notes that, given that people with intersex are created in the image of God, we must allow our theologies to include them in our understandings of humanity and human community,

---

91   While the evangelical tradition is not immune to critique and development, neither should evangelicalism be simply dismissed or ignored. Furthermore the scientific and sociological evidence is not as definitive as has been suggested (Weerakoon and Weerakoon, "Biology"; Toh, "Enculturated or Created?").

92   For science in general, see: Jeeves and Berry, *Science, Life and Christian Belief*, esp. ch.13; McGrath, *Science & Religion*; Polkinghorne, *One World*; *Reason and Reality*. And for medicine and health care in particular, see Messer, *Flourishing*, esp. xiv, xv, 48–50, 103–07, 63, 210. For an outline of a commensurate epistemology, see Sloane, *On Being a Christian in the Academy*. Stackhouse, *Need To Know*.

93   Yarhouse, "Integration" adopts an "integrationist" approach to science-faith interaction.

94   *Understanding Gender Dysphoria*, Ch.2. See also his brief discussion in "Understanding Gender Dysphoria."

95   DeFranza, *Sex Difference in Christian Theology*, Chs.4–6.

and to embody communal practices that include them in our corporate lives. Such strategies can allow for fruitful theological reflection on questions of gender, biology, and identity.

A Theology of (Embodied) Persons-in-Relationship

We need to steer a path between conservative attempts to reify particular cultural constructions of gender as fixed ontological expressions of a determinative creational/biological order of (binary) sex, and "postmodern" attempts to render sex and gender radically indeterminate—or self-determined—categories that deny the givenness of creation and the goodness of creaturely embodiment. I would suggest that the rejection of gender stereotypes and the acknowledgement of the complexities of human embodiment revealed in the phenomenon of intersex need not entail the "queering" of gender and sex. A theological anthropology grounded in nuanced understandings of creation, Christology, and eschatology provides us with a way forward.

The first thing to note is that the biblical texts suggest that we *are* bodies; bodies are not things we inhabit, but the way we inhabit the world as the kind of creatures God has made us.[96] These bodies normally are formed as male or female, and the shape of our bodies informs the character of our relationships with others. Sex and gender *inform* our identity, but we are not *defined* by our sexed bodies or gendered selves.

The creation accounts also indicate that both our nature and identity are fundamentally relational. The "not good" of Gen 2:18 is the absence of relationships of a particular kind: not *sexual* relationships *per se*, but the otherness of fellow creatures who require our commitment and evoke our delight.[97] The primeval community was intended to embody relationships of love, justice, fidelity, and delight between God and humanity, and within the human community, and the expression of fidelity and joyful service in the

---

96   Messer, *Respecting Life*, esp. Ch. 1; *Flourishing*, esp. Ch. 4; Meilaender, *Body, Soul, and Bioethics*, Ch. 2.

97   Westermann, *Genesis*, 10–11, 20–21; Sloane, "Genesis 2–3."

world. It is those relationships that define us and shape our identity—the relationships and the complex gifts, tasks, and responsibilities they entail. Now, it is true that sexual dimorphism—and the sexual relationships and procreative capacity it enables—is a key aspect of human bodily existence. We are mammals—biological entities of a particular kind which reproduce sexually and bear live young; and we are entrusted by God with the gift and task of filling the world and ruling it as God's vicegerents—a task that presupposes the fruitfulness (and blessing) of progeny and an unfolding history of human engagement in God's world (Gen 1:26–31). But the creation accounts focus primarily on the creation of human community and its nature and task, and only secondarily on matters of gender and sexuality.[98]

The embodied and relational nature of human existence is affirmed (and vindicated and transformed) in our new primary identity in Christ.[99] Our redemption and final transformation does not erase our embodied nature; nor does it mean that our gendered and sexed (and sexual) being is somehow jettisoned: "the body is for the Lord, and the Lord for the body" (1 Cor 6:13). Rather, our bodily existence shapes our relationships, making some relationships possible rather than others, and so shapes what identifies and defines us. I am son and brother and husband and father and friend; and both my maleness and the particular forms of masculinity that I express necessarily shape those relationships and the self that they (in)form.

Gender, I would suggest, is another matter. Gender, understood as particular patterns of thought, affect, relationships, and behaviour (including characteristic dress and gesture, and patterns of physical comportment), is largely (but not entirely) culturally constructed or shaped.[100] I say largely (but not entirely) constructed, because some of those patterns are given to us in

---

98   Sloane, "Genesis 2–3," 21–22; Looy and Bouma, "Nature of Gender," 174–76.

99   See O'Donovan, *Resurrection and Moral Order*, esp. 11–75; Wright, *Surprised by Hope*, esp. ch. 10. The vindication of creation renders problematic attempts to "queer" anthropology in light of Christology and the resurrection of Jesus (such as in Stuart, "The Return of the Living Dead"; Sheffield, "Performing Jesus"; Bohache, *Christology from the Margins*). Rather, Gal 3:28 suggests that sex and gender, while not erased (1 Cor 11:2–16; 1 Tim 2:8–15), are not binary categories that determine our identity; our identity is primarily found in Christ.

100   Toh, "Enculturated or Created?"

the shape of our bodies and the ways our different hormonal environments shape thought, affect, behaviour, and so on. Again, while there is a spectrum of kinds of behaviour, etc., rather than a set of rigid types, there do seem to be characteristic patterns of male and female brains and ways of engaging with the world, valuing particular aspects of it, and so on.[101]

Nonetheless, we must not reify these particular patterns of thought, affect, experience, and relationship into rigid ontological categories and assign our constructed visions of "feminine" and "masculine" to female and male bodies (with a degree, I would say, of both arbitrariness and historical and cultural naivety, and even arrogance). Femininity and masculinity are statistical patterns across populations (even more than is true of male and female), and many behaviours and attitudes are gendered differently in different cultural contexts; they are not eternal, trans-cultural, binary categories. We need to allow for a degree of fluidity in expressions of gender (a "permission" that would, most likely, alleviate the distress of at least some people with gender dysphoria);[102] it is not, however, simply a product of autonomous human will as if, no matter the bodily form of my created existence, I can determine that I am female or male or transgendered, or . . .

Implications and Suggestions

Such a view, of course, complicates both simple binary categories *and* their repudiation in queered, fluid sex, sexuality, and gender. We need to recognise that male and female phenotypes (bodily forms) exist as polar rather than binary phenomena: that is to say, at either end of a spectrum of physical types lie (versions of) paradigmatic male and female bodies; and in between these poles there is a variety of male and female bodies, and some that are neither/nor/both/and.[103] A theology that seeks to force the world of human bodies into rigid "male" or "female" types fails to do justice to the realities of the world as it is. Intersex should probably be seen as an inscription

---

101   Weerakoon and Weerakoon, "Biology"; Looy and Bouma, "Nature of Gender," 166–71.
102   "Nature of Gender," 173–74.
103   Ibid., 174–76.

of the brokenness of a fallen world on particular human bodies (a *disability*) given the ways it complicates the biology of reproduction. For one of the ends to which we are ordered as creatures is the procreation of the human species, and so our theology of the body needs to include our procreative capacities.[104] But other variations of maleness and femaleness are complex expressions of the rich variety of God's creation. We need to accommodate this full spectrum of bodily forms in our theology of the (sexed) body. On the other hand, our bodily existence is a given. Our bodies are not mere instruments, infinitely malleable expressions of our untethered wills.[105]

This brings us to two related matters: how do we understand bodies and their relationship to ourselves (note, already, the fraught way this question is framed); and what role should (biomedical) technology play in the (re) shaping of bodies? The apparent body-obsession of contemporary (Western) culture hides an (ironic) hatred and fear of the body and its resistance to our wills.[106] At the empty heart of Western culture lies the absolutised "good" of choice. Our wills, unconstrained by ends to which they should be directed and unfettered from any external moral norms, have become the sole arbiters of the right (and, for that matter, of *rights*).[107] The body has become the resistant matter that the volitional demiurge seeks to dominate and control, conforming it to the image of what we choose (choices which are ironically constrained by the market and technology, which render even our embodied selves into commodities). Such perspectives have come to control much of bioethics and medical technology.[108] Medicine has become a commodity to be purchased from medical technicians, subject only to the constraints of the

---

104   DeFranza suggests that seeing intersex as a consequence of the fall risks their being dismissed as persons (DeFranza, *Sex Difference in Christian Theology*, ch. 4). Her concern can be addressed by seeing sex and gender as a *spectrum* of physical and behavioural and psychological and affective and relational traits rather than reified ontological categories, and human identity as primarily relationally determined. For a discussion of issues of disability, biology, and culture, see Sloane, *Vulnerability and Care*, 96–99.

105   O'Donovan, "Transsexualism and Christian Marriage." While he seems to operate with a relatively unproblematic binary of male and female, he helpfully reflects on issues of psychology and embodiment in relation to gender reassignment.

106   Meilaender, *Body, Soul, and Bioethics*.

107   Hart, "God or Nothingness." See also the reflections in O'Donovan, "Transsexualism and Christian Marriage," esp. 149–52.

108   McKenny, *To Relieve the Human Condition*.

market and the demands of the "client." This false, even idolatrous, vision of medicine must be replaced by a properly Christian account in which medicine exists as an expression of a community's solidarity with and care for frail, finite, embodied beings whose vulnerability has been exposed by illness, infirmity, or misfortune.[109]

In such a view, medicine has a clear, if limited, role to play in the care of people with gender dysphoria or intersex conditions—for we need to care for these people in need. Crucial to the diagnosis of gender dysphoria is the sense that the alienation they experience from their bodies is *distressing*, and is not a matter of choice. Caring for them requires that we do what can rightly be done to alleviate that distress or help them cope with it so as to enable them to function as well as they can as persons and in their relationships. As Yarhouse notes, the key (as in all therapeutic interventions) is to do only that which is required to help a distressed person.[110] As such, radical surgical intervention should be seen as a treatment of last resort, an accommodation to an otherwise intractable disorder. Similarly, if we allow for some kind of spectrum of sexed bodies, we need not engage in complex (and risky) gender assignment surgery on children with intersex conditions. Other strategies will generally allow them space to navigate the world as the bodies they find themselves to be, and to determine for themselves what, if any, medical intervention might be required later in life. In neither case, however, is medicine a tool for the expression of an autonomous human will. This is not a matter of "choosing your own bodily adventure." Furthermore, medicine is not going to be able to "fix" all the problems that people with gender dysphoria or intersex conditions might face. Many of them are the result of particular cultural patterns that are not subject to biomedical control. Indeed, much (but not all) of the distress such people face might be alleviated by the recognition that a wider range of expressions of masculinity and femininity should be allowed—and even encouraged—within Christian communities.[111]

---

109   Sloane, "Christianity and the Transformation of Medicine."
110   Yarhouse, *Understanding Gender Dysphoria*, esp. chs 1, 5–7.
111   Looy and Bouma, "Nature of Gender," 174–76.

In-conclusions

Intersex and gender dysphoria are particular expressions of issues relating to biology and gender that theology needs to address. They rightly call into question rigid binary categories of male/female and feminine/masculine without thereby undermining the notions *per se*. They require us to develop nuanced theologies of the body and understandings of how we relate to each other as embodied beings, and social and technological practices that allow us to deal with our fractured and flawed nature. I have suggested some directions such inquiry should take, as well as what I see as clear limitations on the faithful engagement with these issues. There are many questions I have not addressed, and a number of my suggestions are at best partial and provisional. But such is the nature of theology in a world such as this.

Response: Justine Toh

I want to thank Andrew for the way his paper establishes a useful and nuanced basis from which theological reflection on matters of intersex, gender dysphoria, and gender fluidity can operate. I found particularly illuminating and encouraging Andrew's reminder that science and theology need not be enemies sparring over the same contested territory; nor need one acquiesce entirely to the dictates of the other. Instead, science and theology can "mutually interrogate" each other as conversation partners, with each field having valuable contributions to make to the world in which we live and in relation to our lived experience of it.

I also appreciated the way Andrew emphasised that there are more options available to us than simply, on the one hand, a choice between an inflexible reification of binary sex and gender categories and, on the other, a wholesale rejection of sex and gender norms altogether. I especially welcomed Andrew's tone in pointing out that the complexities of human embodiment, evident in examples of intersex and gender dysphoric individuals, need not "queer" gender and sex beyond recognition. Given how inflammatory these discussions can be in our present context, we need more voices like his to speak on such matters in public.

I would, however, love to press Andrew further on the following. First, I completely agree that our nature and identity are intrinsically relational. While we should always be cautious about drawing too direct a line between the body and our lived experience, it strikes me that some embodied experiences, like those of pregnancy and being a nursing mother, for instance, bear out how fundamentally relational we are. But those experiences are confined to women and, more specifically, mothers. How do we talk more about relationally generated identity in ways that do not reduce, idealise, or idolise women as, fundamentally, child-bearers? And how do we do this in ways that flout the Western autonomous individualist model of self-determination and self-realisation that particularly seems to underwrite decisions for sex reassignment surgery for gender dysphoric individuals—especially given that such surgery can often be devastating for the partners, children, and parents of those "left behind"?

And secondly, while I agree with Andrew that "assigning" a gender to intersex children is no solution, I'm more cautious about his claim that allowing intersex individuals to "determine for themselves what, if any, medical intervention might be required later in life" does not necessarily mean that they will use medicine as a means of expressing their autonomous human will. I want to believe this for myself but I don't share Andrew's confidence—especially in the face of cultural pressures to achieve self-realisation ("love the body you're in"/"be yourself") and the technical know-how that can sculpt bodies after our desires. What makes Andrew so confident that intersex or gender dysphoric individuals can resist the cultural tide? I'd love to hear his ideas.

I've really enjoyed the conversation; it has reminded me that while there are no easy answers, these issues are well worth exploring—and continuing to grapple with. Thanks!

Response to Justine Toh and Andrew Sloane: Patricia and Kamal Weerakoon

Justine has provided an excellent overview of how contemporary gender theory takes fluidity for granted and is therefore "outraged" at classical Christian affirmations of gender dimorphism. She also points out how the way gendered relationships are conducted in church circles reinforces traditional, "secular" concepts of masculinity and femininity— craft-making versus *Courageous*-viewing. Andrew rightly observes how, at the other extreme, it is possible to be so single-sightedly "biblical" as to insist that any sense of gender uncertainty is *only ever* the product of a sinful will.

Our own paper documents how many manifestations of gender variation are unchosen products of prenatal development. We also agree that gender is significantly socially constructed through modelling and habituation. As Andrew says, we are significantly shaped not only by the physical body we inhabit but also by the relationships we share. We agree that churches need to be alert to the socially formative and normative effects of uncritically replicating "traditional" gender stereotypes—and the effect of these stereotypes in alienating those who, for whatever reason, do not conform. Church should always be hospitable to the socially marginalised. Jesus was.

We suggest one way to actually be a "redemptive community" is to extend Andrew's reflections on how we know ourselves as persons-in-relationship, and re-vision the way external society "inscribes" gender upon individuals as a blessing, not an oppressive curse. Part of today's generally accepted radical individualism is an instinctive suspicion towards any external formation of the self. Why should "you" tell "me" anything about "myself"? You're not me—so shut up. Any external formation is necessarily perceived as oppression, to be thrown off, not internalised.

Scripture has a very different view of external formation. God places us in families and communities, and those societies, which are external to us, shape who we are, precisely through the social processes of modelling and habituation. We worship Jesus, who, as second person of the Trinity, is God from eternity to eternity, yet who became not just human, but a gendered man, and not just *a* man, but a son of Abraham, David, Joseph (by family association—Luke 4:22, "isn't this Joseph's son?") and Mary. Those particular located identifications are key to his office as saviour. Jesus redeems external social formation to be a blessing, not a curse.

Therefore, one way we can know ourselves as male or female, a boy or a girl, is through what everyone else says we are. We can, at least *prima facie, trust* those who demonstrably *love* us—our parents, friends, and family, who feed us, clothe us, teach us, and in so many other ways mediate life to us. We can trust them to form us to be healthy men and women, boys and girls. This is not a curse which shackles us but a blessing which liberates us to confidently inhabit that externally affirmed identity—especially in times of uncertainty, like adolescence, when a powerful cocktail of hormones stimulates the brain to develop in ways that are, in the long run, very good and necessary, but can be in the short run unsettling and confusing.

We hasten to add—this is *prima facie* trust, not absolute inscription. As is evident in our own paper, a gender spectrum, significantly shaped by variations in prenatal development, exists. Our aim is to approach the kind of dynamic dialectic Andrew aspires to, which permits a degree of variation while not pretending that our gender identity and physical bodies are merely instruments of our autonomous will.

We ground this permissible, enjoyable variation within basic gender dimorphism—we know ourselves, both as physical bodies, and as persons-in-relationship, as either male *or* female, a boy *or* a girl—because we trust the biblical presentation of binary gender as being good for individual and social health. However, we think we can, without compromising this commitment to basic biblical gender dimorphism, open the question of what does it mean for this *particular* person, as their particular body—with all its particular possibilities and imperfections—in their particular relational network—with all its potentials and limitations—to be a man or a woman, a boy or a girl? But to facilitate this kind of liberating external formation, it is even *more* necessary, as Justine says, for churches to both welcome those who do not conform to traditional gender stereotypes, and to critically review whether their own practices of social modelling and habituation are merely uncritically replicating the practices of this world or encouraging growth in the fruits of the Spirit.

Part Eight

Gender, Mission, and the Reign of God

Gender, Being Missional, and the Reign of God

Karina Kreminski

This year the *Sydney Morning Herald* published three consecutive articles within three weeks which looked at the topic of domestic violence.[1] The interesting thing to note was that the articles focused on the response and culpability of the church regarding this topic. The doctrine of male headship was singled out as a distinctive in Christian theology which could enable the perpetuation of domestic violence towards women. The articles generated an incredible amount of response from Christians and non-Christians alike. It seemed as if everyone had an opinion on this. Whatever our thoughts are regarding this doctrine, two things stood out for me during that time: firstly, our world is very interested in the topic of gender; and secondly, what we decide as the church regarding our theology on gender impacts our broader society. The question is, however, what is the message that we will communicate to our world about the hotly debated topic of gender? Can we offer an alternative that is truly different to the cultural narratives of our society? I wonder if we could even convey glimpses from an upside-down,

---

1   Baird, "Doctrine of headship a distortion"; "Submission is a fraught mixed message"; Young, "Abuse inside Christian Marriages."

alternate reality that we call the kingdom or reign of God. All of this makes the topic of gender a deeply missional issue for us today.

A Reign of God Perspective on Gender

We can't look to our culture for a theological view of gender though it can inform a kingdom of God theology on gender if we critically engage with those narratives. How can we then begin to develop a theology of gender which establishes a missional framework for our engagement with the world? In my opinion, to do this we need to move past our Christian obsession with the binaries of complementarianism and egalitarianism which are problematic categories anyway. We need to present to our world a view of gender that comes from another reality beyond our broken world. As Carolyn Custis James asks in *Half the Church*, "Is Jesus' gospel merely a kinder, gentler version of the world's way of doing things, or does the gospel take us to a completely different, long forgotten way of relating to one another as male and female? When Jesus said, 'my kingdom is not of this world', did he include relationships between men and women?"[2]

What is this "long forgotten" way of relating to each other as men and women? This would be a view of gender that reflects an alternate reality. This would be a paradigm where those who are not yet in the kingdom intuitively realise that this is what they have always longed for. This would be a perspective which goes beyond the current polarisations and sometimes petty internal debates we experience in the church. I long for that. So given that the reign of God is an alternate reality which is growing today and that we live in the tension of the now and not yet, here is my attempt at expressing a kingdom of God perspective on gender which I think we can confidently present to our world.

As I do this, I place at the foundation of this perspective on gender, Elaine Storkey's four characteristics of gender and descriptions of the relationship between men and women which stem from a biblical narrative.

2   James, *Half the Church*, 162.

They are difference, similarity, non-hierarchical complementarity, and union. Firstly, Storkey says that men and women are different. In that sense she critiques the modern view which mostly tries to dissolve difference by highlighting that gender is a social construct and that there is no such thing as essentialism. Secondly, she says that men and women are similar. In essence this is tempering an essentialism which claims, to put it in popular terms, that "men are from Mars and women are from Venus." Instead her point is that we share many similarities. Thirdly, she says that men and women complement each other; however, this does not necessitate hierarchy. Lastly, she points to the importance of union. What she means is that men and women together reflect the image of God and that there is an ontological union between them. I think her four characteristics are helpful for us as we think about what it means to have a theology of gender. The important point is that we need to hold these four characteristics together rather than focusing on one or two. I think that has been one of our problems in the past. When we focus too much on difference, we make the mistake of thinking that it is almost as though men and women live on different planets and that communication is impossible. When we focus on similarities we get concerned that we are abolishing differences, which somehow doesn't ring true for us experientially and biblically speaking. And her emphasis on non-hierarchical complementarity is quite helpful. Men and women need one another, but biblically this does not require a hierarchy of power for good relating.

Therefore, keeping these helpful aspects from Storkey in mind, a kingdom of God perspective on gender has three broad characteristics.

We Are New Creations in Christ

In an article on gender, theologian Cherith Fee Nordling says,

> 'All things are yours,' writes Paul to the women and men
> of the church at Corinth, be it 'the world or life or death
> or the present or the future—all are yours, and you are
> of Christ, and Christ is of God' (1 Corinthians 3:21b–22).

Paul reminds them that, because of God's self-giving generosity, there is no longer any need or place for division over leadership that would limit the gifts of the Spirit poured out equally on women and men alike. To do so would be to go backward to live as 'old creation'. Rather, these diverse women and men, reconstituted by the Spirit are 'new creation'. They share eschatologically in all that belongs to the Son, who has guaranteed an embodied inheritance that does not prioritise gender, class, ethnicity, or anything else.[3]

What she is pointing to is Paul's theology which emphasises that we are a new creation in Christ and that this new status does away with various aspects of the old creation which we are no longer a part of. Those old ways might still tempt us, they might still exist but they are fading as we put on the new nature we have in Christ. The kingdom of God is not of this world—why do we often act as though we are still trapped in it?

One Corinthians 7:31 says that "the present form of this world is passing away." If that is the case then we should engage with the values of the coming reality which has already invaded our earth through Jesus. Gordon Fee applies this logic to Galatians 3:28 which says, "There is no longer Jew or Greek, there is no longer slave or free, there is no longer male and female; for all of you are one in Christ Jesus." He carefully exegetes this verse in his article *Male and Female in the New Creation* and says that Paul is living out his view of the now and not yet of the kingdom by stating that while the old order still exists, it no longer has power to constitute value and social identity in the new creation which is already present.

Gordon Fee says, "That is, even though the categories themselves still function in the present, their significance in terms of old age values has been abolished by Christ and the Spirit."[4] I don't think that what Paul is

---

3   Fee Nordling, "Gender," 497.
4   Gordon Fee, "Male and Female in the New Creation," 179.

saying is that in the new creation there is now no distinction between men and women. He is saying, rather, that some aspects of what used to make men and women distinct are now cancelled out in the new creation. I think he is talking about the power and privilege, the division and the status, that came with those distinctions, which are now no longer a part of the values of the kingdom of God. These things now do not define what it means to be male or female or in fact what it means to be human. What does it mean to be human, to be male or female? When we ask this question we are on the search for our identity and the Bible has more to say about who we are in Christ as a new creation than it does around gender. In a sense we can say that our new identity in Christ relativises our old identity. So in a sense our gender is not of primary importance because ultimately what matters is that we are new creations in Christ which is our new identity. That does not mean gender is abolished but only relativised in comparison with the new thing that Christ has given to us, our identity in him, which trumps all other definitions and distinctions. We should probably be placing more emphasis on our new identity in Christ and what that means rather than making our focus trying to elaborate on our gender distinctions.

Theologian Linda Woodhead is helpful when she writes about our identity in Christ. She says that there is a modern day kind of anxiety about our selfhood and identity, and she feels that Christians have got caught up in that anxiety. Is it our sin which causes us to want to control our identity and then neatly define what is masculine and feminine? Instead Woodhead quotes Colossians 3:3, which says that our "life is hidden with Christ in God" and says that there is so much more to our identity that we cannot know now. She says that Christianity stresses that, "we are always more than we can know. Our identity in this life remains forever beyond our grasp. Our life is something which is hid with God, and which we can never fully know in this life."[5]

So we have glimpses into what our identity as new creations is like but to try and define our identity—and I would say to try and define our

---

5   Linda Woodhead, "God, Gender and Identity," 96.

femininity and masculinity—is something that we won't fully be able to do until we see Jesus face to face. This is helpful because we can humbly say that while we can know some things about ourselves, we can't know everything. This brings a bit of caution to us as we try to establish a theology of gender. We are new creations in Christ but our identity is not fully revealed now.

A Trinitarian Perspective on Identity—Mutual Submission and Surrender of Power.

A second characteristic in a kingdom of God view on gender is a Trinitarian perspective on identity which practises mutual submission and surrender of power. As we are talking about issues to do with identity here, we can look to the one in whose image we are made and, as we do that, we see that God is three persons in the one Godhead. This gives us clues as to how we can interpret our identity and that includes our gender. Of course, we need to be cautious about using the Trinity as a model because God is God and we are not, we can never expect to be who God is. We are standing on sacred ground here.

However, there are characteristics that we can observe about God's identity that we can emulate and in fact, I think we are meant to. Miroslav Volf writes from a Trinitarian perspective and he applies this to the issue of gender. I agree with him when he says that there is no transcultural, eternal definition of manhood and womanhood that we can see from Scripture, so instead of trying to search for them we should instead "let the social construction of gender play itself out guided by the vision of the identity of and relationship between divine persons."[6]

One factor we can identify within the Godhead is that there is distinction between each person. Applied to men and women, we can say that there is also difference between male and female. Even if we go back to Genesis 1 we read that God created humankind in his image, "in the image of God he created them, male and female he created them." That perhaps

---

6   Miroslav Volf, "The Trinity and Gender Identity," 170.

points to difference between men and women. How that works out in terms of then trying to define masculinity and femininity is more difficult and this depends on cultural context which is a powerful factor in constructing these descriptions. Many people have tried to make lists of what it means to be masculine and what it means to be feminine but I think, from my reading, most have failed in this venture. Moreover, I think one fear that many women have is that by emphasising difference, once again our old nature will rise up and enforce division, privilege, and status onto the male–female relationship, usually meaning that the woman is made invisible and subjugated by privileged male power. There are differences between the genders but spelling out that difference takes a lot of wisdom, humility, and discernment.

As we reflect on the Trinity we also see a complementarity that exists between the three persons. While we still maintain our selfhood and see that this is a gift from God, we realise that being human means being interdependent with others. The modern, Western notion of the self as autonomous, self-sufficient, and highly individualistic does not seem to be the manner in which the Trinity operates. How does this apply to gender? Could we imagine a reality where men and women negotiate their identities together as new creations in Christ? We can see this complementarity and negotiation in 1 Corinthians 11:11 where Paul says, "Nevertheless, in the Lord woman is not independent of man, nor is man independent of woman." We can see the same thing relating to husbands and wives in 1 Corinthians 7:4, which says, "The wife does not have authority over her own body but yields it to her husband. In the same way, the husband does not have authority over his own body but yields it to his wife." Paul clearly seems to be describing an interdependence implying complementarity in these verses.

Finally, as we consider the Trinity we also see a mutual submission and a self-giving love between the persons. If we apply this to the relationship between men and women it means that instead of one gender having power over the other, as these roles and unhelpful privileges of the old order fade away, our new ethic as creations in Christ is self-giving love and mutual submission. We see this in Ephesians 5, which shows us that the self sacrifice of Christ is to be a model for relationships between husbands and wives. The mandate is mutual submission. Written in a patriarchal culture where the submission of women was the status quo, wives are told to submit and men are told to love. What is radical here is not that Paul speaks submission to the wife, but that he tells men to love their wives. Moreover, in verses 25–26 he says that husbands are to give themselves up to their wives as Christ gave himself up to the church nurturing, nourishing her, and tenderly taking care of her. This was incredibly radical in that culture.

This kind of surrender of power and living a cruciform existence, particularly as applied to the men, is fraught with risk in our culture today which thrives on power. Volf beautifully captures this and says, "In a world of enmity self-giving is the risky and hard work of love. There are no guarantees that self-giving will overcome enmity and that the evildoers will not try to invade the space that the self has made and crush those willing to give themselves for the good of others. We will have to resist such evildoers without betraying the commitment to self-giving. But though self-giving has no assurance of success, it does have the promise of eternity because it reflects the character of the divine Trinity."[7]

A hard-line hierarchical complementarity which gives a permanent role to the female as submissive and the male as leader and which is restrictive, controlling, stereotyping, and oppressive does not belong in a kingdom of God paradigm. Sadly, this view is sometimes sanctified by the church with the tag line, "Equal in being, unequal in role." My thought is that this is actually a reflection of the darker side of our Western middle-class culture. Rebecca Groothuis claims that it is impossible to maintain that a person can be equal to another if they are in a permanent role of submission to another.[8]

Gordon Fee states that moving in this direction regarding gender can turn us into Pharisees who ask questions such as, "'What constitutes wifely submission?' Or, 'When a husband and wife come to a stalemate in decision

---

7   Miroslav Volf, "The Trinity and Gender Identity," 177.
8   Rebecca Groothuis "Equal in Being, Unequal in Role," 316–17.

making, who has the last word?' One wonders whether Paul would laugh or cry! The gospel of grace and gifting leads to a different set of questions: How does one best serve the interests of the other? How does one encourage the Spirit's gifting in the other? Questions like this cross all gender boundaries."[9] Hierarchical complementarianism does not fit into a kingdom of God view of gender.

Practising Reconciliation

Lastly and briefly, a characteristic of a kingdom of God view on gender is that it focuses on reconciliation. Colossians 1:15 and onwards tells of the supremacy of Christ and it repeats the phrase "all things" several times. It says through Christ "all things" were created, "all things" have been created for him, he is before "all things," Christ hold "all things" together. Then verse 20 says, ". . . through him God was pleased to reconcile to himself 'all things', whether on earth or in heaven by making peace through the blood of his cross." I am sometimes asked, "Why do you focus on gender so much? Shouldn't you just focus on the gospel?" My answer is that when I read that passage all of a sudden the gospel magnifies before my eyes. If the gospel is about bringing the good news of Jesus and his kingdom which has implications of setting free the captives and bringing release to the prisoners, if it is about bringing the peace of God through Jesus by reconciling all things to himself, then everything matters, including gender. Where we see wars and power-plays between men and women that perpetuate lack of unity and peace, suspicion, mistrust, and division, Christ comes to bring restoration and healing. A kingdom of God perspective on gender believes that reconciliation, peace, and unity are possible goals to aim for when it comes to the relationship between men and women.

Christians can present a clear theology of gender to our world which sorely needs to hear about the possibility of a reconciliation between men and women. This "Blessed Alliance"[10] between men and women should

---

9   Gordon Fee, "Hermeneutics and the Gender Debate," 380.

10   James, *Malestrom*, 135.

whisper the presence of another reality. If that reality even remotely begins to reflect the power structures of this world, then we must be immediately suspicious and wonder if it does in fact belong to this alternate world called the kingdom of God. Will we have the courage to represent that kingdom here and now as we join with God on his mission to restore our world?

Restoring All That Was Broken: Gender, Gospel, and the New Creation

David Starling

A Conversation Worth Having

Conversations about gender—even conversations between brothers and sisters within the family of the church—can frequently be difficult interactions to negotiate. Because of the limits of our experience and the partiality of our vision; because of the cultural narratives and assumptions that shape our thinking and our practice, often at a deeper level than we are even conscious of; because of the personal histories—sometimes deeply painful—that inform the way we think and feel about the issues involved; because of the sinful self-interest that biases our motives and our interpretations; because of the weariness and woundedness we feel from past experiences when we tried to have a conversation and it went badly; because of the long history of unequal and oppressive power arrangements within which gender roles have been constructed across the centuries, and the shadow they continue to cast today; because of the multi-stranded entanglements of human experience, and—paradoxically—because of the very richness and complexity of what the Bible says about the subject . . . for all these reasons and more, the gender conversation, in its various forms, is not an easy one for us to have.

Because of that, there is a strong temptation, experienced by all of us in different ways, to buy out of the conversation or to try and shut it down altogether. That can happen in various ways. It can happen when we separate out from one another into disconnected tribes, within each of which a single orthodox opinion prevails, relieving us of the awkward necessity of relating to others whose views differ from our own. It can happen when we replace real conversation with sloganeering or snide remarks—when we are slow to listen, quick to speak, and quick to post on Facebook. It can happen, also, when we consign the topic permanently to the too-hard basket and replace painful conversation with a polite and awkward silence, justifying our disengagement with the rationale that because this is not a "gospel issue" it is not one that we need to focus on.

And yet the conversation goes on, with us or without us on board. And it is a conversation worth having. If the gospel is about the Lordship of Jesus over all things; if it teaches us a wisdom that touches on every aspect of human life and relationships; if the saving purposes of God made known in the gospel embrace the whole of our humanity (and indeed the whole creation), then this is not a topic we ought to shrink back from or push to the margins as unimportant. The gender conversation is a conversation worth having.

Somewhere within the big, swirling ocean of public conversation about gender that we participate in as Christians (and amongst the various private and sub-cultural tributaries that feed into it) is the particular conversation we have been engaged in today: the in-house conversation between Christian brothers and sisters who love the same Lord Jesus and who read and believe the same Scriptures, yet differ on how those Scriptures are to be interpreted and applied to matters of gender. As Karina rightly stresses, that in-house Christian conversation should not be dismissed as petty and inconsequential, irrelevant to the mission of the church; nor can it ever be neatly insulated from the larger conversations of our culture. The way in which we talk about gender as Christian brothers and sisters, the conclusions that we come to, and the practices that anticipate and reflect those conclusions, are all of enormous significance for the way in which we live out the imprint of the Lordship of Jesus in the life of the church and commend the gospel to the world.

Common Ground

When we engage in that conversation—when we talk together about questions of gender with the Scriptures open, with a genuine readiness to listen to one another, with a common commitment to the centrality of the gospel and the mission of God in the world, and with a prayerful and humble desire for our thinking to be shaped by God's word—we find that we have an enormous amount to agree on. Our conversations today have been proof of that, and the same can be said this evening, as we attempt in this last session to draw some threads together and relate the questions of gender to our larger and more basic convictions about the gospel and the mission of God. When I listen as a (broadly) complementarian man to the (broadly) egalitarian perspective outlined by Karina—with due apologies for the inadequacies of those labels—I find so much with which I am in emphatic and earnest agreement.

With Karina, I find myself affirming that there are important *differences* of biology, perspective, and experience between us as men and women that derive in part from the good design of God who made us male and female in the beginning. With Karina, too, I can affirm the crucial *similarities* between us as fellow-bearers of the image of God, as fellow-sinners, and (in Christ) as fellow-members of the Spirit-filled community. With Karina, also, I can affirm and celebrate the *complementarity* within which our maleness and femaleness are to be understood, and agree that this should never be articulated in terms of the superiority of one sex over the other, or the privileging of one at the other's expense. And with Karina, fourthly, I can affirm the *unity* within which the biblical writers call us to live out this vision, side by side within the loving communion of marriage and family and friendship and church.

I could go on: we could speak about the shared understanding that we have on numerous matters about the role that sex and gender play within the shaping of our common life as a society, about the danger of importing into Christian conversation the unexamined assumptions and categories of a secular culture war, and about the responsibility and freedom that all of God's people ought to feel to use their gifts in the service of his mission in the world. There is so much to agree on, and I could, if I chose to, continue in this vein all night. But that would be not so much a conversation as an echo or an Amen. So in the interests of conversation I will turn now to two important points of difference in content or in emphasis between the vision Karina has outlined and the way in which I think the gospel we believe ought to shape our understanding of gender.

Two Points of Difference

Gospel and Creation

The first is a difference of emphasis in the way that we articulate the relationship between the gospel and the present order of the fallen creation that we inhabit. In Karina's account, the emphasis falls heavily on the way in which the gospel disrupts and overturns the current order of things. Our mission, she urges us, requires us to present to the world "a view of gender that comes from another reality beyond our broken world." The "reality beyond our world" that she has in mind is "the reign of God . . . an alternate reality which is growing today." Our view of gender ought to express "the values of the coming reality which has already invaded our earth through Jesus."

There is a powerful truth in this emphasis. Like Hannah in the Old Testament and Mary in the New, Karina draws our attention to the way in which the saving interventions of God lift up the humble and bring down the mighty from their thrones. The God who raised the crucified Jesus from the grave is the God whose gospel turns the world upside down. The gospel that breaks into Caesar's empire with the announcement that Jesus is Lord is an intrusive gospel, a beautiful but devastating disruption to the oppressive structures and value systems of a fallen world.[11]

But this disruptive dimension of the gospel is only half the story of how the salvation in Jesus relates to the world we find ourselves in. If we are to speak of the kingdom of God as an "alternate reality" that has "invaded our earth" (and I'm not entirely convinced that this sort of language is the best terminology to use) we need to stress that the God whose kingdom we are speaking of is the God who established the earth in the first place, and whose wisdom remains deeply embedded in the structure of the creation, underneath all the damage and distortions of sin. The "new creation" that God establishes in Christ is not an alien imposition on this world, or the brand-new invention of an unknown God; it is the restoration and redemption of the original creation that God made in the beginning.[12]

This has implications for how we understand the maleness and femaleness of our bodies, and how we relate to the gender arrangements of the culture we live in. As Karina rightly acknowledges, Paul's "neither male nor female" in Galatians 3 is not a claim about the total erasure of sexual difference in Christ; what is done away with in Christ is not the distinctions within the good creation God made in the beginning, but the divisions and hostilities superimposed on them in a fallen world. When the writers of the New Testament apply the gospel to the gendered roles of men and women in the household and the church, they do not do so in a way that dissolves the particular callings and responsibilities of husbands and wives, fathers and mothers. Grace does not simply endorse the power arrangements of fallen nature, but neither does it destroy or bypass nature altogether; the grace of God in the gospel redeems nature, restoring all that was broken and distorted by the fall.

The "headship" of husbands that Paul speaks of in Ephesians 5 is a case in point. The gospel does not sweep it away into the dustbin of salvation

---

11   Cf. the discussions of the theological vision of the book of Acts in Skinner, *Intrusive God, Disruptive Gospel*, and Rowe, *World Upside Down*.

12   See especially Wright, *Paul and the Faithfulness of God*, 475–94.

history; it redeems it in the pattern of the crucified Christ and his love for the church. "Wives," Paul writes, "submit yourselves to your own husbands as you do to the Lord. For the husband is the head of the wife as Christ is the head of the church" (5:22). "Husbands, love your wives, just as Christ loved the church and gave himself up for her" (5:25). A day is coming when there will be neither marrying nor giving in marriage; but in this age, in the time of the inaugurated kingdom, those of us who do marry are to live out in our marriages a pattern of relationship that reflects the unity and complementarity written into our bodies by God the creator in the beginning, and faithfully anticipates the heavenly marriage between Christ and his people.

Trinity, Mutuality, and Submission

But the pattern of Christ and the church that Paul appeals to in Ephesians 5 is not the only analogy Paul reaches for in teaching us to reframe our understanding of gender in light of the gospel; he also hints in 1 Corinthians 11 at an analogy of some sort between the relationship between a husband and a wife and the relationship between God and Christ. At this point we are, as Karina says, on sacred ground. We would do well to be cautious about transferring too much from the unique relationship between God and Christ to the very different relationship between a husband and a wife, or taking the next step and making inflated claims about the relationships of the immanent Trinity and the extent to which they are meant to find a reflection in our human relationships.

But an analogy of some sort is drawn by Paul in 1 Corinthians 11— even if we stop short of extrapolating from what Paul says here about the relationship between "God" and "Christ" to the eternal relationship between the Father and the Son. And the analogy that Paul draws suggests that the pattern of gender relationships within the redeemed community of the church ought to reflect both the mutuality implied by the original creation story (1 Cor 11:11–12) and, within that framework of difference and mutuality, a particular responsibility carried by husbands which corresponds in some way to the fact that "the head of Christ is God" (1 Cor 11:3).

If we are to take the next step, as Karina does, and ground that analogy explicitly in the eternal, inner-Trinitarian relationships, then it needs to be granted that the equality and mutuality of love between the Father and the Son are never described within the New Testament in the language of "mutual submission," or framed in categories that dissolve the asymmetries of the Father-Son relationship. The Son is the Father's equal in being and in glory, and there is nothing coercive or exploitative about the way in which the Father relates to the Son. But there is still within the witness of the New Testament a consistent distinction between the persons, in which the Father freely shares all that he is and all that he has with the Son, and the Son freely delights to do the will of the Father.[13]

If we are to attempt in some way to image the inner-Trinitarian relationships in the way we live together as men and women in the family and the church, it is *that* Trinity—the Trinity of equal and differentiated relationships made known to us through the way in which they have overflowed into the sendings of the *missio Dei*—that ought to inform our understanding. The relationship between the Father and the Son is a reminder that mutuality of love and equality of honour need not be viewed as inconsistent with distinctions of responsibility and difference of roles.

Any version of those differences and distinctions that uses them to justify a power-arrangement that is "restrictive, controlling, stereotyping, and oppressive" is (as Karina rightly stresses) utterly inconsistent with the teaching of the New Testament and the pattern of mutual love that has been shown to us in the relationship between the Father and the Son. We should not think for a moment that the gospel simply endorses the abusive and exploitative patriarchy of a fallen world. Nor have we been given a comprehensive and detailed blueprint for how these things are to be worked out in every time and every place and every facet of life: there will always be a need for a kind of improvisation and negotiation as we work out how to receive the good gift of our sexual difference and fulfil our complementary responsibilities, within the various situations in which we find ourselves.

---

13   See especially Pannenberg, *Systematic Theology*, 1.308–17; Letham, *The Holy Trinity*, 479–96; Augustine, *On the Trinity*, 4.20.27 and *Answer to Maximus the Arian*, 2.14.89.

But the kind of negotiation that is called for is not the sort that starts with a blank sheet of paper and simply attempts a balancing-out between the desires and ambitions of the two parties; what it is more like is the negotiation and improvisation that take place between fellow-actors in a play or fellow-dancers in a ballet. The various gendered roles we have been given by God to perform are like steps we are to dance together. When we perform our roles as men and women, sisters and brothers, husbands and wives, we are interpreting music that God has written into the creation, following the choreography of the Scriptures, and adapting our steps to the stage on which God's providence has placed us and the cast-members with whom we are performing. In a fallen world, as imperfect dancers on a broken stage, this will not always be easy. Sometimes it will be intensely difficult. But it has the potential, as Peter reminds his readers in 1 Peter 3—even in the most difficult of circumstances—to be radiantly beautiful, and it is of enormous worth in the sight of God.

A Common Task

Interpreting and applying the Scriptures should never be a solitary business. Nor, on those disputable matters in which we come to differing conclusions from one another, should this be regarded as the end of the conversation and a warrant for the withdrawal of fellowship. Each person, as Paul reminds the Christians in Rome, ought to ponder the Scriptures, examine their conscience, and be "fully convinced in their own mind" (Rom 14:5). But we are still to keep welcoming one another, as we have been welcomed by God (cf. Rom 14:1; 15:7), and helping one another to wrestle with the Scriptures and live in the light of what we find there.

We need each other, not only to live out the mandate that we are given in Scripture but even to understand that mandate in the first place. Scripture speaks about *both* the way in which the gospel disrupts and overturns the structures of a fallen world *and* the way in which it redeems the original patterns and order of the good creation God made in the beginning. It paints a picture of our relationships as men and women that emphasises *both* the mutuality and equality that stem from our common inheritance in Christ *and* the distinctions of roles and responsibilities that reflect the differences between us. Those of us whose emphasis falls on one part of the biblical picture ought not to disengage from those whose emphasis falls on another. Our common task as fellow-believers and servants of the same Lord Jesus is to help one another to embrace the whole picture, in all its richness and complexity, and to live it out together to the glory of God.

Epilogue

Epilogue

Edwina Murphy and David Starling

In primary school, to finish a story with the phrase, "And then we all went home," was frowned upon. Well, since the conference, we have all gone home. But that is an unsatisfactory ending, as much in real life as in a juvenile composition. We did manage to play nicely together, which is a start, but are we going to continue to remember our manners? Having been stimulated on a number of fronts by the papers in this book, have we integrated them into our lives? Or have we been so overwhelmed by the flood of information, or conversely, so sheltered by our presuppositions, that we've returned little changed, unable or unwilling to absorb what we've heard?

With this book we want to invite more people into the conversation and encourage the reflection that is necessary to move that conversation forward. But we want to be doers of the word—not just hearers—continuing the talk as we walk in the footsteps of Christ.

Vividly recounted action loses its power when the tale concludes: "And then I woke up." It is our hope that the conference will not be a half-forgotten vision, the book and videos dusty artefacts, but rather that they will be seeds which germinate into life-giving trees. Within the church, yes, embracing our status as brothers and sisters in Christ, but also in our interactions with those around us. How do we model positive relationships between men and women? How is being made male and female in the image of God "good news" for a world in which so many are struggling with their identity? How do we imitate Jesus in relinquishing position and privilege for the benefit of others?

The contributors have planted, others will water. We look forward to the fruit!

Reference List

Ancient Sources

Aristotle. *Politics*. Translated by Benjamin Jowett. New York: Dover, 2000.

Augustine. *De Doctrina Christiana*. Translated by R. P. H. Green. Oxford: Clarendon, 1995.

_____.*On the Soul and its Origin*. Translated by Ernest Wallis. 1887. In *The Nicene and Post-Nicene Fathers*, Series 1, vol. 5, edited by Philip Schaff. Reprint, Grand Rapids: Eerdmans, 1971.

_____.*Sermon 281*. Translated by Edmund Hill. In *The Works of Saint Augustine: A Translation for the 21st Century. Part III—Sermons*, vol. 8, edited by John E. Rotelle, 78–80. Hyde Park, NY: New City, 1994.

_____.*The Trinity*. Translated by Edmund Hill. New York: New City, 2012.

BGU 1208. In *Äegyptische Urkunden aus den königlichen Museen zu Berlin*, Vol. 4, edited by F. Schubart et al., 351. Berlin: Weidmannsche, 1912.

Clement. *1 Clement*. Translated by Michael W. Holmes. In *The Apostolic Fathers: Greek Texts and English Translations*, 3rd ed, 44–131. Grand Rapids: Baker, 2007.

Crates. "The Epistles of Crates." Translated by Ronald F. Hock. In *The Cynic Epistles: A Study Edition*, edited by Abraham J. Malherbe, 54–89. Missoula, MT: Scholars, 1977.

Cyprian. *Ad Quirinum (Testimonies)*. Edited by R. Weber. CCSL 3. Turnhout: Brepols, 1972.

_____.*Epistle 71*. In *The Letters of St. Cyprian of Carthage*, vol. 4, translated and edited by G. W. Clarke, 48–51. New York: Newman, 1989.

_____.*Epistle 61*. In *The Letters of St. Cyprian of Carthage*, vol. 3, translated and edited by G. W. Clarke, 92–94. New York: Newman, 1986.

_____.*On the Dress of Virgins*. Translated by Ernest Wallis. 1867. In *The Ante-Nicene Fathers*, vol. 5, edited by Alexander Roberts and James Donaldson. Reprint, Grand Rapids: Eerdmans, 1965.

_____.*On the Lord's Prayer*. Translated by Ernest Wallis. 1867. In *The Ante-Nicene Fathers*, vol. 5, edited by Alexander Roberts and James Donaldson. Reprint, Grand Rapids: Eerdmans, 1965.

_____.*The Unity of the Catholic Church*. In *St. Cyprian. The Lapsed, The Unity of the Catholic Church*. Translated and annotated by Maurice Bévenot. New York: Newman, 1956.

Danby, Herbert, ed. "Abot 1.1–16." In *The Mishnah*. Oxford: Oxford University Press, 1933.

Demosthenes. *Orations, Volume V: Orations 41–49: Private Cases*. Translated by A. T. Murray. LCL. Cambridge, MA: Harvard University Press, 1939.

Dio Chrysostom. *Discourses 37–60*. Translated by H. Lamar Crosby. LCL. Cambridge, MA: Harvard University Press, 1946.

Diodorus of Sicily. *Library of History*. Edited and translated by Russel M. Geer, Vol. 10 of 12. LCL. Cambridge, MA: Harvard University Press, 1971.

Dionysius of Halicarnassus. *The Roman Antiquities*. Edited and translated by Earnest Cary, Vol. 2 of 7. LCL. Cambridge, MA: Harvard University Press, 1953.

"Genesis." Translated by R. J. V. Hiebert. In *A New English Translation of the Septuagint*, edited by A. Pietersma and B. G. Wright, 1–42. Oxford: Oxford University Press, 2007.

Herodotus. *The Histories*. Translated by A. D. Godley. LCL. Cambridge. Harvard University Press. 1920.

Hesiod. *Theogony. Works and Days. Testimonia*. Edited and translated by Glenn W. Most. LCL. Cambridge, MA: Harvard University Press, 2007.

Hippolytus. *On the Apostolic Tradition*, edited by Alistair Stewart-Sykes. Crestwood, NY: St Vladimir's Seminary, 2001.

_____."A discourse by the much blessed Hippolytus, Bishop and martyr, on the end of the world, and on the antichrist, and on the second coming of our Lord." In *The Ante-Nicene Fathers*, vol. 5, edited by Alexander Roberts and James Donaldson. Reprint, Grand Rapids: Eerdmans, 1965.

Homer. *Iliad, Volume II: Books 13–24*. Translated by A. T. Murray. LCL. Cambridge, MA: Harvard University Press, 1925.

Ignatius, "Philadelphians." In *The Apostolic Fathers: A New Translation and Commentary*. Translated by Robert M. Grant. New York: Thomas Nelson, 1964–68.

Inscriptiones Graecae IX,1. 2nd ed. Edited by Günther Klaffenbach. Berlin: de Gruyter, 1932–1968.

Irenaeus. *Against Heresies*. Translated by Alexander Roberts and James Donaldson. 1867. In *The Ante-Nicene Fathers*, vol. 1, edited by Alexander Roberts and James Donaldson. Reprint, Grand Rapids, MI: Eerdmans, 1963.

Isocrates. *To Demonicus. To Nicocles. Nicocles or the Cyprians. Panegyricus. To Philip. Archidamus*. Translated by George Norlin. LCL. Cambridge, MA: Harvard University Press, 1928.

Josephus. *Jewish Antiquities*. Translated by Ralph Marcus, vol. 6 of 9. LCL. Cambridge, MA: Harvard University Press, 1966.

Jubilees. Translated by O. S. Wintermute. In *The Old Testament Pseudepigrapha*, Vol. 2. Edited by J. H. Charlesworth. Peabody: Hendrickson, 2013.

Musonius Rufus. "That Women too Should Study Philosophy." In *Musonius Rufus: The Roman Socrates*, edited by Cora E. Lutz, 38–43. New Haven: Yale University Press, 1947.

Plato, *Laws, Volume I: Books 1–6*. Translated by R.G. Bury. LCL. Cambridge, MA: Harvard University Press, 1967–68

_____.*Republic*, Volume I: Books 1–5. Edited and translated by Christopher Emlyn-Jones, William Preddy. LCL. Cambridge, MA: Harvard University Press, 2013.

Plutarch. "Advice to the Bride and Groom." In *Plutarch's Advice to the Bride and Groom, and A Consolation to His Wife: English translations, commentary, interpretive essays, and bibliography*, edited by Sarah B. Pomeroy. New York: Oxford University Press, 1999.

_____.*Lives, Volume IX: Demetrius and Antony. Pyrrhus and Gaius Marius*. Translated by Bernadotte Perrin. LCL. Cambridge, MA: Harvard University Press, 1920.

Polybius. *The Histories*. Edited and translated by W. R. Paton. Revised by F. W. Walbank and Christian Habicht. LCL. Cambridge, MA: Harvard University Press, 2012.

Ptolemy. *Tetrabiblos*. Translated by Frank Egleston Robbins, Vol. 1. LCL. Cambridge, MA: Harvard University Press, 1940.

Res gestae divi Augusti: Text, translation, and commentary. Edited and translated by Alison E. Cooley. Cambridge: Cambridge University Press, 2009.

Sophocles. *Ajax. Electra. Oedipus Tyrannus.* Edited and translated by Hugh Lloyd-Jones. LCL. Cambridge, MA: Harvard University Press, 1994.

Tertullian. *On Baptism.* Translated by S. Thelwall. 1867. In *The Ante-Nicene Fathers*, vol. 3, edited by Alexander Roberts and James Donaldson. Reprint, Grand Rapids: Eerdmans, 1963.

_____.*On Prescription Against Heretics.* Translated by Peter Holmes. 1867. In *The Ante-Nicene Fathers*, vol. 3, edited by Alexander Roberts and James Donaldson. Reprint, Grand Rapids: Eerdmans, 1963.

"Tobit." Translated by A. A. Di Lella. In *A New English Translation of the Septuagint*, edited by A. Pietersma and B. G. Wright, 456–77. Oxford: Oxford University Press, 2007.

The Martyrdom of Perpetua and Perpetua and Felicitas. In *The Acts of the Christian Martyrs*, edited by Herbert Musurillo, 106–31. Oxford: Clarendon Press, 1972.

The Martyrdom of Polycarp. In *The Acts of the Christian Martyrs*, edited by Herbert Musurillo, 2–21. Oxford: Clarendon Press, 1972.

The Martyrs of Lyons. In *The Acts of the Christian Martyrs*, edited by Herbert Musurillo, 62–85. Oxford: Clarendon Press, 1972.

The Septuagint with Apocrypha: Greek and English. Translated by L. C. L. Brenton. 1851. Reprint, Peabody, MA: Hendrickson, 2011.

The Shepherd of Hermas. In *The Apostolic Fathers: Greek Texts and English Translations*, edited by Michael W. Holmes, 454–685. 3rd ed. Grand Rapids: Baker, 2007.

Modern Sources

ABC News. "Christopher Cullen sentenced to 30 years' jail for murder of estranged wife in Sydney's south." ABC News (July 2, 2015). http://www.abc.net.au/news/2015-07-02/cullen-sentenced-to-22-years-jail-for-murdering-wife/6588950.

"Academy of Korean Studies." http://terms.naver.com/entry.nhn?docId=578314&cid=46647&categoryId=46647.

Adams, Daniel J. "Church Growth in Korea: A Paradigm Shift from Ecclesiology to Nationalism." In *Perspectives on Christianity in Korea and Japan: The Gospel and Culture in Asia*, 13–28. Lewiston, NT: Edwin Mellen, 1995.

Ainsworth, Claire. "Sex Redefined." *Nature* 518 (2015) 288–91.

Alexander, T. Desmond. *From Eden to the New Jerusalem: Exploring God's Plan for Life on Earth*. Nottingham: IVP, 2008.

Alsup, Wendy. "Practical Theology for Women." http://www.theologyforwomen.org/.

Alter, Adam. *Drunk Tank Pink: The Subconscious Forces that Shape How We Think, Feel, and Behave*. London: Oneworld, 2013.

Amat, Jacqueline. *Passion de Perpétue et de Félicité suivi des Actes*. Paris: Cerf, 1996.

American Psychiatric Association. *Diagnostic and Statistical Manual of Mental Disorders*. 5th ed. Washington, DC: American Psychiatric Association, 2013.

Anderson, Nicole, and Katrina Schlunke, eds. *Cultural Theory in Everyday Practice*. South Melbourne: Oxford University Press, 2008.

Arendt, Hannah. *The Human Condition*. Charles R Walgreen Foundation Lectures. Chicago: University of Chicago Press, 1958.

Arnold, Clinton E. *Ephesians*. ZECNT. Grand Rapids: Zondervan, 2010.

Ash, Christopher. *Marriage: Sex in the Service of God*. Leicester: IVP, 2003.

Atkinson, James. *The Trial of Luther*. London: Batsford, 1971.

Aune, Kristin. "Evangelical Christianity and Women's Changing Lives." *European Journal of Women's Studies* 15, no.3 (2008) 277–94.

Australian Bureau of Statistics. "4442.0 – Family Characteristics and Transitions, Australia, 2012–13." http://www.abs.gov.au/ausstats/abs@.nsf/mf/4442.0.

_____. "3310.0 – Marriages and Divorces, Australia, 2013." http://www.abs.gov.au/ausstats/abs@.nsf/mf/3310.0.

_____. "3236.0 – Household and Family Projections, Australia, 2011 to 2036." http://www.abs.gov.au/ausstats/abs@.nsf/Latestproducts/3236.0Main%20Features42011%20to%202036?opendocument&tabname=Summary&prodno=3236.0&issue=2011%20to%202036&num=&view=.

_____. "Young Adults Then and Now: 4102.0 – Australian Social Trends, April 2013." http://www.abs.gov.au/AUSSTATS/abs@.nsf/Lookup/4102.0Main+Features40April+2013#livingar.

Australian Greens. "Equality for LGBTI Australians." http://greens.org.au/LGBTI.

_____. "Scripture Books Promote Dangerous Messages on Sex, Sexuality and Gender." http://greens.org.au/node/11021.

_____. "Sexual Orientation and Gender Identity." http://greens.org.au/policies/vic/sexual-orientation-and-gender-identity.

Bae, Choon Sup. "Ancestor Worship and the Challenges It Poses to the Christian Mission and Ministry." PhD. diss. University of Pretoria, 2007. http://repository.up.ac.za/bitstream/handle/2263/25045/Complete.pdf?sequence=10

Bae, Yo-Han. "A Confucian Analysis of Lee Su-Jeong's Confessional Essay." *Korea Presbyterian Journal of Theology* 38 (2010) 481–504.

Baird, J. "Doctrine of headship a distortion of the gospel message of mutual love and respect." *Sydney Morning Herald* (February 27, 2015). http://www.smh.com.au/comment/doctrine-of-headship-a-distortion-of-the-gospel-message-of-mutual-love-and-respect-20150226-13q2xc.html#ixzz3n9vjEMWY

_____. "Submission is a fraught mixed message for the church." *Sydney Morning Herald* (February 13, 2015). http://www.smh.com.au/comment/submission-is-a-fraught-mixed-message-for-the-church-20150212-13d9nw.html#ixzz3n9v9yrif

Bal, Mieke. *Lethal Love: Feminist Readings of Biblical Love Stories.* Bloomington: Indiana University Press, 1987.

Baldwin, H. Scott. "*authenteō* in Ancient Greek Literature (Appendix 2)." In *Women in the Church: A Fresh Analysis of 1 Timothy 2:9–15,* edited by T. R. Schreiner et al., 269–305. Grand Rapids: Baker Book House, 1995.

Balentine, S. E. *Leviticus.* Interpretation. Louisville: John Knox, 2002.

Balthasar, Hans Urs von. *The Glory of the Lord: A Theological Aesthetics. Vol. 1: Seeing the Form.* Translated by Erasmo Levia-Merikakis. 2nd ed. San Francisco, USA: Ignatius, 2009.

Barclay, John M. G. *Colossians and Philemon.* NTG. Sheffield: Sheffield Academic, 1997.

Barnes, Marc. "Masculine and Feminine Time." http://www.patheos.com/blogs/badcatholic/2015/8/masculine-and-feminine-time.html.

Barth, Markus, et al. *Colossians: A New Translation with Introduction and Commentary.* AB. New York: Doubleday, 1994.

Bartky, Sandra L. "Foucault, Femininity, and the Modernisation of Patriarchal Power." In *Writing on the Body: Female Embodiment and Feminist Theory,* edited by Katie Conboy, Nadia Medina and Sarah Stanbury, 129–154. New York: Columbia University Press, 1997.

Barton, Stephen C. *Life Together: Family, Sexuality and Community in the New Testament and Today.* Edinburgh: T&T Clark, 2001.

Bauckham, Richard. *Jesus and the Eyewitnesses: The Gospels as Eyewitness Testimony.* Grand Rapids: Eerdmans, 2006.

Bauer, Walter. "ὅμοιος" and "πλευρά." In *A Greek–English Lexicon of the New Testament and Other Early Christian Literature,* Third edition, revised and edited by F. W. Danker. Chicago: University of Chicago Press, 2000, 706 and 824.

James R. Beck, ed. *Two Views on Women in Ministry.* Rev. ed. Counterpoints. Grand Rapids: Zondervan, 2005.

Believe Out Loud. "Christianity and LGBT Equality." http://www.believeoutloud.com/background/christianity-and-lgbt-equality.

Belleville, Linda. L. "Women in Ministry: An Egalitarian Perspective." In *Two Views on Women in Ministry*, edited by J. R. Beck, 19–103. Rev. ed. Grand Rapids: Zondervan, 2005.

Benhabib, Seyla. "Feminist Theory and Hannah Arendt's Concept of Public Space." *History of the Human Sciences* 6, no. 2 (1993) 97–114.

Beuken, W. A. M. "Isaiah Liv: The Multiple Identity of the Person Addressed." In *Language and Meaning*, edited by James Barr, 29–70. Leiden: Brill, 1974.

Bevans, S. B. *Models of Contextual Theology.* Maryknoll: Orbis Books, 2002.

Bilezikian, Gilbert G. *Beyond Sex Roles: What the Bible Says about a Woman's Place in Church and Family.* 3rd ed. Grand Rapids: Baker, 2006.

Bird, Michael F. *Colossians and Philemon.* NCCS. Eugene, OR: Wipf & Stock, 2009.

Blanchard, Ray. "The Concept of Autogynephilia and the Typology of Male Gender Dysphoria." *Journal of Nervous and Mental Disorders* 177 (2008) 616–23.

Blenkinsopp, Joseph. "The Structure of P." *Catholic Biblical Quarterly* 38 (1976) 275–92.

Blocher, Henri. *In the Beginning.* Leicester: IVP, 1984.

————.*The Songs of the Servant: Isaiah's Good News.* London: IVP, 1975.

Block, Daniel I. "Marriage and Family in Ancient Israel." In *Marriage and Family in the Biblical World*, edited by K. M. Campbell, 33–102. Downers Grove: IVP, 2003.

Boa, Ai-Min, and Dick F. Swaab. "Sexual Differentiation of the Human Brain: Relation to Gender Identity, Sexual Orientation and Neuropsychiatric Disorders." *Frontiers in Neuroendocrinology* 32, no.2 (April 2011) 214–26.

Bohache, Thomas. *Christology from the Margins.* London: SCM, 2008.

Boo, Gil-man. "Looking through One-Hundred Years of Christianity through Publications: Sin Hak Walpo (Created in December 1900, Published by Methodist Denomination)." *Kook Min Il Bo*, 12 January 2011.

Bradshaw, Paul F., Maxwell E. Johnson, and L. Edward Phillips. *The Apostolic Tradition: A Commentary.* Minneapolis: Fortress, 2002.

Bremen, Riet van. *The Limits of Participation: Women and Civic Life in the Greek East in the Hellenistic and Roman Periods.* Amsterdam: J. C. Gieben, 1996.

Brenner, A. "Identifying the Speaker-in-the-Text and the Reader's Location in Prophetic Texts: The Case of Isaiah 50." In *A Feminist Companion to Reading the Bible: Approaches, Methods and Strategies*, edited by Athalya Brenner and Carole Fontaine, 136–50. Sheffield: Sheffield Academic Press, 1997.

Brown, Francis. "גאל." In *The Brown-Driver-Briggs Hebrew and English Lexicon.* Peabody: Hendrickson, 2007, 617.

Brueggemann, W., and D. Hankins. "The Invention and Persistence of Wellhausen's World." *Catholic Biblical Quarterly* 75 (2013) 15–31.

Bruenig, Elizabeth S. "The Failure of Macho Christianity." *The New Republic* (February 24, 2015). http://www.newrepublic.com/article/121138/mark-driscoll-and-macho-christianity.

Bunge, Marcia J. *The Child in Christian Thought.* Grand Rapids: Eerdmans, 2001.

Burin, Margaret. "'I am not a man or a woman': What it means to be genderqueer." ABC News (September 1, 2015). http://www.abc.net.au/news/2015-09-01/what-it-means-to-be-genderqueer/6727080.

Burrow, Rufus, and Michael G. Long. *A Child Shall Lead Them: Martin Luther King Jr., Young People, and the Movement.* Minneapolis: Fortress, 2014.

Butler, Judith. *Bodies That Matter: On the Discursive Limits of "Sex."* New York: Routledge, 1993.

_____. *Gender Trouble: Feminism and the Subversion of Identity*. New York: Routledge, 1990.

_____. *Gender Trouble: Feminism and the Subversion of Identity*. Routledge Classics. 3rd ed. New York: Routledge, 2006.

Butler, Rex D. *The New Prophecy & "New Visions": Evidence of Montanism in* The Passion of Perpetua and Felicitas. Washington, DC: Catholic University of America Press, 2006.

Byrd, Aimee. "John Piper's Advice for Women in the Workforce." http://www.mortificationofspin.org/mos/housewife-theologian/john-pipers-advice-for-women-in-the-workforce#.VvIXW_t97IV.

Calvin, Jean. *The Epistles to Timothy*. Calvin's New Testament Commentaries. Edinburgh: Oliver & Boyd, 1964.

_____. *Institutes of the Christian Religion*. Translated by John Thomas McNeill and Ford Lewis Battles. 2 vols. Philadelphia: Westminster, 1960.

Carey, Hilary M. "Companions in the Wilderness? Missionary Wives in Colonial Australia, 1788–1900." *Journal of Religious History* 19 (1995) 227–48.

_____. "Conversion, Gender Order and the Wellington Valley Mission, 1832–43." In *Religious Change, Conversion and Culture*, edited by Lynette Olson. Sydney Studies in Society and Culture, 241–73. Sydney, 1996.

Carey, Hilary M., and David A. Roberts, eds. "The Wellington Valley Project. Letters and Journals Relating to the Church Missionary Society Mission to Wellington Valley, NSW, 1830–45. A Critical Electronic Edition. 2002." http://www.newcastle.edu.au/school/hss/research/publications/the-wellington-valley-project.

Carlson, Richard F, ed. *Science and Christianity: Four Views*. Downers Grove: IVP, 2000.

Carson, D. A. *Exegetical Fallacies*, 2nd ed. Grand Rapids: Baker Books, 1996.

_____. "'Silent in the Churches': On the Role of Women in 1 Corinthians 14:33b–36." In *Recovering Biblical Manhood and Womanhood: A Response to Evangelical Feminism*, edited by John Piper and Wayne Grudem, 140–53. Wheaton: Crossway, 1991.

Carvosso, Benjamin. "Methodism in Van Diemen's Land." *Wesleyan Methodist Magazine* 55 [third series vol. 11] (1832) 245.

Cavanaugh, William T. *Torture and Eucharist*. Oxford: Blackwell, 1998.

Chandler, Matt. "Should a Boyfriend 'Lead' His Girlfriend?" desiringgod.org. http://www.desiringgod.org/interviews/should-a-boyfriend-lead-his-girlfriend#full-audio.

Chang, Christine Sungjin. "John Ross and Bible Women in the Early Protestant Mission of Northern Korea and Eastern China." The Institute of Cross-Cultural Studies in Seoul National University. *Rethinking Mission* (March 2008) 1–14. http://www.rethinkingmission.org/pdfs/Rossandbiblewomen%20(2).pdf.

Childs, Brevard S. *Isaiah*. The Old Testament Library. Louisville: Westminster John Knox, 2001.

Cho, Sun-Hye. "The Missionary Work and Social Network of Mattie Wilcox Noble." *Christianity and History in Korea* 39 (September 2013) 33–68.

Choi, Hyaeweol. "The Visual Embodiment of Women in the Korea Mission Field." *Korean Studies* 34 (2010) 90–126.

_____. "The Missionary Home as a Pulpit: Domestic Paradoxes in Early Twentieth-Century Korea." In *Divine Domesticities: Christian Paradoxes in Asia and the Pacific*, 29–56. Canberra: ANU Press, 2014. http://press.anu.edu.au/wp-content/uploads/2014/10/prelim.pdf.

Chong, Kelly H. *Deliverance and Submission: Evangelical Women and the Negotiation of Patriarchy in South Korea*. Harvard East Asian Monographs 309. Cambridge, MA: Harvard University Asia Center, 2008.

Chou, Fang-Lan. "Bible Women and the Development of Education in the Korean Church." In *Perspectives on Christianity in Korean and Japan: The Gospel and Culture in East Asia*, 30–45. Lewiston, NT: Edwin Mellen, 1995.

Christian Democratic Party. "All Australian Schools Must Stop Teaching 'Queer Sex.'" https://www. christiandemocraticparty.com.au/media-releases/all-australian-schools-must-stop-teaching-queer-sex/.

_____."CDP National Charter." http://www.christiandemocraticparty.com.au/about-the-cdp/cdp-national-charter/.

_____."2015 NSW Election Policy Snapshot." https://www.christiandemocraticparty.com.au/2015-nsw-election/2015-nsw-election-policy-snapshot/.

Clark, Allen D. *A History of the Church in Korea*. Seoul: Christian Literature Society, 1971.

Clarke, S. J., and W. Norris. *The One and the Many: A Contemporary Thomistic Metaphysic*. Indiana: University of Notre Dame Press, 2001.

Clines, David J. A. *What Does Eve Do to Help? And Other Readerly Questions to the Old Testament*. Sheffield: JSOT Press, 1990.

Coakley, Sarah. *God, Sexuality, and the Self: An Essay 'On the Trinity'*. Cambridge: Cambridge University Press, 2013.

Cobb, L. Stephanie. *Dying To Be Men: Gender and Language in Early Christian Martyr Texts*. New York: Columbia University Press, 2008.

Colapinto, John, "The True Story of John / Joan." *The Rolling Stone* (December 11 1997) 54–97. http://www. healthyplace.com/gender/inside-intersexuality/the-true-story-of-john-/-joan/.

Colson, Chuck. "Blurred Biology: How Many Sexes Are There?" https://www.breakpoint.org/commentaries/5213-blurred-biology.

Conron, Kerith J. et al. "Transgender Health in Massachusetts: Results from a Household Probability Sample of Adults." *American Journal of Public Health* 102 (2012) 118–122.

Conzelmann, Hans. *1 Corinthians: A Commentary on the First Epistle to the Corinthians*. Hermeneia. Philadelphia: Fortress, 1975.

Cook, Kaye V., and Howard E. Frost. "Being Single in a Couples' World: Gender Roles, Identity, and Contentment." *Priscilla Papers* 7, no. 4 (1993) 1–8. http://www.cbeinternational.org/resources/article/being-single-couples%E2%80%99-world?page=show.

Cooper, Kate. "The Bible Woman." *The Korea Magazine* (January 1917) 6–10.

Cornwall, Susannah. "'State of Mind' versus 'Concrete Set of Facts': The Contrasting of Transgender and Intersex in Church Documents on Sexuality." *Theology & Sexuality* 15, no. 1 (2009) 7–28.

Council of Biblical Manhood and Womanhood. "Appendix 2, The Danvers Statement." In *Recovering Biblical Manhood and Womanhood: A Response to Evangelical Feminism*, edited by John Piper and Wayne Grudem, 477–82. Wheaton: Crossway, 1991.

Creegan, Nicola Hoggard, and Christine D. Pohl. *Living on the Boundaries: Evangelical Women, Feminism, and the Theological Academy*. Downers Grove: IVP, 2005.

Critchley, Simon. "Introduction." In *The Cambridge Companion to Levinas*, edited by Simon Critchley and Robert Bernasconi, 1–32. Cambridge: Cambridge University Press, 2002.

Crosby, Emilye. *Civil Rights History from the Ground Up: Local Struggles, a National Movement*. Athens, GA: University of Georgia Press, 2011.

Crouch, Andy. "Sex Without Bodies." *Christianity Today* 57 (2013) 74.

Cruickshank, Joanna. "'If God . . . See Fit To Call You Out': 'Public' and 'Private' in the Writings of Methodist Women, 1760–1840." In *Religion in the Age of Enlightenment*, 55–76. New York: AMC Press, 2010.

Danker, Frederick W. *Benefactor: Epigraphic Study of a Graeco-Roman and New Testament Semantic Field*. St. Louis: People Lovers, 1982.

Davidson, Richard J., and Bruce S. McEwen. "Social Influences on Neuroplasticity: Stress and Interventions to Promote Well-Being." *Nature Neuroscience* 15 (2012) 689–95.

Davis, Daniel M. "The Impact of Christianity upon Korea, 1884–1910: Six Key American and Korean Figures." *Journal of Church & State* 94:4 (Autumn 1994) 795–822. http://search.ebscohost.com/login.aspx?dir ect=true&AuthType=cookie,ip,url,cpid&custid=s9398328&db=aph&AN=9412303786&site=ehost-live&scope=site

DeFranza, Megan K. *Sex Difference in Christian Theology: Male, Female and Intersex in the Image of God.* Grand Rapids: Eerdmans, 2015.

Diamond, Milton, "Sex and Gender Are Different: Sexual Identity and Gender Identity Are Different." *Clinical Child Psychology and Psychiatry* 7/3 (2002) 320–34.

_____."Sexual Identity: Monozygotic Twins Reared in Discordant Sex Roles and a BBC Follow-Up." *Archives of Sexual Behavior* 11/2 (1982) 181–86.

Diamond, Milton, and H. Keith Sigmundson. "Sex Reassignment at Birth: Long-Term Review and Clinical Implications." *Archives of Pediatric Adolescent Medicine* 151/3 (1997) 298–304.

Dickson, John P. *Hearing Her Voice: A Case for Women Giving Sermons.* Rev. ed. Grand Rapids: Zondervan, 2013.

Dictionary of the Old Testament Prophets. Downers Grove: IVP, 2012.

Dix, Gregory. "General Introduction." In *The Treatise on the Apostolic Tradition of St. Hippolytus of Rome, Bishop and Martyr,* edited by Gregory Dix, 11–51. London: SPCK, 1937.

_____. *Jurisdiction in the Early Church: Episcopal and Papal.* London: Church Literature Association, 1975.

Dobbs-Allsopp, F. W. "The Syntagma of *Bat* Followed by a Geographical Name in the Hebrew Bible: A Reconsideration of Its Meaning and Grammar." *Catholic Biblical Quarterly* 57 (1995) 451.

Duhm, Bernhard. *Das Buch Jesaia.* GHAT. Göttingen: Vandenhoeck & Ruprecht, 1922.

Dumas, Daisy. "The in-betweeners." Sydney Morning Herald (Aug 1, 2015). http://www.smh.com.au/good-weekend/the-inbetweeners-20150730-ginojq.html.

Dumbrell, William J. "The Purpose of the Book of Isaiah." *Tyndale Bulletin* 36 (1985) 111–28.

Dunn, James D. G. *The Epistle to the Galatians.* London: Continuum, 1993.

_____. *Jesus Remembere:. Christianity in the Making.* Grand Rapids: Eerdmans, 2003.

Durber, Susan. *Of the Same Flesh: Exploring a Theology of Gender.* Waterloo: Christian Aid UK, 2014.

Eastman, Susan G. *Recovering Paul's Mother Tongue: Language and Theology in Galatians.* Grand Rapids: Eerdmans, 2007.

Edwards, Owen, and Nathan Paylor. "A Play for Harmony: Reviewing Complementarian Theologies of Gender in Contemporary Evangelicalism." Paper presented at *Missio Dei* conference, Sheffield, 2015. https://www.academia.edu/10255538/A_Play_for_Harmony_-_Complementarianism_and_Modern_Evangelical_Theologies_of_Gender.

EFCA Spiritual Heritage Committee. "A Church Statement on Human Sexuality: Homosexuality and Same-Sex 'Marriage', A Resource for EFCA Churches." (2013). http://go.efca.org/resources/document/resource-homosexuality-and-same-sex-marriage.

Eldredge, John and Stasi Eldredge. *Captivating: Unveiling the Mystery of a Woman's Soul.* Nashville: Thomas Nelson, 2005.

Eliot, Lise. "Girl Brain, Boy Brain?" http://www.scientificamerican.com/article/girl-brain-boy-brain/.

Erikson, Erik H. *Identity, Youth, and Crisis.* New York: W. W. Norton, 1968.

Evans, Rachel Held. *A Year of Biblical Womanhood: How a Liberated Woman Found Herself Sitting on Her Roof, Covering Her Head, and Calling Her Husband "Master."* Nashville: Thomas Nelson, 2012.

Fausto-Sterling, Anne. *Sexing the Body: Gender Politics and the Construction of Sexuality*. New York: Basic, 2000.

Fee, Gordon. "Hermeneutics and the Gender Debate." In *Discovering Biblical Equality: Complementarity without Hierarchy*, edited by R. Pierce and R. M. Groothuis, 364–81. Downers Grove: IVP, 2005.

—————."Male and Female in the New Creation." *Discovering Biblical Equality: Complementarity without Hierarchy*, edited by R. Pierce and R. M. Groothuis, 172–85. Downers Grove: IVP, 2005.

Ferguson, Everett. "Early Christian Martyrdom and Civil Disobedience." *JECS* 1 (1993) 73–83.

Fiore, Benjamin. *The Function of Personal Example in the Socratic and Pastoral Epistles*. Rome: Biblical Institute Press, 1986.

Foulkes, Francis. *The Letter of Paul to the Ephesians: An Introduction and Commentary*. TNTC. 2nd ed. Leicester: IVP, 1989.

Frederick, T. V. "An Interpretation of Evangelical Gender Ideology: Implications for a Theology of Gender." *Theology & Sexuality* 16, no.2 (2010) 183–92.

Frend, W. H. C. *The Donatist Church: A Movement of Protest in Roman North Africa*. Oxford: Clarendon Press, 1952.

—————.*The Early Church: From the Beginnings to 461*. 3rd ed. London: SCM Press, 1991.

—————.*The Rise of Christianity*. London: Darton, Longman and Todd, 1984.

Fretheim, T. E. *Exodus*. Interpretation. Louisville: John Knox, 1991.

Frey, Lulu. "The Bible Woman." *Korea Mission Field* 3:2 (1907) 42.

Fulton, Karen, Ruth Gouldbourne, and Sharon James. "Biblical Truth and Biblical Equality: A Review Article on Two Recent Books from IVP on Evangelical Feminism and Biblical Manhood and Womanhood." *Evangelical Quarterly* 78, no. 1 (2006) 65–84.

Fung, Ronald Y. K. *The Epistle to the Galatians*. NICNT. Grand Rapids: Eerdmans, 1988.

Gagnon, Robert A. J. *The Bible and Homosexual Practice: Texts and Hermeneutics*. Nashville: Abingdon, 2001.

Gagnon, Robert A.J., and Dan O. Via. *Homosexuality and the Bible: Two Views*. Minneapolis: Fortress, 2003.

Gallagher, Sally K., and Christian Smith. "Symbolic Traditionalism and Pragmatic Egalitarianism: Contemporary Evangelicals, Families, and Gender." *Gender and Society* 13, no. 2 (April 1999) 211–33.

Gay Christian Network, "The Great Debate." https://www.gaychristian.net/greatdebate.php.

Gellman, Jerome. "Gender and Sexuality in the Garden of Eden." *Theology and Sexuality* 12 (2006) 319–35.

Gerhardsson, Birger. *The Reliability of the Gospel Tradition*. Peabody: Hendrickson, 2001.

Gesenius, Friedrich Wilhelm. "נָגַד." *Gesenius' Hebrew-Chaldee Lexicon to the Old Testament Scriptures*, English translation by Samuel Prideaux Tregelles. London: Samuel Bagster and Sons, 1857. <https:/www.blueletterbible.org/lang/lexicon/lexicon.cfm?strongs=H5048&t=NIV>

Gilmore, D. D. *Misogyny: The Male Malady*. Philadelphia: University of Pennsylvania Press, 2001.

Glancy, Jennifer. "Protocols of Masculinity in the Pastoral Epistles." In *New Testament Masculinities*, edited by Stephen D. Moore and Janice Capel Anderson, 235–64. Atlanta: SBL, 2003.

Goldingay, John, and David Payne. *Isaiah 40–55. Volume I, Introduction and Commentary on Isaiah 40.1–44.23*. ICC. London: T&T Clark, 2006.

—————."Justice and Salvation for Israel and Canaan." In *Reading the Hebrew Bible for a New Millenium: Form, Concept and Theological Perspective*, edited by D. Ellens, W. Kim, M. Floyd, and M. Sweeney, 169–87. Harrisburg: Trinity, 2000.

—————."The Theology of Isaiah." In *Interpreting Isaiah: Issues and Approaches*, edited by D. G. Firth and H. G. M.Williamson, 169–90. Nottingham: Apollos, 2009.

Goldstein, Jill M. et al. "Normal Sexual Dimorphism of the Adult Human Brain Assessed by In Vivo Magnetic Resonance Imaging." *Cerebral Cortex* 11, no.6 (2001) 490–97.

Gombis, Timothy G. *The Drama of Ephesians: Participating in the Triumph of God*. Downers Grove: IVP, 2010.

_____."A Radically New Humanity: The Function of the *Haustafel* in Ephesians." *JETS* 48, no. 2 (2005) 317–30.

Grayson, James H. *Early Buddhism and Christianity in Korea: A Study in the Implantation of Religion*. Leiden: Brill, 1985.

_____.*Korea: A Religious History*. Rev. ed. Routledge: Curzon: 2002.

Green, Emma. "The Real Christian Debate on Transgender Identity." The Atlantic (June 4, 2015). http://www.theatlantic.com/politics/archive/2015/06/the-christian-debate-on-transgender-identity/394796/.

Grenz, Stanley J. *Sexual Ethics: An Evangelical Perspective*. Louisville: WJK, 1997.

_____.*The Social God and the Relational Self: A Trinitarian Theology of the Imago Dei*. Louisville: WJK, 2001.

Groothuis, Rebecca. "Equal in Being, Unequal in Role: Exploring the Logic of Women's Subordination." In *Discovering Biblical Equality: Complementarity without Hierarchy*, edited by R. Pierce and R. M. Groothuis, 301–33. Downers Grove: IVP, 2005.

Grudem, Wayne, ed. *Biblical Foundations for Manhood and Womanhood*. Wheaton: Crossway, 2002.

Grudem, Wayne. *Evangelical Feminism & Biblical Truth: An Analysis of More Than One Hundred Disputed Questions*. Wheaton: Crossway, 2012.

_____."Review Article: Should We Move Beyond the New Testament to a Better Ethic? An Analysis of William J. Webb, *Slaves, Women and Homosexuals: Exploring the Hermeneutics of Cultural Analysis*." *JETS* 47 (2004) 299–346.

_____."Wives Like Sarah, and the Husbands Who Honor Them, 1 Peter 3:1–7." In *Recovering Biblical Manhood & Womanhood: A Response to Evangelical Feminism*, edited by John Piper and Wayne Grudem, 194–208. Wheaton: Crossway, 1991.

Guthrie, Donald. *The Pastoral Epistles*, 7th ed. Grand Rapids: Eerdmans, 1975.

Hahm, Pyong-Choon. *The Korean Political Tradition and Law: Essays in Korean Law and Legal History*. 2nd ed. Royal Asiatic Society of Great Britain and Ireland: Korea Branch. Seoul: Hollym International Corporation, 1971.

Hall, Stuart G. "Women among the Early Martyrs." In *Martyrs and Martyrologies: Papers Read at the 1992 Summer Meeting and the 1993 Winter Meeting of the Ecclesiastical History Society*, edited by Diana Wood, 1–22. Oxford: Blackwell Publishers, 1993.

Hammett, J. S. "Human Nature." In *Theology for the Church*, edited by D. L. Akin, 285–335. Rev. ed. Nashville: B&H, 2014.

Hampson, Margaret Daphne. *Swallowing a Fishbone? Feminist Theologians Debate Christianity*. London: SPCK, 1996.

Hardenbrook, Weldon. "Where's Dad? A Call for Fathers with the Spirit of Elijah." In *Recovering Biblical Manhood and Womanhood*, edited by John Piper and Wayne A. Grudem, 384–83. Wheaton: Crossway, 1991.

Harding, Mark. *Tradition and Rhetoric in the Pastoral Epistles*. New York: Peter Lang, 1998.

Hardy, E. R. "The Decline and Fall of the Confessor-Presbyter." *StPatr* 15 (1984) 221–25.

Harper, G. G. "Time for a New Diet? Allusions to Genesis 1–3 as Rhetorical Device in Leviticus 11." *Southeastern Theological Review* 4 (2013) 179–195.

Harries, Richard, Peter Forster, John Gladwyn, and Michael Scott-Joynt. *Some Issues in Human Sexuality: A Guide to the Debate*. London: Church House, 2003.

Harris, William V. *Restraining Rage: The Ideology of Anger Control in Classical Antiquity*. Cambridge: Harvard University Press, 2001.

Harrison, Alan P. *Incessant Theology*. UK: Lulu.com, 2014.

Hart, David B. *Atheist Delusions: The Christian Revolution and Its Fashionable Enemies*. New Haven: Yale University Press, 2009.

_____.*The Beauty of the Infinite: The Aesthetics of Christian Truth*. Grand Rapids: Eerdmans, 2003.

_____."God or Nothingness." In *I Am the Lord Your God: Christian Reflections on the Ten Commandments*, edited by Carl E. Braaten and Christopher R. Seitz, 55–76. Grand Rapids: Eerdmans, 2005.

Hauerwas, Stanley. *After Christendom? How the Church Is To Behave if Freedom, Justice, and a Christian Nation Are Bad Ideas*. Sydney: ANZEA, 1991.

Heffernan, Thomas J. *The Passion of Perpetua and Felicity*. Oxford: Oxford University Press, 2012.

Hégy, P., and J. Martos. "Understanding the Dynamics of Gender Roles: Towards the Abolition of Sexism in Christianity." In *Equal at the Creation: Sexism, Society, and Christian Thought*, edited by J. Martos and P. Hegy, 181–202. Toronto: University of Toronto, 1998.

Hellerman, Joseph H. *The Ancient Church as Family*. Minneapolis: Fortress, 2001.

_____.*When the Church Was a Family: Recapturing Jesus' Vision for Authentic Christian Community*. Nashville: B&H, 2009.

Hempton, David. *Methodism: Empire of the Spirit*. New Haven: Yale University Press, 2005.

Hess, Richard S. "Equality With and Without Innocence." In *Discovering Biblical Equality: Complementarity without Hierarchy*, edited by Ronald W. Pierce and Rebecca Merrill Groothuis, 79–95. Leicester: IVP, 2004.

Hesselgrave, D. J. "Contextualization That Is Authentic and Relevant." *International Journal of Frontier Missions* 12, no.3 (July, 1995) 115–20.

Hezser, Catherine. *Jewish Literacy in Roman Palestine*. *Texts and Studies in Ancient Judaism*. Tübingen: Mohr Siebeck, 2001.

Hines, Melissa. "Prenatal Endocrine Influences on Sexual Orientation and on Sexually Differentiated Childhood Behavior." *Frontiers in Neuroendocrinology* 32 (2011) 170–82.

Hofius, Otfried. "The Fourth Servant Song in the New Testament Letters." Translated by Daniel P. Bailey. In *The Suffering Servant: Isaiah 53 in Jewish and Christian Sources*, edited by Bernd Janowski and Peter Stuhlmacher, 163–88. Grand Rapids: Eerdmans, 2004.

Horsley, G. H. R., ed. *New Documents Illustrating Early Christianity: A Review of the Greek Inscriptions and Papyri*. Vol. 4. North Ryde: The Ancient History Documentary Research Centre, Macquarie University, 1979.

Hugenberger, Gordon P. "Women in Church Office: Hermeneutics or Exegesis? A Survey of Approaches to 1 Tim 2:8–15." *JETS* 35, no.3 (1992) 341–60.

Huizenga, Annette Bourland. *Moral Education for Women in the Pastoral and Pythagorean Letters: Philosophers of the Household*. Boston: Brill, 2013.

Hunsinger, G. *How to Read Karl Barth: The Shape of his Theology*. New York: Oxford University Press, 1993.

Hunt, Everett N. *Protestant Pioneers in Korea*. New York: Orbis, 1980.

Hunt, S. "Women's Ministry in the Local Church: A Covenantal and Complementarian Approach." *Journal of Biblical Manhood and Womanhood* 11, no.2 (Fall 2006) 37–47.

Hurley, James B. *Man and Woman in Biblical Perspective: A Study in Role Relationships and Authority*. Leicester: IVP, 1981.

Huston, Matt. "None of the Above." *Psychology Today* 48, no. 2 (Mar/Apr2015) 28–30.

Imms, Miriam E. *Wesleyan Methodist Cemetery Brown's River: The Firth Burial Ground and Diaries*. Hobart: Self-published, 1995.

Ireland, Judith. "'No Gender December': Greens Senator Calls for End to Gender-Based Toys." *The Sydney Morning Herald* (December 2, 2014). http://www.smh.com.au/federal-politics/political-news/no-gender-december-greens-senator-calls-for-end-to-genderbased-toys-20141201-11y4ro.html.

Isbell, Charles D. "The Limmûdîm in the Book of Isaiah." *JSOT* 34, no. 1 (2009) 99–109.

James, Allison, and Alan Prout, eds. *Constructing and Reconstructing Childhood: Contemporary Issues in the Sociological Study of Childhood*. London: Falmer, 1999.

James, Carolyn Custis. *Half the Church: Recapturing God's Global Vision for Women*. Grand Rapids: Zondervan, 2010.

_____.*Malestrom: Manhood Swept into the Currents of a Changing World*. Grand Rapids: Zondervan, 2015.

James, Sharon. *God's Design for Women: Biblical Womanhood for Today*. Darlington: Evangelical Press, 2002.

Jang, Jin Gyeong. "A Study of Education of Korean Bible Women and Their Missionary Work for Korean Women during the Early Period of Korean Protestantism." *Journal of Christian Education and Information Technology* 21 (December 2008) 221–46.

Jeeves, Malcolm A., and R.J. Berry. *Science, Life and Christian Belief: A Survey and Assessment*. Leicester: Apollos, 1998.

Jensen, Anne. *God's Self-Confident Daughters: Early Christianity and the Liberation of Women*. Translated by O. C. Dean Jr. Louisville: Westminster John Knox, 1996.

Jensen, Peter. "Men and Women Are Different, and So Should Be Their Marriage Vows." *Sydney Morning Herald* (August 29, 2012). http://www.smh.com.au/it-pro/men-and-women-are-different-and-so-should-be-their-marriage-vows-20120828-24yo6.html.

Jensen, Peter, et al. "9/84 Ordination of Women to the Priesthood of the Anglican Church." http://www.sds.asn.au/site/103242.asp?ph=cp.

Jenson, Robert W. *Systematic Theology. Volume 1: The Triune God*. New York: Oxford University Press, 1997.

Jeppesen, Knud. "Mother Zion, Father Servant: A Reading of Isaiah 49–55." In *Of Prophets' Visions and the Wisdom of Sages: Essays in Honour of R. Norman Whybray on His Seventieth Birthday*, edited by H. A. McKay and D. J. A. Clines. Sheffield: JSOT Press, 1993. Leiden: Brill, 1994.

Jnews. "Australia Election: Rudd Defends Gay-Marriage Stance." https://www.youtube.com/watch?v=gGMsVoQqpSA.

Johnson, Gregg. "The Biological Basis for Gender-Specific Behaviour." In *Recovering Biblical Manhood and Womanhood*, edited by John Piper and Wayne Grudem, 280–93. Wheaton: Crossway, 2006.

Jones, P. "Sexual Perversion: The Necessary Fruit of Neo-Pagan Spirituality in the Culture at Large." In *Biblical Foundations for Manhood and Womanhood*, edited by W. Grudem, 257–73 Wheaton: Crossway, 2002.

Joo, Sun Ae. *History of Korean Presbyterian Women*. Seoul: Presbyterian Church of Korea Women's Union, 1978.

Joosten, J. *People and Land in the Holiness Code: An Exegetical Study of the Ideational Framework of the Law in Leviticus 17–26*. VTSup 67. Leiden: Brill, 1996.

Judge, E. A. *The First Christians in the Roman World: Augustan and New Testament Essays*, edited by James R. Harrison. Tübingen: Mohr Siebeck, 2008.

Judkis, Maura. "Always Super Bowl 2015 Commercial: Redefining 'Throw Like a Girl'." *Washington Post* (Feb 1, 2015). http://www.washingtonpost.com/news/style-blog/wp/2015/02/01/always-super-bowl-2015-commercial-redefining-throw-like-a-girl/.

Kaiser, Walter C. "Genesis." In *Hard Sayings of the Bible*, edited by Walter C. Kaiser, Jr., Peter H. Davids, F. F. Bruce, and Manfred Brauch, 87–136. Downers Grove: IVP, 1996.

Kang, Dorcas Kim. "Mrs. Dorcas Kim Kang: A Recipient of Abounding Grace." In *Victorious Lives of Early Christians in Korea*, compiled by Noble Mattie Wilcox, 81–85. Seoul: Kyujang, 1985.

Keller, K. *Jesus, Justice, and Gender Roles: A Case for Gender Roles in Ministry*. Grand Rapids, Zondervan, 2012, Kindl Edition.

Kelly, J. N. D. *A Commentary on the Pastoral Epistles*. Black's NT Commentaries. London: Adam & Charles Black, 1972.

Kidson, Lyn. "1 Timothy: An Administrative Letter." *Early Christianity* 5, no.1 (2014) 97–116.

Kilburn, Michael. "Spivak, Gayatri Chakravorty." https://scholarblogs.emory.edu/postcolonialstudies/2014/06/19/spivak-gayatri-chakravorty/.

Kilby, Karen. "Perichoresis and Projection." *New Blackfriars* 81 (2000) 432–45.

Kim, Kyung-Mi. "Women's Labor and Economic Activities in the Late Chosŏn: Focusing on Upper Class Women in 18th to 19th Century." *Korean Women's Studies* 28, no.4 (December 2012) 85–116.

Kim, Kyung-ran. "'Jikyok' (Occupational Classification) and Its Meaning of Women in Chosun Dynasty." *History and Discourse* 51 (December 2008) 39–68.

Kimmel, Michael. *The Gendered Society*. New York: Oxford University Press, 2013.

Kitzler, Petr. *From Passio Perpetuae to Acta Perpetuae: Recontextualizing a Martyr Story in the Literature of the Early Church*. Berlin: de Gruyter, 2015.

Klawiter, Frederick C. "The Role of Martyrdom and Persecution in Developing the Priestly Authority of Women in Early Christianity." *Church History* 49 (1980) 251–61.

Knight, George W. III. *The Role Relationship of Men and Women: New Testament Teaching*. Rev. ed. Chicago: Moody, 1985.

Knox, David Broughton, et al. "8/87 the Ministry of Women." http://www.sds.asn.au/site/103254.asp?ph=cp.

Koks, S. J. Immanuel. "Being Masculine in My Disabled Male Body." In *Reconsidering Gender: Evangelical Perspectives*, edited by Myk Habets and Beulah Wood, 171–86. Eugene, OR: Pickwick, 2011.

Korpel, Marjo C. A. "The Female Servant of the Lord in Isaiah 54." In *On Reading Prophetic Texts: Gender-Specific and Related Studies in Memory of Fokkelien Van Dijk-Hemmes*, edited by Bob Becking and Meindert Dijkstra, 153–67. Leiden: Brill, 1996.

Köstenberger, Andreas J. "A Complex Sentence Structure in 1 Timothy 2:12." In *Women in the Church: A Fresh Analysis of 1 Timothy 2:9–15*, edited by T. R. Schreiner et al., 81–103. Grand Rapids: Baker, 1995.

Köstenberger, Andreas J., and David W. Jones. *God, Marriage and Family: Rebuilding the Biblical Foundation*. Wheaton: Crossway, 2004.

Köstenberger, Andreas J., and Thomas R. Schreiner, eds. *Women in the Church: An Analysis and Application of 1 Timothy 2:9–15*. Grand Rapids: Baker, 2005.

Kraus, Helen. *Gender Issues in Ancient and Reformation Translations of Genesis 1–4*. Oxford Theological Monographs. Oxford: Oxford University Press, 2011.

Kreukels, Baudewijntje P. C., Thomas D. Steensma, and Annelou L. C. de Vries. *Gender Dysphoria and Disorders of Sex Development: Progress in Care and Knowledge*. New York: Springer, 2014

Kroeger, Richard Clark, and Catherine Kroger. *I Suffer Not a Woman: Rethinking 1 Timothy 2:11–15 in Light of Ancient Evidence*. Grand Rapids: Baker, 1992.

Krueger, Christine L. *The Reader's Repentance: Women Preachers, Women Writers, and Nineteenth-Century Social Discourse*. Chicago: University of Chicago Press, 1992.

Landry, Donna, and Gerald MacLean, eds. *The Spivak Reader: Selected Works of Gayatri Chakravorty Spivak*. New York: Routledge, 1996.

Lang, Judith. *Ministers of Grace: Women in the Early Church*. Slough: St. Paul Publications, 1989.

Lee, Hyo-chae. "Protestant Missionary Work and Enlightenment of Korean Women." *Korea Journal* 17, no.11 (November 1977) 33–50.

Lee, Jung-Sook. "Human Rights of Women Clergy in Korean Protestant Church." *Asian Women* 42 (May 2003) 113–81.

Lee, Young Mee. "Biblical Interpretation in the Early Korean Christianity and Its Influence on Women's Status." *Canon & Culture* 1, no.2 (Autumn 2007) 43–74.

_____."Biblical Interpretation of Korean Early Church and Its Ripple Effect: Centred on Its Influence on Women's Status." In *Biblical Interpretation of Korean Early Church Before and After Pyongyang Bible Conference in 1907*, 521–46. Seoul: IKTINOS, 2007.

Lefkowitz, Mary R. "The Motivations for St. Perpetua's Martyrdom." *Journal of the American Academy of Religion* 44 (1976) 417–21.

Leiow, Martti. "Imperatives and Other Directives." In *The Language of the Papyri*, edited by T. V. Evans et al., 97–119. Oxford: Oxford University Press, 2010.

Letham, Robert. *The Holy Trinity in Scripture, History, Theology, and Worship*. Phillipsburg: P&R, 2004.

Levinas, Emmanuel. *Otherwise Than Being: Or Beyond Essence*. Translated by Alphonso Lingis. Pittsburgh: Duquesne University Press, 1998.

_____.*Totality and Infinity*. Translated by Alphonso Lingis. Dordrecht: Kluwer, 1991.

Levinson, Daniel J. *The Seasons of a Man's Life*. New York: Knopf, 1978.

Lewis, C. S. *Reflections on the Psalms*. First Mariner Books ed. Boston: Mariner Books, 2012 [orig. 1958].

Liddell, Henry George, and Robert Scott. *A Greek–English Lexicon*. Revised by H. S. Jones and R. McKenzie. 9th ed. Oxford: Clarendon, 1996.

_____."ὅμοιος," *A Greek–English Lexicon*, Ninth edition, revised by Sir Henry Stuart Jones, with the assistance of Roderick McKenzie, 1124–25. Oxford: Clarendon, 1996.

Lincoln, Andrew T. *Ephesians*. WBC. Dallas: Word, 1990.

Liptak, Yeong Woo. "Bible Women: Evangelism and Cultural Transformation in the Early Korean Church." PhD diss., Southern Baptist Theological Seminary, 2014.

Loader, William R. G. *Sexuality in the New Testament: Understanding the Key Texts*. Louisville: WJK, 2010.

Looy, Heather, and Hessel Bouma III. "The Nature of Gender: Gender Identity in Persons Who Are Intersexed or Transgendered." *Journal of Psychology and Theology* 33 (2005) 166–78.

Low, Maggie. *Mother Zion in Deutero-Isaiah: A Metaphor for Zion Theology*. Studies in Biblical Literature. New York: Peter Lang, 2013.

Luther, Martin. "Marburg Colloquy, 1529." In *Great Debates of the Reformation*, edited by Donald J. Ziegler, 71–107. New York: Random House, 1969.

MacDonald, Margaret Y. "Can Nympha Rule This House? The Rhetoric of Domesticity in Colossians." In *Rhetoric and Reality in Early Christianities*, 99–120. Edited by Willi Braun. Waterloo, ON: Wilfrid Laurier University Press, 2005.

Mack, Phyllis. *Heart Religion in the British Enlightenment: Gender and Emotion in Early Methodism*. Cambridge: Cambridge University Press, 2008.

Maier, C. *Daughter Zion, Mother Zion; Gender, Space and the Sacred in Ancient Israel*. Minneapolis: Fortress, 2008.

Maier, Harry O. "The Politics of the Silent Bishop: Silence and Persuasion in Ignatius of Antioch." *The Journal of Theological Studies* 55, no. 2 (2004) 503–19.

Malherbe, Abraham J., ed. *The Cynic Epistles: A Study Edition*. Missoula, MO: Scholars Press, 1977.

Malherbe, Abraham J. "The Virtus Feminarum in 1 Timothy 2:9–15." In *Renewing Tradition: Studies in Texts and Contexts in Honor of James W. Thompson*, edited by Mark W. Hamilton et al., 193–224. Eugene, OR: Pickwick, 2007.

Mann, T. W. *The Book of the Torah: The Narrative Integrity of the Pentateuch*. Atlanta: John Knox, 1988.

Markschies, Christoph. "The *Passio Sanctarum Perpetuae et Felicitatis* and Montanism?" In *Perpetua's Passions: Multidisciplinary Approaches to the* Passio Perpetuae et Felicitatis, edited by Jan N. Bremmer and Marco Formisano, 277–90. Oxford: Oxford University Press, 2012.

Marshall, I. Howard, and Philip H. Towner. *A Critical and Exegetical Commentary on the Pastoral Epistles*. ICC. London: T&T Clark, 2004.

Martyn, J. Louis. *Galatians: A New Translation with Introduction and Commentary*. AB. New York: Doubleday, 1997.

Marx, A. *Lévitique 17–27*. Commentaire de l'Ancien Testament 3b. Geneva: Labor et Fides, 2011.

Mathew, Susan. *Women in the Greetings of Rom 16.1–16: A Study of Mutuality and Women's Ministry in the Letter to the Romans*. Library of New Testament Studies 471. London; New York: Bloomsbury, 2013.

Mathews, Greta A., et al. "Personality and Congenital Adrenal Hyperplasia: Possible Effects of Prenatal Androgen Exposure." *Hormones and Behavior* 55 (2009) 285–91.

Mathews, Kenneth A. *Genesis 1–11:26*. NAC. Nashville: B&H, 1996.

McCarthy, Margaret M., et al. "Sex Differences in the Brain: The Not So Inconvenient Truth." *The Journal of Neuroscience* 32, no. 7 (2012) 2241–47.

McCrindle Research. *Australian Communities Report*. http://mccrindle.com.au/resources/Australian-Communities-Report_McCrindle-Research.pdf.

——————."A Demographic Snapshot of Christianity and Church Attenders in Australia." http://mccrindle.com.au/the-mccrindle-blog/a-demographic-snapshot-of-christianity-and-church-attenders-in-australia.

McGrath, Alister E. *Science & Religion: A New Introduction*. 2nd ed. Malden, MA: Wiley-Blackwell, 2010.

McHugh, Paul. "Surgical Sex: Why We Stopped Doing Sex Change Operations." *First Things* (November 2004). http://www.firstthings.com/article/2004/11/surgical-sex.

McKean, Erin. *The Hundred Dresses: The Most Iconic Styles of Our Time*. London: Bloomsbury, 2013.

McKenny, Gerald P. *To Relieve the Human Condition: Bioethics, Technology, and the Body*. Albany: University of New York Press, 1997.

McKinney, Jennifer. "Sects and Gender: Reaction and Resistance to Cultural Change." http://digitalcommons.spu.edu/cgi/viewcontent.cgi?article=1030&context=weter_lectures.

Meilaender, Gilbert. *Body, Soul, and Bioethics*. Notre Dame: University of Notre Dame Press, 1995.

Messer, Neil G. *Flourishing: Health, Disease, and Bioethics in Theological Perspective*. Grand Rapids: Eerdmans, 2013.

——————.*Respecting Life: Theology and Bioethics*. London: SCM, 2011.

Mettinger, Tryggve N. D. *A Farewell to the Servant Songs: A Critical Examination of an Exegetical Axiom*. Scripta Minora. Lund: CWK Gleerup, 1983.

Meyer-Bahlburg, Heino F. L., "Sex Steroids and Variants of Gender Identity." *Endocrinology and Metabolism Clinics of North America* 42, no.3 (2013) 435–52.

Meyers, Carol. *Rediscovering Eve: Ancient Israelite Wisdom in Context*. New York: Oxford University Press, 2013.

Milbank, John. "Can a Gift Be Given? Prolegomena to a Future Trinitarian Metaphysic." *Modern Theology* 11 (1995) 119.

——————.*Theology and Social Theory: Beyond Secular Reason*. Oxford: Blackwell, 2006.

Miscall, P. D. "Isaiah: New Heavens, New Earth, New Book." In *Reading between Texts: Intertextuality and the Hebrew Bible*, edited by Danna Nolan Fewell, 41–56. Literary Currents in Biblical Interpretation. Louisville: WJK, 1992.

——————.*Isaiah*. Readings: A New Biblical Commentary. Sheffield: Sheffield Academic, 1993.

Mitchell, Jessie. "'The Nucleus of Civilisation': Gender, Race and Australian Missionary Families, 1825–1855." In *Evangelists of Empire? Missionaries in Colonial History*, edited by Amanda Barry et al., 103–14. Melbourne: University of Melbourne Press, 2008.

Moffett, Samuel A. *The First Letters from Korea (1890–1891)*. Seoul: Presbyterian Theological Seminary Institute of Missions, 1975.

_____.*Missionary Samuel Moffett's Missionary Letters: 1890–1904*. Translated into Korean by In-soo Kim. Seoul: PCTS Press, 2000.

Moffett, Samuel H. *A History of Christianity in Asia*. 2 vols. Maryknoll: Orbis, 1998, 2005.

Money, John, and Anke A. Ehrhardt. *Man & Woman, Boy & Girl: The Differentiation and Dimorphism of Gender Identity from Conception to Maturity*. Baltimore: Johns Hopkins University, 1972.

Moo, Douglas J. *The Letters to the Colossians and to Philemon*. Grand Rapids: Eerdmans, 2008.

Moore, Russell. "What Should the Church Say to Bruce Jenner?" http://www.russellmoore.com/2015/04/24/what-should-the-church-say-to-bruce-jenner/.

Morales, L. M., ed. *Cult and Cosmos: Tilting toward a Temple-Centred Theology*. Biblical Tools and Studies. Leuven: Peeters, 2014.

Morales, L. M. *The Tabernacle Pre-Figured: Cosmic Mountain Ideology in Genesis and Exodus*. Biblical Tools and Studies. Leuven: Peeters, 2012.

Morris, Leon. *The First and Second Epistles to the Thessalonians*. NICNT. Grand Rapids: Eerdmans, 1991.

Morse, MaryKate. "Gender Wars: Biology Offers Insights to a Biblical Problem." *Priscilla Papers* 20, no. 1 (2006): 3–8. http://www.cbeinternational.org/resources/article/gender-wars.

Moss, Candida R. *Ancient Christian Martyrdom: Diverse Practices, Theologies, and Traditions*. New Haven,: Yale University Press, 2012.

Moule, C. F. D. *The Birth of the New Testament*. London: A&C Black, 1981.

Mounce, William D. *Pastoral Epistles*. WBC. Nashville: Nelson, 2000.

Mouw, R. J. *He Shines in All That's Fair: Culture and Common Grace*. Grand Rapids: Eerdmans, 2001.

Mowczko, Margaret. "The Chiasm in 1 Corinthians 11:2–16." http://newlife.id.au/equality-and-gender-issues/the-chiasm-in-1-corinthians-11_2-16/.

_____."The Consensus and Context of 1 Timothy 2:12." http://newlife.id.au/equality-and-gender-issues/the-consensus-and-context-of-1-timothy-212/.

_____."Every Verse in the Septuagint that Contains 'boēthos.'" http://newlife.id.au/every-verse-that-contains-boethos-in-the-septuagint/.

_____."A Suitable Helper." http://newlife.id.au/equality-and-gender-issues/a-suitable-helper/.

Mustanski, B., Laura Kuper, and George J. Greene. "Development of Sexual Orientation and Identity." In *APA Handbook of Sexuality and Psychology, Vol. 1: Person-Based Approaches*, ed. Deborah L. Tolman et. al., 597–628. Washington, DC: American Psychological Association, 2014.

Musurillo, Herbert. "Introduction." In *The Acts of the Christian Martyrs*, edited by Herbert Musurillo, xi–lxxiii. Oxford: Clarendon Press, 1972.

Neitz, Mary Jo. "Gender and Culture: Challenges to the Sociology of Religion." *Sociology of Religion* 65, no. 4 (2004) 391–402.

Nicole, R. "Biblical Egalitarianism and the Inerrancy of Scripture." In "An Evangelical Tradition," 4–9. http://www.cbeinternational.org/sites/default/files/An-Evangelical-Tradition-web.pdf.

Nihan, C. *From Priestly Torah to Pentateuch: A Study in the Composition of the Book of Leviticus*. Forschungen zum Alten Testament 2/25. Tübingen: Mohr Siebeck, 2007.

Noble, Mattie W. "A Bible Institute in Korea." *Women's Missionary Friend* 38, no.11 (November 1906) 399–400. http://babel.hathitrust.org/cgi/pt?id=mdp.39015039671758;view=1up;seq=889

_____.*The Journals of Mattie Wilcox Noble 1892–1934*. Seoul: The Institute of the History of Christianity in Korea, 1993.

Nordling, Cherith. "Gender." In *The Oxford Handbook of Evangelical Theology*, edited by Gerald R. McDermott, 497–511. Melbourne: Oxford University Press, 2010.

North, C. R. *The Suffering Servant in Deutero-Isaiah: An Historical and Critical Study*. 2nd ed. London: Oxford University Press, 1956.

North, Helen. "The Mare, the Vixen, and the Bee: *Sophrosyne* as the Virtue of Women in Antiquity." *Illinois Classical Studies* 2 (1977) 35–48.

_____.*Sophrosyne: Self-Knowledge and Self-Restraint in Greek Literature*. Ithaca: Cornell University Press, 1966.

Nussbaum, Martha C. "The Professor of Parody: The Hip Defeatism of Judith Butler." *New Republic* 220 (1999) 37–45.

O'Brien, Anne P. *God's Willing Workers: Women and Religion in Australia*. Sydney: UNSW Press, 2005.

_____."Women in the Churches before 1992: 'No Obtrusive Womanhood.'" In *Preachers, Prophets and Heretics: Anglican Women's Ministry*, edited by Elaine Lindsay and Janet Scarfe, 30–54. Sydney: UNSW Press, 2012.

O'Brien, Peter Thomas. *Colossians–Philemon*. WBC. Waco: Word, 1982.

O'Donovan, Oliver. *The Church in Crisis: The Gay Controversy and the Anglican Communion*. Eugene: Cascade, 2008.

_____.*The Desire of the Nations: Rediscovering the Roots of Political Theology*. Cambridge: Cambridge University Press, 1996.

_____.*Principles in the Public Realm: The Dilemma of Christian Moral Witness*. Oxford: Clarendon, 1984.

_____.*Resurrection and Moral Order: An Outline for Evangelical Ethics*. 2nd ed. Grand Rapids: Eerdmans, 1994.

_____."Transsexualism and Christian Marriage." *Journal of Religious Ethics* 11 (1983) 135–162.

Oakley, Ann. *Sex, Gender and Society*. Towards a New Society. London: Temple Smith, 1972.

Olson, Roger. "Tensions in Evangelical Theology." *Dialog: A Journal of Theology* 42, no. 1 (2003).

Ortlund Jr., R. C. "Male-Female Equality and Male Headship: Genesis 1–3." In *Recovering Biblical Manhood and Womanhood: A Response to Evangelical Feminism*, edited by J. Piper and W. Grudem, 95–112. Wheaton: Crossway, 1991.

Osiek, Carolyn. "Did Early Christians Teach, or Merely Assume, Male Headship?" In *Does Christianity Teach Male Headship? The Equal-Regard Marriage and Its Critics*, edited by David Blankenhorn, Don S. Browning and Mary Stewart Van Leeuwen, 23–27. Grand Rapids: Eerdmans, 2004.

_____."The Ministry and Ordination of Women According to the Early Church Fathers." In *Women and Priesthood: Future Directions*, edited by Carroll Stuhlmueller, 59–68. Collegeville, MN: Liturgical Press, 1978.

_____."The Widow as Altar: The Rise and Fall of a Symbol." *SecCent* 3 (1983) 159–69.

Ott, Kate. "Children as An/other Subject: Redefining Moral Agency in a Postcolonial Context." *Journal of Childhood and Religion* 5, no. 2 (2014) 1–23.

Packer, J. I. "The Challenge of Biblical Interpretation: Women." In *The Proceedings of the Conference on Biblical Interpretation* 1988. Nashville: Broadman, 1988.

Padgett, A. G. *As Christ Submits to the Church: A Biblical Understanding of Leadership and Mutual Submission*. Grand Rapids: Baker, 2011.

Padilla, C. R. "Liberation Theology—An Appraisal." In *Freedom and Discipleship in an Anabaptsist Perspective*, edited by D. Schipani, 34–50. Maryknoll: Orbis, 1989.

Palmer, Parker J. *To Know as We are Known: Education as a Spiritual Journey*. San Francisco: Harper, 1993.

Pannenberg, Wolfhart. *Systematic Theology*. 3 vols. Grand Rapids: Eerdmans, 1991.

Papanikolaou, Aristotle. "Person, Kenosis and Abuse: Hans Urs Von Balthasar and Feminist Theologies in Conversation." *Modern Theology* 19, no. 1 (2003) 41–65.

Park, Bokyoung. "A Possibility of Women's Ministry among Korean Evangelical Churches." *Journal of Presbyterian College and Theological Seminary* 44, no.2 (July 2012) 333–357.

Payne, Philip B. "The Bible Teaches the Equal Standing of Man and Woman." *Priscilla Papers* 29 (2015) 3–10.

_____.*Man and Woman, One in Christ: An Exegetical and Theological Study of Paul's Letters*. Grand Rapids: Zondervan, 2009.

_____."1 Timothy 2.12 and the Use of Οὐδε To Combine Two Elements To Express a Single Idea." *NTS* 54 (2008) 235–53.

Perschbacher, Wesley J. "*Boētheō.*" *The New Analytical Greek Lexicon*. Peabody: Hendrickson, 1990, 72.

Pettersen, Alvyn. "Perpetua – Prisoner of Conscience." *VC* 41 (1987) 139–53.

Petty, John. *The History of the Primitive Methodist Connexion from its Origin to the Conference of 1859*. London: R. Davies, 1860.

Phillips, J., and P. Vandenbroek. *Domestic, Family and Sexual Violence in Australia: An Overview of the Issues*. Australian Parliamentary Research Paper, Oct, 2014. http://parlinfo.aph.gov.au/parlInfo/download/library/prspub/3447585/upload_binary/3447585.pdf;fileType=application/pdf.

Piper, John. "A Vision of Complementarity: Manhood and Womanhood Defined According to the Bible." In *Recovering Biblical Manhood and Womanhood*, edited by John Piper and Wayne Grudem, 31–59. Wheaton: Crossway, 2006.

_____."Should Women Be Police Officers?" http://www.desiringgod.org/interviews/should-women-be-police-officers.

_____.*What's the Difference? Manhood and Womanhood Defined According to the Bible*. Wheaton: Crossway Books, 2001.

Piper, John, and Wayne A. Grudem, eds. *Recovering Biblical Manhood and Womanhood*. Wheaton: Crossway Books, 1991.

Poirier, Michel. "Note sur la *Passio Sanctarum Perpetuae et Felicitatis*: Félicité était-elle vraiment l'esclave de Perpétue?" *StPatr* 10 (1970) 306–9.

Polkinghorne, John C. *One World: The Interaction of Science and Theology*. Philadelphia: Templeton Foundation Press, 2007.

_____.*Reason and Reality: The Relationship between Science and Theology*. London: SPCK, 1991.

Pomeroy, Sarah B. *Women in Hellenistic Egypt: From Alexander to Cleopatra*. New York: Schocken Books, 1984.

Presbyterian Church in the U.S.A. Board of Foreign. "The Missions in Korea." In "Historical Sketches of the Mission under the Care of the Board of Foreign Missions of the Presbyterian Church U.S.A," 1–33. http://www.ebooksread.com/authors-eng/presbyterian-church-in-the-usa-board-of-foreign/historical-sketches-of-the-missions-under-the-care-of-the-board-of-foreign-missi-ser/page-15-historical-sketches-of-the-missions-under-the-care-of-the-board-of-foreign-missi-ser.shtml

Procter & Gamble. "Our Epic Battle #Likeagirl." http://always.com/en-us/about-us/our-epic-battle-like-a-girl.

Purcell, David W., et al., "Childhood Sexual Abuse Experienced by Gay and Bisexual Men: Understanding the Disparities and Interventions To Help Eliminate Them." In *Unequal Opportunity: Health Disparities Affecting Gay and Bisexual Men in the United States*, edited by Richard J. Wolitski, Ron Stall, and Ronald O. Valdiserri, 72–96. New York: Oxford University Press, 2007.

Quinn, Regina Ammicht. "Dangerous Thinking: Gender and Theology." *Concilium* 4 (2012) 13–25.

Quinn-Miscall, Peter D. *Reading Isaiah: Poetry and Vision*. Louisville: WJK, 2001.

Rabinowitz, Peter J. *Before Reading: Narrative Conventions and the Politics of Interpretation*. Columbus: Ohio State University Press, 1987.

Rad, Gerhard von. *Genesis: A Commentary*. Old Testament Library. Rev. ed. London: SCM, 1972.

_____.*Old Testament Theology, Volume Two: The Theology of Israel's Prophetic Traditions*. Translated by D. M. Stalker. Edinburgh: Oliver and Boyd, 1965.

Reaoch, Benjamin. *Women, Slaves, and the Gender Debate*. Philipsburg, NJ: P&R, 2012.

Reinfrank, Alkira. "Transgender, intersex people say they are ostracised from playing sport in Australia." ABC News (August 23, 2015). http://www.abc.net.au/news/2015-08-23/gender-diverse-community-ostracised-from-playing-sports/6710778.

Resource777. "Does 'Bible Say Slavery Is a Natural Condition'? Response to Kevin Rudd by N.T. Wright." https://www.youtube.com/watch?v=pOrP73kq5Ps.

Rhie, Deok-Joo. "Religious Experience and Formation of Feministic Consciousness of Church Women by the Early Revival Movement in Korea." *Christianity and History in Korea. Special Edition. The Great Revival Movement of 1907 and the Korean Church* 26 (March 2007) 39–74.

_____."Freedom and Emancipation, and Practice: Understanding the History of Early Korean Christian Women." In *The Korean Church and Women*, 10–102. Seoul: IVP, 2013.

Richters, Juliet et al. "Sexual Identity, Sexual Attraction and Sexual Experience: The Second Australian Study of Health And Relationships." *Sexual Health* 11, no.5 (2014) 451–60.

Roberts, C. R. *Creation and Covenant: The Significance of Sexual Difference in the Moral Theology of Marriage*. New York: T&T Clark, 2007.

Robinson, Donald. *Faith's Framework: The Structure of New Testament Theology*. Sutherland, NSW: Albatros, 1985.

_____.*Ordination for What?* Sydney: Anglican Information Office, 1992.

Rowe, Christopher Kavin. *World Upside Down: Reading Acts in the Graeco-Roman Age*. Oxford: Oxford University Press, 2009.

Rubin, Gayle. "Thinking Sex: Notes for a Radical Theory of the Politics of Sexuality." In *Pleasure and Danger: Exploring Female Sexuality*, edited by Carol S. Vance, 267–319. London: Routledge and Kegan Paul, 1984.

Ryu, Dae Young. "Religion Meets Politics: The Korean Royal Family and American Protestant Missionaries in late Joseon Korea." *Journal of Church & State* 55, no.1 (March 2013) 113–33.

_____."Understanding Early American Missionaries in Korea (1884–1910): Capitalist Middle-Class Values and the Weber Thesis." *Archives de Sciences Sociales des Religions*, 93–117 (January–March 2001). https://assr.revues.org/20190.

Safe Schools Coalition. "OMG My Friend's Queer." http://www.safeschoolscoalition.org.au/uploads/d82dbcaf5e76d8e1c8b52799ace021ca.pdf.

_____."What We Do." http://www.safeschoolscoalition.org.au/.

Salih, Sarah. *Judith Butler*. London: Routledge, 2002.

Sanlon, Peter. *Plastic People: How Queer Theory Is Changing Us*. London: Latimer Trust, 2010.

Saucy, Robert L. "Paul's Teaching on the Ministry of Women." In *Women and Men in Ministry: A Complementary Perspective*, edited by Robert L. Saucy and Judith K. TenElshof, 291–310. Chicago: Moody, 2001.

Sawyer, John F. A. "Daughter of Zion and Servant of the Lord in Isaiah: A Comparison." *Journal for the Study of the Old Testament* 44 (1989) 89–107.

Schaper, J. "The Pharisees." In *The Cambridge History of Judaism* 3, edited by W. D. Davies, et al. Cambridge: Cambridge University Press, 1999.

Schmitt, John J. "The City as Woman in Isaiah 1–39." In *Writing and Reading the Scroll of Isaiah: Studies of an Interpretive Tradition*, edited by Craig C. Broyles and Craig A. Evans, 96–119. Leiden: Brill, 1997.

_____."The Gender of Ancient Israel." *Journal for the Study of the Old Testament* 26 (1983) 115–25.

_____."Israel and Zion—Two Gendered Images: Biblical Speech Traditions and Their Contemporary Neglect." *Horizons* 18, no. 1 (1991) 18–32.

_____."The Motherhood of God, and Zion as Mother." *Revue Biblique* 92 (1985) 557–69.

_____."The Wife of God in Hosea 2." *Biblical Research* 34 (1989): 5–18.

Scholer, David M. "1 Timothy 2:9–15 and the Place of Women in the Church's Ministry." In *Women, Authority and the Bible*, edited by Alvera Mickelsen, 193–224. Downers Grove: IVP, 1986.

Schreiner, Thomas R. "William J. Webb's *Slaves, Women and Homosexuals*: A Review Article." *SBJT* 6 (2002) 46–65.

_____.*Paul, Apostle of God's Glory in Christ: A Pauline Theology*. Downers Grove: IVP, 2006.

Schultz, Daniel. "Transitions: Caitlyn Jenner, Gender Identity, and Christians Behaving Badly (Again)." *Religion Dispatches* (June 5, 2015). http://religiondispatches.org/transitions-caitlyn-jenner-gender-identity-and-christians-behaving-badly-again/.

Seitz, Christopher. *Zion's Final Destiny: The Development of the Book of Isaiah: A Reassessment of Isaiah 36–39*. Minneapolis: Fortress, 1991.

Seth, Michael J. "Korean Education: A Philosophical and Historical Perspective." In *Korean Education*, 3–16. The Sigur Center Asia Papers. Washington, DC: The George Washington University, 2005. https://www.gwu.edu/-sigur/assets/docs/scap/SCAP24-KoreanEd.pdf

Shack, Jennifer. "A Text without 1 Corinthians 14:34–35? Not according to the Manuscript Evidence." *JGRChJ* 10 (2014) 10.4.

Sheffield, Tricia. "Performing Jesus: A Queer Counternarrative of Embodied Transgression." *Theology & Sexuality: The Journal of the Institute for the Study of Christianity & Sexuality* 14, no. 3 (05//2008): 233–58.

Shen, Erica Y. et. al. "Epigenetics and Sex Differences in the Brain: A Genome-Wide Comparison of Histone-3 Lysine-4 Trimethylation (H3k4me3) in Male and Female Mice." *Experimental Neurology* 268 (2015) 21–29.

Silva, Moises. "διδάσκω." In *New International Dictionary of New Testament Theology and Exegesis*, edited by M. Silva, 1.714–17. 2nd ed. Grand Rapids: Zondervan, 2014.

Skelton, Tracey. "Children, Young People, Unicef and Participation." *Children's Geographies* 5, no. 1/2 (2007) 165–81.

Skinner, Matthew L. *Intrusive God, Disruptive Gospel: Encountering the Divine in the Book of Acts*. Grand Rapids: Baker, 2015.

Sloane, Andrew. "Aberrant Textuality? The Case of Ezekiel the (Porno) Prophet." *Tyndale Bulletin* 59, no. 1 (2008) 53–76.

_____."'And He Shall Rule over You': Evangelicals, Feminists, and Genesis 2–3." In *Tamar's Tears: Evangelical Engagements with Feminist Old Testament Hermeneutics*, edited by Andrew Sloane, 1–29. Eugene, OR: Pickwick, 2012.

_____."Christianity and the Transformation of Medicine." In *Christianity and the Disciplines: The Transformation of the University*, edited by Oliver D. Crisp et al., 85–99. London: T&T Clark, 2012.

_____."Gender, Biology and Identity—Theological Reflections." In *The Gender Conversation*, edited by David Starling and Edwina Murphy, Sydney: Morling Press, 2016.

_____.*On Being a Christian in the Academy: Nicholas Wolterstorff and the Practice of Christian Scholarship*. Carlisle: Paternoster, 2003.

_____.*Vulnerability and Care: Christian Reflections on the Philosophy of Medicine*. London: T&T Clark, 2016.

Smith, C. *God's Good Design: What the Bible Really Says about Men and Women*. Kingsford: Matthias Media, 2012.

Soltau, T. Stanley. *Korea: The Hermit Nation and Its Response to Christianity*. London: World Dominion Press, 1932.

Spencer, A. B. *Beyond the Curse: Women Called to Ministry*. Nashville: Nelson, 1985.

Spencer, William David. "Marriage and Singleness as Teaching Tools of the Image of God." *Priscilla Papers* 23, no. 3 (2009) 5–7.

Spivak, Gayatri Chakravorty. *Outside in the Teaching Machine*. New York: Routledge, 1993.

Stackhouse, John G. *Need To Know: Vocation as the Heart of Christian Epistemology*. Oxford: Oxford University Press, 2014.

Stansall, Max. *Alive to the Great Work: Stories and Artefacts from Wesley Church, Hobart 1820–1977*. Hobart: Wesley Church, 1977.

Stark, Rodney. *The Rise of Christianity: A Sociologist Reconsiders History*. Princeton, N.J.: Princeton University Press, 1996.

Starling, David I. "Ephesians and the Hermeneutics of the New Exodus." In *Reverberations of the Exodus in Scripture*, edited by R. Michael Fox. 139–59. Eugene, OR: Wipf & Stock, 2014.

—————. "'Not as the Gentiles': The Ethics of the Earliest Christians." In *Into All the World: Emergent Christianity in its Jewish and Greco-Roman Context*, edited by Mark Harding and Alanna Nobbs. Grand Rapids: Eerdmans, forthcoming.

Starling, Nicole. "Between Two Paradigms: Harriet Pullen and the Earliest Australian Female Preachers." *Journal of Religious History* 39 (2015) 399–419.

Steensma, Thomas D., and Peggy T. Cohen-Kettenis. "More Than Two Developmental Pathways in Children with Gender Dysphoria?" *Journal of the American Academy of Child & Adolescent Psychiatry* 54, no.2 (2015) 147–48.

Steinhauser, Kenneth B. "Augustine's Reading of the *Passio sanctarum Perpetuae et Felicitatis*." *StPatr* 33 (1997) 244–49.

Stewart-Sykes, Alistair. "Introduction." In *Hippolytus. On the Apostolic Tradition*, edited by Alistair Stewart-Sykes, 11–52. Crestwood, NY: St Vladimir's Seminary Press, 2001.

Stone, Bebb Wheeler. "Second Isaiah: Prophet to Patriarchy." *Journal for the Study of the Old Testament* 56 (1992) 85–99.

Storkey, Elaine. "Evangelical Theology and Gender." In *The Cambridge Companion to Evangelical Theology*, edited by Timothy Larsen and Daniel J. Treier. Cambridge Companions to Religion, 161–76. Cambridge, New York: Cambridge University Press, 2007.

—————. *Origins of Difference: The Gender Debate Revisited*. Grand Rapids: Baker, 2001.

Stryker, Susan. "My Words to Victor Frankenstein above the Village of Chamounix: Performing Transgender Rage." In *The Transgender Studies Reader*, edited by Susan Stryker and Stephen Whittle, 244–256. New York: Routledge, 2006.

Stryker, Susan and Nikki Sullivan. "King's Member, Queen's Body: Transsexual Surgery, Self-Demand Amputation and the Somatechnics of Sovereign Power." In *Somatechnics: Queering the Technologisation of Bodies*, edited by Nikki Sullivan and Samantha Murray, 49–63. Farnham: Ashgate, 2009.

Stuart, D. K. *Exodus*. New American Commentary. Nashville: B&H, 2006.

Stuart, Elizabeth. "The Return of the Living Dead." In *Post-Christian Feminisms: A Critical Approach*, edited by Lisa Isherwood and Kathleen McPhillips, 211–22. Aldershot: Ashgate, 2008.

Stuhlmacher, Peter. "Isaiah 53 in the Gospels and Acts." Translated by Daniel P. Bailey. In *The Suffering Servant: Isiaah 53 in Jewish and Christian Sources*, edited by Bernd Janowski and Peter Stuhlmacher, 147–62. Grand Rapids: Eerdmans, 2004.

—————. *Paul's Letter to the Romans: A Commentary*. Translated by Scott J. Hafemann. Louisville: Westminster, 1994.

Swain, Shurlee. "In These Days of Female Evangelists and Hallelujah Lasses: Women Preachers and the Redefinition of Gender Roles in the Churches in Late Nineteenth-Century Australia." *Journal of Religious History* 26 (2002) 65–77.

Tachibana, Makoto. "Epigenetic Regulation of Mammalian Sex Determination." *The Journal of Medical Investigation* 62, no.1/2 (2015) 19–23.

Tamez, Elsa. *Struggles for Power in Early Christianity.* Translated by Gloria Kinsler. Maryknoll: Orbis, 2007.

Taylor, Charles. *A Secular Age.* Cambridge, MA: Harvard University Press, 2007.

Thielman, Frank. *Ephesians.* BECNT. Grand Rapids: Baker, 2010.

Thiselton, Anthony. *New Horizons in Hermeneutics: The Theory and Practice of Transforming Biblical Reading.* Grand Rapids: Zondervan, 1992.

Thom, Johan C. "The Mind Is Its Own Place: Defining the Topos." In *Early Christianity and Classical Culture: Comparative Studies in Honor of Abraham J. Malherbe,* edited by Thomas H. Olbricht et al., 555–73. Leiden: Brill, 2003.

Thomas, H. A. "Zion." In *Dictionary of the Old Testament Prophets,* edited by Mark J. Boda and J. Gordon McConville, 907–14. Downers Grove: IVP, 2012.

Thurston, Bonnie Bowman. *The Widows: A Women's Ministry in the Early Church.* Minneapolis: Fortress, 1989.

Tobia, Jacob. "I Am Neither Mr, Mrs nor Ms but Mx." *The Guardian* September 1, 2015. http://www.theguardian.com/commentisfree/2015/aug/31/neither-mr-mrs-or-ms-but-mx.

Toh, Justine. "Encultured or Created? Gender and Sex in the Context of Caitlyn Jenner's 'New Normal'." In *The Gender Conversation,* edited by David Starling and Edwina Murphy. Sydney, Morling Press, 2016.

Towner, Philip. H. *The Goal of Our Instruction: The Structure of Theology and Ethics in the Pastoral Epistles.* JSNTSup. Sheffield: JSOT Press, 1989.

———. *The Letters to Timothy and Titus.* NICNT. Grand Rapids: Eerdmans, 2006.

Tracy, Steven. R. "Patriarchy and Domestic Violence: Challenging Common Misconceptions." *Journal of Evangelical Theological Society* 50 (2007) 576–78.

Trevett, Christine. *Montanism: Gender, Authority and the New Prophecy.* Cambridge: Cambridge University Press, 1996.

Trible, Phyllis. *God and the Rhetoric of Sexuality.* Overtures to Biblical Theology. Philadelphia: Fortress Press, 1978.

Trigg, Joseph W. "Martyrs and Churchmen in Third-Century North Africa." *StPatr* 15 (1984) 242–46.

Tripp, Paul David. "Man Does Not Live by Man Skills Alone." http://www.christianitytoday.com/ct/2015/march-web-only/man-does-not-live-by-man-skills-alone.html?start=2.

Trueman, Carl. "An Accidental Feminist?" http://www.alliancenet.org/mos/postcards-from-palookaville/an-accidental-feminist#.VvIW9_t97IU.

UN Women. "International Day of the Girl Child." http://www.unwomen.org/en/news/in-focus/girl-child.

———. "The United Nations Fourth World Conference on Women." http://www.un.org/womenwatch/daw/beijing/platform/girl.htm.

UNICEF. "A Statistical Snapshot of Violence against Adolescent Girls" https://www.unicef.ch/sites/default/files/attachments/a_statistical_snapshot_of_violence_against_adolescent_girls.pdf

———. "State of the World's Children 2015." http://www.unicef.org/publications/files/SOWC_2015_Summary_and_Tables.pdf.

———. "Under-Five Mortality." http://data.unicef.org/child-mortality/under-five.html.

United Nations. "Convention on the Rights of the Child." http://legal.un.org/avl/ha/crc/crc.html.

Valenze, Deborah M. *Prophetic Sons and Daughters: Female Preaching and Popular Religion in Industrial England.* Princeton: Princeton University Press, 1985.

Van Caenegem, Eva, et al. "Prevalence of Gender Nonconformity in Flanders, Belgium." *Archives of Sexual Behavior* 44, no.5 (2015) 1281–87.

Van Leeuwen, Mary Stewart. *Gender and Grace: Women and Men in a Changing World.* Leicester: IVP, 1990.

_____.*My Brother's Keeper: What the Social Sciences Do (and Don't) Tell Us about Masculinity.* Downer's Grove: IVP, 2009.

Vanhoozer, Kevin J. "A Drama-of-Redemption Model: Always Performing?" In *Four Views on Moving beyond the Bible to Theology,* edited by Gary T. Meadors, 151–99. Grand Rapids: Zondervan, 2009.

Volf, Miroslav. "Soft Difference: Theological Reflections on the Relation between Church and Culture in 1 Peter." *Ex Auditu* 10 (1994) 15–30.

_____."The Trinity and Gender Identity." In *Gospel and Gender: A Trinitarian Engagement with Being Male and Female in Christ,* edited by C. D. Achison and A. Torrance, 155–78. T&T Clark: London, 2003.

_____.*Exclusion and Embrace: A Theological Exploration of Identity, Otherness, and Reconciliation.* Nashville: Abingdon, 1996.

Wagner, Ellasue. "A Korean Home." *The Korea Mission Field* 4, no.6 (June 1908) 90.

Waldenfels, Bernhard. "Levinas and the Face of the Other." In *The Cambridge Companion to Levinas,* edited by Simon Critchley and Robert Bernasconi, 63–81. Cambridge: Cambridge University Press, 2005.

Wallien, Madeleine S. C., and Peggy T. Cohen-Kettenis. "Psychosexual Outcome of Gender-Dysphoric Children." *Journal of the American Academy of Child and Adolescent Psychiatry* 47 (2008) 1413–23.

Walsh, Bruce. "Bruce Jenner Is Not a Woman. He Is a Sick and Delusional Man." http://www.theblaze.com/contributions/bruce-jenner-is-not-a-woman-he-is-a-sick-and-delusional-man/.

Walton, John H. *Ancient Near Eastern Thought and the Old Testament: Introducing the Conceptual World of the Hebrew Bible.* Nottingham: Apollos, 2007.

_____.*Genesis.* NIVAC. Grand Rapids: Zondervan, 2001.

_____.*The Lost World of Genesis One; Ancient Cosmology and the Origins Debate.* Downers Grove: IVP, 2009.

Wansbrough, Henry. *Jesus and the Oral Gospel Tradition.* JSNTSup. Sheffield: JSOT Press, 1991.

Ware, Bruce. "Gender Moves?" https://www.e-n.org.uk/2015/06/features/gender-moves/.

Webb, Barry. "Zion in Transformation: A Literary Approach to Isaiah." In *The Bible in Three Dimensions: Essays in Celebration of Forty Years of Biblical Studies in the University of Sheffield,* edited by D. Clines et al., 65–84. JSOTSup. Sheffield: JSOT Press, 1990.

Webb, William J. *Slaves, Women and Homosexuals: Exploring the Hermeneutics of Cultural Analysis.* Downers Grove, IL: InterVarsity, 2001.

Webster, K., et al. *Australians' Attitudes to Violence against Women: Full Technical Report, Findings from the 2013 National Community Attitudes towards Violence Against Women Survey.* https://www.vichealth.vic.gov.au/media-and-resources/publications/2013-national-community-attitudes-towards-violence-against-women-survey

Weeks, Jeffrey. *Sexuality.* New York: Routledge, 2010. Kindle edition.

Weerakoon, Patricia, and Kamal Weerakoon. "The Biology of Sex and Gender." In *The Gender Conversation,* edited by David Starling and Edwina Murphy. Sydney: Morling Press, 2016.

Wegenast, Klaus. *Das Verständnis der Tradition bei Paulus und in den Deuteropaulinen.* WMZANT. Neukirchen Kreis Moers: Neukirchener Verlag, 1962.

_____."Teach." In *New International Dictionary of New Testament Theology,* edited by Colin Brown, 3.759–81. Grand Rapids: Zondervan, 1992.

Weinfeld, M. "Sabbath, Temple and the Enthronement of the Lord: The Problem of the *Sitz im Leben* of Genesis 1:1–2:3." In *Mélanges bibliques et orientaux en l'honneur de H. Cazelles*, edited by A. Caquot and M. Delcor, 501–12. Alter Orient und Altes Testament. Kevelaer: Butzon & Bercker, 1981.

Weiss, H. F. "Didaskalia." In *Exegetical Dictionary of the New Testament*, edited by Gerhard Schneider and Horst Robert Balz, 1.316–17. Grand Rapids: Eerdmans, 1993.

Welles, Charles Bradford. *Royal Correspondence in the Hellenistic Period: A Study in Greek Epigraphy*. New Haven: Yale University Press, 1934.

Wenham, Gordon J. *The Book of Leviticus*. NICOT. Grand Rapids: Eerdmans, 1979.

—————.*Genesis*. 2 vols. WBC. Waco: Word, 1987.

Wesley Church, Hobart. "Minute Book of Leaders' Meetings 4/8/1830 – 28/12/1842." Tasmania Archives Office NS499/1/158.

—————."Minute Book of the Wesleyan Library Committee 19/9/1825 – 25/8/1845." Tasmania Archives Office NS499/1/232.

—————.*Rules and Regulations of the Wesleyan Library, to Which Is Annexed a Catalogue of Books Contained Therein*. Tasmania: Andrew Bent, 1827. Tasmania Archives Office NS499/1/3155.

West, Candace, and Don H. Zimmerman. "Doing Gender." *Gender & Society* 1, no.2 (1987) 125–51.

West, Janet. *Daughters of Freedom*. Sutherland: Albatross, 1997.

Westermann, Claus. *Genesis: A Practical Commentary*. Translated by David E. Green. Grand Rapids: Eerdmans, 1987.

Westfall, Cynthia Long. "The Meaning of *authenteō* in 1 Timothy 2:12." *JGRChJ* 10 (2014) 138–73.

Whiteway, Eleanor, and Denis R. Alexander. "Understanding the Causes of Same-Sex Attraction." *Science & Christian Belief* 27, no.1 (2015) 17–40.

Wieland, George M. *The Significance of Salvation: A Study of Salvation in the Pastoral Epistles*. Milton Keynes: Paternoster, 2006.

Wigram, George V. "עלצ." In *Englishman's Hebrew Chaldee Concordance of the Old Testament* (1923). http://biblehub.com/hebrew/strongs_6763.htm.

Willey, Patricia Tull. *Remember the Former Things: The Recollection of Previous Texts in Second Isaiah*. SBL Dissertation Series. Atlanta: Scholars Press, 1997.

Williams, Craig. "Perpetua's Gender. A Latinist Reads the *Passio Perpetuae et Felicitatis*." In *Perpetua's Passions: Multidisciplinary Approaches to the Passio Perpetuae et Felicitatis*, edited by Jan N. Bremmer and Marco Formisano, 54–77. Oxford: Oxford University Press, 2012.

Williams, Rhiannon. "Facebook's 71 Gender Options Come to UK Users." http://www.telegraph.co.uk/technology/facebook/10930654/Facebooks-71-gender-options-come-to-UK-users.html.

Williams, Rowan. *Lost Icons*. London: Continuum, 2003.

Williams, Roy. *Post-God Nation? How Religion Fell Off the Radar in Australia and What Might Be Done To Get It Back*. Sydney: Harper Collins, 2015.

Willmer, Haddon, and Keith White. *Entry Point: Towards Child Theology with Matthew 18*. London: WTL Publications, 2013.

Wilshire, Leland E. "Servant-City: A New Interpretation of the Servant of the Lord in the Servant Songs of Deutero-Isaiah." *Journal of Biblical Literature* 94, no. 3 (1975) 356–67.

Wilson, Helen W., and Cathy S. Widom. "Does Physical Abuse, Sexual Abuse, or Neglect in Childhood Increase the Likelihood of Same-Sex Sexual Relationships and Cohabitation? A Prospective 30-Year Follow-Up." *Archives of Sexual Behavior* 39 (2010) 63–74.

Witherington, Ben. *Women in the Earliest Churches*. Cambridge: Cambridge University Press, 1988.

Wolters, Albert M. "An Early Parallel of *authentein* in 1 Tim 2:12." *JETS* 54 (2011) 673–84.

_____."A Semantic Study of *authentēs* and its Derivatives," *Journal for Biblical Manhood and Womanhood* 1, no.11 (Spring 2006) 44–65.

Woodhead, Linda. "God, Gender and Identity." In *Gospel and Gender: A Trinitarian Engagement with Being Male and Female in Christ*, edited by C. D. Achison and A. Torrance, 84–104. London: T&T Clark, 2003.

Woude, Annemarieke van der. "Can Zion Do without the Servant in Isaiah 40–55?" *Calvin Theological Journal* 39, no. 1 (2004) 109–16.

Wright, N. T. "Jesus, Israel and the Cross." *Society of Biblical Literature Seminar Papers* 24 (1985) 75–95.

_____.*Paul and the Faithfulness of God*. London: SPCK, 2013.

_____.*Women's Service in the Church: The Biblical Basis*, conference paper for the symposium "Men, Women and the Church," St John's College, Durham, UK (September 4th 2004). http://ntwrightpage.com/Wright_Women_Service_Church.htm.

_____.*Surprised by Hope*. London: SPCK, 2007.

Wright, Stephen J. *Dogmatic Aesthetics: A Theology of Beauty in Dialogue with Robert W. Jenson*. Minneapolis: Fortress, 2014.

Yarhouse, Mark A. "Integration in the Study of Homosexuality, GLBT Issues, and Sexual Identity." *Journal of Psychology & Theology* 40, no. 2 (2012) 107–11.

_____."Understanding Gender Dysphoria." *Christianity Today* 59, no. 6 (2015) 44–50.

_____.*Understanding Gender Dysphoria: Navigating Transgender Issues in a Changing Culture*. Downers Grove: IVP, 2015. Kindle edition.

_____.*Understanding Gender Dysphoria: Navigating Transgender Issues in a Changing Culture*. Downers Grove: IVP, 2015.

Yi, Duk-joo. "Freedom and Liberation, and Practice: Understanding the History of Early Korean Christian Women (1887–1920)." In *The Korean Church and Women*, 13–25. Seoul: IVP Korea, 2013.

Young, Iris M. "Throwing Like a Girl: A Phenomenology of Feminine Body Comportment, Motility and Spatiality." *Human Studies* 3 (1980) 137–156.

Young, Isabella. "Abuse inside Christian Marriages—A Personal Story." *Sydney Morning Herald* (March 2, 2015). http://www.smh.com.au/comment/smh-editorial/abuse-inside-christian-marriages-a-personal-story-20150301-13rrvr.html#ixzz43fyQJOUe.

Zenger, E., ed. *Einleitung in das Alte Testament*. 7th, rev. & exp. ed. Stuttgart: Kohlhammer, 2008.

Zucker, Kenneth J., and Anne A. Lawrence. "Epidemiology of Gender Identity Disorder: Recommendations for the Standards of Care of the World Professional Association for Transgender Health." *International Journal of Transgenderism* 11, no.1 (2009) 8–18.